MW01039395

AN OBITUARY FOR “WISDOM LITERATURE”

An Obituary for "Wisdom Literature"

The Birth, Death, and Intertextual Reintegration of a Biblical Corpus

WILL KYNES

OXFORD
UNIVERSITY PRESS

Great Clarendon Street, Oxford, OX2 6DP,
United Kingdom

Oxford University Press is a department of the University of Oxford. It furthers the University's objective of excellence in research, scholarship, and education by publishing worldwide. Oxford is a registered trade mark of Oxford University Press in the UK and in certain other countries

First Edition published in 2019

Published in the United States of America by Oxford University Press
198 Madison Avenue, New York, NY 10016, United States of America

British Library Cataloguing in Publication Data
Data available

Library of Congress Control Number: 2018938573

ISBN 978–0–19–877737–3

To my parents, Bill and Susan Kynes,
who introduced me to wisdom.

Hear, my child, your father's instruction,
and do not reject your mother's teaching;
for they are a fair garland for your head,
and pendants for your neck.

Proverbs 1:8–9

Acknowledgements

This book is about the importance of viewing texts through multiple perspectives rather than uncritically maintaining a single vantage point. In keeping with this thesis, I have greatly profited from interacting with scholars, colleagues, and friends (not mutually exclusive groups) who have kindly taken the time to provide their perspectives on my work as it was developing. I could never hope to encompass the breadth or depth of either their contributions to this work or my gratitude to them in this short space.

I began research on this book during my time as Liddon Research Fellow and Tutor in Theology at Keble College, Oxford. I am grateful for the time and resources provided by the college, along with the camaraderie of its Senior Common Room. Markus Bockmuehl and Christopher M. Hays were particularly helpful interlocutors. Many of my other colleagues in the Department of Theology and Religion at Oxford left their mark on this work, as well. Fortuitously, the Senior Old Testament Seminar hosted a series on Wisdom while I was at Oxford, to which I was invited to contribute. That paper became the foundation for this book. Both in the lively discussion that followed it and in further conversations I especially profited from the insight of John Barton, John Day, Susan Gillingham, John Jarick, and Hugh Williamson.

Colleagues at my current institution, Whitworth University, have also encouraged me in my research and offered feedback along the way. I am particularly grateful to James Edwards, Jerry Sittser, Adam Neder, and Jonathan Moo, who read parts of the work and made valuable suggestions for improvement. My colleagues in English, Fred Johnson and John Pell, helped me think about genre, and Nate King contributed his expertise in philosophy. I am also grateful to Whitworth University and the Weyerhaeuser Center for Christian Faith and Learning for providing funding to support my research. Christina Dolan-Derks, Cara Elston, Nancy Bunker, and Barbara Carden in the library tracked down books and articles with unflagging efficiency and kindness. The Whitworth students funded by the Welch Family Foundation who helped me with the book as research assistants, Michael Bouterse, Luke Olsen, Katrina Ulnick, Christopher Pieper, and Sophia Ridgeway also went above and beyond my expectations and made significant contributions to this work.

Others beyond these institutions also shed light on the various arenas of knowledge addressed in this book, kindly reading chapters or engaging with developing arguments: Matthew Crawford on Patristic Interpretation, Paul Michael Kurtz and Michael Legaspi on German intellectual history, Michael V. Fox, Tremper Longman, Richard Schultz, Choon-Leong Seow, Mark Sneed, Raymond Van Leeuwen, and Stuart Weeks on Wisdom Literature, and Kevin Vanhoozer on genre. Katharine Dell, my former Ph.D. supervisor at Cambridge, continued to be an invaluable guide in wisdom, both in the Hebrew Bible and beyond.

I am also grateful to Manfred Lautenschläger for funding the Manfred Lautenschläger Award for Theological Promise and Michael Welker for organizing it. The award not only helped fund this research but also steered it toward completion through the insightful feedback I received at the colloquium at Heidelberg University. Tom Perridge and Karen Raith at Oxford University Press were also instrumental in getting this project off the ground and then bringing it in for a safe landing.

Each of those mentioned above (and many others) contributed beneficially to some part of this work (the faults that remain are all my own, of course), but one person has been constant in her support across its duration: my wife, Vanessa. I cannot thank her enough. My daughters, Karis, Charlotte, and Hannah have also cheered me on with their infectious joy. My parents have also encouraged me onward, as they have done throughout my life. As they have consistently reminded me, I have much to be grateful for.

Reprinted by permission of Bloomsbury Academic, an imprint of Bloomsbury Publishing Plc.

Schlegel, Friedrich. *Dialogue on Poetry and Literary Aphorisms*. Translated by Ernst Behler & Roman Struc. © 1968 Pennsylvania State University Press. Reprinted by permission.

Friedrich Schlegel's "Lucinde" and the Fragments. Translated by Peter Firchow. © 1971 University of Minnesota Press. Reprinted by permission.

Fig. 4.2 Orion constellation in three dimensions from Chaisson, Eric, and Steve McMillan. *Astronomy Today*. 1997, Media edition. 2nd edn. ©1997. Reprinted by permission of Pearson Education, Inc., New York: New York.

Contents

Figures and Tables

Abbreviations

AB	Anchor Bible
ACCS	Ancient Christian Commentary on Scripture
ACW	Ancient Christian Writers. 1946–
AIL	Ancient Israel and Its Literature
AOAT	Alter Orient und Altes Testament
ArBib	The Aramaic Bible
ASTI	*Annual of the Swedish Theological Institute*
ATANT	Abhandlungen zur Theologie des Alten und Neuen Testaments
ATD	Das Alte Testament Deutsch
BBB	Bonner biblische Beiträge
BCOTWP	Baker Commentary on the Old Testament Wisdom and Psalms
BETL	Bibliotheca ephemeridum theologicarum lovaniensium
Bib	*Biblica*
BJS	Brown Judaic Studies
BJRL	*Bulletin of the John Rylands Library*
BTB	*Biblical Theology Bulletin*
BThSt	Biblisch-theologische Studien
BWANT	Beiträge zur Wissenschaft vom Alten und Neuen Testament
BZAW	Beihefte zur Zeitschrift für die alttestamentliche Wissenschaft
CBQ	*Catholic Biblical Quarterly*
CBQMS	Catholic Biblical Quarterly Monograph Series
CBR	*Currents in Biblical Research*
CCSL	Corpus Christianorum: Series latina
CFThL	Clark's Foreign Theological Library, 4th series
ConBOT	Coniectanea biblica: Old Testament Series
CSEL	Corpus scriptorum ecclesiasticorum latinorum
CurBS	*Currents in Research Biblical Studies*
DSD	*Dead Sea Discoveries: A Journal of Current Research on the Scrolls and Related Literature*

ErFor	Erträge der Forschung
ETL	*Ephemerides theologicae lovanienses*
EvT	*Evangelische Theologie*
ExpTim	*Expository Times*
FAT	Forschungen zum Alten Testament
FAT II	Forschungen zum Alten Testament II
FC	Fathers of the Church
FOTL	Forms of the Old Testament Literature
FRLANT	Forschungen zur Religion und Literatur des Alten und Neuen Testaments
HAR	*Hebrew Annual Review*
HBM	Hebrew Bible Monographs
HBS	Herders biblische Studien
HBT	*Horizons in Biblical Theology*
HR	*History of Religions*
HS	*Hebrew Studies*
HTKAT	Herders Theologischer Kommentar zum Alten Testament
HTR	*Harvard Theological Review*
HUCA	*Hebrew Union College Annual*
ICC	International Critical Commentary
Int	*Interpretation*
JAJSup	Journal of Ancient Judaism. Supplements
JANESCU	*Journal of the Ancient Near Eastern Society of Columbia University*
JAOS	*Journal of the American Oriental Society*
JBL	*Journal of Biblical Literature*
JBQ	*Jewish Bible Quarterly*
JBR	*Journal of Bible and Religion*
JQR	*Jewish Quarterly Review*
JR	*Journal of Religion*
JSJSup	Supplements to the Journal for the Study of Judaism
JSNTSup	Journal for the Study of the New Testament Supplement Series
JSOT	*Journal for the Study of the Old Testament*
JSOTSup	Journal for the Study of the Old Testament Supplement Series
JTC	*Journal for Theology and the Church*

JTISup	Journal of Theological Interpretation Supplements
JTS	*Journal of Theological Studies*
KAT	Kommentar zum Alten Testament
LBS	The Library of Biblical Studies
LGRB	Lives of Great Religious Books
LHBOTS	Library of Hebrew Bible/Old Testament Studies
LNTS	Library of New Testament Studies
NCB	New Century Bible
NIB	The New Interpreter's Bible
NIBCOT	New International Biblical Commentary on the Old Testament
NICOT	New International Commentary on the Old Testament
NLH	*New Literary History*
NSKAT	Neuer Stuttgarter Kommentar, Altes Testament
OLZ	*Orientalistische Literaturzeitung*
OTL	Old Testament Library
OtSt	Oudtestamentische Studiën
PG	Patrologia Graeca
PL	Patrologia Latina
RB	*Revue biblique*
RevExp	*Review and Expositor*
RTP	*Revue de théologie et de philosophie*
SBLDS	Society of Biblical Literature Dissertation Series
SBLSymS	Society of Biblical Literature Symposium Series
SBS	Stuttgarter Bibelstudien
SHR	Studies in the History of Religions
SJT	*Scottish Journal of Theology*
Spec	*Speculum*
STDJ	Studies on the Texts of the Desert of Judah
SVT	Scholia in Vetus Testamentum
TBT	*The Bible Today*
THL	Theory and History of Literature
THOTC	Two Horizons Old Testament Commentary
TLZ	*Theologische Literaturzeitung*
TOTC	Tyndale Old Testament Commentaries

TRu	*Theologische Rundschau*
TSAJ	Texts and Studies in Ancient Judaism
TTFL	Theological Translation Fund Library
TTH	Translated Texts for Historians
VT	*Vetus Testamentum*
VTSup	Supplements to Vetus Testamentum
WBC	Word Biblical Commentary
WMANT	Wissenschaftliche Monographien zum Alten und Neuen Testament
WO	*Die Welt des Orients*
ZAW	*Zeitschrift für die alttestamentliche Wissenschaft*

Introduction

> Amalia: I always shudder when I open a book where the imagination and its works are classified under headings.
>
> (Schlegel 1968 [1800], 76)

The rise of Wisdom Literature in less than a century from obscurity to ubiquity is one of biblical studies' great rags-to-riches stories. In her ascent from "orphan" to "Queen Mother" (Crenshaw 1976, 1), Wisdom Literature became "the Cinderella of biblical studies" (Weeks 2016b, 3). Before the close similarities between Proverbs and Egyptian instructional literature came to light in the early twentieth century, Wisdom Literature was generally ignored. Now, Wisdom Literature is everywhere. Hardly a biblical text has escaped association with it. Wisdom's influence has even extended beyond biblical studies to play a prominent role in recent works by theologians, such as David Ford (2007) and Paul Fiddes (2013).

In Wisdom Literature's climb to prominence, if not quite dominance, however, a number of vital questions about the category have been left unanswered. Its definition, theology, setting, and delimitation remain elusive, leaving interpreters "grasping after the wind" (Sneed 2015a). The category has widespread implications for the texts included within it, whether they number three (Proverbs, Job, and Ecclesiastes), five (adding Ben Sira and Wisdom of Solomon), or seven (adding Psalms and Song of Songs as well) (see Scott 1971, 19). It also affects the interpretation of a seemingly ever-increasing number of texts across the Hebrew Bible and beyond associated with it on the grounds of related content, scribal origin, or didactic intent. Its fundamental weaknesses can no longer be ignored.

Interpreters have not, of course, completely overlooked the many difficulties the category poses. However, this has not hindered its rapid growth in popularity over the course of the twentieth and early twenty-first centuries. In fact, as I will argue, this weakness has been its strength, as a reliance on a vague, abstract, ill-defined, circularly justified, modernly developed, and extrinsically imposed definition of the category has enabled scholars to extend the boundaries of Wisdom Literature indefinitely, leading to a pan-sapiential epidemic in biblical scholarship. The many disagreements about the definition of Wisdom Literature have become more pressing in recent times, though, and the questions have begun to mount, both in number and urgency. Was there a "Wisdom tradition"? What are the boundaries of "Wisdom"? Is the "Wisdom Literature" category useful? When they have been discredited, concepts are not shackled in handcuffs but in scare quotes. As the titles of the articles asking these questions demonstrate, those scare quotes have already begun to appear.[1]

What has happened that "Wisdom Literature," so recently the belle of the biblical studies ball, should have the shimmering coach of scholarly enthusiasm transform into a rotting pumpkin beneath her? In this book, I will argue the chimes of midnight have rung for two interrelated reasons. The first, dealt with in Part I of this book, is metacritical. The field is finally coming to terms with the weaknesses of an unwieldy scholarly category developed in mid-nineteenth-century Germany to meet the ideological demands of that time and place. Despite (or more likely because of) those weaknesses, this category has spread across the canon like a virus. The second reason, addressed in Part II, is methodological. Biblical scholarship has begun to put aside its commitment to strictly separated, binary in-or-out, taxonomic approaches to genre and instead to incorporate more recent developments in genre theory, which has made efforts to define and maintain a distinct category like Wisdom less compelling. Together, these factors set the stage for the intertextual reintegration of Wisdom Literature back into the canon in Part III.

PART I: HISTORICAL METACRITICISM

As the articles mentioned above indicate, both the very nature of the Wisdom Literature category and its broader effects on the field have

[1] "Is the 'Wisdom Tradition' a Tradition?" (Sneed 2011); "Deciding the Boundaries of 'Wisdom': Applying the Concept of Family Resemblance" (Dell 2015); "Is 'Wisdom Literature' a Useful Category?" (Weeks 2016a).

begun to encounter more careful interrogation. Katharine Dell questions how far the category should extend. Mark Sneed focuses on one of the conclusions drawn from the category, the associated "wisdom tradition" in ancient Israel. However, similarly to Stuart Weeks, I believe the category "Wisdom Literature" itself is to blame for many of the difficulties faced in its interpretation. Biblical scholars may continue to attempt to define Wisdom Literature better and to debate what that category reveals about other texts and ancient Israelite thought. However, since these efforts constantly refer back to an assumed and unexamined consensus that Proverbs, Ecclesiastes, and Job provide the essence of Israelite Wisdom Literature, the time is ripe to examine that consensus, determine when and how it arose, and confront its lasting impact on the study of the Hebrew Bible. James Crenshaw (2010, 10) claims a "mysterious ingredient" links the diverse Wisdom Literature together. Perhaps, instead of pouring more flour into this poisoned soup, we can find the wild vine that provided this ingredient and avoid it as we start foraging for a new meal. For too long, the category has simply been presupposed. Now, with its lack of assured results compounding with and encouraging its expanding application, such a historical and conceptual re-evaluation of Wisdom Literature and its presuppositions is desirable (Marböck 2006, 201), even necessary, lest further scholarly conclusions be built on a foundation liable to crumble beneath them.

The first three chapters of this book take on this metacritical task. In chapter 1 The Rise and Impending Demise of Wisdom Literature: The Modern Scholarly Wisdom Tradition and the Threat of Pan-Sapientialism, after summarizing the growing doubts about the Wisdom Literature category, I trace the development of Wisdom scholarship in the twentieth century, focusing on the debates over the category's delimitation, which force the question of its definition. Over the course of the century, scholars struggled to provide a definition for Wisdom Literature that was not merely a restatement of the scholarly consensus handed down to them in the critical tradition. Without clear definitional limits, the diversity of those contents constantly encouraged the category to expand, drawing more and more of the canon into Wisdom's "influence." Recently, that expansion has reached a pan-sapiential extreme, with some associating the entire canon with "wisdom scribes." The consistent circular appeals back to the initial scholarly consensus in an attempt to limit this expansion have inspired questions about the viability of the consensus itself.

Drawing in the similar sapiential expansion in scholarship on the Psalter, the Dead Sea Scrolls, and the ancient Near East and comparing the analogous spread of Deuteronomism, I argue that in all these cases, attempts to define the category resort eventually to the scholarly consensus concerning which biblical texts make up its core. This "universal consensus" has become the cornerstone supporting the sapiential superstructure, and yet the origins of this consensus have not been identified, leaving a hazardous lacuna in biblical scholarship.

The examination of current Wisdom scholarship invites the historical investigation into its origins that follows in chapters 2 The Ancestry of Wisdom Literature: Ancient Tradition or Modern Invention? and 3 The Birth of Wisdom Literature: The Nineteenth-Century Origin of the Wisdom Corpus. I begin that quest in early Jewish and Christian interpretation, reaching as far back into history as possible to search for indications of the category's existence. Current scholars appeal to various "vestiges" of the Wisdom Literature category in early interpretation that include early views on the structure and order of the canon, the association of a group of books with Solomon, the ancient recognition of shared traits between texts, and the title Wisdom applied to several books. However, when closely examined, this evidence does not justify the common assertion that Wisdom Literature has an ancient pedigree. To the degree that a category approaching the modern one existed at all, its contents and definition differed significantly, making it not merely quantitatively, but qualitatively different from the current category. This indicates that Wisdom as we know it is instead an invention of modern scholarship.

Chapter 3 The Birth of Wisdom Literature: The Nineteenth-Century Origin of the Wisdom Corpus aims, then, to identify the precise scholarly world in which the Wisdom category arose, understand what aspects of that environment inspired its creation, and evaluate the lasting effects that origin has had on its interpretation.[2] Working backwards from Wisdom's commonly accepted scholarly discovery in the early twentieth century by following citations in biblical scholarship, I identify Johann Bruch as the "Wellhausen of Wisdom." His *Weisheits-Lehre der Hebräer: Ein Beitrag zur Geschichte der Philosophie* (*Wisdom Teaching of the Hebrews: A Contribution to the History of Philosophy*)

[2] See, similarly, Nathan MacDonald (2003), who argues "monotheism" as a concept originated in the early English Enlightenment connected to "distinctly modern ideas" that explain the "yawning gap" between it and the Hebrew Bible (52).

(1851) is the first work to draw together a developing concept of a Wisdom Literature genre and present it systematically and comprehensively. As the subtitle indicates, contemporary philosophy looms large both in his work and in that of the primary scholars who influenced it. As a result, a suspicious correspondence appears between the post-Enlightenment ideals of his time and the traits Bruch associates with Wisdom Literature, as its non-theocratic spirit pursues free thought. Scholars could so easily look into the well of Wisdom Literature and see their own reflections because the level of abstraction necessary to justify a category that included texts as diverse as Proverbs, Ecclesiastes, and Job left ample room for them to import their own presuppositions of what wisdom should be into the interpretation of these texts. It is little surprise then that Wisdom Literature continues to be associated with modern values, such as humanism, internationalism, secularism, and empiricism (see Miller 2015, 90–3).

The invention of Wisdom Literature within biblical studies is similar to the creation in rhetoric of the four "forms" or "modes" of discourse: Description, Narration, Exposition, and Argumentation. This classification system originated between 1850 and 1900, was adopted almost universally in the 1890s and remained influential well into the 1930s. Like other rhetorical theories developed during that time, it was advanced to address the discipline's decline and make it "once more a vital discipline, in step with the age" (Kitzhaber 1990, 222). These "convenient abstractions" were ideally suited to the increasingly rigid, abstract, and academic atmosphere of nineteenth-century rhetorical theory, and yet they have cast a long shadow that continues to obscure the field (Kitzhaber 1990, 138–9, 226). One rhetorician laments, "Our discipline has been long in knuckling from its eyes the sleep of the nineteenth and early twentieth centuries, and the real lesson of the modes is that we need always to be on guard against systems that seem convenient to teachers but that ignore the way writing is actually done" (Connors 1981, 455). The convenience of the forms of discourse, which "served well the particular nexus of situational, cultural, and generic contexts in which they operated," their "createdness" as "academic constructs rather than 'naturally' occurring genres," and their distorting "oversimplification" together draw them into question and have left the field "tainted" (Devitt 2004, 100, 121–2; see also D'Angelo 1984). Wisdom Literature originated for similar reasons at a similar time and has had a similar effect.

The term "religion" itself appears to be another example of this anachronistic scholarly projection on antiquity (see Lash 1996; Nongbri

2013). Providing an illuminating parallel to the oppositional development of Wisdom Literature and salvation history, Peter Harrison (2015) recounts how religion as a category was developed from the seventeenth century onward in opposition to "science," creating unnecessary conflict between them. Like Wisdom Literature, this modern invention also distorts through abstraction, which contributes to the category's reification, expansive inclusion, and self-replication of scholarly views. Like the picture on the cover of a jigsaw puzzle, argue Carlin Barton and Daniel Boyarin (2016, 6–7; cf. 3), the category "religion" guides the reconstruction of the fragments of an ancient world, and, in so doing, risks predetermining how the pieces will fit together. Therefore, they enjoin a "self-critical consciousness" regarding the imposition of modern categories, which have the tendency to carry Western values with them. Abandoning predetermined abstract scholarly categories like these, they claim, will increase the necessity and potential of careful examination and comparison of each piece of the puzzle from every angle in order to fit them together.

Similarly, by contextualizing biblical scholarship in the same way that the discipline attempts to contextualize the biblical text, this first part of the book "foregrounds the background" (Kurtz 2016, 568) and participates in a broader metacritical genre in biblical scholarship. I follow the lead of Hans Frei, whose *The Eclipse of Biblical Narrative* (1974) helped to define "the almost legendary category of analysis of analyses of the Bible" (vii). He argued Enlightenment interests forced the question of ostensive reference on the biblical narratives, detaching them from the "real" historical world to judge them by external standards (3–4). The recent proliferation of studies making this type of argument indicates a growing recognition of metacriticism's potential to reinvigorate a discipline stumbling under the weight of its historical-critical past, fragmented present, and uncertain future (e.g., Childs 2000, xv; Legaspi 2010, 6). Jonathan Sheehan (2005) traces the development of the "Enlightenment Bible," its authority transposed from theological to cultural grounds. Diane Banks (2006) explains the current unresolved conflict in the writing of Israel's history between empirical or "scientific" research and theological commitments as a "dilemma" that "has driven controversy in scholarly biblical studies since the nineteenth century" (225). Ward Blanton (2007) recounts the lasting effects of the contest between New Testament scholars and philosophers to define Christian origins during the nineteenth and early twentieth centuries in Germany. Christopher Seitz (2007) describes how the interpretation of the prophets was transformed in the late eighteenth century by replacing their canonical ordering with one based on the historical reconstructions of their composition. Michael Legaspi (2010) identifies Johann David Michaelis's central role in the eighteenth-century creation of the "academic Bible," which now stands in opposition to the "scriptural Bible" (viii). Stephen Moore and Yvonne Sherwood (2011) argue challenges to the morality of the Bible in the late seventeenth and eighteenth centuries led to an objectifying approach to the Bible as historical "text" and, thus, the "invention of the biblical scholar" (60–1).

As they turn their gaze onto their own discipline, these scholars make the history of biblical scholarship itself a character in the story of the interpretation of the biblical text. This character interacts with others, most prominently the Enlightenment and its effects, whose methods and motives are variously evaluated, but whose continuing effect on biblical scholarship is undeniable. The Bible also plays its part, but in a supporting role, as it primarily receives the action of the scholarly protagonists, who variously reorder, reinvent, or even kill it.

Biblical scholarship has a prominent part in my study as well, but I am not telling its story. The Wisdom Literature category drives the plot: what were its precursors; when was it developed, by whom, and why; what effect has it had; how did it die; and what should follow it? In writing Wisdom Literature's "obituary," I assess the category's life and legacy, ancestors, parents, birth, troubled upbringing, decline, death, and afterlife. By doing so, I adapt a second genre, the "biography" of influential texts, such as those in Princeton University Press's Lives of Great Religious Books series. Here the text moves from object to subject and takes a starring role, as its tale is told from birth to the present. Whether it is Genesis (Hendel 2013), Job (Larrimore 2013), or the *Book of Common Prayer* (Jacobs 2013), in each case, the texts "live" through their interactions with readers, and those readings reveal as much, if not more, about the readers, their commitments, their assumptions, and their understandings of reality as they do about the texts (e.g., Hendel 2013, 10; Larrimore 2013, 6). These "biographies" examine the origins and effects of these influential texts, whereas I consider the same questions not for the texts themselves, but for their communal life as a corpus.

A good biography depicts its subject's character through his or her relationships with others. Telling Wisdom Literature's story involves, therefore, documenting its influence on those who have come into contact with it. As a scholarly construct, Wisdom Literature's primary interactions are with interpreters, who invented the category and have since debated nearly every feature associated with it, including, recently, its very existence. To demonstrate the category's distorting effects on interpretation, I have been forced to focus on examples from recent scholarship where, in my estimation, it has led even the most careful interpreters astray. Indeed, these examples are most effective when they appear in the work of the most learned, influential, and well-respected scholars. Incidentally, the large bodies of work scholars of this caliber have produced on Wisdom Literature also offer greater opportunity to discover such incidences of the category's influence. My intent is not to denigrate their contributions but to argue that if even the interpretations of scholars like these may be mistaken, the paradigm they inherited must be at fault. Many of these interpreters have noted various problems with that paradigm, but they can hardly be blamed for doing the most they could within it. Despite the popular perception, a paradigm shift is a collective, not an individual, accomplishment. As I argue in chapter 4 The Universe of Texts: The Intertextual Network of Genres from Multiple Perspectives, the cultural context in which one stands limits what one can see but should not call the clarity of one's eyesight into question.

Because I am recounting the life of a constructed category rather than a concrete text that still lives on, though it may already be experiencing its "afterlife" (Hendel 2013, 4–5), this biography can include the subject's death. Arguments for the "end" of various subjects have recently become a genre in themselves. Carlos Lozada (2013) identifies Francis Fukuyama's article "The End of History?" (1989) as the Patient Zero of a growing "end-of" craze, which recently included *The End of Men* and *The End of Sex*, along with the ends of power, money, illness, war, faith, and reason. Before Fukuyama coined "the end-of" title, Tryggve Mettinger wrote *A Farewell to the Servant Songs* (1983), which critically evaluates and dismisses Bernhard Duhm's hypothesis in favor of an integrated reading of Isaiah 40–55. Other contributions in theology and religious studies include *The Beginning and the End of "Religion"* (Lash 1996), and, more recently, *The End of Biblical Studies* (Avalos 2007), *Theology and the End of Doctrine* (Helmer 2014), *The End of the Timeless God* (Mullins 2016), and *The End of Protestantism* (Leithart 2016).

These "ends," as Lozada argues, take various forms. Some only countenance the possibility of an end, taking refuge in a question mark. Fukuyama's first foray into the genre would fit into this category, as would mine, a paper titled, "The Nineteenth-Century Beginnings of 'Wisdom Literature,' and Its Twenty-First-Century End?" (2012b).[3] Some of these "ends" actually only declare a meaningful change in their subject, such that it has only ended *as we know it*. Others play on "purpose" as the secondary definition of "end." There is also the 'if-only-they-listened-to-me' end, in which the end is aspired for rather than asserted. Finally, the end of a concept may be declared, in which case it is not aspects of reality but our perception of them that changes so radically that the old concept fades away.

This book primarily fits into that final category. As a way of conceptualizing biblical literature, the Wisdom Literature category has lost its vitality and come to an end; the biblical texts themselves and wisdom as a concept live on. However, aspects of the other four types of ends are evident in my argument as well. The end declared here is, in some sense, aspirational. Some may even follow Mark Twain and respond that reports of Wisdom Literature's death are an exaggeration. The category is still very much in operation in biblical scholarship: introductions to Wisdom Literature continue to be published, conference sessions continue to convene, courses continue to be taught. However, Twain's quip works because he is speaking of his own death; Wisdom Literature cannot do the same. If Wisdom Literature lives, it does so only in our heads. And, in this way, she may live on far beyond her death, as many deceased do. Reading an obituary of the departed may then aid in dispelling denial.

The word "end" is not in my title, so I do not attempt to play on its meaning, but the ideologically convenient purpose Wisdom Literature was created to serve is a crucial feature of my argument. In this sense, the end (purpose) of Wisdom Literature leads to the end (demise) of Wisdom Literature. Also, I am in some sense arguing that the category must end *as we know it*, since I do not deny the validity and value of grouping together texts that have a particular interest in the concept of wisdom or any of the other traits associated with the Wisdom Literature category. I simply argue that using these affinities to classify the texts and isolate them from others in the canon distorts their interpretation according to post-Enlightenment presuppositions. This grouping must be considered only one of many in which the texts

[3] Published as Kynes 2016. A revised version of this essay appears in chapter 3 The Birth of Wisdom Literature: The Nineteenth-Century Origin of the Wisdom Corpus. Reprinted by permission.

could be read, no different than collections of texts which share an interest in other concepts, such as righteousness, justice, or holiness. And, finally, more have joined Wisdom Literature's mourning party since 2012, so I no longer temper my position with a question mark, but I acknowledge the possibility that the category may somehow survive the current scholarly onslaught. It has weathered sustained attacks before. If the concerns raised in the following chapters are addressed, perhaps it will turn out that she was not dead but only sleeping.

Lozada makes another observation about this "end-of" genre relevant to the argument presented here: its popularity is inspired by an uncertain era, when the old structures are questioned and new ones are constantly competing. The argument for the end of Wisdom Literature made here is indeed shaped as much by its historical setting as those for its beginning a century-and-a-half ago. The metacritic is not immune from metacriticism. Just as I believe those earlier interpreters wanted to find a category of biblical texts that reflected their ideals (rationalism, empiricism, universalism, etc.), I must admit that I find such an idea difficult to believe; it seems too good to be true, particularly now, as confidence in such ideals is crumbling. However, the strength of this current era of thought (whether we call it postmodern or something else) is its emphasis on developing interpreters' self-awareness of the situated nature of their interpretation. This becomes the foundation of the second part of my argument.

PART II: GENRE METHODOLOGY

Given its weaknesses, how did Wisdom Literature's hermeneutical hegemony last so long, and why is it collapsing now? Metacriticism only supplies part of the answer. Bruch may have personally wanted Wisdom Literature to thrive as the canonical record of unfettered philosophical reflection, but few likely embraced the category for this reason consciously. Several of those who first read his work accepted the category despite recognizing its reflection of contemporary scholarly desires (see section 3.4 Implications), but most, particularly after it gained notoriety in the 1920s, simply received it as part of the status quo. And, even so, wanting something to be true does not make it false, though it should inspire a healthy dose of skepticism, particularly when objective support is lacking.

Something else carried the corpus along: the method employed for identifying and interpreting genres of biblical texts. An approach to genre that used literary affinities to classify texts into a Linnean taxonomy of "species" of literature had dominated literary scholarship since the Enlightenment (Fishelov 1993, 19–52; Beebee 1994, 2–3). This drive to organize knowledge inspired the nineteenth-century development of German modern research universities (Wellmon 2015) and guided their theological studies (Purvis 2016). Though Gunkel's form-critical method broke with the literary criticism of his day, it was perhaps even more rigid in its categorization of genres (Newsom 2005, 437–8). Mixed forms were degenerate; they made it difficult to explain the correspondence between literary genre and historical *Sitz im Leben*. Once the Wisdom Literature category was invented and applied to Proverbs, Ecclesiastes, and Job, a taxonomic approach to genre perpetuated the classification. Each now *was* in its essence a "Wisdom text."

But, now, finally, biblical scholarship is beginning to catch up with the rest of literary criticism and to shed these essentialist, taxonomic assumptions about genre. Whether the struggles to define Wisdom Literature are cause or effect of this transition is difficult to determine, but those addressing the topic have been some of the early adopters of new (at least to biblical studies) approaches to genre, such as family resemblance and prototype theory. Old habits die hard, however, and even these innovators still maintain the category and many of its taxonomically dependent trappings, such as the "sapiential tradition" (Wright 2010, 302), often recruiting the new genre approaches to their defense. The approach I develop in chapter 4 The Universe of Texts: The Intertextual Network of Genres from Multiple Perspectives does have a number of similarities with these approaches, such as recognizing that genre categories need not be exclusive (e.g., Dell 2015, 152–3), but it more radically relativizes genres, without simply diffusing their power, while providing a fuller understanding of the process through which they are created, including the contributions of cultural perspectives.

Paired with a metacritical analysis of the category's development and the presuppositions on which it depends, and which depend upon it, the application of more recent nominalist approaches to genre encourages a more radical reimagining of the nature of the affiliations that draw Proverbs, Ecclesiastes, and Job together in the Hebrew Bible. In order to understand the essentially intertextual nature of genres, in chapter 4 The Universe of Texts: The Intertextual Network of Genres from Multiple Perspectives, I have drawn together recent research on networks, emergence, and conceptual blending to develop a new approach to genre. My novel contribution is to combine the insights of these theories to take the constellation metaphor occasionally applied to genres and make it three-dimensional. This accounts for the subjectivity cultural and historical location inevitably injects into genre creation, while maintaining the stable objectivity of textual meaning. As readers view this three-dimensional network of texts from different perspectives, they notice different similarities between texts that have a particular resonance for their own culture, making genres inevitably selective, self-reflective, and subjective phenomena. Thus, any given text may contribute to multiple genres, and only through recognizing those multiple genres, viewing the text's interactions with others from various perspectives, is its full meaning, its true location in the vast textual network, evident. Seeing genres in this way, as dynamic groupings rather than static classifications, redirects the hermeneutical power of genre. It still illuminates similarities and differences between texts, but it does not restrict them to a single "horizon of expectation" (see section 4.2 The Rebirth of Genre). Instead, it seeks to increase that illumination from as many angles as possible, dispelling the stark shadows that a single spotlight creates.

Wisdom Terminology

The approach to genre advocated here may also shed some light on the terminological confusion within the field. The word "wisdom" is used with several meanings in biblical scholarship (see section 1.4.4 Pan-Deuteronomism).

Wisdom Literature as a Category

I am primarily concerned here with "Wisdom Literature" as a category of biblical books. When "Wisdom" is capitalized, it refers to the literary category and is used here interchangeably with the fuller title. The quotation marks encompassing the category's title reflect the fact that it is a scholarly convention. For ease of reading, I will henceforth dispense with them. Though I will argue that biblical interpretation would be better off with this convention discarded, its previous prominence cannot be ignored. Some who share some of my concerns about the Wisdom category have argued that the label, or something like it, may need to be maintained as a term of convenience to prevent having constantly to list all the books previously associated with it (Fox 2015,

79; Weeks 2016a, 23). The term has been freighted with such meaning, however, that the day is quite distant when we can speak of "wisdom texts" and simply mean "texts concerned with the concept of wisdom." On the other hand, intending anything more with the term would be a return to the scholarly convention.[4] Until that day comes, the scare quotes or prefix "so-called" is necessary to remind readers that this scholarly convention is only one of many ways the texts may be grouped together.

Wisdom as a Genre

Wisdom Literature is also a genre. Indeed, the words "category" and "genre" are frequently used interchangeably in the study of Wisdom (e.g., Wolfers 1995, 49; Dell 2006, 5–6). In one sense, this is perfectly reasonable. After all, as the glossary in David Duff's *Modern Genre Theory* defines it, a "genre" is "A recurring type or category of text, as defined by structural, thematic and/or functional criteria" (Duff 2000b, xiii). However, speaking of genres as "categories" encourages them to be thought of in taxonomic terms, as defining what a text *is* rather than the group of texts with which it shares some salient similarity. This practice is therefore best avoided. It can be quite helpful, on the other hand, to speak of literary categories as "genres." After all, as I argue in chapter 4 The Universe of Texts: The Intertextual Network of Genres from Multiple Perspectives, according to the nominalist understanding of genre, literary categories *are* genres, since a genre is simply a group of texts gathered together due to some perceived significant affinity between them. Recognizing this prevents any special pleading that seeks to protect the Wisdom Literature category from genre analysis. If literary categories are treated as genres, then they may profit from the recent gains in genre theory rather than being cordoned off from them. So, as I see it, literary categories, such as Wisdom Literature, should be considered genres, but genres should not be considered literary categories.

If they attempt this distinction, biblical scholars, however, tend to make it in precisely the opposite way. Gerald Sheppard (2000, 396) declares, "the term 'wisdom' in the phrase 'biblical wisdom literature'

[4] Fox (2015, 79–80) first entertains "didactic wisdom literature" as a potential alternative and then lands on "ethical instruction" in light of Egyptian parallels. Neither label, in his view, would apply to Job.

does not indicate a genre, but names a corpus of literature within the scriptures." Similarly, John Collins (1997, 265) writes, "There is universal agreement that wisdom does not constitute a literary genre, and that it can find expression in various literary forms." Maurice Gilbert (2003, 15) likewise argues that enough "harmony" exists between the five Wisdom books (including Ben Sira and Wisdom of Solomon) to justify considering them a unified corpus, but adds that their differences prevent them from employing the same "literary genres," which he equates with "literary forms." What these interpreters likely mean is that the Wisdom texts do not all share the same literary structure or form, and, indeed, Collins (1997, 281) concludes that Wisdom Literature coheres "in its use as instructional material rather than in literary form, strictly defined." However, as Duff's definition above indicates, structure is only one feature that may constitute a genre.

Further, any line drawn between Wisdom Literature as a category and various smaller "wisdom forms" or "wisdom genres" (Murphy 1981, 3 and *passim*) can only be arbitrary, because no agreement exists about the relative size of "genres" as opposed to "subgenres" (Duff 2000a, 17), or, as Collins (1997, 266) proposes for Wisdom Literature, "macro-genres." John Gammie (1990), for example, makes an impressive attempt to provide a taxonomy of genres in Wisdom Literature (complete with chart, 47), which divides it into two secondary genres (paraenetic literature and reflective essays) and a series of sub-genres. However, this only demonstrates the difficulty of distinguishing levels in a hierarchy of genres. Wisdom Literature is, after all, a secondary genre of biblical literature, which is a secondary genre of sacred literature, and so on. Nor does a clear line distinguish genre from "mode," a broader and more abstract means of grouping texts, which Sneed (2011, 57) has argued is a better characterization of Wisdom.

Additionally, the distinction between genre and form (as well as the German *Form* and *Gattung*) is unclear and broadly disregarded, both in literary studies (see Duff 2000a, 17) and in biblical form criticism (see Blum 2003, 32–5; Weeks 2013, 17, 19).[5] Even when "form" is used exclusively to identify texts "formally," forms, like genres, can be identified at multiple levels. When Crenshaw (2010, 12) speaks of the for-

[5] I will not attempt to clear up the terminological confusion in form criticism, which made Gunkel himself uncomfortable (see Blum 2003, 33 n. 2; Koch 1969 [1964], 3). For example, Anthony Campbell (2003, 24) claims "genre" is an appropriate translation of *Gattung*, while Klaus Koch (1969 [1964], 5 n. 5) argues, "[I]t is useless to try to differentiate between 'type' (*Gattung*) and 'form' (*Form*)."

mal characteristics of Wisdom Literature, for example, he mentions proverbs and debates, though the debate in Job incorporates multiple proverbs. Form criticism is facing its own challenges and surviving by becoming indistinguishable from genre theory (see, e.g., Blum 2003, 45; Weeks 2013, 18–19), so I will simply employ genre theory and leave the debates about form criticism's future to others (see Sweeney and Ben Zvi 2003).

Wisdom Schools

Wisdom Literature is also associated with schools as pedagogical institutions and with a distinct school of thought analogous to those in Greek philosophy, variously described as a movement, tradition, or class in ancient Israel.[6] The connection of wisdom with schools in ancient Israel slightly predates the clear delineation of the Wisdom Literature category, and suppositions about the worldview of the "sages" who produced that literature are made long before form criticism came onto the scene (see chapter 3 The Birth of Wisdom Literature: The Nineteenth-Century Origin of the Wisdom Corpus). However, the form-critical connection between literary genre and historical *Sitz im Leben* has encouraged the two questions to be treated as mutually reinforcing, with traits abstracted from the Wisdom category, not wisdom as a concept, projected onto the Wisdom schools, movement, etc. (hence, the capital "W"). This only contributes to the circularity which plagues the study of Wisdom Literature (Barton 1996a, 37; Van Leeuwen 2003, 73).[7]

Such historical questions are valuable, but they should not be allowed to drive the discussion of the purported existence and nature of the Wisdom Literature category in the way they have in the past. Form criticism should be treated as a one-way street (Weeks 2013, 18), rather than a roundabout. We may be able to take similarities between the "Wisdom" texts and draw some conclusions about the group called "the wise" in ancient Israel and the setting in which they taught, but we cannot take this group and use it to justify the Wisdom

[6] See Fox (2015, 69), who denies the existence of both types of Wisdom school.

[7] According to the form-critical method, as Koch (1969 [1964], 27) explains, "The regulations and needs of a particular sphere of existence determine and form the respective manners of speech and writing, just as in reverse the customary linguistic forms help to determine the face of a particular way of life."

category. The content of the עצה ("counsel") attributed to this purported class in Jer. 18:18 is never delineated. In fact, the existence of such a distinct group is, like the category, facing serious questions. Doubts have been raised about this common interpretation of Jer. 18:18 (see section 2.1.1 Hebrew Order and section 2.4 The Title "Wisdom"). Others have challenged this view based on the way "wisdom vocabulary" is used in the Hebrew Bible,[8] the interconnections between Proverbs and texts across the canon (Dell 2006), and the nature of ancient Near Eastern scribal culture. Recent studies have revealed a much more integrated scribal setting, in which scribes produced various genres and even mixed them (Sneed 2015a, 67–182). Yoram Cohen (2013, 60–2), for example, believes the texts grouped together on collective tablets or *Sammeltafeln* and in a catalogue from the Old Babylonian period indicate an awareness of a distinct Wisdom genre at the time. However, some of these *Sammeltafeln* include prayers, hymns, and laments along with these "Wisdom" texts.[9] Cohen appropriately concludes, therefore, that proverbs and Wisdom texts were not studied in isolation but in the complex interplay of types of literature in the scribal education.

Some attempt to link this entire variegated scribal enterprise with Wisdom (van der Toorn 2007a, 58), but it is one thing for all the scribal domains to be considered *nēmequ* ("wisdom") and quite another for them to be associated with traits abstracted from the Wisdom corpus (see section 1.4.4 Pan-Deuteronomism). This association, a holdover from the earlier exclusive association between scribes and wisdom, creates more problems than it solves. As the definition of Wisdom Literature has become more inclusive, so has the role of the "sage." Crenshaw (1993, 161 n. 1), for example, chastises John Gammie and Leo Perdue for the "impossible design" of their volume, *The Sage in Israel and the Ancient Near East* (1990), which operates on "the underlying assumption that sapiential influence has permeated the entire Hebrew Bible," leading to essays that "approach the ludicrous" and "put forth highly dubious interpretations of the facts."

[8] See Whybray (1974, 15–31). He observes, for example, the lack of "the wise" among lists of officials and other significant groups (e.g., 1 Kgs. 4:1–6; 2 Kgs. 24:10–16; 1 Chr. 28:1) and the fact that official royal counselors are never called "wise" (17).

[9] Further, he is forced to assume that two unidentified texts in the catalogue are also Wisdom compositions to match the rest in his proposed grouping.

We can concede the historical existence of "the wise," of a sophisticated scribal institution, or even schools in ancient Israel,[10] but to draw any conclusions about distinct views held in these settings requires identifying a group of texts that reflects those views. This just forces upon us the question of the viability of the Wisdom category once again. Speaking of the situation in Egypt, Nili Shupak (2015, 280) writes, "The special nature of wisdom literature stems from its literary genre rather than from the group of people responsible for creating it." Given that in Israel, Isaiah and Jeremiah criticize "the wise" based on their failure to conform to principles evident in Proverbs (Van Leeuwen 1990, 299; see section 7.2.2.4 Inspired Instruction), we cannot draw a simple correspondence between the group described in the Hebrew Bible and the texts often associated with them. Arguments for the ideological distinctiveness of the Wisdom movement, tradition, worldview, or even theology depend logically on the literary category, not the other way around. But even if such a category exists, the worldview distilled from a literary genre cannot comprehend the worldview of those who composed the texts it contains (Van Leeuwen 2003, 83–4; Sneed 2011, 59–60). In fact, if the genre is a later critical creation, it reveals just as much, if not more, about the worldview of the readers who grouped the texts together.

One can start with the Wisdom corpus and derive features that, to a greater or lesser degree, set them apart from other texts in the canon, such as their emphasis on order or on individuals. Annette Schellenberg (2015) has recently provided an excellent example of how this might be done. The question is why one would start with that group of texts in the first place. If the answer is, because we can derive distinct features from them, then the problem becomes evident. Schellenberg (2015, 116 n. 3) acknowledges that "it is one's preconceptions that determine where to see the center of the wisdom tradition" before she proceeds to "concentrate on the five wisdom books of the Old Testament" in "defending the traditional consensus"

[10] For a recent contribution to this continuing debate, see Rollston 2010. He finds evidence of "formal, standardized education" but refrains from using the "polarizing" term "school" (95). On the positive pole is André Lemaire (1984), who argues for numerous schools, while on the negative are Crenshaw (1985, 113) and Weeks (1994, 153), who finds the available evidence "very weak indeed."

(Schellenberg 2015, 120–1). Therefore, when she observes that the distinct ideas she has discovered are all "connected with one another" (138), we can ask, who has done the connecting? The death of the category will both require and enable all these conclusions built upon it to be reconsidered.

Wisdom as a Concept

Finally, there is wisdom (חכמה) as a concept (now with a lower-case "W"). The Hebrew word broadly defined refers to "a high-degree of knowledge and skill in any domain" (Fox 2000, 32). However, it appears across the Hebrew Bible in contexts that range from women spinning goats' hair into linen (Exod. 35:25–6; cf. Prov. 31:24) to God creating the world (Jer. 10:12; Prov. 3:19). Referencing texts from the Torah, Former and Latter Prophets, and Writings, Michael Fox (2000, 33) lays out the word's semantic breadth, which includes (a) "skill"; (b) "learning"; (c) "perceptiveness"; (d) "cleverness"; (e) "prudence"; and (f) "sagacity." Fox argues, however, that though חכמה and related words have the same meaning in Proverbs, the "*concept* of wisdom has changed," adding an ethical feature to the intellectual power it represents (Fox 2000, 29; emphasis original). Such a change is reasonable; words and concepts acquire new meanings in different contexts. However, that being the case, if the word חכמה and the concept of wisdom are primarily interpreted in the context of the Wisdom Literature category, as is commonly the case in biblical scholarship, then the features associated with the category are bound to shape their interpretation. For example, Norman Whybray's (1974) attempt to "investigate afresh" the meaning of this term across the Hebrew Bible only ends up reinforcing its restriction by sapiential assumptions, since he considers all non-intellectual usage of the term as "non-significant" (5, 83; see Van Leeuwen 2010, 418). We do not want to "throw out the baby out with the bathwater" (Schellenberg 2015), of course, but the water has become murky enough that distinguishing baby from bathwater is far from straightforward. In arguing that Wisdom Literature as a genre category is dead, I am not seeking to bury the concept of wisdom with it, but to unencumber the concept of the presuppositions with which the category has entangled it. The death of Wisdom Literature will be new life for wisdom.

PART III: THE REINTEGRATION OF WISDOM LITERATURE

According to the understanding of genre developed in Part II, the shared interest in wisdom as a concept in the so-called Wisdom Literature is only one of the many selective, self-reflective, and subjective ways the texts it contains could be associated. Wisdom is *a* genre *grouping* for these texts rather than *the* genre *category* for them. After the death of Wisdom Literature as a category, its hold on both wisdom as a concept and the interpretation of the texts long associated with it will disintegrate, allowing them to reintegrate into the canonical elements from which they came, creating an occasion for new interpretations of wisdom and the texts associated with the concept to be born and old interpretations to be resurrected. Part III of this book, therefore, begins to explore how freedom from the fetters of the category gives both the texts and the concept of wisdom new life by applying the multiperspectival network approach to genre developed in Part II to the three Hebrew Bible texts commonly classified as Wisdom Literature.

The classification of each book as Wisdom Literature has some justification, and the comparisons the category inspires have offered new insight into their meaning. However, the exclusive application of this category has distorted their interpretation. First, it has discouraged comparison with other texts, leading to their isolation from the rest of the Hebrew Bible. Though studies of Wisdom influence re-engaged the Wisdom texts with those across the canon, they did so on the basis of a distinct Wisdom movement, thereby forestalling any real dialogue between the Wisdom texts and the rest of the canon. Wisdom may influence other texts, but, by definition, it eschews significant influence from other traditions. This lack of dialogue even appears in scholarly practice, as Wisdom specialists create separate traditions of interpretation from those studying other biblical texts.

This canonical separation has led naturally to theological abstraction. Extracting the texts from the broader theological conversation in the Hebrew Bible and grouping them together around features abstract enough to comprehend their diversity, such as didacticism, universalism, humanism, naturalism, pragmatism, and intellectualism (to paraphrase Hunter 2006, 23), is bound to reinforce this line of interpretation. Job becomes the philosophical investigation of a "problem,"

Qoheleth becomes an advocate for natural philosophy, and Proverbs becomes "theoretical" and dogmatically rigid in its fixation on creation and order.

Separating the Wisdom books from the canon and interpreting them at this abstract level leads to the hermeneutical limitation of these texts, as their potential meaning is constrained within the imposed category and the characteristics derived from it. The interpretation of each book is conformed to those characteristics, as the category itself guides the interpretive questions asked, the answers given, and the methods employed for reaching them. Given its history, the Wisdom Literature category is simply too flimsy a foundation on which to exclude the possibility of a significant relationship between prophetic or historical texts and Job or between legal texts and Ecclesiastes or Proverbs. Even when this *a priori* line of argumentation is not used, its influence may be evident when these connections are simply ignored or conformed to preconceptions about the category and understood merely as traces of Wisdom influence.

Putting the categorical presupposition aside, I map out the textual network surrounding each text by documenting the range of various genres or textual groupings in which it has been read across interpretive history. Each generic grouping views the text from a different perspective that reveals additional salient features. Integrated together they depict the texts more fully, adding new depth and complexity to their interpretation. This approach also provides new insight into the depiction of wisdom as a concept in the Hebrew Bible, since breaking down the category boundary similarly limits the importation of characteristics abstracted from it into the interpretation of that concept while also inviting more texts in to fill out its meaning.

The three chapters in the third part of this book, then, each provide a consolidation of previous research on the genre of each so-called Wisdom text. Unlike previous surveys of the genres of these texts, I do not start with the assumption that each is best characterized as Wisdom Literature, with any other genre groupings subservient to that classification. Neither do I argue that the text is best classified as something else. Instead, in keeping with the approach to genre developed in Part II, I argue that there are many different ways of grouping texts together, and each reveals something about the meaning of the books.

I start with Job because others have previously recognized the Wisdom category's inability to comprehend it, which has led to more discussion of the various genre groupings that may elucidate its meaning. Rather than attempt to squeeze Job into some alternative genre as these previous studies have done, I make an initial foray into triangulating its meaning amongst them all. Previous genre proposals for the book demonstrate the selective nature of genre, as each responds to some significant feature of the book that it shares with other texts. None, however, can fully encompass the multitudes it contains. The polyphonic dialogue within the book, between lawsuit and lament, prophecy and parody, drama and didacticism, overflows into a dialogue amongst its readers.

The interpretation of Ecclesiastes throughout the centuries reveals well the self-reflective nature of such inevitably selective approaches to genre, as the text's thorough ambiguity invites multiple, divergent, and often contrasting interpretations. The illumination diverse readers provide on various aspects of a text is projected from a particular position and reflects back from the text onto that interpretive location. Jews and Christians, ancients, moderns, and postmoderns, all see something of themselves in the text. These viewpoints inspire multiple textual groupings for the book across history, apparent in early canon lists, ancient Near Eastern parallels, and literary affinities in form, tone, and content. The pluralism that besets the interpretation of Ecclesiastes may actually be its strength if it can be integrated into a clearer perception of its motley allure.

Though Proverbs is the natural starting point for most studies of wisdom in the Hebrew Bible, I address it last for precisely this reason. Grasping the selective and self-reflective aspects of genre, which come across more clearly in Job and Ecclesiastes, will reveal the subjective imposition of the Wisdom category even on Proverbs, the quintessential Wisdom book. Starting with Proverbs encourages readers to assume that the modern characterization of Wisdom Literature emerges from that text, but, in fact, that characterization is projected upon it, obscuring its complexity. To ground my alternative reading, I take the connection the book's Solomonic attribution creates between it and the definition of wisdom narrated in 1 Kings 1–11 seriously. The Kings account does not share modern interpreters' reticence to integrate intellectual wisdom with other features of Israelite religion from its history, law, cult, and prophecy. Could the restriction of Proverbs and its depiction of wisdom from those spheres be a subjective modern construction?

In the conclusion, then, I explore how recognizing that, as a selective, self-reflective, and subjective modern scholarly creation, the

Wisdom Literature category is not "real" could revitalize the interpretation of wisdom as a concept in the Hebrew Bible along with the texts associated with it. Scraping off the interpretive patina that has built up on the concept through its close association with the category will enable readers to see the concept anew. If conceptions of wisdom in ancient Israel are to be accurately understood, wisdom must be considered first as a concept, not as the uniting feature of a category that first emerged more than two millennia later.

CONCLUSION

When comparing Wisdom Literature to Cinderella, Weeks (2016b, 3–4) quotes a seventeenth-century epilogue to the tale that observes that the parvenu's virtues were useless without a godmother to get her to the ball. As Weeks tells Wisdom's tale, she languished in the kitchen overshadowed by her stepsisters, salvation history and covenant, until the mid-twentieth century when Walther Zimmerli (1963) took on the role of fairy godmother, though the ball gown he dressed her in did not quite fit. In my telling, nineteenth-century biblical scholars, with Bruch in the lead, wield the magic wand of taxonomic genre theory to create the Wisdom Literature category and transform an assortment of post-Enlightenment ideals into the horses that would draw her into the modern age. They made her beautiful, as they understood beauty, and sent her off to find her prince. For us to see the biblical text clearly, however, that conjured princess will have to disappear, for she blinds us to its true nature, and, perhaps, the virtues that were there all along.

Part I

Historical Metacriticism

1

The Rise and Impending Demise of Wisdom Literature

The Modern Scholarly Wisdom Tradition and the Threat of Pan-Sapientialism

> Modern historical research itself is not only research, but the handing down of tradition.
>
> (Gadamer 2004 [1960], 285)

Biblical scholarship is currently suffering from a Wisdom Literature category that is plagued by definitional deficiency, amorphous social location, and hemorrhaging "influence," among other maladies.[1] Weeks describes well the symptoms of Wisdom's illness in his *An Introduction to the Study of Wisdom Literature* (Weeks 2010a). His clear, concise, and critical evaluation of the category highlights the lack of assured results that afflict the field with an incisive force that suggests a better title for his book might have been, "A *Conclusion* to the Study of Wisdom Literature." A basic problem in defining the precise referent of the term "Wisdom Literature" confronts us from the outset. An opening discussion of the difficulty of defining the genre has become *de rigueur* in introductions to Wisdom Literature (see, e.g., Gilbert 2003; Hunter 2006; Crenshaw 2010), but Weeks is more willing than most to admit the significant challenges of this undertaking. He declares, "[B]iblical scholarship does not operate with a consensus about the definition of wisdom literature as a genre—if, indeed, it is a genre in any meaningful sense" (Weeks 2010a, 85). Despite these disagreements, a widespread consensus has developed that Wisdom, however its essence is defined, is the

[1] An earlier version of this chapter was published as Kynes 2015a. Reprinted by permission.

classification of a group of texts in the Hebrew Bible centered on Proverbs, Ecclesiastes, and Job and often including Ben Sira, Wisdom of Solomon, certain psalms, and even occasionally the Song of Songs (see Introduction).

1.1 SYPMTOMS OF WISDOM'S ILLNESS

One challenge Weeks discusses is the development of a genre definition that can account for the diversity in form and content of these so-called Wisdom texts (similarly, Dell 2000, 348–9). This leads to attempts made at a high point of abstraction in the methodology or worldview supposedly shared by the texts, such as their secularism, universalism, or empiricism (Weeks 2010a, 108–26).[2] However, these common Wisdom assumptions are difficult to uncover, with the result that "what we find is going to depend very much on the ways in which we approach the texts" (108). This facilitates the importation of modern presuppositions, such as a distinction between natural theology and revelation or between universal and national conceptions of God (115–16, 119). The search for distinct elements of Wisdom thought is often, therefore, "driven by assumptions which lie outside the texts themselves," as the debate revolves on a circle in which theories about the content of the category and theories about its origin are alternatively used to justify one another (107).

Second, according to Weeks (2010a, 21), parallel ancient Near Eastern Wisdom texts "belong firmly within the broader religious, cultural, and literary traditions of the regions within which they each emerged" so that, if these parallels prove anything, it is only that the biblical works and their authors were likely similarly integrated in Israelite society rather than participants in some international Wisdom movement. In his earlier work, *Early Israelite Wisdom*, Weeks (1994, 7) argues that evidence for a distinct "wisdom school," either physical or philosophical, remains elusive. I would add that it has long been noted by Egyptologists and Assyriologists, and yet is often forgotten, that the term "Wisdom Literature" was adopted into their fields from biblical scholarship

[2] Brown (2014, 3), for example, claims, "Biblical wisdom seeks the common good along with the common God. Wisdom's international, indeed universal appeal constitutes its canonical uniqueness." For examples of this tendency toward theological abstraction, see chs 5–7 in this volume.

(Whybray 2005, 7; see section 1.4.3 Wisdom in the Ancient Near East). This means that appeals to ancient Near Eastern parallels to justify the category run into significant problems of circularity. Grouping the disparate ancient Near Eastern texts that parallel the range of diverse features in Proverbs, Ecclesiastes, and Job into a distinctive ancient Near Eastern Wisdom Literature is dependent on the classification of those three books together as biblical Wisdom. Therefore, these parallels cannot be used to justify the classification itself.

Third, Weeks (2010a, 133) claims, "Attempts to connect wisdom literature with royal administrators and with education are based on a lot of speculation and a certain amount of misunderstanding: we can hardly regard the case as proven." His *Early Israelite Wisdom* is a sustained critique of the "assured result" of Wisdom Literature's origins in the education of administrators. In fact, the evidence from other ancient Near Eastern societies suggests that a scribal class would have been just as responsible for texts of other genres as for Wisdom (Weeks 2010a, 130, 134) (see Introduction: Wisdom Schools).

Fourth, arguments for Wisdom influence, though inspired by the conception of Wisdom as something "historically and ideologically distinct," have in turn called into question that very distinctiveness by becoming so widespread, including texts from Genesis to Esther (similarly, Dell 2006, 12). This suggests that we should instead see these links as evidence of the shared cultural context of the biblical authors and "the broad interconnectedness of biblical literature" (Weeks 2010a, 136, 140–1). Recognizing the seriousness of this symptom, which I devote much of this chapter to diagnosing, Weeks (2010a, 141) concludes, "With so much Israelite discourse rendered 'wise' almost by definition, we must begin to suspect that 'wisdom' has become more of a liability than an asset in our discussions, and that debates about origin and influence would do well to retire the term."

Weeks does not, of course, retire Wisdom completely; it appears in the title of his book, after all. He acknowledges that Wisdom Literature defies simple classification by either intrinsic or extrinsic criteria, which causes attempts to apply the classification to "either make the criteria hopelessly vague, or adjust the contents of the corpus" (Weeks 2010a, 142). However, he presses on to provide his own definition, apparently choosing the former option. Weeks (2010a, 144) declares:

> [W]isdom is not specifically a genre, a movement, or a school of thought. Since it is far from clear, moreover, that the wisdom texts were identified

> as a distinct corpus by contemporary readers, we should probably not strive too hard to identify some classification that the writers might themselves have used. Perhaps we can do no better than to speak of their works loosely as products of a wisdom tradition, which drew on long-established genres linked to exhortation or disputation, was marked by a characteristic style of discourse, and focused on particular problems surrounding individual human life.

Weeks is admittedly more pessimistic than some other scholars about what can be said about Wisdom,[3] but his lack of confidence in the scholarly conclusions about its definition, ancient Near Eastern comparative support, setting, and influence suggests Wisdom scholarship is not currently in a particularly strong position. It would seem that what Gerhard von Rad (1972 [1970], 7–8) observed four decades ago may apply now with even greater force. He claimed that "wisdom . . . is by no means directly rooted in the sources," having instead "first emerged in the scholarly world." Therefore, the possibility exists that it suggests "something which never existed," which could be "dangerously prejudicing the interpretation of varied material." He complained that the rise of scholarly interest in Wisdom had only succeeded in making the concept increasingly unclear (a fact to which Weeks's work testifies), and, thus, he declared, "The question is therefore justified whether the attractive codename 'wisdom' is nowadays not more of a hindrance than a help, in so far as it disguises what stands behind it rather than depicts it properly." Similarly, Matthew Goff (2010, 325) has recently observed,

> [T]he prospects of wisdom as a viable category of genre can seem rather bleak. One might suppose that in the next generation of scholarship the term "wisdom" might seem like a rather antiquated scholarly term, such as the amphictyony, the putative tribal federation of ancient Israel, or the Elohist source.

Indeed, a recent volume edited by Sneed (2015c) asks, *Was There a Wisdom Tradition?* The category, if not on life support, is certainly in critical condition.

Goff (2010, 334–5), like von Rad (1972 [1970], 7) and Weeks (2010a, 144), however, thinks the Wisdom category is worth preserving despite its significant difficulties as long as scholars are willing to acknowledge

[3] For a criticism of the lengths to which Weeks goes in this regard, see Dell's review (2012).

that it is a subjective, modern projection onto the texts, which could be mistaken (see, similarly, Fox 2012, 232). In chapter 2 The Ancestry of Wisdom Literature: Ancient Tradition or Modern Invention? and chapter 3 The Birth of Wisdom Litertature: The Nineteenth-Century Origin of the Wisdom Corpus, I document the category's modern origin, but in this chapter, a brief overview of the past century of Wisdom study will suggest that this scholarly tradition may, in fact, be the source of Wisdom's definitional difficulties. As a result, the survival of Wisdom study will require significant changes in lifestyle. I suggest that the discussion of biblical Wisdom exercise more hermeneutical restraint, cut back on its exclusive claims to define the texts it includes and their historical origins, and add more intertextual connections to its interpretive diet.

These alterations are radical enough to leave Wisdom unrecognizable as a category, transforming it into something else entirely. The intertextual alternative I propose will demand the death of Wisdom Literature as a distinct category of texts and its reintegration into the canonical elements from which it was constituted. This will lead to its eventual resurrection in a new form, one with recognizable continuity and yet profound discontinuity with its current broken and taxonomically bound existence. It may be one of several genre groupings in which the so-called Wisdom texts are read, but it can no longer be considered their exclusive categorization. The prescribed treatment is bold and experimental, but Wisdom no longer has a choice. If it continues on its current course, the term risks succumbing to meaninglessness, either as an unexamined scholarly "consensus" or as an all-encompassing and indistinct umbrella term, thereby, indeed, acting as more of a hindrance than a help. The treatment of this ailment must, however, be determined by a diagnosis of its underlying causes, and this begins with the patient's history.

1.2 PATIENT HISTORY

According to common accounts, Wisdom developed as a distinct subject of scholarly study soon after the turn of the twentieth century. Though I argue in chapter 3 The Birth of Wisdom Literature: The Nineteenth-Century Origin of the Wisdom Corpus that closer study of the history of Wisdom interpretation reveals this date to be at least half a century too late, the discovery of a definite literary relationship between Prov. 22:17–24:22 and the Egyptian Instruction of Amenemope in 1924 did indeed ignite new scholarly interest in the subject (Erman 1924a, b; see Scott 1970, 23–4; Crenshaw 1976, 5–6).[4] Bolstered by the concurrent embrace of Gunkel's trailblazing form-critical work in his commentaries on Genesis (1901) and the Psalms (1926), and the discovery of further ancient Near Eastern parallels, Wisdom Literature burst onto the scene. By the outbreak of World War II, a deluge of research addressed many of the questions that continue to shape the study of Wisdom, such as the extent of parallels from the ancient Near East, the structure of Wisdom thought, and the identification and social setting of Wisdom forms (Crenshaw 1976, 6).[5] As I demonstrate in chapter 3 The Birth of Wisdom Literature: The Nineteenth-Century Origin of the Wisdom Corpus, many of these issues had already been raised in the nineteenth century, but the attention Wisdom received during this period certainly exposed them to a broader audience.

Despite the initial interest in Wisdom, its contribution to biblical scholarship more broadly remained unclear. After World War II, Wisdom's shine faded. The enthusiasm for finding connections between biblical Wisdom texts and those from the ancient Near East became a liability when a new scholarly movement brought the theological significance of Israelite history and Hebrew thought to the fore. Crenshaw (1976, 1–2) offers G. Ernest Wright (1952, 104) and Horst D. Preuss (1970, 393–417) as representative bookends for this trend. Both considered Wisdom's affinity with foreign Wisdom an indication of a worldview they did not hesitate to call "pagan." Wisdom began to be considered a *Fremdkörper* ("foreign body") in the Hebrew Bible (Gese 1958, 2) and treated as a virtual "vermiform appendix" to Old Testament theology (Scott 1970, 39). In fact, in the first volume of von Rad's *Old Testament Theology*, Wisdom is a *literal* appendix, tacked on at the end as "Israel's answer" to YHWH (von Rad 2001 [1957–60], 1:355, 418–59). During this period the common and continuing tendency to define Wisdom negatively, by what it lacks, is pronounced. The absence of revelatory content, Israel's covenant with YHWH, the law revealed at Sinai, and YHWH's intervention in history on behalf of his chosen

[4] Rudolf Smend (1995, 264) notes as well the discovery of Aramaic fragments of Aḥiqar in 1906, along with other ancient Near Eastern parallels recognized in the last two decades of the nineteenth century.

[5] For further bibliography from this period, see Baumgartner 1933, 259–61; Scott 1970, 23 n. 3.

people all contribute to the definition and consequent marginalization of Wisdom.[6] Characterized as secular, empirical, humanistic, international, and universal, it found only a secondary place in relation to the sacred traditions and specific Yahwistic beliefs that loomed large in the theological thought of this period, suffering "the fate of one who is insufficiently Hebraic at a time when a premium is placed on Hebrew thought" (Crenshaw 1976, 2; see also Murphy 1969, 290).

Over the course of the 1960s, however, the emphasis on Israelite history that had marginalized Wisdom eventually fell into disfavor itself. Perhaps due to a new appreciation for its "universalism" (Crenshaw 1976, 3; see also Crenshaw 2010, 1–2) and "secularism" (Sheppard 1980, 2), Wisdom's relationship to the rest of the canon swung to the opposite pole as studies on purported Wisdom influence proliferated. According to these studies, Wisdom played a formative role in books across the canon, including the primeval history (Genesis 1–11), the Joseph story (Genesis 37–50), Exodus, Deuteronomy, the Succession Narrative (2 Samuel 9–20; 1 Kings 1–2), Esther, the historical books as a whole, Isaiah, Jeremiah, Ezekiel, Daniel, Amos, Jonah, and Habakkuk.[7] Wisdom, once disregarded, now gained new prominence, inspiring Roland Murphy (1969, 290) to ask, "Where has Old Testament wisdom failed to appear?"

The arguments for Wisdom influence were based on affinities in vocabulary, subject-matter, and worldview (Crenshaw 1976, 9). The same types of arguments continued to be made with ancient Near Eastern texts (though with greater caution), so in this period the number of texts connected to the Wisdom movement was expanding in both directions at once, across the canon as well as the ancient Near East, with the biblical Wisdom texts testifying to ancient Near Eastern influence on Israelite Wisdom, and other biblical texts from across the canon revealing Wisdom's influence in Israel. Thus, though this development was an about-face in regard to the relationship between Wisdom and the rest of the canon, it continued to see Wisdom as something distinct in Israel, defined to a large degree by its contact and similarity with other texts from the ancient Near East. This attempt

[6] See Zimmerli (1963), who provides an influential and yet flawed response at the time (Weeks 2016b). Murphy's (1975, 2000) attempts to address the issue are, in my view, more effective, since they treat the conflict between Wisdom and Yahwism as a problem of scholars' own making.

[7] For discussion and relevant bibliography, see Crenshaw 1969; Whybray 1974, 1–2; Crenshaw 1976, 9–13; Morgan 1981; Weeks 2010a, 135.

at the reintegration of Wisdom with the rest of the canon did not make Wisdom more Israelite, but Israel more sapiential, as the emphasis on Wisdom's *influence* suggests. As a result, von Rad could both place Wisdom in a poorly integrated appendix to his Old Testament theology and argue that in postexilic Israel "the entire theological thinking of late Judaism came more or less under the sway of wisdom: at any rate it found in the general concept a unity and an all-embracing binding factor such as Israel had not possessed until then" (von Rad 2001 [1957–60], 1:441).

However, each connection with another text diluted that very distinctiveness of Wisdom that influence studies had depended on to be both convincing and significant (Weeks 2010a, 140).[8] The texts and associated features that defined Wisdom expanded as the popularity of these studies initiated a chain reaction, in which arguments for one purported Wisdom-influenced text invited the association of yet another with Wisdom. Thus, Hans Walter Wolff's (1964) conclusion that Amos's intellectual home was the wisdom of tribal society built on Johannes Fichtner's (1949) earlier argument that the prophet Isaiah was a product of a Wisdom school (see Scott 1970, 36–7). Similarly, Whybray's (1968) argument for Wisdom influence in the Succession Narrative (2 Samuel 9–20; 1 Kings 1–2) and Shemaryahu Talmon's (1963) reading of Esther as Wisdom both grew out of von Rad's (1953) earlier suggestion that the Joseph narrative (Genesis 37, 39–50) was an example of the didactic literary novel as a form of Wisdom Literature (see Crenshaw 1969, 129; Sheppard 1980, 8–9). Referring to all these studies and more, Donn Morgan (1981) is able to discover elements of the Wisdom tradition in non-Wisdom traditions across the Hebrew Bible. Fueled by the tendency "to describe as 'wisdom thinking' not just concepts which are found in every wisdom text, but concepts which are found in any wisdom text" (Weeks 2010a, 107–8), from its place as an appendix, Wisdom was spreading like an infection throughout the Hebrew Bible.

Crenshaw (1969) recognized the threat of this enthusiasm for Wisdom influence and attempted to provide a methodological antibiotic to limit the infection. His basic argument, as becomes clear in a later article (1976, 9–13), is that these purported Wisdom-influenced texts were either not distinctive enough from the rest of the canon or

[8] See Crenshaw's counter-arguments below, which consistently aim to demonstrate that these influence studies do not reflect a sufficiently distinct view of Wisdom.

not united enough with Wisdom to justify the sapiential association. For example, Crenshaw (1969, 135–7) argues that von Rad's argument that the Joseph narrative is designed to demonstrate courtly wisdom fails because, on the one hand, the anthropological concern that he claims connects the story with Wisdom is found in texts across the canon, and, on the other hand, numerous "nonwisdom themes" appear, such as appeals to special revelation and theophanic visions, sacrifice, and *Heilsgeschichte*. Crenshaw's approach assumes, however, that Wisdom is composed of a discrete group of texts that can be distinguished formally and thematically from the rest of the canon. His attempts to justify this broadly shared scholarly assumption reveal the weakness of this constraint on Wisdom.

Crenshaw (1976, 9) claims that one of the "distinct disadvantages" of these influence studies is that "they cannot escape circular reasoning" due to the fact that "the wisdom corpus alone (itself the result of a subjective decision on the part of each interpreter) defines what is in the last resort 'wisdom.'" Using Whybray's work as an example, he explains, "If, then, the succession narrative is by definition wisdom, a study of thematic considerations in wisdom literature and in the 'historical' account turns up nothing that contradicts the hypothesis and proves nothing unassumed from the outset." When it comes to his own study of Wisdom based on the limited grouping of Proverbs, Job, Ecclesiastes, Sirach, Wisdom of Solomon, and a few psalms, Crenshaw (1976, 5) admits the "subjective nature" of his "assumption."[9] Nevertheless, he claims elsewhere, "However much the five books ... differ from one another, they retain a mysterious ingredient that links them together in a special way" (Crenshaw 2010, 10).

Crenshaw's restricted Wisdom corpus is itself essentially just a series of studies in Wisdom influence that have been generally accepted, so it shares this liability to the charge of circularity. His attack on the expansion of Wisdom reveals the weakness of the category's current limits, which causes the grouping either to disintegrate or to expand indefinitely as each added text contributes further aspects to what defines Israelite Wisdom. Though he never acknowledges this dilemma, he does fear that influence studies will eviscerate Wisdom of meaning by constantly extending its definition (Crenshaw 1976, 13).

[9] Crenshaw would later question the existence of "Wisdom psalms" altogether. See section 1.4.1 Wisdom in the Psalter below.

These studies challenge Wisdom study more fundamentally, however, by exposing its circularity.

Though he employs family resemblance to maintain the Wisdom genre, Raymond Van Leeuwen (2003, 65; cf. 82–3) clearly recognizes its potential for circular justification:

> The questions are basic and seem to entail a vicious hermeneutical circle, for *how* one understands wisdom determines where one finds wisdom, while the (interpreted) texts are in turn presented as evidence for one's account of wisdom. Researchers inevitably bring to their exegetical work a variety of unstated theoretical and methodological assumptions. (Emphasis original)

David Fishelov (1993, 148) argues the inevitable hermeneutic circle of genre production can avoid becoming vicious if it describes "conspicuous patterns of similarity between the texts" and demonstrates "that these generic characteristics have been real factors in literary history, shaping how writers cope with a subject and building expectations in readers." As I argue in chapter 4 The Universe of Texts: The Intertextual Network of Genres from Multiple Perspectives, the question then becomes, who decides which patterns of similarity are "conspicuous" and when and why have those characteristics become "real factors" in literary history?

In his effort to curb Wisdom influence studies in his initial salvo, Crenshaw (1969, 132) is forced to resort to circular reasoning himself, arguing that "wisdom influence can only be proved by a stylistic or ideological peculiarity found primarily in wisdom literature," in spite of the fact that the content of Wisdom Literature was exactly what was up for debate.[10] With this appeal to the general consensus (even more pronounced in Crenshaw 1974, 227), his work likewise "proves nothing unassumed from the outset." Thus, his oft-cited definition of Wisdom Literature merely lists the features of texts in his Wisdom corpus (Crenshaw 2010, 12):

> [F]ormally, wisdom consists of proverbial sentence or instruction, debate, intellectual reflection; thematically, wisdom comprises self-evident intuitions about mastering life for human betterment, gropings after life's secrets with regard to innocent suffering, grappling with finitude,

[10] Dell (1991, 62 n. 23) recognizes this circularity in Crenshaw's approach to limiting Wisdom, while Sheppard (1983, 479) notes a similar circular reliance on the traditional grouping of Wisdom books in Morgan's (1981) attempt to expand the discussion of Wisdom influence.

> and quest for truth concealed in the created order and manifested in a feminine persona. When a marriage between form and content exists, there is wisdom literature.[11]

More than two decades after his initial arguments against Wisdom influence, with the debate raging on, Crenshaw (1993, 176) admits that "conclusive criteria" for distinguishing which texts derive from a "sapiential milieu" are still lacking. These criteria remain elusive. The "mysterious ingredient" that links the Wisdom texts together is evidently still the subjective presuppositions of modern interpreters. Thus the problem, the traditional Wisdom corpus, with the difficulties it poses to definition, becomes the solution to the problem of Wisdom's spread across the canon.

For a generation, Crenshaw's retrenchment of Wisdom in the traditional scholarly Wisdom corpus has dominated Wisdom scholarship. However, recently, in the midst of a "great bloom" of Wisdom research (Witte 2012, 1159),[12] Crenshaw's valiant effort to save Wisdom from its own internal inconsistencies has begun to lose its hold on the field. Increasingly, it is cited to be criticized, as new approaches to Wisdom are offered. Crenshaw's definition is said to be "only really a way of encapsulating the problem of definition, rather than of solving it" (Weeks 2010a, 142–3). In light of evidence from Qumran, it is charged with illegitimately tying sapiential instruction to "a particular kind of content or a single worldview" (Collins 1997, 278; cf. 266). Due to the diverse worldviews represented in Qumran "Wisdom" texts, its marriage between form and content "ends in divorce" (Goff 2010, 325; cf. 318, citing Collins 1997, 280). Its "list-of-features approach" to genre, which depends on "binary logic" and cannot account for "the diversity inherent in the wisdom tradition," should be replaced with a prototype-theory approach that allows for "fuzzy" generic borders (Wright 2010, 292, 314; cf. 290). The previous generation's infection of influence

[11] Crenshaw does go on to leave room for some fuzziness in the boundaries of the Wisdom category by writing, "Lacking such oneness, a given text participates in biblical wisdom to a greater or lesser extent." However, from his exclusion of historical narratives (1969) to his denial of Wisdom psalms (2000), he has consistently drawn clear lines around it.

[12] The attraction of Wisdom's international character remains in scholarship, though Markus Witte (2012, 1160) adds further reasons for its recent popularity, such as its reflections on the limits of human knowledge and freedom, the relationship of the individual and community, conceptions of life and ethics, and representations of God in the world.

has developed a resistance to Crenshaw's antibiotic, and, as will become apparent, has returned stronger.

1.3 DISCUSSION AND DIAGNOSIS

Sneed provides the most extensive recent attack against the traditional approach to Wisdom that Crenshaw's influential work represents. His article "Is the 'Wisdom Tradition' a Tradition?" is exemplary in the way it raises important questions to which it offers provocative answers that have ignited a healthy discussion among scholars interested in Wisdom. It provides, therefore, an opportunity to diagnose the current stage of the scholarly Wisdom tradition's progression. Sneed (2011, 53–4) takes issue with the common view, which he associates with Crenshaw, that the "wisdom tradition" involves a worldview distinct from those of the priests and prophets, providing an anti-revelatory alternative to Yahwism. In order to argue instead that Wisdom complemented other biblical literature, Sneed appeals to two recent developments in scholarship since those influence arguments of a previous generation: the first involves a new understanding of the nature of genres and the second re-envisions the scribal setting in which biblical texts were produced and preserved.

1.3.1 A Case of Pan-Sapientialism

First, according to Sneed (2011, 52, 54–7), this new understanding of the nature of literary genre asserts its independence from worldviews, which are too large for a genre to convey,[13] from setting (*contra* Gunkel), since genres may be used in more than one setting, and even from ontological existence. In contrast with "generic realism," which considers genres to be stable, static, ontological categories, and thus focuses on determining their specific features and which texts are in and out, Sneed (2011, 66–7), following Kenton Sparks (2005, 6–7), advocates a "generic nominalism" that recognizes that genres are taxonomic inventions with loose, constantly shifting boundaries. However,

[13] Priests, for example, "had lives"; they had to deal with non-cultic activities for which cultic laws would offer little guidance. Similarly, various features of Israelite life are not addressed in Wisdom Literature (Sneed 2011, 60).

Sneed (2011, 57) argues that Wisdom should not even be considered a genre at all, but a "mode," which is a broader, more abstract category (e.g., *comic* play or *heroic* epic, or, in the Bible, *legal* material or *historical* books). The abstraction of modes, which in the case of Wisdom Literature "represents, in many ways, an arbitrary collection of only loosely connected works," actually in itself suggests that speaking of corresponding settings or "worlds" and, presumably, worldviews is inappropriate for Wisdom.

Sneed (2011, 68) follows the exemplary definitions he provides from Derek Kidner, John Goldingay, and Richard Clifford in the widespread practice of defining Hebrew Wisdom negatively, claiming much of its distinctiveness can be explained by recognizing that "[i]t is not historical; it is not apocalyptic (except for hybrid examples in early Judaism); it is not prophetic, and so on." However, he argues, Wisdom is not opposed to these other features of Israelite thought. Instead, as one of several "complementary" modes in the Hebrew Bible (54), its focus simply lies elsewhere. Thus, with its primary purpose the enculturation of elite youth, the Wisdom mode is defined by two broad characteristics: didacticism and moralizing, which, though evident in other modes, are "more overt and distilled" in Wisdom (68–9).

Second, Wisdom's educational function supports Sneed's main opposition to a separate "wisdom tradition." Wisdom's complementary relationship to the rest of the Hebrew Bible is grounded, he argues, in the texts' common scribal origins, in which "scribal scholars," such as "the wise" in Prov. 22:17; 24:23, were responsible, not only for producing the Wisdom Literature, but also for "the preservation, composition, utilization, and instruction of the other literary genres of our Hebrew Bible" (Sneed 2011, 62–4).[14] This scribal role should be "given more weight" in the biblical authors' worldview than other roles they may have simultaneously held, such as Ezra's role as priest. Though the Israelite scribal scholars were not "one homogeneous whole," Sneed claims, "their worldview was largely the same, especially in light of their common academic heritage and common goals in teaching." The Wisdom Literature, then, particularly Proverbs, was central in the

[14] Sneed cites McKenzie (1967, 4–9); Weinfeld (1967, 249–62); Clifford (1997, 1, 7); Sparks (2005, 56); and van der Toorn (2007a, 75–108, 143–72). He also refers to David Carr's view that the Wisdom Literature was employed in the initial training of all biblical authors (see Carr 2011, 410). Sneed's citations of each, with the exception of van der Toorn, explicitly connect this scribal setting to Wisdom (though see van der Toorn 2007a, 58).

academic development of scribes, serving as a primer (see Carr 2005), but, since he claims the other genres and traditions were also taught and studied in this setting, the entire Bible similarly contributed to scribal training (Sneed 2011, 66, 71). Thus, in effect, Sneed deals away with a purported distinctive Wisdom tradition by arguing the whole Hebrew Bible came from the same tradition, and that this tradition was actually shaped by Wisdom, with "these same Israelite wisdom writers or scribal scholars" producing and preserving all the biblical texts (62–3).

Ludger Schwienhorst-Schönberger (2013, 127–8) provides a potential diagnosis to explain the pan-sapiential propensity in Sneed's work when he identifies two opposing tendencies in Wisdom scholarship: one, exemplified by von Rad, aims toward integrating the Wisdom Literature with the rest of the canon and makes it the center (*Mitte*) of Old Testament theology,[15] and the other, exemplified by Preuss, emphasizes Wisdom's distinctiveness in a way that makes it theologically problematic and pushes it toward the edge (*Rand*). As the brief survey above suggests, the past century of Wisdom scholarship could be interpreted as a pendulum swinging between these two extremes, constantly overcorrecting and thereby missing the golden mean between them, and most recently attempting to make the edge the center. Thus, even in his attempt to limit early Wisdom influence studies, Crenshaw (1969, 142 n. 54) demonstrated his unease with the reigning paradigm by acknowledging that those studies offered a "reminder that we have compartmentalized Israelite society far too rigidly." Sneed's work could then be understood as a swing back toward an integrated view of Wisdom after Crenshaw's efforts to restrict its spread.

However, Sneed's problematic methods for reaching his conclusion suggest more is at stake than how to balance the medications properly to manage the tensive relationship between Wisdom and the rest of

[15] Murphy (1967, 407 n. 2) suggests von Rad's attractive presentation of Wisdom in his *Old Testament Theology* was a possible impetus for Wisdom influence studies, but he also criticizes von Rad for relegating Wisdom to a "peripheral or secondary" position as Israel's response to God (1969, 290). This demonstrates the conflicted nature of the interpretation of Wisdom and von Rad's complex involvement in its development in the twentieth century. Murphy's (1969, 290) observation that the entire Old Testament might legitimately be considered "Israel's answer" to YHWH may be the key to reconciling these apparently contradictory effects of von Rad's work: characterizing Wisdom as response rather than revelation marginalized it when Hebrew thought was valued but enabled its popularization when universal ideas became more popular.

the canon. Sneed's attempt to distinguish the Wisdom mode from other modes of biblical literature indicates he does not intend to advocate pan-sapientialism. This makes the pan-sapiential tendency of his argument all the more revealing of the current state of scholarly affairs. While employing his loose approach to genre, he never clearly explains how he reaches the conclusions above about what Wisdom is and is not concerned with. His reticence to list a number of Wisdom texts from which he distills these essential traits is understandable given his opposition to a taxonomically focused generic realism. However, in its place, Sneed (2011, 66–7) offers only the admittedly "arbitrary" and "loosely connected" mode of Wisdom Literature, and a nominalist view of genre, which understands genre as "an unstable entity, constantly changing and dynamic," so that one could, for example, include Daniel, the Song of Songs, and Wisdom psalms, or exclude Job. When Sneed combines his nominalist view of the Wisdom genre, or "mode," with a scribal setting shared with the entire Hebrew Bible, he takes these recent developments in the discussion of Wisdom to an untenable extreme. If the worldview of those who composed and preserved the biblical texts militates against a distinctive Wisdom worldview because the same "scribal scholars," which Sneed and the scholars he cites associate with Wisdom, composed and preserved them all, Wisdom and non-Wisdom alike, then would not their worldview ultimately define the entire Bible? Sneed's approach to genre enables anything to be considered Wisdom, while the shared scribal setting enables everything to be considered Wisdom, and if Wisdom can mean anything and everything, then it means nothing.

1.3.2 Failed Treatments

Sneed's combination of the redefinition of genre with a widespread scribal setting makes clear the pan-sapiential potential of these two responses to the traditional approach to delimiting Wisdom. However, scholars have already recognized the lack of control suggested by each approach individually and attempted to provide some methodological limits to the sapiential expansion they facilitate. The failure of the proposed solutions to maintain the Wisdom category while limiting its spread, apart from appealing circularly to the scholarly consensus, suggests that the problem with Sneed's argument does not stem ultimately from his methods or their combination but from the Wisdom category itself.

1.3.2.1 Refining Genre Methodology

First, in regard to genre, Benjamin Wright provides a more methodologically developed generic nominalist approach to the Wisdom genre in his study of Wisdom at Qumran by incorporating a prototype theory of genre. Wright (2010, 291, 297) acknowledges the lack of consensus on what constitutes Wisdom as a literary genre and the fact that its existence could be questioned altogether. However, because scholars "almost universally agree" on a group of Wisdom books, he believes it legitimate to discuss Wisdom as a genre. He suggests the prototype theory of genre, which does not require the identification of clearly defined classificatory criteria, may enable the category's continued use (297–8). Taking this approach, he begins with the prototypical exemplars of the genre by "general consensus" (Proverbs, Ecclesiastes, Job, Ben Sira, and Wisdom of Solomon) and distills four properties that serve as a template for judging other potential members: (1) pedagogical form and intent; (2) concern for acquiring wisdom through study and learning; (3) engagement with earlier sapiential tradition; and (4) interest in practical ethics (298–9; cf. 294–5). Though other texts may share several of these traits, what is important for a prototype approach is the structural relations between them (301). This approach, then, provides two primary advantages over the more traditional taxonomic list-of-features approach: it removes the need to worry about whether borderline cases belong in the genre or not, and it enables the borders between genres to be blurred and overlap (302–3).

Despite its methodological clarity, Wright's article is a clear example of the *ex post facto* justification of Wisdom that characterizes the current discussion. Beginning with the scholarly consensus on the contents of the genre, he looks for a means of explaining it, finding one in prototype genre theory. What the field lacks is an analysis that reaches back before the Wisdom category became a "fact" to the origins of this grouping that scholars must go to such lengths to justify. The basis for the categorization of this "universally" agreed-upon group of Wisdom texts remains "a legitimate question" (Collins 2010, 429).

1.3.2.2 Examining Scribal Setting

Second, in regard to scribal setting, Dell (2000, 350) observes that in the earlier discussion of Wisdom influence the question of whether these affinities with Wisdom resulted from an early formative influence on the authors' thought or from later literary editing was never answered (see Dell 2000, 352–3). Though few did so explicitly, the earlier "influence" arguments in the 1960s and 70s tended to explain the affinities between those texts and Wisdom with the first explanation (as the term "influence" suggests). The fact that the Wisdom books are predominantly dated later than the texts that purportedly demonstrate Wisdom influence is potentially problematic for this view (see Weeks 2010a, 136). However, Carr (2005, 2011) has recently proposed a historical justification by placing Wisdom Literature at the heart of the enculturation of Hebrew scribes.

The latter view of later sapiential editing built on a notion that Wisdom came to dominate the theology of late Judaism, which is already evident in von Rad's *Old Testament Theology* (2001 [1957–60], 1:441). Sheppard (1980, 13) proposed a means through which this thinking seeped back into earlier texts by taking the use of Wisdom as a "hermeneutical construct," already recognized in Ben Sira 24 by von Rad (1972 [1970], 245), and arguing that it was applied in the editing of texts across the Hebrew Bible.[16] He initially provided Eccl. 12:13–14; Hos. 14:10; Psalms 1 and 2; and 2 Sam. 23:1–7 as examples, but similar arguments expanding on his thesis soon followed, so that, for example, scribal Wisdom was seen to be involved in the editing of the Psalter (Wilson 1992) and the Book of the Twelve (Van Leeuwen 1993). By attributing the entire canon to "scribal scholars," Sneed combines the school setting with that of scribal editing and conflates Wisdom as an early formative influence with the later sapiential editing of texts of other genres. Thus, he consistently links "composition and/or preservation" in his description of these scribal scholars' role in the shaping of the canon (Sneed 2011, 54; cf. 63, 71). In so doing, he demonstrates the diachronic pincer movement by which Wisdom has invaded the broader canon.

Dell's response to such arguments is again indicative of the current state of Wisdom scholarship. Though the influence of Wisdom on biblical material beyond the "so-called wisdom books" was "significant,"

[16] Sheppard's method "depends on locating redactional layers which evaluate canonical non-wisdom literature in terms of the sacred wisdom tradition" (1980, 120), but he fails to provide a clear means of distinguishing between "wisdom" and "non-wisdom" texts. The evidence he does provide of an early Wisdom category in the epilogue of Ecclesiastes is unable to substantiate the inclusion of Job or the exclusion of Song of Songs (128; cf. 159). For this evidence, see section 2.4 The Title "Wisdom."

Dell (2000, 353) argues, "if we want a stable definition of what wisdom literature proper actually includes, we need to restrict it to that material containing in large measure the forms, content, and context of wisdom and this brings us back to the mainline wisdom books." She continues,

> It is interesting that the tradition has preserved wisdom as a separate entity with its own forms, content, and theology and it may well have belonged to a distinctive context in the social world of the Israelites. This suggests that consideration of its literature should focus on the major biblical wisdom books plus a few wisdom psalms, and that the issues of wisdom influence elsewhere in the Old Testament, and its context of origin and development, should have these books as their point of reference.

Her supposition that the tradition has preserved Wisdom as a separate entity, especially if that entity is associated with the "mainline wisdom books," is based on modern views of the definition of Wisdom Literature that, as I argue in subsequent chapters, only gained prominence in the mid-nineteenth century; it is a *scholarly* tradition. This, in the end, is the final recourse she (and the field more broadly) has available to limit Wisdom's spread so that it can have a "stable definition."

1.3.3 The Looming Epidemic

The diverse contents of the Wisdom corpus have consistently given attempts to define its distinctive features a certain instability, characterized by vague, abstract, and potentially all-encompassing definitions (see Weeks 2010a, 108), such as a "shared approach to reality" (Murphy 1978, 47–8), which is broad enough to make all literature Wisdom Literature (Whybray 1982a, 186). Crenshaw considered his work a dam to hold back the spread of Wisdom throughout the Hebrew Bible. Wisdom, held in its own distinctive reservoir by Crenshaw's appeal to the consensus, has, now that that dam has started to crumble, begun to rush across the canon again. If Crenshaw's definition of Wisdom circularly both starts and ends with the scholarly tradition, this more recent approach's start in a traditional consensus, the justification for which scholars are increasingly recognizing to be problematic, leaves it without a way to end apart from an appeal back to that same consensus.

Sneed's work is a prime example of how a broad discomfort with the marginalization of Wisdom from the rest of the Hebrew Bible and its theology has led, not so much to a theologization of Wisdom in scholarship akin to the one once proposed to have existed within the Israelite Wisdom movement itself,[17] as to a sapientialization of the theology of the Hebrew Bible.[18] Thus, Sneed (2011, 64) can cite approvingly Clifford's (1997, 1) view: "Rather than wisdom books influencing other biblical books, however, it is more likely that wisdom thinking was in the main stream of biblical literary production whence its style and ideas radiated throughout biblical writings." The Wisdom worldview is seen as "an important part of the background for most of the literature in the Old Testament" (Høgenhaven 1987, 99–100). So, Carr (2011, 407) argues, " 'In the beginning' was the writing-supported teaching of 'the wise.' " Or, as Dell (2000, 370) writes, "The richness and diversity of wisdom, and the extent of its influence, lead one to suspect that wisdom's proper place is at the heart of the Israelite experience of God." The appendix has become the heart. From there, it threatens to infect the entire canonical corpus. In fact, Yoram Hazony (2012, 284–5 n. 26), in his study of the "philosophy of Hebrew Scripture," argues that Proverbs is no more a work of Wisdom Literature than Genesis, Judges, Jeremiah, or Esther, since they all "were composed largely in an effort to attain and inculcate worldly wisdom." He concludes, "Indeed, I look forward to a time when most of the Hebrew Bible, if not all of it, will be recognized as 'wisdom literature.' " If current trends continue, he may not have to wait long.[19]

1.4 ANALOGOUS CASES

Observing efforts to identify Wisdom texts within other literary corpora supports the diagnostic analysis above. Building on the contents and criteria of the canonical Wisdom category, each demonstrates its

[17] e.g., McKane 1970. For criticism of this view, see, e.g., Dell 2000, 357–8; Crenshaw 2010, 82–8.

[18] See Clements 1995, 269 and the subtitle of Sheppard's influential book, *Wisdom as a Hermeneutical Construct: A Study of the Sapientializing of the Old Testament*. For more on this book, see section 1.3.2.2 Examining Scribal Setting. For recent discussion of sapiential influence on texts across the Hebrew Bible, see Saur 2011a, 447–8; Witte 2012, 1173–4.

[19] Hazony shares his concern for justifying the place of the Hebrew Bible in the study of philosophy with the originator of the category, Johann Bruch, and his work is a culmination of the trajectory Bruch initiated (see chapter 3 The Birth of Wisdom Literature: The Nineteenth-Century Origin of the Wisdom Corpus).

expansive and distorting effect. By then contributing to conceptions of the category, they further compound those effects.

1.4.1 Wisdom in the Psalter

The study of Wisdom in the Psalter, the *kleine biblia*, as Luther called it, is a microcosm of the issues facing the canonical Wisdom category. Interpreters created the "Wisdom psalms" subcategory out of the broader collection of texts in the Psalter based on criteria derived from the Wisdom Literature, such as vocabulary, forms, themes, and didactic intent (Weeks 2005, 292). Depending on what combination of those features they have emphasized, scholars have placed that label on various assortments of psalms, ranging from five (Hurvitz 1988) to thirty-nine (Jacquet 1975–79).[20] Rather than consider these purported Wisdom psalms as further evidence of Wisdom influence, scholars commonly add them to the category itself. This both demonstrates the tenuous distinction between Wisdom influence and Wisdom membership and further broadens the borders of the category both canonically, into the Psalter, and conceptually, into other aspects of Israelite life. These psalms are taken, for example, as evidence of the "intellectualization of the cultic tradition" (Oeming 2008, 161). Given the diversity of Wisdom's contents, these psalms primarily resonate with a single Wisdom book, just as the Dead Sea Scrolls and ancient Near Eastern texts do. Taking the most notable examples, Psalm 37 is similar to instruction on retribution in Proverbs, Psalm 49 to reflection on the brevity of human life in Ecclesiastes, and Psalm 73 to complaints against the prosperity of the wicked in Job (Saur 2015, 187–99, esp. 195; similarly, Dell 2000, 368). Constructing these diverse texts into a common category on top of the fissured foundation of the broader Wisdom category both reveals and deepens those cracks.

First, none of these psalms is *only* like its closest Wisdom parallel. Each has its own distinctive features, so using these affinities to label them "Wisdom psalms" leaves a semantic excess unaccounted for. As a result, the category has indistinct boundaries that make determining a limit to Wisdom's influence in the Psalter difficult. Going further than he had when he recognized the same issue for the broader category, Crenshaw (2000, 15), therefore, rejects the Wisdom psalms designation entirely, arguing instead that these psalms merely reflect

[20] See the table in Cheung 2015, 188–90.

some of the themes in Wisdom Literature. His arguments have not prevailed, however. Instead, the nebulous category has expanded across the Psalter. The criteria for identifying these psalms derived from those developed to encompass the diverse Wisdom texts is, by necessity, abstract. Though attempts are made to restrict it to more "objective" features, such as vocabulary and forms, few of these are actually either limited to or shared by all the Wisdom texts, and thus a higher criterion must be at play. This inevitably ends up being some form of didacticism (e.g., von Rad 1972 [1970], 48; Cheung 2015, 37). And yet, didacticism is such a broad concept that it can easily apply to any psalm—Whybray (1995b, 154) even claims liturgical texts naturally have a didactic function (see Crenshaw 2000, 15). This capacious genre definition, then, encourages and enables a corresponding historical proposal, in which a "process of sapientializing the Psalter" was carried out through the redactional placement of Wisdom psalms at "macro-structurally central points" (Saur 2015, 198). At the extreme, this has led the entire Psalter to be associated with Wisdom (Ceresko 1990, 217, 230; Wilson 1992, 138; Oeming 2008).

Second, the purported Wisdom psalms put significant pressure on the form-critical commitment to attaching each literary genre to a particular *Sitz im Leben*. On this view, a Wisdom psalm would not merely represent the intersection of genres, but of distinct traditions, the scribal and the cultic (Weeks 2005, 304). Westermann (1984, 203), therefore, treats such psalms as an impossibility, since Wisdom and worship are two different "realms." Others have developed speculative historical proposals to explain the apparent "fusion" of the two traditions (e.g., Lemaire 1990).[21] Those mentioned above, who solve this problem by attributing the final form of the Psalter to the editorial work of scribal scholars shaping it according to their interests, give this tradition the final word, just like similar proposals for the canon as a whole, such as Sneed's. A simpler, less speculative solution is simply to conclude that "wisdom, in its important links with the worshipping life of the people of Israel, was not so sharply separate from other areas of Israelite life as scholars have traditionally maintained" (Dell 2000, 369). Further, separating the literary features associated

[21] See the discussion in Weeks 2005, 305. Some of these explanations are rather creative. James Ross (1978, 169) suggests the mix of sapiential and cultic language in Psalm 73 results from the author visiting both the temple and a Wisdom school on the same day.

with Wisdom from "the precarious exercise of traditio-historical reconstruction" (Cheung 2015, 187; similarly, Weeks 2005, 305) will avoid both imposing a conflict between Wisdom and worship and the temptation to subsume the latter under the former.

These generic and historical proposals have hermeneutic effects, which creates a third problem. Categorizing a psalm as Wisdom tends to obscure those features of the psalm that do not correspond to the category's definition. For example, Clinton McCann (1987) notes that the sapiential reading of Psalm 73 generally corresponds with its interpretation as a *Problemgedichte*, in which the psalmist struggles with the problem of righteous suffering. Those who read the psalm as a song of thanksgiving, however, claim the psalmist is recounting his gratitude to God for his deliverance from affliction or for the solution to the problem of divine retribution he has obtained. McCann proposes that the tension between these two major form-critical proposals is actually intrinsic to the psalm itself, and that recognizing it provides the key to understanding the psalm's theology.[22] Applying either label to the psalm would evaporate this tension fundamental to its meaning. However, even this may falsely limit its interpretation because Psalm 73 is more complex than that simple clash of two forms, but is, in fact, "at the same time confession, reflection, prayer, instruction, narrative, and proclamation" (Hossfeld and Zenger 2005, 224). McCann (1987, 249) claims, "[T]he difficulty of classifying Psalm 73 serves as an invitation to pay less attention to the type of Psalm 73 and more attention to its individuality." However, he does not in fact interpret the psalm in isolation without recourse to other texts, but in comparison to both other "Wisdom" texts and other "thanksgiving" texts, which provide the general theological categories that he sees colliding within it. The psalm's individuality, then, becomes evident through an intertextual analysis that uncovers its inter-generic affinities to multiple types (see chapter 4 The Universe of Texts: The Intertextual Network of Genres from Multiple Perspectives).[23]

[22] For more on how this tension contributes to the interpretation of the psalm and the way the Job poet capitalizes on it in the dialogue between Job and his friends, see Kynes 2012a, 161–79.

[23] Van Leeuwen (2003) similarly argues that the "interactive whole whose theological function is greater than the sum of its parts" created by the "twin" Psalms 111 and 112, linked by structure, vocabulary, theology, and repetition, is obscured by the classificatory division between them, which associates the former with thanksgiving and the latter with Wisdom. Weeks (2015, 22–4) makes a similar argument for Psalm 34.

The fourth problem mirrors the third. Wisdom books may have affinities with certain psalms that are not mediated by the features of the category, and these too may be overlooked thanks to the category's influence. Wisdom's categorical lens may encourage this in two ways. It may leave interpreters blind to connections outside of its vision, such that, for example, the links between Proverbs and the cultic entrance liturgy in Psalm 15 are widely overlooked (see section 7.2.2.3 Cultic Guidance).[24] Or, when an affinity between a Wisdom text and a psalm is recognized, the focus on Wisdom may blur other features of the psalm with which the Wisdom text resonates. For instance, the primary psalms to which Job alludes have been classified as Wisdom psalms primarily due to their connection with the book, orienting the dialogue between them toward sapiential interests and obscuring Job's engagement with praise and lament (see Kynes 2012a, 190). Also, as Brown (2005a) demonstrates, rhetorical similarities between a psalm and a Wisdom text like Proverbs may actually create an opportunity to distinguish their divergent emphases, rather than associate them together. Brown (2005a, 93–6) takes, for example, the instructional exordium of Psalm 78 (vv. 1–2) with its close parallels to Proverbs (1:2, 6) as an invitation, not to associate the psalm with Wisdom, but to sharpen the complementary contrast between what the two texts teach.

Dell (2000, 368) observes, "If we only possessed the Psalter and no wisdom literature, we might not immediately recognize the wisdom psalms as substantially different from other discursive psalms or laments." Thus, she claims the debate over the Wisdom psalms "highlights the problem of deciding the boundaries of the wisdom genre." It does more than that, though. It also exposes the problems at the heart of the genre itself, as reliance on an abstract definition derived from a diverse group of texts encourages categorical expansion, historical speculation, and hermeneutical distortion.

1.4.2 Wisdom at Qumran

Recent research on Wisdom in the Dead Sea Scrolls provides a second parallel to the attempts to bring the pan-sapiential epidemic in the Hebrew Bible under control, which is related by both analogy and

[24] The psalm only appears in six of the sixty-one lists in Cheung's table (2015, 188–90).

extension to that phenomenon.[25] Qumran scholars had an advantage over Hebrew Bible scholars, however; they were able to approach their texts as a blank slate without previously established consensuses on which books were Wisdom and which were not (Newsom 2010, 276–7). This *tabula rasa* was quickly piled up with scholarly assumptions, however, and is no longer available (Collins 2010, 425). This has fostered widespread debate, though a generally agreed-upon group of primary Qumran Wisdom texts has emerged.[26] In this discussion, however, a number of the same problematic tendencies have arisen as in the pan-sapiential epidemic in the study of the Hebrew Bible.

Goff's approach to defining Wisdom at Qumran, though it stands somewhere between a chastened list-of-features approach and a family resemblance approach, is nearly indistinguishable from Wright's prototype-theory approach to the question (see section 1.3.2.1 Refining Genre Methodology). Both start with the general scholarly consensus on Wisdom texts in the Hebrew Bible (Goff 2010, 319, 331; Wright 2010, 298) and draw in Qumran texts that interact with this tradition to greater or lesser degrees, integrating other features, such as Torah or apocalyptic interests. For both, this follows a chain-reaction process similar to that in Wisdom influence studies. Texts are associated with Wisdom because of a particular affinity with a single Wisdom text, such as 4QInstruction with Ben Sira, or even a section within it, such as 4QWiles of the Wicked Woman with Proverbs 7 (Wright 2010, 304–6). This has the effect of expanding the definition of Wisdom (see Collins 2010, 424), so that, according to Goff, Ben Sira links Proverbs to the Torah, which then allows the Qumran texts 4Q185 and 4Q525, which share this trait, to be connected to Wisdom, while 4QInstruction takes Proverbs in a different direction, toward apocalypticism,[27] enabling the book of Mysteries and the Treatise of the Two Spirits to be considered Wisdom texts as well (Goff 2010, 330, 322). As a result, Goff concludes that "one can consider a Qumran composition a wisdom text, even if it has little in common with biblical wisdom or includes much that is

[25] For a survey of the extensive relevant literature, see Goff 2009.

[26] 4QInstruction (1Q26, 4Q415–418, 423) (also known as *musar le-mebin*), the book of Mysteries (1Q27, 4Q299–301), 4QWiles of the Wicked Woman (4Q184), 4QSapiential Work (4Q185), 4QWords of the Maśkîl (4Q298), 4QWays of Righteousness (4Q420–421), 4QInstruction-like Composition B (4Q424), and 4QBeatitudes (4Q525). See Goff (2010, 316–17).

[27] Wright (2010, 305) argues, however, that 4QInstruction was primarily associated with Wisdom through its similarity to Ben Sira, not Proverbs.

alien to older sapiential texts" (321).[28] To hold these disparate texts together, both scholars end up with short lists of rather vague and abstract common Wisdom traits. The two "somewhat ambiguous" defining features Goff (2010, 327–8, 330) identifies, noetic purpose and participation in the traditional Israelite Wisdom sapiential discourse exemplified by Proverbs, closely resemble the first and third of Wright's four features (see section 1.3.2.1 Refining Genre Methodology). Whether the various developments in the genre are seen as texts at the boundaries of multiple genres, as Wright would put it, or as "several types of sapiential discourse," which may stem from different traditions, as Goff says, the genre has spread so far in both their treatments that, as Goff (2010, 334) declares, "Engagement of a given wisdom composition with other sapiential texts must be established, rather than assumed on the basis of the genre label." This being the case, however, the value of the genre label is drastically reduced, since it can provide little interpretive guidance. As Goff puts it, once the Qumran texts are considered, "[W]isdom as a literary category, which was somewhat loose to start with, is now even looser" (335).[29]

The progression from scholarly consensus to vague definition to chain-reaction extension and consequent dilution of the genre's interpretive significance common to these two studies is shared by attempts to define Wisdom in the Hebrew Bible. The failed efforts of both scholars, in my opinion, to begin with the general consensus from Hebrew Bible scholarship and provide definitions of Wisdom at Qumran that give the genre a definition distinct enough to provide interpretive guidance and prevent potential pan-sapiential expansion are due not to their erudite efforts, but to the unwieldy Wisdom category handed down to them in the scholarly tradition. In order to encapsulate the diverse Wisdom texts in the Hebrew Bible, this classification is already so nebulous and notional that any attempt to categorize other texts on this basis "threatens to become an all-encompassing category" (Tanzer 2005, 42, quoting Collins 1994, 2).

[28] By tracing the affiliations between texts, Goff's analysis resembles a family resemblance approach. The chain reactions in Goff's article, however, validate the concern that "a family resemblance theory can make anything resemble anything" (Swales 1990, 51).

[29] As Collins (2010, 424) observes, Wright's prototype theory approach provides no check against further expansion, as the addition of each of these texts at the borders of Wisdom expands its sphere and affects the definition of the genre.

1.4.3 Wisdom in the Ancient Near East

The situation in Qumran scholarship in the past half-century is similar to the one scholars faced with ancient Near Eastern texts in the half-century before that: an opportunity to evaluate texts that had appeared unencumbered by a tradition of generic classification. Here also, however, those studying both ancient Egyptian (Williams 1981, 1; Lichtheim 1996, 261) and ancient Mesopotamian texts (Lambert 1960, 1; Beaulieu 2007, 3) defined ancient Near Eastern Wisdom Literature based on the scholarly consensus on the biblical Wisdom corpus (Murphy 1981, 9).[30]

Because the ancient Near Eastern Wisdom Literature category is based on extrinsic scholarly comparison rather than explicit intrinsic ancient association or categorization, the antiquity of the texts does not necessarily extend to the genre classification itself. It may merely be a modern invention, a literary comparison to which ancient readers, including the authors of the biblical texts, would have been oblivious. Therefore, I would characterize the situation in the opposite way David Lambert (2015, 570) does when discussing Job:

> Scholars today might group the book with "wisdom" texts, but, in truth, that designation speaks more to its origins—there are attestations of the dialogue form in wisdom literature from elsewhere in the ancient Near East—than to its place in the canon, for its proverbial content is somewhat limited, even in comparison to Ecclesiastes.

Yes, Job fits poorly in a canonical Wisdom category, but, still, that category originated in an attempt to find a place in the canon for the book: it is a *biblical* category, only later projected onto ancient Near Eastern texts. This fact may be empirically verified by comparing the mid-nineteenth-century date the category developed in biblical scholarship (see chapter 3 The Birth of Wisdom Literature: The Nineteenth-Century Origin of the Wisdom Corpus) with the dates when the ancient Near Eastern texts were discovered and then classified as Wisdom Literature, which only began in the late nineteenth century and significantly accelerated after the discovery of parallels between Amenemope and Proverbs

[30] Paul-Alain Beaulieu claims, "In ancient Mesopotamia, there was no such concept or category as wisdom literature" (2007, 3). Similarly, Giorgio Buccellati (1981, 44) rejects Wisdom as a genre, intellectual or spiritual movement, or literary corpus in ancient Near Eastern literature since "wisdom themes" are broadly diffused throughout a range of literary forms and social settings.

in 1924. Ancient Near Eastern material is notably lacking from the nineteenth-century discussion of the category (Smend 1995, 263). If those texts were known before the biblical Wisdom category was developed, one wonders whether it would have been developed at all, or whether scholars would have been content to categorize Proverbs, Ecclesiastes, and Job with the separate groups of ancient Near Eastern texts with which each shared the greatest affinities, as they are generally willing to group Song of Songs with ancient Near Eastern love poetry. However, though such classifications would better avoid the threat of pan-sapientialism, they would still constrain the books' interpretations unnecessarily, as I will argue in Part II of this book.

The classification of texts from the ancient Near East as Wisdom Literature does not speak to the "origins" of either those texts or biblical texts like Job. This does not mean, of course, that certain ancient Near Eastern texts do not show striking similarities to Job, Proverbs, or Ecclesiastes when compared according to particular characteristics.[31] Nor does it suggest that these comparisons cannot aid in the interpretation of those books, or even that their authors were unaware of similar texts or, at the least, the conventions they represent.[32] It simply means that calling such similarities proof of an "ancient" Wisdom genre is misleading because it invites the general characteristics distilled from the modern, biblical category to be projected onto the texts while masquerading as objective ancient evidence. The similarities between the biblical texts and ancient Near Eastern texts are real; their incorporation into broader theories of ancient Wisdom Literature is a modern scholarly construct and must be treated that way. Those textual similarities direct attention to notable features of the biblical books; however, they do not always correspond with what would be expected if those features are filtered through assumptions about the Wisdom category.

To create a category of ancient Near Eastern Wisdom Literature, texts that resembled Proverbs, such as the Instruction of Ptahhotep or

[31] Because the discussion of potential ancient genre parallels for Ecclesiastes has been particularly wide ranging, I discuss the problems of this comparative approach in more depth in chapter 6 The Intertextual Network of Ecclesiastes and the Self-Reflective Nature of Genre.

[32] The apparent dependence of Prov. 22:17–24:22 on Amenemope is the most prominent example, but it is not alone. The affinities between Job, Ecclesiastes, and Proverbs, respectively, and various ancient Near Eastern genres are addressed in chapters 5–7 in this volume.

the Mesopotamian Instructions of Shuruppak, and others that resembled Ecclesiastes or Job, such as the Egyptian Dialogue between a Man and His Ba or the Mesopotamian Ludlul Bēl Nēmeqi were all grouped together. Just as texts in the Psalter or from early Judaism do, these additional texts stretch the conception of Wisdom in various ways, as they incorporate aspects foreign to the traditional understanding of biblical Wisdom. For example, John Gray repeatedly notes that the Babylonian texts that have the most affinities with Job also share them with psalmic laments. He claims that both the Babylonian texts and Job reflect the conventional language of that common literary type, which was used in fast-liturgies in Mesopotamia and Israel and concludes, "All those texts indicate how intimately wisdom in the ancient Near East was connected with religion" (Gray 1970, 268; cf. 255, 256, 263). Similarly, Paul-Alain Beaulieu (2007, 8–11) discusses how the Mesopotamian reflections on pious suffering were set in the context of exorcism, which indicates the "fully integrated nature of wisdom, religion, ritual, and divination" in Mesopotamian texts. In fact, he observes, exorcism, divination, and rites of intercession were all characterized as *nēmequ* ("wisdom") or associated with Ea, the god of wisdom, so attempting to define Wisdom based on the Mesopotamian understanding would lead to an extensive corpus quite unlike the traditional characterization of biblical Wisdom Literature (12). This literary intermingling is reflected in the integrated nature of scribal culture across the ancient Near East (see Introduction: Wisdom Schools).

It is little surprise, then, that in scholarship on the ancient Near East, as in study of the Psalter and Dead Sea Scrolls, Wisdom Literature has continued to expand, becoming "a mixed bag" stretched to the point that it can no longer carry meaning.[33] It now includes texts as diverse as the Epic of Gilgamesh[34] and the "preceptive hymns" Hymn to Ninurta and The Šamaš Hymn.[35] Once again, using the biblical Wisdom corpus as an unexamined starting point leads to the expansion

[33] Veldhuis (2003, 29), cited in Cohen (2013, 10). See the discussion in Cohen 2013, 9–12. He cites several Assyriologists (Buccellati, Vanstiphout, and Alster) who consider Wisdom Literature "a harmful, outdated, and unusable genre designation." For Cohen's attempt to find ancient evidence for the genre, see Introduction: Wisdom Schools.

[34] e.g., van der Toorn 2007b, 21. See also, Beaulieu (2007, 7), who claims, the work's sapiential themes "cannot easily be separated from the larger context of religion and ritual." Van der Toorn (2007b, 22) also includes Etana, the Series of the Fox, Sidu, and the Series of the Poplar among the ancient Near Eastern Wisdom texts.

[35] See Lambert 1960, 118–38 and discussion in Scott 1970, 32.

of the genre and weakening of its hermeneutical significance, and therefore the potential distortion of the interpretation of its contents.

1.4.4 Pan-Deuteronomism

The difficulties in defining Wisdom at Qumran, in the ancient Near East, and in the Psalter, which can, in all three cases, be traced back to the consensus regarding the content of biblical Wisdom, indicate that this scholarly tradition is the source of the pan-sapiential infection. However, a further analogous case demonstrates that methodological factors have contributed to its spread. This struggle to quarantine a category that threatens to spread across the canon is not a unique phenomenon within biblical studies. In 1999 a collection of essays undertook an evaluation of the growing "pan-Deuteronomism" before "the fever" reached "epidemic proportions" (Schearing 1999, 13). Continuing the analogy in his contribution to the volume, Crenshaw (1999, 146, 145) notes the "astonishing" likeness this pan-Deuteronomistic tendency in scholarship bears to "a pan-sapientialism [that] infected much research relating to the Hebrew Bible" thirty years before. He charges both with circular reasoning and a lack of widely agreed-upon controlling criteria, though he identifies five criteria commonly employed by both: (1) phraseological similarities; (2) thematic considerations; (3) social location; (4) creative adaptation; and (5) oppositional ideology (146). Robert Wilson (1999, 78) similarly observes that "although a growing number of scholars agree that much of the Hebrew Bible is Deuteronomistic, they do not agree on what makes it Deuteronomistic."

As the methodological reflections by Wilson, Richard Coggins, and Norbert Lohfink included in the volume indicate, pan-Deuteronomism shares a number of other similarities with recent Wisdom scholarship beyond their common recourse to circular reasoning, lack of adequate controls, and use of similar criteria.

1. Associated "movement." Just as "speculation" and "misunderstanding" characterize discussion of the Wisdom "movement" in ancient Israel (Weeks 2010a, 133), so evidence is also lacking for the purported tradents of Deuteronomism and the "movement" or "tradition" to which they belonged (Coggins 1999, 26–7; see also Lohfink 1999). Coggins (1999, 32) even entertains the idea that the "Deuteronomists" were not a group at all, but that

instead the similar rhetoric that enables scholars to infer their existence is no more than "just a kind of language" used for particular types of religious prose.

2. Terminology. Confusion results from the use of "wisdom" (often used interchangeably with "scribal" and "sapiential") to refer to a concept, a genre, and a movement, with illegitimate transfers from one category occasionally made to another. As a result, "scribal circles become 'wisdom circles' and schools become 'wisdom schools' almost by default, and therefore anything scribal or educational becomes 'wisdom' as well" (Weeks 2010a, 141). It only confuses the issue to call the Egyptian scribal school, for example, a "Wisdom School" (Fox 1996, 229). Crenshaw (1969, 130 n. 4) attempted to introduce distinct terms to differentiate the books as "wisdom literature" from *paideia*, the Wisdom movement, and *hokmah*, the approach to reality, though this terminology never caught on. Deuteronomism is similarly plagued by terminological confusion. "Deuteronomic" and "Deuteronomistic" are often used in an overlapping fashion, muddling together the name for a book, a literary process, and an ideological movement. Using the terms this way "is to invite a breakdown in understanding" (Coggins 1999, 34–5).
3. Chain-reaction expansion. Just as a chain-reaction process has enabled the expansion of Wisdom across the canon (see above), Lohfink (1999, 39) explains how through a similar process the starting point for determining what is "Deuteronomistic" has expanded from simply the book of Deuteronomy (or even just the law in Deuteronomy 12–26), to the commonly accepted canon of Deuteronomistic texts (Deuteronomy, the Former Prophets, and parts of Jeremiah), to texts that share features with that broader canon, even if they lack direct connections with Deuteronomy. For both phenomena, this extension has reached a point where every part of the canon, and nearly every book, has been associated with each (Coggins 1999, 22–3; Wilson 1999, 68; see above).
4. Recourse to scholarly consensus. A recourse to the scholarly consensus emerged above as a repeated response to the threat of pan-sapientialism. Lohfink takes a similar approach to attempt to limit "pan-Deuteronomistic chain reactions." He suggests reserving the word "Deuteronomistic" only for describing textual affiliation, so that only books "within the *basic Deuteronomistic*

> *canon already known*" may be designated "Deuteronomistic," and beyond that, it could serve only as an adjective for specific phenomena such as "Deuteronomistic formulation" (1999, 39; emphasis added). The semantic distinction Lohfink attempts to make is analogous to the one in Wisdom study between Wisdom Literature and literature that demonstrates Wisdom influence (see above).

Along with their methodological similarities, it appears the two scholarly phenomena may now face the same drastic alternatives: either a nearly all-encompassing embrace or abandonment. The Wisdom category now seems poised between capacious proposals like Sneed's and the potential demise entertained by von Rad, Goff, and Weeks. Pan-Deuteronomism may force a similar choice. Thus, on the one hand, Wilson (1999, 82) argues that the extensive literary activity attributed to the Deuteronomists may make it necessary "to explore the possibility that Deuteronomism was a wide-ranging movement that was much more diverse than scholars commonly think and that was active over a very long period of time." However, on the other hand, he continues, "Recent research may in fact have demonstrated, unwittingly, that the concept of Deuteronomism has become so amorphous that it no longer has any analytical precision and so ought to be abandoned." He concludes, "Current trends in Deuteronomistic research may thus force scholars to take seriously the possibility that if everybody is the Deuteronomist, then there may be no Deuteronomist at all."[36] Thus, there appear to be two potential courses of treatment for biblical scholarship's sapiential appendicitis: amputating the infected category or letting the contagion spread throughout Hebrew Bible interpretation. The significant difficulties of defining the Wisdom genre given the diversity of its contents have left previous mediating approaches untenably unstable.

1.5 PRESCRIBED TREATMENT

These common traits suggest that the scholarly conclusions extrapolated from the similarities between texts in each of these two groupings have exceeded the available evidence. The response to this

[36] Since texts such as Song of Songs and Esther "attest no Deuteronomistic influence at all," the term pan-Deuteronomism does not strictly apply (McKenzie 1999, 270), but the same cannot be said for Sneed's proposal regarding the pervasive influence of "scribal scholars."

situation has generally been to address arguments for sapiential or Deuteronomistic influence in given texts piecemeal in order to determine where the line of plausibility was crossed. I propose a different approach. The intertextual connections on which these conclusions are based could be interpreted in another way altogether. Lohfink, for example, claims the use of "Deuteronomistic" content or language in later works may be better explained simply as the result of the widespread familiarity with the Deuteronomistic writings gained in an educational context. Similar to the way Chronicles takes up passages from the Deuteronomistic History, and yet is not considered "Deuteronomistic" as a result (McKenzie 1999, 269), other writers could refer their readers to Deuteronomy or other Deuteronomistic texts through allusions and citations, perhaps even in their redaction of earlier books, without being involved in a Deuteronomistic "movement" (Lohfink 1999, 65; see also McKenzie 1999, 264).[37] Thus, the connections between the texts associated with each movement and other biblical texts could be the result of scribal familiarity and intertextual citation or allusion rather than of a unified, distinct "school," "movement," or "tradition" in Israelite culture.[38] Noting the "fact of resemblance or dependence" is both more precise and more accurate than the use of vague terms such as Deuteronomism, sapientialism, or wisdom influence because "in the final analysis, writers work directly or indirectly with texts, and with their recollections of texts, not with abstractions" (Weeks 2016a, 18).

I will return to the question of intertextual interpretation in Part II, but the vital point here is that using such connections to create a genre with an associated movement in ancient Israel is a scholarly construct. Admittedly, the formation of such hermeneutical constructs is unavoidable. Texts cannot be read in isolation, and they do not always provide their own genre labels. As Fox (2015, 75–6) observes, scholars have devised numerous categories after the fact to classify phenomena, such as "detective story" or "phoneme." He argues the influence of

[37] Lohfink offers the intentional citation of Jeremiah in Zech. 1:1–6, the plusses in the MT of Jeremiah, and imitations of the Deuteronomistic prose of Jeremiah in Daniel 9 and Baruch as examples.

[38] Thus, while attempting to preserve the "so-called Deuteronomistic History," Thomas Römer (2003, 250–1) envisions a "Deuteronomistic library" of independent scrolls later linked together "by cross-references and the creation of an overarching structure." The distinction between this and the formation of the canon as a whole depends on the presupposition of a separate "Deuteronomistic" movement.

contemporary intellectual and religious ideas need not invalidate these concepts, and they can be applied today with any erroneous historically situated "extraneous assumptions" set aside. Fox does acknowledge, though, that biblical scholarship may be "crippled" by ideological influences "when the ideology predetermines the conclusion."

Metacritical analysis is therefore required to determine whether this is the case (particularly when the scholarly results fit their scholarly setting rather too conveniently), and that same analysis should evaluate which of the questionable assumptions behind those conclusions are indeed "extraneous," and which cannot be set aside without drawing the entire category into question. Therefore, though Fox disputes some of my conclusions here, his comments invite the type of study that produced them. An imposed category is not necessarily problematic, but it becomes so when it creates a new center of gravity for a group of texts, drawing them away from the rich variety of their original context toward its own extrinsically imposed presuppositions. Such constructs may be inevitable, but they are not infallible.

Every genre is such a construct, the formalization of intertextual comparisons made by a group of readers (see chapter 4 The Universe of Texts: The Intertextual Network of Genres from Multiple Perspectives). Attempts to identify links with Wisdom in other texts in the Hebrew Bible (i.e., "Wisdom influence"), in the Psalter, at Qumran, or in the ancient Near East are simply extensions of the same process that originally brought Proverbs, Ecclesiastes, and Job together. Some of these similarities may be the results of later biblical authors intentionally referencing earlier texts ("diachronic" intertextuality) and others may only be the products of readerly comparison ("synchronic" intertextuality) (see Kynes 2013a, 202). As long as the possibilities of other connections are acknowledged, discussions of such similarities are unproblematic. However, the reification of these intertextual connections through their connection to a particular ancient "tradition" or "movement" complete with its own social setting and group of authors and tradents sets unwarranted boundaries on the interpretation of the so-called Wisdom books (see Nickelsburg 2005, 36; Weeks 2013, 19, 24). I would agree with Weeks (1999, 27), who is willing to use the title Wisdom Literature for Proverbs, Ecclesiastes, and Job "so long as this is taken simply as a description of subject-matter, and not of form or origin" (see also Van Leeuwen 2003, 67). Fox (2015, 82, 83) ends up saying much the same thing. While arguing against the existence of both Wisdom schools and a distinct faction of the wise, he claims that as a modern heuristic concept Wisdom Literature may be used to reflect affinities scholars see between texts, but that the texts may be put in other sets as well.

As I argue in chapter 3 The Birth of Wisdom Literature: The Nineteenth-Century Origin of the Wisdom Corpus, however, the presuppositions imported into the category at its creation threaten to distort its contents. Fox (2015, 82), for example, claims that Wisdom Literature does not to appeal to revelation or laws. Comparing these texts solely to one another may indeed lead one to that conclusion, but comparing them to other texts, such as Job with the Psalms, Ecclesiastes with Genesis, or Proverbs with Deuteronomy, would suggest otherwise (see chapters 5 The Intertextual Network of Job and the Selective Nature of Genre, 6 The Intertextual Network of Ecclesiastes and the Self-Reflective Nature of Genre, and 7 The Intertextual Network of Proverbs and the Subjective Nature of Genre, respectively). More than that, using appeal to revelation or lack thereof as a criterion for defining a category is a modern concern. Sneed, then, provides half of the solution to the problem of Wisdom's marginalization produced by the modern scholarly Wisdom tradition in his appeals to a nominalist view of genre that is open to placing the texts in multiple groupings. But, his argument, which attempts to connect his Wisdom "mode" with a setting in scribal education and then expands this setting to the entire Hebrew Bible, brings the entire canon within those boundaries instead of breaking them down.

The efforts to define Wisdom Literature, whether in the Psalter, at Qumran, in ancient Near Eastern texts, or in the Hebrew Bible, resort eventually to the scholarly consensus concerning which biblical texts make up the category's core. With the other arguments resting upon it, this factor carries all the weight in the current debates about Wisdom, and yet little research has been put into how this consensus developed, leaving it a "grey area" in biblical scholarship (Dell 2013c, 605–6 n. 2). If an understanding of Wisdom based on the scholarly consensus either turns circularly back on itself or expands indefinitely, then perhaps that consensus is itself the problem. Instead of starting and ending at this point or starting here and never ending, I propose evaluating how this modern tradition started and interrogating its driving presuppositions to determine how they may be affecting the current discussion of the ancient Wisdom tradition.

Miller (2015, 94, 95, 109) has recently started with the "intuition" that the Wisdom genre exists, with Job, Proverbs, and Ecclesiastes as its "acknowledged 'prototypes,'" and attempted to uncover the attributes of the texts that inspired that intuition for the scholars who first identified the genre. The three he proposes—instructive rhetoric, realized eschatology that advocates for a successful life in the present, and experiential epistemology—each needs some qualification to fit all three books and not apply to many others in the canon. However, if we can discover the actual origin of the category in scholarship, we will not have to guess at those intuitions. We can read the justifications scholars originally gave for the category and understand the reasons behind them.

Indeed, because genres are social phenomena, the social situation in which the Wisdom genre was formed will provide valuable insight into its meaning. And, though biblical scholarship assumes it to be the case, that situation may not be ancient Israel. If the Wisdom genre as it is currently understood is indeed a modern construct, then attempts to interpret its social dimensions must start with the time when it developed before they address a purported setting in ancient Israel. Though genres are inevitable, they are not innocent; they shape the interpretations of texts, often conforming them to the image of their beholder, which is another reason to question their infallibility. Will Wisdom Literature survive? At this point, any steps forward will require a leap backwards to the origin of the category.

2

The Ancestry of Wisdom Literature

Ancient Tradition or Modern Invention?

> Differentiation is the cutting edge of the modernization project, sundering cruelly what tradition had joined.
>
> (Cuddihy 1974, 10)

Despite its widespread influence on biblical interpretation, the origin of the Wisdom Literature categorization has been lost, forgotten, leaving its identification a gray area in biblical scholarship. Though Dell (2013c, 605–6 n. 2) observes that Wisdom's parentage has so far eluded scholars, she notes a widespread view that "vestiges of early nomenclature of this material as 'wisdom' goes back to patristic times." These "vestiges," to which scholars appeal for early evidence of the category, include early views on the structure and order of the canonical books, the association of a group of books with Solomon, the ancient recognition of shared traits between books, and the title "Wisdom" applied to several texts. In this chapter, I aim to dispel the murky shadows enveloping the corpus's ancestry by evaluating this evidence to determine whether it justifies the common assertion that the Wisdom category has an ancient pedigree.

2.1 CANONICAL STRUCTURE AND ORDER

Markus Witte (2012, 1160), for example, argues that the arrangement of the individual books in the Hebrew Bible, the Septuagint, and corresponding early descriptions of the canon all reflect a classification of the texts into historical, prophetic, and sapiential, or didactic, categories. As he proceeds to point out, none of these early canonical structures offers the developed definition of the Wisdom genre that arose with later critical study, but the organization of the canon is often considered an early acknowledgement of the similarity between the Wisdom books. According to this view, the difference between this early category and current views would be merely quantitative, not qualitative—though we may have refined our understanding of Wisdom in light of critical scholarly developments, the thinking goes, we are still referring to the same basic category. For example, Robert Wright (2005, xvii), comments,

> In the early church the critical study of the books of the Bible was not so far advanced that the ancient commentators were preoccupied with the questions of dates, authorship, setting, context, source, genre and structure that energizes so many scholars today. There was a developing sense already then, however, that the books of Proverbs and Ecclesiastes, together with the book of Job and certain of the Psalms, did have some of the common features that over time would lead them to become known collectively as the Wisdom literature of the canonical Old Testament.

He goes on to speak of the early grouping of Proverbs, Ecclesiastes, and Song of Songs in both the East and West, however, not the group of texts he lists above (Wright 2005, xvii). These differing collections *then* and *now* are problematic for his ensuing attempt to summarize the basic message of "the Wisdom literature collectively, then as now," particularly since he fails to note the difference. This, however, is a widespread practice, and Wright is to be applauded for engaging with early interpretation of the so-called Wisdom texts at all, since it is too often simply ignored. Once that evidence is more closely examined, it becomes clear that its testimony to a developing Wisdom category is not as straightforward as it may at first appear.

Josephus, to whom Witte refers, and Philo provide descriptions of the canon from the first century of the common era. Josephus divides his twenty-two-book Hebrew canon into three groups: five books of Mosaic law, thirteen prophetic books, and four books that "contain hymns to God and instructions for people on life [*ὕμνος εἰς τὸν θεὸν καὶ τοῖς ἀνθπώποις ὑποθήκας τοῦ βίου*]" (*Ag.Ap.* 1.8, or 1.40; trans. Barclay 2007, 30). Philo similarly refers to the texts the Therapeutae take into their "sacred chambers" as "laws and oracles delivered through the prophets, and psalms and the other books through which knowledge and piety are increased and perfected [τὰ ἄλλα οἷς ἐπιστήμη καὶ εὐσέβεια συναύξονται καὶ τελειοῦνται]" (*Contempl.* 25; trans. Winston 1981, 46).

Neither of them list the books in these categories, leaving their exact contents disputed. The four books in Josephus's final category are generally considered to be the Psalms and the three Solomonic books, Proverbs, Ecclesiastes, and Song of Songs, leaving Job to be included among the prophets.[1] It is unclear whether he considers all four texts in this grouping a mix of hymns and instructions for life, or, as appears to be the case in Philo's list, he has two separate categories in mind.[2] The content of Philo's final category is even more uncertain. Debate even exists over whether "the other (books)" (τὰ ἄλλα) are canonical or non-canonical texts.[3] It also seems unlikely that this "other" is exclusive, as if only these "other books" fostered and perfected knowledge and piety, as opposed to the rest of the collection, so Philo does not provide any insight into their distinctive character. Combined, these two early witnesses tell us, at the most, only that there were at least three books, likely Proverbs, Ecclesiastes, and Song of Songs, that were considered part of the canon but were categorized neither as Law nor Prophets, and which could be considered, at least in part, and not necessarily exclusively, to teach precepts for human life and foster knowledge and piety. Thus when Goff (2010, 332) claims Josephus "had some understanding, however vague, of a category of literature that roughly approximates our designation 'wisdom literature,'" the understanding is vague and the approximation rough indeed.

The enumerated lists of canonical books that begin to appear in the second century provide more specificity but little more clarity to the question of a potential wisdom category. These lists testify to two broad approaches to ordering the books of the Hebrew Bible, one

[1] e.g., Beckwith 1986, 80, 227 n. 43; Leiman 1989, 53–4; Barclay 2007, 30 n. 165, 166. Rufinus provides potential support for this ordering when he follows a sequence similar to Josephus's (*Symb.* 37–8; trans. Kelly 1955, 72–3). In his list, Job is immediately after the prophets, with the Psalms and "three which Solomon bequeathed to the churches" following after, though he does not demarcate a third division (Ellis 2004, 672 n. 86).

[2] Steve Mason and Robert Kraft (1996, 221) argue Josephus is distinguishing between four genres (laws, tradition/history, hymns, and advice), but that these distinctions are made purely for the sake of his Gentile readers and do not correspond to canonical divisions. They conclude, "There are simply too many variables and insufficient evidence to reconstruct Josephus' personal knowledge of any categorization of biblical materials" (231).

[3] E. Earle Ellis (1992, 8–9) takes the former view, while Roger Beckwith (2004, 54–5) takes the latter.

Hebrew and the other Greek.[4] Nahum Sarna (2007, 576) offers a common view when he claims the tripartite division of the canon in the Hebrew tradition resulted from historical development rather than topical or stylistic categorization, while the Greek order reflects the efforts of Hellenistic Jews to bring this "more or less random" collection into "a more systematic arrangement." This would make the Greek, and not the Hebrew, structure of the canon a potential witness to early views on the Wisdom genre.

2.1.1 Hebrew Order

The third, Writings section of the Hebrew order, in which all the so-called Wisdom texts are located, does seem particularly haphazard, and early references seem to suggest it was little more than a miscellany of later texts added to the established groupings, Law and Prophets. The prologue of Ben Sira appears to refer to this section as simply "the other books of our ancestors," and the lack of an established title for a third section of books in Philo and Josephus reflects this undefined character. Aside from a single reference to "the law of Moses, the prophets, and the psalms" (Luke 24:44), the New Testament does not even indicate an awareness of a third canonical division, elsewhere only mentioning "the law and the prophets" (e.g., Matt. 7:12; Luke 16:16; Acts 13:15; Rom. 3:21).

Roger Beckwith (1986, 149, 163), however, argues that despite its imprecise and apparently late-developed title, the Writings section resulted from the intentional subdivision of a larger collection called the Prophets in the mid-second century BCE.[5] The logic behind this division, he claims, is reflected in the titles of the three sections, which are determined, not by the sequential history recounted in some of their books, but by the other genre prominent in each. Thus, the

[4] Though the Hebrew and Greek orders are sometimes distinguished as "Jewish" and "Christian," respectively, the Hebrew order appears in some Christian texts (e.g., Jerome's *Prologus Galeatus*) and the Greek order may be pre-Christian, so that distinction is a misnomer. Of course, the Christian texts that refer to the Hebrew order are in Latin and Greek, so even a linguistic categorization is imperfect.

[5] Beckwith's theory is rather speculative, particularly when he attempts to attribute this division to Judas Maccabaeus around 164 BCE on the basis of 2 Macc. 2:14–15. Even so, books eventually placed in the third division of the Hebrew Bible, such as Job, Daniel, and Psalms, were indeed occasionally referred to as prophetic literature (McDonald 2007, 110). For more on Job's connections with prophecy, see section 5.2.1.5 Prophecy and section 5.2.3.3 Metaprophecy.

history from conquest to exile in the Prophets is joined to "oracular, visionary books by named prophets," and the exilic and postexilic history in the Writings is combined with "lyrical and proverbial, sapiential books" (Beckwith 1986, 157). Though his historical reconstruction differs, Sarna (2007, 578) ends up saying something similar, that the Writings "were excluded from the prophetic collection because their inspiration appeared to be human rather than Divine, or because they did not otherwise conform to the special ideological content or historical-philosophical framework of that corpus."

Both these explanations, however, fall short of giving the Writings a generic unity, leaving them defined primarily by what they are not (law or prophecy), rather than by what they are. In fact, Beckwith (1986, 164) concludes that the third division is left with its vague title because "there existed no convenient generic term, corresponding to 'the Prophets'... which would cover both the lyrical and the sapiential books." The Writings category may indeed have interpretive significance, then, but only in the sense that the texts in this grouping neither fit well in the other two categories, nor conform to a unified genre themselves, even if the historical texts are set aside. The texts in the Writings are unified primarily by their idiosyncrasy (see de Pury 2003, 25–6).

Beckwith (1986, 157) does refer to one rabbinic text (y. Mak. 2:4–8) to suggest that "Wisdom" may have been a title used for the final section. Aside from the limited nature of this evidence, the diversity of texts that would be included in this category (even excluding the historical texts) would not suggest something like the modern category of Wisdom was in view.[6] The same can be said for R. B. Y. Scott's (1961, 5) attempt to correlate the tripartite Hebrew canon with the torah of the priests, the word of the prophets, and the advice of the wise mentioned in Jer. 18:18. He argues the Writings "represent that element in OT literature most closely associated with wisdom, and least dominated by priestly and prophetic ideas." However, the lengths to which he is forced to go to justify this statement demonstrate how poorly it accounts for the collection as a whole. First, he expands the Wisdom corpus to include Psalms and Song of Songs "according to the ancient

[6] Leiman (1991, 70–2) also notes the mention of "Wisdom" (חכמה), "Prophets" (נביאים), and "Torah" (תורה) in Yalqut Shimeoni Tehillim 702. This has been considered evidence of the early designations of the tripartite canon. However, since the third section is nowhere else designated חכמה, Leiman argues it more likely refers here to Proverbs, which is quoted, or the Solomonic books, since they are each associated with Solomon's wisdom (see section 2.2 Solomonic Association).

Catholic reckoning" (cf. section 2.1.2 Greek Order below). Then, he calls Ruth a "parable," Lamentations a "small psalter," argues Daniel 1–6 and Esther "turn in part on the superior wisdom of Jewish piety," and appeals to the description of Ezra "as endowed with divine wisdom" (Ezra 7:25). Finally, he conveniently overlooks Chronicles and the priestly and prophetic features of any of these texts. This evidence hardly supports a canonical division unified by its association with wisdom.[7]

Joseph Blenkinsopp (1995, 1–5) is more forthright that Wisdom is "clearly inadequate" as a designation for this "heterogeneous collection" on a "purely literary level." However, he argues the Writings were associated with an "authoritative sapiential tradition." The example he provides, Song of Songs, is the most natural, and therefore the least compelling indication that texts across the Writings were associated with this tradition. Though scribes may have been instrumental in the inclusion of the Writings in the canon, and sages may have taken over the prophetic claim to mediate revelation, as he argues, these factors cannot justify classifying the Writings as Wisdom without inviting pan-sapientialism by suggesting that anything the scribes touched turned into Wisdom.

In Jewish tradition, there were subcategories within the Writings (Brandt 2001, 128–30); however, these do not appear to be based on genre either. As with the Prophets, the Talmud refers to three larger books of the Writings: Psalms, Proverbs, and Job (b. Ber. 57b; Sarna 2007, 581–2). These three books, traditionally known as the *Sifrei Emet*,[8] are united both by their relative size and by a distinctive form of cantillation. This system of accents may have set these books off as the three "poetical books" (Fox 2000, 4), though the accents could also be the effect of a grouping made on a different basis rather than its cause. Rabbinic reflection on the grouping, however, describes the books' differences rather than their affinities, associating Psalms with piety, Proverbs with wisdom, and Job with punishment (b. Ber. 57b). This suggests the rabbis are themselves attempting retroactively to provide

[7] Robert Gordis (1968, 19–20) makes a similarly forced attempt to relate all of the books in the Writings with wisdom, in which he is forced to admit how "tenuous" the links appear.

[8] This title may be translated "Books of Truth," though *emet* is apparently derived from an acronym for the Hebrew titles of the three books: איוב, משלי, תהלים. Following the order of the books in the Talmud and Ben Asher tradition, the acronym *Ta'am* (תא"ם) was also used.

hermeneutical significance to a grouping that may have originally arisen for another reason, such as relative length or distinctive cantillation. The other traditional grouping, the Megilloth, groups Ecclesiastes with Song of Songs, Ruth, Lamentations, and Esther.[9] Debates over the date and reasoning behind these groupings aside, they provide little support for an ancient Wisdom category, since they separate the so-called Wisdom books.[10] In its repeated attempts to associate books within these traditional groupings with the traits piety, wisdom, and punishment, b. Berakhot 57b does associate Ecclesiastes with wisdom along with Proverbs, though it also speaks of Ezekiel in the same way. If this is taken as an indication of a Wisdom category, the association of Job with punishment and the Song of Songs with piety would distinguish these books from it.

There have been efforts to identify genre subcategories within the Writings by other means, however. One suggestion made by Bernhard Lang (1998) is that the collection follows Greek precedents by presenting an anthology of exemplary texts in four literary genres: Poetry, Wisdom, Historiography, and Novella. Though it may be reasonable to conclude "both Jews and Christians were aware of the Greek canons of sacred and literary collections" (McDonald 2013, 47), Lang simply assumes the early existence of a Wisdom category consisting of Proverbs, Ecclesiastes, and Job, even as he implicitly acknowledges a "sapiential" Solomonic corpus of Proverbs, Ecclesiastes, and Song of Songs would have been more likely at the time (51, 54). Lang's approach would also group the texts irrespective of their order in any surviving canon list. Albert de Pury (1999; 2003) also compares the Writings to Greek literary canons, though he claims each book in the Writings belongs to its own genre. He does, however, group Job, Proverbs, Ecclesiastes, and Song of Songs as the "humanistischen Ketubim" for their common avoidance of issues of salvation and cultic history. He provides no

[9] b. Berakhot 57b only refers to three shorter books, Song of Songs, Ecclesiastes, and Lamentations, though Esther is appended, perhaps as a later redaction.

[10] Timothy Stone (2013, 211) challenges the common assumption that the Megilloth grouping is late and results from liturgical practice. Adapting Steinberg's view (see below) to the Masoretic Text (MT) order, he claims the five books can be divided into a "wisdom corpus" (Ruth, Song of Songs, and Ecclesiastes), associated with Proverbs (and possibly Job), which precedes them, and a "national-historical corpus" (Lamentations and Esther), associated with Daniel and Ezra-Nehemiah, the books following them. To make this connection between the Megilloth grouping and the Wisdom category, Stone must, however, break down the grouping and associate texts within it with texts outside of it.

evidence of early recognition of this common feature of the books, though.

While Lang's approach would group the texts irrespective of their order in any surviving canon list, Julius Steinberg (2006, 444–54) sees implicit subcategories, which reveal ancient views on genres, evident in the order of the Writings found in b. B. Bat. 14b. It is unclear, however, whether the order of the texts was considered significant for their interpretation, given that before the development of the codex, the texts would have been preserved as a group of scrolls (Barton 1996b, 81). Perhaps, though, b. B. Bat. 14b lists how the scrolls were arranged in a book room (Sarna 1971), or on larger scrolls that could contain several texts (Haran 1993). Even so, the rabbinic text does not explain the significance of its order beyond the vague, likely *post hoc* reference to a progression from destruction to consolation across several sequences of books. Two prominent explanations attribute the actual reason for the order to either the size of the books (e.g., Beckwith 2004, 58), or the relative chronological date of their traditional authors (e.g., Sarna 2007, 581). Neither of these would be particularly significant for questions of genre.

Steinberg argues, however, that the list in b. B. Bat. 14b presents the texts in two sub-collections, a "wisdom series" (Job, Proverbs, Ecclesiastes, and Song of Songs) and a "national-historical series" (Lamentations, Daniel, Esther, and Ezra-Nehemiah), which both move from sorrow to joy, and are together bracketed by the Psalms (with Ruth appended as an introduction) and Chronicles. Though Steinberg uses this schema to provide a wealth of fresh insight into both the meanings of the individual texts in the Writings and the collection as a whole, I remain unconvinced that ancient Jewish readers had such strict distinctions in mind, particularly in light of the close connections between Job and the book of Psalms, which often lies immediately before Job in Hebrew lists, including b. B. Bat. 14b and the Masoretic Text (MT) (see Kynes 2012a, 2015b). Steinberg's schema is not reflected in the MT, the other major witness to the order of the canonical books,[11] and it relates only superficially to the content of the books,

[11] Depending on the categorizations of manuscripts and the date to which the search is extended, there are between twenty-nine and seventy different orders just for the Writings. These orders only begin to multiply after the twelfth century, though. Before that there are only two orders, b. B. Bat. 14b and the MT, as represented in the Aleppo and Leningrad codices (Stone 2013, 3–4). See also Brandt 2001, 125–71.

leaving it "too general to be meaningful" (Stone 2013, 185).[12] His "wisdom series" appears, like Lang's exemplary Wisdom collection, to be an anachronistic projection of the modern category onto the ancient list.[13] Both approaches illuminate the texts in various valuable ways, but neither can draw its conclusions about an ancient Wisdom category without simply assuming its existence at the outset or circularly relying on the very thesis the study is setting out to prove.

2.1.2 Greek Order

The Hebrew canon does not, therefore, appear to be arranged based on genre. Beckwith claims it was the force of Jewish tradition that restrained attempts to order the books according to literary character, contents, or supposed authorship. However, he argues, when its "curb" is removed, "the desire at once finds unlimited scope, and orderings are adopted in Greek, Latin and Syriac lists and Bibles which bear little relation to those found in Jewish and Hebrew sources" (Beckwith 1986, 182). As a result, according to John Barton (2007b, 135), "the Christian division of the canon...is into historical, Wisdom, and prophetic books, and this does seem to reflect an awareness of genre distinctions." Though some would dispute the relative antiquity and Christian origin of the Greek order (e.g., Orlinsky 1974, 851–2; Ellis 1992, 44–5), it does appear that the textual distribution within the Greek lists is more likely "due to the characteristically Alexandrian desire to arrange the books according to their literary character or contents, or their supposed authorship" (Swete 1902, 218).

Even so, the contents of the Greek section that generally comes third in these lists, which commonly includes Job, Psalms, Proverbs, Ecclesiastes, and the Song of Songs, and often Ben Sira and Wisdom of Solomon, is a poor approximation of the current view of Wisdom

[12] When modifying Steinberg's view, Stone attempts to justify connections between the texts on more concrete intertextual connections between the texts. See n. 10 above.

[13] The texts could be grouped in any number of ways, and where those groupings correspond to modern views, it is difficult to prove that those modern categories are not being projected onto the collection. For example, I could imagine successive pairings in the b. B. Bat. order that would also reflect similarities between texts and yield significant insight into their meaning but cross each of the boundaries that Steinberg suggests between his series and the texts that bracket them: Ruth–Psalms and Job; Proverbs and Ecclesiastes; Song of Songs and Lamentations; Daniel and Esther; Ezra–Nehemiah and Chronicles.

Literature.[14] The few general references to the texts in this category from the early church merely classify them as "the books written in verse" (Cyril of Jerusalem, *Catech.* 4.35; trans. McCauley and Stephenson 1968, 136–7).[15] In fact, like the Writings collection, these texts seem to be grouped more by their lack of fit with the other categories in the Greek Old Testament, Law, History, and Prophecy, than their coherence with one another. After all, poetic form does not actually distinguish them well from other texts, many of which are similarly poetic. Given that four of these seven books are attributed to Solomon and Ben Sira is also closely associated with wisdom early on, the title *libri didactici* or "pedagogical books" that eventually arises for this collection in the Latin tradition is understandable. However, given its contents, this category does not equate with "Wisdom Literature," as some would suggest (e.g., Lemche 2008, 6).[16] The texts in this section are too diverse—didacticism is only characteristic of some of them (Barton 2007a, 25). The association of this collection with wisdom may be retroactive, like the rabbis' attempt to explain the *Sifrei Emet*, as readers sought some general theme to hold together a grouping that was not originally collected for a thematic reason. I have yet to find evidence of

[14] Job appears to sit particularly uncomfortably in this collection (see Brandt 2001, 181). In the three early LXX manuscripts extant from the fourth and fifth centuries, Vaticanus, Sinaiticus, and Alexandrinus, Psalms is always first, Proverbs, Ecclesiastes, and Song of Songs are always grouped together in that order, as are Wisdom of Solomon and Ben Sira, but Job appears in a different position every time (see Beckwith 1986, 194; Brandt 2001, 183).

[15] See also the late-fourth-century "Poem to Seleucus" by Amphilochius of Iconium (lines 271–5) (Oberg 1969, 37) and John of Damascus, *De fide orthodoxa* (4.17; trans. Chase 1958, 375). The *Apostolic Constitutions* compares biblical literature with "heathen books," and says, "For if thou hast a mind to read . . . books of wisdom or poetry, thou hast those of the Prophets, of Job, and the Proverbs, in which thou wilt find greater depth of sagacity than in all the heathen poets and sophisters, because these are the words of the Lord, the only wise God" (1.2.6; trans. Roberts et al. 1886, 7:393). Here, the labels "wisdom" and "poetry" appear to apply to the Prophets just as well as to Job and Proverbs. For more, see the chart of early designations for the "poetic books" in Brandt 2001, 205.

[16] In the early eighteenth century, Chambers' *Cyclopedia* (1728) does define the term "sapiential" as "an Epithet applied to certain Books of Scripture, calculated for our Instruction and Improvement in Prudence, or Moral Wisdom; Thus called in Contradistinction to Historical and Prophetical Books. The Sapiential Books are Proverbs, Canticles, Ecclesiastes, the Psalms, and Job; though some reckon this last among the Historical Books" (see Weeks 2016a, 5). Chambers appears to be following the Latin tradition. That the Song of Songs and Psalms fit comfortably in his category while Job's inclusion is less certain suggests different criteria are being used than that which distinguishes the modern Wisdom category.

a clear distinction between didactic and lyrical poetic texts in this category before the nineteenth century (see section 3.1 Wisdom's Date of Birth).[17] The closest approximation of such a subcategory is the collection of texts associated with Solomon, though this classification is not as close as it may first appear.

2.2 SOLOMONIC ASSOCIATION

The association between texts attributed to Solomon is strong in both Jewish and Christian traditions.[18] The rabbis connect the three Solomonic books to phases of his life, explaining that "when a man is young he composes songs; when he grows older he makes sententious remarks; and when he becomes an old man he speaks of the vanity of things" (Cant. Rab. 1:1). Christian interpreters attempt in various ways to make theological sense of the works attributed to Solomon (see Starowieyski 1993, 406–8). Hippolytus of Rome associates the message of each book with a separate person of the Trinity: Proverbs communicates the wisdom of the Father, Ecclesiastes the Son's arrival into the world, and Song of Songs the joy and consolation of the Spirit (*In Cant.* 1.3–5; trans. Smith 2009, 250–2).[19] Origen connects each book with a stage in the progression of philosophical reflection. The Greek sequence of knowledge consisting of Ethics, Physics, and Enoptics (or moral, natural, and inspective knowledge) was actually borrowed from Solomon, he argues, who teaches them in Proverbs, Ecclesiastes, and Song of Songs, respectively (*Comm. Cant.* prologue; trans. Lawson 1957, 40–4). And John Cassian links the books with different aspects of earthly life to be renounced in favor of spiritual contemplation: "fleshly things and the earthly vices" (Proverbs), "all that is accomplished under the sun" (Ecclesiastes), and "everything that is visible"

[17] Junilius (or Junillus) does divide the poetic books into *Proverbia* ("proverbs") (Proverbs, Ben Sira, Wisdom, and Songs of Songs) and *Dogmatica* ("plain teaching") (Ecclesiastes) (Brandt 2001, 205; Maas 2003, 86). For Junilius, Wisdom and Song of Songs are among a secondary group of books that "may be added" to the canon, along with Job, which he categorizes as history.

[18] For Christian identification of three or even five of the "poetic books" with Solomon, see the tables in Brandt 2001, 205–6.

[19] Hippolytus also claims that Proverbs and Song of Songs are a selection of the 3,000 parables and 5,000 songs attributed to Solomon in 1 Kgs. 5:12 [ET 4:32] (*In Cant.* 1.10–15; trans. Smith 2009, 256–65).

(Song of Songs) ("Third Conference: On Renunciations," IV.4; trans. Ramsey 1997, 124).

The Council of Carthage refers to "five books of Solomon,"[20] and the record of the Septuagint order in Cassiodorus's *Institutiones* and *Codex Amiatinus* does the same, listing them as Proverbs, Wisdom of Solomon, Ben Sira, Ecclesiastes, and Song of Songs, even though Ben Sira was not attributed to the wise king and Wisdom of Solomon was widely considered not to be his work either. Augustine observes that some attribute these five books to Solomon, though, despite their semblance in style, "the critics are convinced that [Wisdom of Solomon and Ben Sira] are not from his pen" (*Civ.* 17.20; trans. Walsh and Honan 1954, 73).[21] Thus, this Solomonic connection could potentially indicate more than traditional views on authorship, reflecting instead something like a genre category. Edwin Bissell (1880, 231) provides a number of examples of the broad usage of both the association with Solomon and the term "Wisdom" to refer to a number of books. Both Wisdom of Solomon and Ben Sira were occasionally referred to as "Wisdom" (*ἡ Σοφία*), and Jerome cites a passage from Ben Sira (3:21) under the title "book of Wisdom" (*Liber Sapientiæ*) (*Pelag.* 1.33; trans. Hritzu 1965, 280). Augustine cites Prov. 1:26 as *in quodam libro Sapientiæ* (*Ep.* 140.75; Golbacher 1904, 222),[22] and the Latin fathers would at times use *apud Salomonem* to cite texts from any of the five books associated with Solomon (see Cyprian, *Test.*, 3.6.12;[23] Jerome, *Comm. Ezech.*, 33.1). Finally, he observes, in old Roman missals, these five books are known as "*libri Sapientiales*." Similarly, Leiman (1991, 173 n. 317) lists several passages from early Jewish literature in which Proverbs (b. Ber. 4a; Sot. 44a), Ecclesiastes (b. Meg. 7a), and Song of Songs (Song 1:1 in the Peshitta; Shir. Rab. 1:1) are referred to as the products of Solomon's "wisdom" (חכמה). Thus, as Brevard Childs (1979, 551, 579) argues, these Solomonic attributions may suggest

[20] Canon XXIV (Greek XXVII); Latin text and English translation in Westcott 1896, 448, 550–1.

[21] He initially attributes Wisdom of Solomon to "Jesus Sirach" (*Doctr. chr.* 2.8.13; trans. Green 1995, 69) but later retracts this view (*Retract.* 2.30.2; trans. Bogan 1968, 125). He places all five books associated with Solomon among the Prophets while grouping Job with the "historiography" (*Doctr. chr.* 2.8.13; trans. Green 1995, 69).

[22] Wilfred Parsons (1953, 124) translates this as "in one of the *books* of Wisdom," which suggests a category more strongly than the singular in the quotation.

[23] The citation given here is the one provided by Bissell. In Weber and Bévenot 1972, 94, it is 3.6.3–4, where Cyprian cites Sir. 27:5 as "apud Solomonem" (both spellings appear).

Solomon was considered "the traditional source of Israel's sapiential learning (as Moses was of Torah and David of psalmody)," so that references to Solomon could serve to "classify the material within its genre."[24]

The correlation between Solomonic attribution and sapiential genre categorization has its difficulties, however. First, both the Jewish and Christian attempts to explain the progression between the books in the Solomonic corpus are clearly efforts to make sense of the diversity of the collection (Stone 2013, 186–7). This suggests the Solomonic attribution inspired the grouping of the texts and not vice versa. Also, in this grouping Job is excluded,[25] and the Song of Songs is included.[26] To exchange this grouping for the modern one, the category's definition had to change significantly. The primary basis for the old category, Solomonic attribution, had to be discarded, and new defining features had to be developed (Sheppard 2000, 372, 378), such as the books' common "universalistic, humanistic, philosophical" character, as Franz Delitzsch (1864, 5) would put it in the mid-nineteenth century, or the disproportionate use of the term "wisdom," or some other shared "underlying perspectives" (e.g., Hunter 2006, 20, 24). Though the early collection developed an association with wisdom, changes in both the contents and defining characteristics of the classification suggest the ancient category is qualitatively and not merely quantitatively different than the modern one.[27] Even the "wisdom" associated with the ancient grouping is different than that later used to define the Wisdom category.

[24] Similarly, David Meade (1987, 44–72) sees in the Solomonic attribution "a theological claim to an authoritative tradition, a distinctive Israelite wisdom tradition which began to take national form in the reign of Solomon" (53). Fox (2000, 57), however, claims that other so-called Wisdom texts from the ancient Near East mention sages as their purported authors, not as indicators of a body of traditional material.

[25] Dell (1991, 87) argues the lack of attribution to Solomon or another "famous wisdom author" is a potential argument for Job's place "very much on the edge of the wisdom context."

[26] As Magne Saebø (1998, 276) observes, "It is not because of an allegedly wisdom character that [Song of Songs] has been attributed to Solomon, but the other way round."

[27] Clifford (1998, 17), for example, declares, "The wisdom books are traditionally grouped together because of their association with Solomon (Prov. 1:1; 10:1; 25:1; Qoh. 1:1; Cant. 1:1) *and* because of their common themes and style" (emphasis mine). In fact, one has to choose. Moreover, to say these four books (or even three of them) have the same style requires quite a broad understanding of style.

2.3 COMMON TRAITS

The lack of a Wisdom category does not mean that common characteristics of the so-called Wisdom texts like those Delitzsch mentioned were completely ignored by early interpreters. Origen's influential association of the Solomonic corpus with philosophy is occasionally seen, for example, to provide an early definition of the Wisdom category (Wright 2005, xxv; Sneed 2011, 69). However, Origen has a different group of texts in mind. He does not include Job, placing the book between Ezekiel and Esther, far removed from the Solomonic corpus in his canon list (Eusebius, *Hist. eccl.* 6.25; trans. Deferrari 1953, 2:48; see Ellis 2004, 661).[28] He also operates with a different conception of philosophy, a "divine philosophy" that culminates in the Song of Songs, which in his view, "instils into the soul the love of things divine and heavenly" (*Comm. Cant.* prologue; trans. Lawson 1957, 41; see Trigg 1998, 13, 46). Though Origen speaks of the "the seeker after wisdom" progressing through this curriculum, the wisdom he has in mind will lead one to "reach out for the things unseen and eternal" (trans. Lawson 1957, 44). This is not the practical, humanistic wisdom of the contemporary category.

Similarly, according to the view attributed to him and condemned in the Fifth General Council in 553, Theodore of Mopsuestia believed Proverbs and Ecclesiastes were the products of Solomon's human experience, not divine inspiration, thereby anticipating those who would define Wisdom by its humanistic "non-revelatory speech" (see Crenshaw 1974, 226).[29] He was likewise charged with denying direct divine inspiration to Job and Song of Songs.[30] According to the

[28] Brandt (2001, 213), relying on Heinzgerd Brakmann (1997, 573), argues that the early division of the Hebrew Bible into historical, sapiential, and prophetic books is evident in Origen's liturgical *lectio continua*, which works through the three sections, History, Wisdom, and Prophets, in a three-year cycle. Brakmann does not, however, list the texts that made up the Wisdom reading or whether that title was applied to them at the time. The *Apostolic Constitutions* describe the liturgical reading of "the books of Job and of Solomon, and of the sixteen prophets" after texts from the Pentateuch and History (2.57; trans. Roberts et al. 1886, 7:421).

[29] The statement from the Fifth General Council reads: "Among the things that were written for the instruction of mankind the books of Solomon should be counted, that is, Proverbs and Ecclesiastes, which he composed in his own person for the benefit of others, since he had received not the grace of prophecy but the grace of wisdom, which is clearly different from the former, according to the words of the blessed Paul" (Acts IV.72; trans. Price 2009, 1:262).

[30] See Zaharopoulos 1989, 46–50, 87–8. He argues that Theodore believed that the author of Job drew on source material just as the priests who authored the historical books of the Hebrew Bible did. Rather than completely rejecting these books' inspiration,

Council, he claimed Job was written by "a wise pagan" who embellished a simple folk tale with "superfluous" speech and "pagan knowledge" out of an "improper love of empty honour," and Song of Songs was "a domestic and nuptial song for the banquets of Solomon, with as its theme the insults uttered against his bride" (Acts IV.72–7, 80; trans. Price 2009, 262–7). These views may be the source of the disputed status of these two books (as well as Ezra-Nehemiah and Esther) in several later Antiochene canon lists, with Proverbs and Ecclesiastes joining them in the Florence Codex, a Peshitta manuscript from the ninth century (Beckwith 1986, 191, 195–6).

Doubt is also expressed about the revelatory character of the Solomonic books (though not Job) in Jewish tradition, which likely contributed to their disputed canonical status as well (Beckwith 2004, 64, 71). Thus, one Minor Tractate of the Talmud (Avot de-R. Natan A1, 2) claims the ancients stored the Solomonic books away, "because they spoke [mere] parables and did not belong to the Scriptures," supporting this judgment with apparently erotic or hedonistic passages from each of the three books (Prov. 7:7, 10–20; Eccl. 11:9; Song 7:10, 11–12) (Beckwith 1986, 284). Similarly, a passage in the Tosefta proclaims, "Ecclesiastes does not make the hands unclean because it is [merely] Solomon's wisdom" (Tos. Yad. 2:14).

Further research into early interpretation of the so-called Wisdom books would likely produce additional examples of ancient Jewish and Christian readers identifying similarities between those texts that anticipate modern views of the Wisdom genre. For example, another passage in the Tosefta (Tos. Sabb. 13:1) explains the exclusion of the Writings from the lectionary because reading them on the Sabbath might lead to the reading of common writings on that sacred day. Beckwith (1986, 146–8) thinks this prohibition may be inspired by the fact that several of the Writings are "secular in appearance" and "shared the entertaining quality of secular literature." Also, a text attributed to John Chrysostom (1859) refers to Proverbs, Ben Sira, Ecclesiastes, and Song of Songs as "advice" (*τὸ συμβουλευτικόν*) (*Synopsis Scripturae sacrae*; PG 56:316).[31] None of this is surprising. The texts do share a

Theodore likely attributes different types of inspiration to different biblical books (see also Starowieyski 1993, 411). Junilius's view, possibly derived from Theodore, is similar (see above n. 17; Price 2009, 262 n. 159, 265 n. 169).

[31] *συμβουλευτικόν* is one of Aristotle's three forms of rhetoric (*Rh.* 1358b; translated as "deliberative" by Freese [1926]), which may have inspired this classification.

number of common features; the Wisdom category was not created *ex nihilo*. What is unlikely to be found, though, is any evidence that these shared characteristics were considered to be isolated in Proverbs, Ecclesiastes, and Job to such a degree that they could be considered a distinctive category.

2.4 THE TITLE "WISDOM"

Even so, Whybray (1982a, 181–2) argues that a "specialized meaning" for Wisdom "was recognized at a very early date, as is shown by the titles given to certain Biblical [*sic*] or Apocryphal books," which "reflect an early recognition that certain Old Testament books are especially concerned to teach something called 'wisdom.'" Ben Sira ends with a superscription identifying it as the "Wisdom of Yeshua son of Eleazar son of Sira" (Sir. 51:30; see Skehan and Di Lella 1987, 3, 579–80). Though this may be a later addition (Goff 2010, 333), it could still testify to an early connection between the book and Wisdom. Early interpreters, such as Athanasius (*Easter Letter* 39.20; trans. Brakke 2010, 61), used "Wisdom of Sirach" as a title for the book, though other titles were used as well, such as the rabbinic title "Instruction of Ben Sira" (Skehan and Di Lella 1987, 3–4). There is, of course, another text known as Wisdom of Solomon (in the Greek tradition), the Book of Wisdom (in the Latin tradition), or simply Wisdom (Winston 1979, 65). Both these texts, however, push the boundaries of the Wisdom genre as it is currently conceived by, for example, incorporating the history of Israel (Ben Sira 44–9; Wisdom 11–19) or merging Wisdom with Torah (e.g., Sir. 19:20; 24:1–34) or apocalyptic (e.g., Wisdom 5). They are "obvious exceptions" to the humanism, internationalism, and secularism often associated with the corpus (Miller 2015, 91–2). The titles of the books may not have been intended to identify their genres (Goff 2010, 333), but if they indicate the "specialized meaning" of wisdom, then one wonders whether it should be applied to the books in the Hebrew Bible. One could perhaps say that the biblical Wisdom genre is among the other "ancient biblical phraseology, patterns and genres [that] are applied in the literature of the Second Temple period to new religious phenomenon" (Kister 2004, 18 n. 24). Or perhaps only parts of these books fit into the biblical Wisdom genre, as Gilbert (1984, 307) says of the Wisdom of Solomon. Either way the differences between these texts and the Hebrew Bible Wisdom corpus discount the use of their titles as justification for the biblical category.

None of those so-called Wisdom books in the Hebrew canon has a similar title: Proverbs' superscription identifies the book as "the proverbs of Solomon" (משלי שלמה), Ecclesiastes calls itself "the words of Qoheleth" (דברי קהלת), and Job lacks a superscription (see Goff 2010, 332–3). Proverbs does state its purpose to instruct in wisdom (among other things) in its second verse, the medieval Tosefot to b. B. Bat. 14b refers to Proverbs as ספר החכמה "The Book of Wisdom," and early Christian interpreters occasionally referred to the book as Solomon's "Wisdom."[32] Since such designations are absent in manuscripts of Proverbs, they are better considered descriptions of the book's content than titles (Fox 2000, 53). However, even when Ecclesiastes and Song of Songs are considered together with Proverbs as Solomon's wisdom or resources for gaining wisdom (as in Origen above), such references do not indicate that "wisdom" has a "specialized meaning" that identifies a category of books. Rather, wisdom appears to describe pious knowledge generally.

Nowhere in the Bible is "wisdom" used to identify a category of texts. The closest we come is Jer. 18:18, where "the counsel" (עצה) of "the wise" (חכם) is mentioned, alongside "the instruction" (תורה) of "the priest" (כהן) and "the word" (דבר) of "the prophet" (נביא). However, the most this text would provide is evidence for a specialized meaning for "the wise" as a class in Israel, not for a group of books, despite the common assumption that members of this class authored the biblical Wisdom texts. Even here, though, an argument could be made for the general meaning of "wisdom" as pious knowledge. Carr (2011, 406) observes that in a parallel construction in Ezek. 7:26, "the elders" replace "the wise" as the third group in addition to "the prophet" and "the priest." This suggests, I would argue, that "the wise" in Jer. 18:18 characterizes anyone who has attained wisdom, as could be assumed of the elders and hoped of any counselors to the king, which may be the group in mind in both passages (Van Leeuwen 1990, 304–5), and is not a specialized term for a specific class in Israel.[33] Carr, following Whybray (1974, 2–23), points out that this is how the word is generally used,

[32] This according to Eusebius's recording of Melito (*Hist. eccl.* 4.26; trans. Deferrari 1953, 1:266). According to Eusebius (*Hist. eccl.* 4.22; trans. Deferrari 1953, 1:256), "the all-virtuous Wisdom" was a common designation for Proverbs in the second century.

[33] A stronger argument could be made for "counsel" or "advice" (עצה) as a genre term, since it is associated with these wise elders in both texts and paralleled with the

often in contrast with the "fool," which is certainly not intended to indicate a particular social group (2011, 405).[34]

The collocation of "the words of the wise" (דברי חכמים) with "collections" (אספות) and "books" (ספרים) in Eccl. 12:11–12 suggests evidence of a Wisdom genre to some; however, the contents of this purported genre are unclear, with the following possibilities proposed: the Solomonic books (Sheppard 1980, 128), Proverbs and Ecclesiastes in close association with Deuteronomy (Wilson 1984), or even "the words of the wise whatever they may be" (Fox 1999, 376). Choon-Leong Seow (1997, 386) denies that "the words of the wise" has a technical meaning here and argues that the passage refers to wisdom teachings generally rather than to a specific corpus. Significantly, either way, the passage provides little evidence for Job's inclusion.

Ben Sira supports this generalized understanding of wisdom. For example, when Ben Sira asks God to grant his audience "wisdom of heart to judge his people in righteousness" (45:26), Menahem Kister (2004, 14 n. 6) asks, "Would we have identified 'wisdom' in this verse as identical with that of 'wisdom literature' if we had not known that its author was Ben Sira?" Even Sir. 38:34b–39:3, which Stephen Dempster (2008, 111–13) uses as evidence of a tripartite division of the canon due to its mention of law, wisdom, and prophecies in subsequent cola,[35] could actually be understood to communicate this generalized sense of "wisdom." The text reads:

> 38:34b How different the one who devotes himself
> to the study of the law of the Most High!
> 39:1 He seeks out the wisdom of all the ancients,
> and is concerned with prophecies;
> 39:2 he preserves the sayings of the famous
> and penetrates the subtleties of parables;
> 39:3 he seeks out the hidden meanings of proverbs
> and is at home with the obscurities of parables.

However, just as "prophecies" is paralleled in the next line with "sayings of the famous" (van der Kooij 1998, 35), so "law of the Most High" is paralleled with "wisdom of all the ancients" after it, and therefore

productions of the other two groups. Research would then have to be done into how well this term would apply to the texts now associated with Wisdom, particularly Job.

[34] However, the "fools" were suggested as a social group early on in the development of the Wisdom genre (see section 3.2.3 Heinrich Ewald).

[35] See also Lebram 1968, 180; Skehan and Di Lella 1987, 451–2.

"wisdom" here represents pious knowledge generally and not a specific category of books.[36] Dempster (2008, 111 n. 133) even understands "the famous" in 39:2a in light of "wisdom of all the ancients" in 39:1a, thereby acknowledging the parallel between them, which is reflected in the identical syntax of the two stichoi. He also claims "wisdom of all the ancients" acts "as a variant for 'the ancestral books' in the Prologue" (112 n. 135). There Ben Sira's grandson refers to "the Law and the Prophets and the *other books of our ancestors*." This would mean that both the Law and the Prophets were considered "ancestral books," as well. If "ancestral books" is a variant for "wisdom of all the ancients," then the latter phrase in Sir. 39:1 would also refer to the Law and the Prophets, not to a separate category of books (notice "other" is missing here). This would agree with the following lines of the Prologue, which implicitly refer to the entire canon as texts "pertaining to instruction and wisdom" since, after reading these texts, Ben Sira "was himself *also* led to write something pertaining to instruction and wisdom." As Dempster (2008, 112) says, "These three categories of books have been responsible for Israel's wisdom." Blenkinsopp (1995, 163) goes further, claiming Ben Sira here "identifies Israel's wisdom as the law, the prophets, and the other writings." Indeed, from the Second Temple period onward, Kister argues, " 'Knowledge' and 'wisdom' became loose terms for the intellectual teachings of every circle. The continuity of the biblical wisdom tradition, often presumed because of the similarity in terminology or phraseology is just as often an illusion" (Kister 2004, 19; see also Stone 1984, 389).

2.5 MEDIEVAL INTERPRETATION

Even when medieval interpretation is considered, a category corresponding to the modern Wisdom corpus remains elusive. The *Ordines romani* (*Roman Liturgical Instructions*) describing liturgy from the sixth and seventh centuries divide scripture readings among the seasons, with "the Books of Solomon" in between summertime and

[36] If Ben Sira were referring to the parts of the tripartite canon here, it is odd that he would put wisdom, presumably representing the Writings, before Prophecy, since this violates the Masoretic order, which he follows in Sir. 46:1–49:10 (Leiman 1991, 150–1 n. 135).

the middle of fall and Ezekiel, the Minor Prophets, and Job between Epiphany and the ides of February (cited in van Liere 2014, 210). In Isidore of Seville's *Etymologiae*, which, after its completion in the seventh century, "was arguably the most influential book, after the Bible, in the learned world of the Latin West for nearly a thousand years" (Barney et al. 2006, 3), his discussion of the groupings of the biblical books follows the Hebrew ordering, with so-called Wisdom books integrated into the *Hagiographia* in the third division (6.7; trans. Barney et al. 2006, 135).

In another work of lasting influence, Cassiodorus records the canonical divisions of "Jerome," "Augustine," and "the Septuagint."[37] The Jerome list follows the Hebrew, putting Job and the three books associated with Solomon in the *Hagiographia*. The Augustine list groups Job with the histories and lists three books by Solomon (Proverbs, "Ecclesiasticus" [Ecclesiastes], Song of Songs) and two by Sirach afterwards among the Prophets (see n. 21 above). In the Septuagint list Job is with the historical books, though at the end of the list, and the five books of Solomon (Proverbs, Wisdom of Solomon, Ben Sira, Ecclesiastes, Song of Songs) are between Psalms and the prophetic books (*Institutiones* 1.12–14; trans. Halporn and Vessey 2004, 135–7). These same lists appear in the *Codex Amiatinus* from the eighth century. Cassiodorus divides his own discussion of the Old Testament into six sections: Octateuch, Kings, Prophets, Psalms, Solomon (the five books), and Hagiographa (including Job).

A typical thirteenth-century Bible included Job with Tobit and Esther at the end of a sequence of historical books, with the Psalms next, followed by the five books of Solomon (van Liere 2014, 54–5).[38] The Council of Trent (1546) follows the same order for these books (van Liere 2014, 56). Therefore, the title of Beryl Smalley's *Medieval Exegesis of Wisdom Literature* (1986) is anachronistic. Though, as she argues, there may have been great interest in texts now included in the category, she offers no explicit evidence that medieval interpreters

[37] For the reliability of these attributions, which are often associated instead with Hilary of Poitiers and Epiphanius, bishop of Cyrus, and the relationship between Cassiodorus's work and *Codex Amiatinus*, see Meyvaert 1996.

[38] When Frans van Liere (2014, 266) lists the books in this typical Bible in his appendix, he groups Job in a section labeled "Wisdom Books." He does not provide information on which northern French Bible provided the basis for this order, so it is unclear whether this heading is original or a projection of the modern category onto the list (though the fact that he does not use the division in his earlier description of the list suggests the latter).

believed they were interpreting "Wisdom Literature" at the time, beyond the Solomonic association (e.g., Smalley 1986, 40–2).[39] Though much more work remains to map the interpretive contours of this largely unexplored terrain, even if something closer to the modern Wisdom category existed in the Middle Ages, its absence in the early nineteenth century (see chapter 3 The Birth of Wisdom Literature: The Nineteenth-Century Origin of the Wisdom Corpus) would suggest it had since been forgotten.

CONCLUSION

Whether or not the continuity of the biblical Wisdom tradition is illusory, as Kister suggests, this examination of the ancient "vestiges" of a purported Wisdom category indicates its existence in early interpretation is, at the least, arguments for Wisdom's ancient pedigree rest on rather flimsy foundations. To the degree that a category approaching the modern one existed at all, its contents and definition differed significantly, making it not merely quantitatively, but qualitatively different from the current category. This indicates that von Rad (1972 [1970], 7) was right to claim Wisdom "first emerged in the scholarly world" (see also Weeks 2010a, 144).

This does not, in itself, mean that the category should be rejected. Numerous categories that are necessary for understanding the ancient world, such as those that describe grammatical phenomena, are scholarly creations of which the ancients were ignorant. The later development of a category does not invalidate its usefulness, but, in the case of Wisdom, it does mean, as von Rad observed, that "[i]t belongs, therefore, to the fairly extensive number of biblical-theological collective terms whose validity and content are not once for all established and which have to be examined from time to time from the point of view of whether they are being correctly used." Scholarship, he argues, may have "gone too far in an uncritical use of this collective term," and, as a result distorted the interpretation of its contents (von Rad 1972 [1970], 7). It is indeed suspicious that traits commonly attributed to Wisdom,

[39] At one point, Smalley (1986, 23) even distinguishes between Job and the Solomonic "sapiential books," a classification she applies to the texts, but one that better represents how they were likely seen at the time.

such as rationalism, empiricism, humanism, and universalism, are prominent modern concerns. It would not be that unusual, though, for interpreters to import the traits they valued into their definition of wisdom. The concept of wisdom has been "transformed by the changing needs and aspirations of successive epochs, centuries, and even generations," such that it has consistently "described the highest knowledge men were capable of and the most desirable patterns of human behavior" and "mirrored man's conception of himself, of the world, and of God" (Rice 1958, 2; cited in Fox 2000, 29–30). In Judaism, the torah "overflows with wisdom" (Sir. 24:24), while in Christianity, Christ is the "wisdom of God" (1 Cor. 1:24); "Each community tended to 'decode' canonical wisdom according to their respective commitments" (Berry 1995, 63).[40] Biblical interpreters have demonstrated a tendency to apply the "Wisdom" label to "[a]ny form of knowledge that is recognized as good" (Collins 1994, 2). Given the subjective nature of identifying "good" knowledge, one begins to wonder whether this new emperor is in fact well enough attired to merit the growing throng craning to get a glimpse of his garments. A proper evaluation of Wisdom must therefore venture into the category's birth in that modern scholarly world.

[40] For more on how early Jews and Christians interpreted the concept of wisdom (as opposed to the purported category) in line with these commitments, see Wilken 1975 (e.g., 11, 48, 70–1).

3

The Birth of Wisdom Literature

The Nineteenth-Century Origin of the Wisdom Corpus

Definitions of genre can hardly be stated, before they are falsified.
(Fowler 1982, 42)

If Wisdom's lineage cannot be traced back to early Judaism or Christianity, then where did it come from? I will pursue the answer to that question in this chapter from the opposite end of history, working back through the potential origins suggested by previous scholars and following chains of citation to the earliest point at which something that modern scholars would recognize as their category can be found. This is the moment when Wisdom, which may have gestated for some time, entered the world, took its first breath, and received its name.

3.1 WISDOM'S DATE OF BIRTH

Once again Weeks (2010a, 21–2) provides a starting point. He claims that the channeling off of the Wisdom Literature from the mainstream of Israelite theology, and its association with a separate group with concerns distinct from the historical and prophetic books became a scholarly commonplace after World War II. At this time, a widespread emphasis on history in Old Testament scholarship fused with a conception of the foreign nature of Wisdom Literature, inspired by parallels discovered in the 1920s (see section 1.2 Patient History).[1] The surveys

[1] Weeks (2016a, 12) has recently revised his view to incorporate the earlier evidence of the category below, though he still argues that "it was the twentieth century that put [the wise men and their books] in uniform and set them to march together."

of scholarly trends composed by members of the Society for Old Testament Study appear to support Weeks's contention: Wisdom receives a single mention in the 1925 volume, a few pages in 1938, and only in 1951 a chapter of its own.[2] Though interest in the category did grow over the course of the twentieth century, the category itself had developed earlier.

Crenshaw (1976, 3) suggests that Johannes Meinhold was the first to recognize the separate existence of Wisdom as a category in his *Die Weisheit Israels in Spruch, Sage und Dichtung* (1908).[3] However, two years earlier John Genung published *The Hebrew Literature of Wisdom in the Light of To-day: A Synthesis* (1906), and before that W. T. Davison published *The Wisdom-Literature of the Old Testament* (1894). Both works testify to an earlier acceptance of the category in the nineteenth century.[4] Whybray (1995a, 1–2) also claims Meinhold is the first to devote an entire book to the Wisdom Literature, but he sees evidence of the category even further back in S. R. Driver's *An Introduction to the Literature of the Old Testament* (1891). Driver (1891, 369, 385) claimed that Israel's "wise men" took the nation's creed for granted, focusing instead on humanistic, practical, universal, reflective, and often natural investigation, and he even referred to Job as "a product of the Wisdom-Literature." Carl Heinrich Cornill (1891, 226) also claims Proverbs, Job, Ecclesiastes, Ben Sira, and Wisdom of Solomon are "usually designated" ("zu bezeichnen pflegt") as the "Weisheitsliteratur" in his introduction to the Old Testament published the same year (English translation 1907, 420). In that year, Genung (1891, 92–4) also provides the same list of "so-called Wisdom literature," which he proceeds to associate with "the wise" in Jer. 18:18 and describes as humanistic, non-revelatory, rationalistic, empirical, universalistic, individualistic,

[2] See Peake 1925; Eissfeldt 1938, 104–8; Baumgartner 1951. For this progression, see Smend 1995, 257.

[3] Crenshaw is apparently following Walter Baumgartner (1933, 261). Though he is less specific, Ludger Schwienhorst-Schönberger (2013, 119) has also recently dated the separation of Wisdom from Law and Prophecy to the beginning of the twentieth century.

[4] Previous scholarship on Wisdom interpretation in the nineteenth century has not addressed the development of the category itself. Smend (1995) surveys interpretation of Proverbs as representative of the category as a whole. Dell (2013c) similarly surveys scholarship on the Wisdom books without attempting to identify the category's origin, acknowledging that it has not yet been discovered (605–6 n. 2). J. W. Rogerson (1984) generally ignores the Wisdom Literature in his work on nineteenth-century biblical scholarship, claiming it was "treated, in the spirit of Herder, as essentially poetic compositions" (257).

and secular. He writes, "What the Hebrews called Wisdom corresponds to what other nations call philosophy.... It is man thinking for himself, interpreting what he sees about him and above him by the free exercise of reason, spiritual insight, faith." Another decade before these three works, Eduard Reuss (1881, 487) was already speaking of the "Wisdom Books" as he claimed that a summary chapter on this literature and its spirit could be found in most introductions of recent times, including in commentaries on the Proverbs. He explained that the Hebrew term *Chokmah* does not need to be used for this literature, just as it is unnecessary to refer to prophetic texts as *Nabi*-literature.

Reuss's discussion suggests that the idea of Wisdom Literature was already widespread, but the fact that he had to explain its title indicates it was not yet firmly established. A survey of introductions to the Old Testament in the second half of the nineteenth century demonstrates this. One need look no further than the tables of contents to see that changes were afoot. Poetry, consisting of Psalms, Job, Proverbs, Ecclesiastes, Song of Songs, and Lamentations continued as the dominant category into the second half of the nineteenth century.[5] For some, this category was divided into lyrical poetry (Psalms, Song of Songs, and Lamentations) and didactic poetry (Proverbs, Job, and Ecclesiastes),[6] and eventually the latter collection achieved a category of its own as Wisdom Literature. An early example is Theodor Nöldeke (1868). He groups Proverbs, Ben Sira, Ecclesiastes, Wisdom of Solomon, and Job separately, though he refers to them as *Lehrdichtung*, not *Weisheitsliteratur*, and speaks of them at one point as the "didaktischen Poesie des Alten Testaments" (156). Emil Kautzsch (1894, 206, 211) draws a thicker line between them by no longer classifying the "lyrical" and "didactic" books as subdivisions of Hebrew poetry but instead treating the "so-called poetical books" (Psalms and Song of Songs) separately from the "so-called Chockma (Wisdom) Literature" (Proverbs, Job, and Ecclesiastes).[7]

In addition to indicating the category's growing scholarly acceptance, Driver's and Reuss's introductions provide insight into its development, since both refer back to earlier scholars' influence on their

[5] See, e.g., Davidson 1862; Vatke 1886; Wright 1891.

[6] See, e.g., Keil (1859, 321–2), who admits that the two categories cannot be distinguished sharply because there are didactic psalms and Job is written in a lyrical style.

[7] The English translation (1899) reflects these distinctions in its more detailed table of contents.

views of Wisdom.[8] Driver (1891, 369) cites Delitzsch and T. K. Cheyne for the view that Israel's wise men were the "Humanists" of Israel. However, Delitzsch cites an even earlier influence: Johann Bruch in his *Weisheits-Lehre der Hebräer* (*Wisdom Teaching of the Hebrews*) (1851). Delitzsch (1873, 38) claims Bruch "was the first to call special attention to the Chokma or humanism as a peculiar intellectual tendency in Israel" (trans. 1874–75, 1:46). In Cheyne's (1887, 178) list of further literature, to which Driver refers, this same work by Bruch is the earliest mentioned, with the exception of an 1837 commentary on Proverbs by Lowenstein, written in Hebrew. Bruch is also the primary resource for his Strasbourg colleague, Reuss. Otto Zöckler (1867) also interacts with Bruch's work repeatedly and at some length in his Proverbs commentary (e.g., 3–5, 7, 14, 16). Hermann Schultz (1869, 2:186) introduces the section on "Die Weisheit des Israeliten" ("The Wisdom of the Israelites") in his Old Testament theology with references to two works: Bruch's and Gustav Oehler's *Die Grundzüge der alttestamentlichen Weisheit* (*The Fundamentals of Old Testament Wisdom*) (1854). Both in this work, and in his description of Wisdom in his Old Testament theology (Oehler 1873–74, 2:49, 276–9), Oehler primarily interacts with Bruch when discussing the Wisdom corpus, though he, like Schultz, disputes several of Bruch's characterizations of the movement associated with it (see section 3.4 Implications). These various streams of interpretation all seem to flow from the same source: Bruch's *Weisheits-Lehre der Hebräer*.

3.2 BRUCH'S INFLUENCES

Little has been written about Bruch or his work. He does not appear, for example, in Hans-Joachim Kraus's history of Old Testament historical-critical research (1982). Born in Pirmasens in 1792, he was educated in Strasbourg, where he became a professor in the faculty of theology and

[8] In tracing influence between biblical scholars here, I rely on direct citation of one work by another, which explicitly indicates knowledge of the earlier work. Influence does not always work in the same way, though. As I demonstrate, scholars may adapt or reject ideas from works that have "influenced" their own. For the influence of various philosophers on biblical scholars, I have largely relied on previous research on the topic, though I indicate explicit mentions of the philosophers or their distinctive ideas when they appear in the context of the discussion of biblical Wisdom.

eventually rector of the University from 1871–72. He died in 1874. He sought, according to his own words, after "a conception of Christianity which is in harmony with the most secure results of science and the undeniable principles of reason" (Gerber 1955). Anthony Steinhoff (2008, 51–2) offers Bruch as an example of Alsatian liberalism in the mid-nineteenth century. These liberals carried on the rationalist commitment to Protestant liberty, which involved the freedom to examine critically all truths, including religious ones, and suspicion of ecclesiastical authority, even as they reaffirmed biblical authority and the validity of the Confession of Augsburg, and took interest in the sentimental dimension of faith. They also sought to address contemporary cultural and intellectual questions in order to demonstrate religion's continuing relevance. Later, as the "arch-liberal" member of the Lutheran Directory in Strasbourg from 1866–74, Bruch was instrumental in holding off orthodox conservative challenges (Steinhoff 2008, 71, 166). Many of these aspects of his thought are evident in his description of "the wise" and the literature they produced, particularly free thought and distaste for religious authority, which contributes to his effort to defend the relevance of religion.

Before discussing the sources Bruch credits with contributing to his own work on Wisdom, it is important to observe a stream of interpretation he does not mention: any early Jewish or Christian classifications of biblical texts as Wisdom. Bruch's omission is likely due to the fact that, as chapter 2 The Ancestry of Wisdom Literature: Ancient Tradition or Modern Invention? demonstrated, such classifications do not exist. The ancient groupings that do appear, such as the Solomonic collection, the *Sifrei Emet*, or the Poetic section of the Septuagint, are inconsistent in their contents, both with one another and with the modern category. Further, these groupings do not appear to be built around the philosophical nature of Wisdom Literature that distinguishes it for Bruch. With the help of his acknowledged influences in the early nineteenth century, Bruch is inventing something new, a category that has not previously been applied to the biblical canon.

Bruch (1851, 4) does mention an enthusiasm for discussing the philosophy of the Hebrews in the seventeenth century, which is evident most prominently in *Introductio ad historiam philosophiae ebraeorum* (1702) by Johann Franz Budde [Buddeus]. This work is unlike the modern categorization of Wisdom, however, since Budde traces the history of philosophy from Adam's wisdom through Joseph, Moses, and others from Hebrew antiquity.[9] Among the discussions of Hebrew philosophy or wisdom closer to him both conceptually and chronologically, Bruch (1851, 4–5) mentions the work of four scholars in particular: Johann Lorenz Blessig's (1810) description of Proverbs as the philosophical literature of the Hebrews in his forward to Johann Georg Dahler's commentary on that book; W. M. L. de Wette's distinction between practical philosophy in Proverbs and speculative philosophy in Genesis 1, Psalms 37 and 73, Job, and Ecclesiastes in the second edition of his *Lehrbuch der hebräisch-jüdischen Archäologie* (*Handbook of Hebrew-Jewish Archaeology*) in 1830 (first edn 1814); Friedrich Umbreit's high praise of the wisdom of the Hebrews in his Proverbs commentary of 1826; and Heinrich Ewald's argument for the development of independent scholarship ("Wissenschaft") or philosophy and speculative reflection in the time of Solomon (Ewald 1843–55) and his article on Israelite intellectual movements (Ewald 1848). Also, though he does not mention it here as influential on his views, later in the book (178–9 n.), Bruch demonstrates an awareness of Wilhelm Vatke's *Biblische Theologie* (*Biblical Theology*) of 1835. Bruch concludes that this diversity of opinions justifies an investigation of whether and to what extent a Hebrew philosophy existed, which is the task he goes on to undertake (Bruch 1851, 5–6). (For a graphic representation of the sources of Bruch's work and its influence, see Figure 3.1 on the following page.)

These acknowledged influences on Bruch's work shed light on the emergence of Wisdom Literature as a category in the first half of the nineteenth century. The most striking feature of this development is the strong pull of the philosophical currents of the time.[10] Immanuel Kant, as the headstream of many of these currents, offers an indication of the direction they would flow in his comments on Jewish "religion" in his *Die Religion innerhalb der Grenzen der blossen Vernunft* (*Religion within the Limits of Reason Alone)* (1793). According to Kant, "Judaism is really not a religion at all" (trans. Greene and Hudson 1960, 116–18).

[9] Budde is participating in the earlier trend to depict Israelite figures, especially Moses, as philosophers that preceded and excelled their Greek counterparts (see Mahlev 2014, 241–9; Levitin 2015, 113–229).

[10] Blessig's comments are too brief to merit discussion. For a discussion of de Wette, Ewald, and Vatke and their lasting impact on Old Testament scholarship through taking it from Romanticism to Idealism, see Kraus 1982, 174–208, esp. 208. Kraus does not mention their interpretation of Wisdom, though he does discuss the influence of contemporary philosophy on their work.

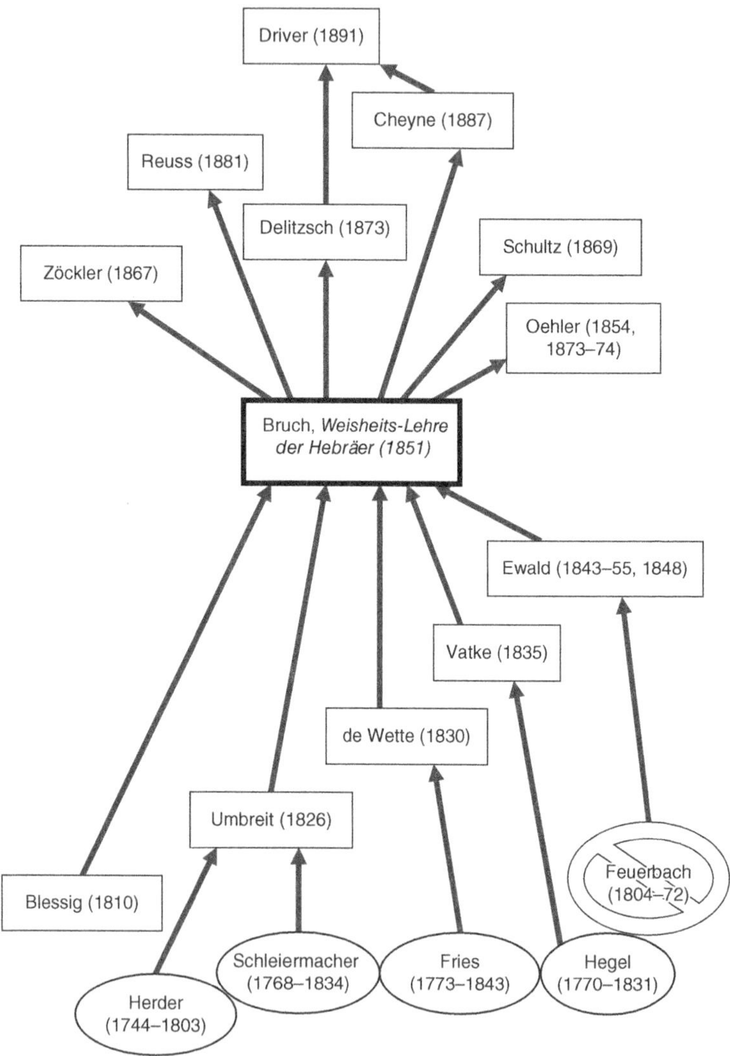

Fig. 3.1. Influences on Bruch's work and its influence on later scholarship

He writes, "The Jewish faith was, in its original form, a collection of mere statutory laws upon which was established a political organization; for whatever moral additions were then or later appended to it in no way whatever belong to Judaism as such." Its political organization is a "theocracy." Its commands are "coercive laws" that "relate merely to external acts." It lacks the belief in a future life fundamental to religious faith. Its exclusive claim to be "a special people chosen by God for Himself" falls short of setting up the "universal church." Kant claims the efforts of contemporary Christians, like those at its beginning, to present Christianity as a continuation of Judaism reveal the fundamental problem they face: "the discovery of the most suitable means of introducing a purely moral religion in place of the old worship, to which the people were all too well habituated, without directly offending the people's prejudices." Kant himself acknowledges that Judaism prepared the way for Christianity to arise, but only when its patriarchal character had been lost, its political constitution unsettled, and the power of its priests diminished. By this time it "was already interfused, by reason of moral doctrines gradually made public within it, with a religious faith—for this otherwise ignorant people had been able to receive much foreign (Greek) wisdom. This wisdom presumably had the further effect of enlightening Judaism with concepts of virtue and, despite the pressing weight of its dogmatic faith, of preparing it for revolution."

Though Bruch does not mention a debt to his work, Georg Lorenz Bauer offers an early example of how ideas like these filtered into Old Testament scholarship.[11] Throughout his *Beylagen zur Theologie des alten Testaments* (*Addenda to the Theology of the Old Testament*) (1801), he contrasts the narrow-minded particularism of Israelite folk-religion with a philosophically sophisticated universalism associated with wisdom (see Schwáb 2013, 21–3). Bauer struggles to reconcile Solomon's writings, where he speaks of God "in such an enlightened and right way," with his behavior in the historical books, where he is depicted worshipping "only a national God in Jehovah." He concludes, "It is undeniable that the historical books follow more the general principles of popular religion than the concepts that wiser and more talented Israelites acquired through reflection and scholarly education" (152; trans. Schwáb 2013, 21). He mentions that some hold that Job is the product of a Solomonic-era "Weisenversammlung" ("collection of wise men"),[12] which may explain how the author reached such a "height of insight and wisdom" that "he fully forgot his Israelite prejudices, popular religion, and national beliefs and taught a religion and morality

[11] Bruch (1851, 40 n. 1) does mention Bauer's *Handbuch der Geschichte der hebräischen Nation* (1800) at one point, so he was not ignorant of his scholarship.

[12] Herder initially proposed this setting for the book, which was followed by several other scholars in the latter eighteenth century (Witte 2007, 104–5).

of pure reason" (Bauer 1801, 154–5; translation mine). Though Bauer never speaks explicitly of a Wisdom corpus, he claims Proverbs comes second to Job (along with the Psalms) in its import for religion and ethics in the Old Testament (135) and makes the same judgment regarding the conception of God in Ecclesiastes (240). He concludes his work by proclaiming that Israel's wise men offer the purest and most elevated conceptions of God, in contrast to the national ideas and prejudices of the priests and prophets (254–5).

3.2.1 W. M. L. de Wette

Writing soon after Bauer, de Wette, whom Bruch mentions, echoes several of these sentiments, though he adapts them in light of his well-known affinity to the philosophy of Jakob Friedrich Fries (e.g., Smend 1962, 171). Friesian philosophy bears a close resemblance to Kantian idealism but emphasizes the ability of intuition to discover truth. This subjectivist approach enabled de Wette to employ the critical method to discover the deeply felt religious experience in the Old Testament books that his aesthetic interests deemed worthwhile.[13] Prior to the work cited by Bruch, de Wette (1807) combined the Psalms, Job, and Ecclesiastes to describe Hebrew religion as characterized by *Unglück* or "misfortune," a theme adopted from Fries (Rogerson 1984, 41). Though he presents these works as common witnesses to the existential affliction tormenting Hebrew experience, he does not suggest that they together comprise some kind of "Misfortune" category of biblical literature. In fact, Job and Ecclesiastes are each presented as eccentric and isolated within the canon (de Wette 1807, 286–8, 306). The author of Job had shed the fetters of the usual faith in providence and the widely oppressive particularism of the theocracy, breaking free from the sphere of Hebrew religion and producing a work that stood by itself, supported by nothing and supporting nothing. Ecclesiastes is similarly isolated, strange and mysterious, and set off from the rest of the Hebrew Bible. The concept of wisdom is not absent from the work, but it is not presented as a particular category of texts or of worldview (e.g., de Wette 1807, 298).

[13] See the fuller discussion of Fries, his philosophy, and his influence on de Wette, which began when de Wette attended his lectures in Jena and extended into a life-long friendship, in Rogerson 1984, 36–44.

Instead Ecclesiastes is described as a great work of skeptical philosophy, and Job is at times associated with it in this regard. Both books are seen as rejecting the doctrine of retribution, but this concept is considered a general trait of Hebrew religion, and not simply the worldview of Proverbs, a text scarcely mentioned in de Wette's discussion.

De Wette develops the theological sentiment behind his presentation of Job's rejection of the oppressive particularism of the theocracy in his *Biblische Dogmatik* (*Biblical Dogmatics*) of 1813.[14] There he divides Hebrew religion between universalism and particularism. Universalism involves the general doctrines of faith, the doctrines of God, the world, and humanity. Particularism relates to the political and ecclesiastical features of Israelite life and everything associated with the theocracy, including the priests and prophets, judges and kings, law, offerings and festivals (Smend 1962, 171). De Wette (1831, 73) presents Hebrew philosophy as the Israelites' abstract ideas about God, including the deity's omnipotence, omniscience, ubiquity, and eternity. These doctrines are not found exclusively in the Wisdom Literature (a term he does not use). When he does mention wisdom, it is as one of these traits of God, and de Wette (1831, 80) again finds this described in a range of texts not limited to Proverbs, Job, and Ecclesiastes.[15] De Wette reproaches the Hebrews for confusing the symbol with what it represented by exchanging the universal for the particular in their devotion to the theocracy and cult. As Smend (1962, 172) observes, this view found a significant following, which is not surprising because it performed an important apologetic function. The cosmopolitan humanists of the eighteenth century, such as Kant, were inclined to reject the Old Testament as a document of a particularistic spirit characterized by nationalism and statutory instead of moral laws. Rather than dispute their charges, de Wette could acknowledge them from the outset but declare that they were only the degeneration of the main, universal idea of Hebrew religion. At the same time, he could avoid being accused of neglecting these features of the religion, since they contributed fundamentally to his depiction of its development.

[14] References here are to the third edition (1831).

[15] De Wette refers to Pss. 33:11; 40:6; 104:24; Job 12:13; 28:23ff.; 38; Prov. 8:22ff.; and Isa. 55:8ff.

3.2.2 Friedrich Umbreit

The work of Umbreit, the next scholar Bruch mentions, demonstrates the influence of Johann Gottfried Herder and Friedrich Schleiermacher.[16] This becomes clearly evident in his discussion of the nature of wisdom as a concept and its relationship to poetry and Hebrew religion generally in his Proverbs commentary (Umbreit 1826). In his opening description of wisdom, he differentiates between the longing spirit of poetry and the inner peace of wisdom and claims that Job and Ecclesiastes are sometimes classified as poetic and other times as philosophical because they represent this conflict (Umbreit 1826, iv). In this way his interpretation of these books stands between de Wette's emotional existential interpretation and Bruch's more abstract philosophical reading.[17] Umbreit (1826, vii) refers to Kant and Herder in his discussion of the differences between Eastern and Western metaphysics. Similar to Schleiermacher (1893 [1799], 52–3, 107 n. 7), he declares that a conception of religion as direct feeling of the existence of the divinity belongs naturally to the Orient, as opposed to the cold systematic approach of the West. Then, drawing on the declaration in Prov. 1:7 that the fear of God is the beginning of wisdom, he claims that religion and wisdom are as indivisible as the root of a tree and its trunk (Umbreit 1826, vii–ix). Wisdom, he argues, does not contradict the law, and its proper essence is revealed in the covenant (xxxvi–xxxviii). He then gives an overview of Israelite history, which includes a description of the prophets as sages in Israel (xliv). Thus, his approach mixes Romanticism with a traditional, unified biblical theology.

3.2.3 Heinrich Ewald

Ewald styled himself an objective, neutral interpreter, and even attacked de Wette and Vatke for allowing their philosophical theories to determine their interpretations of Israelite history (Rogerson 1984, 93; see also Kraus 1982, 199). The influence of contemporary philosophy on his work is most evident, therefore, in his response to it, though

[16] Reading Schleiermacher's *Dogmatics* shaped Umbreit's understanding of religion, and at his death Delitzsch claimed he had continued Herder's work of fully appreciating the human side of the Old Testament without denigrating its divine attributes (Rogerson 1984, 136–7).

[17] In his Job commentary, Umbreit (1824, xxxviii) describes Job as a combination of aesthetic-reflective poetry and skeptical philosophy.

the impact of philosophers such as Kant and Schiller on his fundamental ideas is undeniable (Kraus 1982, 208). Indeed, during his depiction of the rise of the wisdom schools in the centuries following David's reign, he makes his philosophical concerns explicit. Like Umbreit, Ewald (1848, 99) closely links wisdom with religion, declaring that for wisdom to be true and beneficial it must be grounded in God himself, and even claiming that the fear of God is not merely the beginning of wisdom, but that it *is* wisdom. However, in addition to the rise of a circle of the wise, he envisions a contrasting group of "mockers" (לצים) and "fools" (נבלים), who are mentioned in Proverbs and several prophetic texts (100).[18] He claims that in the seventh century these "happy libertines" found philosophical defenders for their views. History shows, he declares, that if a time is favorable for practical atheism, theoretical atheism is soon to follow, "as we have adequately experienced also in Germany again in the last fifteen years" (102). He claims the Words of Agur in Prov. 30:1–14 reflect the views of one of these "atheists" in Israel, which Ewald compares to "our Feuerbachs," who have demonstrated the "atheism" of Friedrich Theodor Vischer and David Friedrich Strauss (two Hegelian-influenced scholars at Tübingen) only more logically and audaciously. Just as Agur did, Ewald claims, "So the philosophers of our day also ask which reasonable man could consider as real such a being as the God depicted in the Bible?" (102).

Though Bruch (1851, 57–8) rejects Ewald's conception of wisdom schools in favor of a nonprofessional group of those who were no longer satisfied in the national religion, Ewald's view was influential on later interpreters (e.g., Delitzsch 1873, 37–8). Ewald does not appear, however, to have a developed view of Wisdom as a category. In the introduction to his commentary on Job, he describes the book as "the most sublime didactic poem of the Bible" (Ewald 1836, 60; trans. 1882, 71), but then classifies it as a drama and primarily compares it with the experience of the sufferer in the Psalms and Lamentations; Proverbs and Ecclesiastes and the word "wisdom" are never mentioned. His commentaries on Proverbs, Ecclesiastes, Job, and Psalms were originally published between 1835 and 1839 under the title *Die poetischen Bücher des Alten Bundes* (*The Poetic Books of the Old Covenant*).

[18] See, e.g., Prov. 13:1; 15:12; Hos. 7:5; Isa. 28:14. This idea is adopted by a number of later commentators, e.g., Bruch (1851, 65); Delitzsch (1873, 32–3).

3.2.4 Wilhelm Vatke

A final evident influence on Bruch's work is Vatke. Though he escapes Ewald's mention, Vatke was closely associated with Strauss in his affinity for Hegel (see Kraus 1982, 194–9; Rogerson 1984, 70–1). He dedicated a large portion of his biblical theology to explaining how his Hegelian views guided his depiction of the development of Israelite religion, and this is evident in his discussion of Wisdom Literature. The Hegelian influence on biblical scholarship in the mid-nineteenth century was an issue of considerable contention, with conservative scholars like Ernst Hengstenberg vehemently denouncing it, which may explain why Bruch does not acknowledge Vatke more explicitly.

Following Hegel in seeing religion as developing from the lower to the higher, Vatke reverses the relationship between the universal and the particular depicted by de Wette. Instead of being a pure original idea that degenerated into particularism, in Vatke's view Hebrew religion sheds earlier particularistic nature worship for postexilic universalistic monotheism. In the Persian period, with the political interests of the nation pushed into the background, the "wisdom teachers" (*Weisheitslehrer*) emerge in Proverbs, Job, and Ecclesiastes,[19] and the freer prophetic spirit lives on in the "teachings of the wise" (*Lehren der Weisen*), in which the particularistic elements, so far as was possible, were stripped or subordinated to general spiritual and humanistic interests (Vatke 1835, 561, 563). Proverbs and Job, which Vatke dates to the fifth century, and Ecclesiastes, which he dates even later, are the synthesis of the earlier conflict between the thesis and antithesis of the priests and prophets, and thus, in the Wisdom texts, the particularism of the Jewish nationality disappeared (Vatke 1835, 563–4; cf. 570–2). Vatke may have been the first to posit a late date for Proverbs (Dell 2013c, 608), and considering how the Wisdom books fit into his Hegelian view of the progressive development of Israelite religion, one can see how he arrived at this conclusion.[20] To Rogerson (1984, 78) it is "obvious that Vatke's views about the development of religion led him to interpret the Old Testament material according to his preconceived notions."

[19] In a footnote, he also refers to Psalms 34, 37, and 78 and Mal. 3:16.

[20] The late dating of the Wisdom books was not originally, therefore, a result of their being "devalued" as the replacement of God's increasingly distant salvific work in Israel with pagan thinking (cf. Miller 2015, 96).

3.3 WEISHEITS-LEHRE DER HEBRÄER

Therefore, by presenting his work as an investigation of the "philosophy" of the Hebrews, Bruch follows a growing trend of drawing on contemporary philosophy in order to present the Wisdom Literature as Israel's own philosophy. He even claims not only to be writing for theologians but also for philosophers (Bruch 1851, xiv). In fact, like the interpreters before him, Bruch appears to have one eye on the biblical text and the other on the latest philosophical works, which he would have known well after writing *Études philosophiques sur le christianisme* (*Philosophical Studies on Christianity*) (1839), which had recently been translated, with his help, into German (1847).[21] In this work, he discusses all of the philosophers mentioned above, with the exception of Fries and Feuerbach.

Weisheits-Lehre der Hebräer begins, similarly to Schleiermacher's *Über die Religion: Reden an die Gebildeten unter ihren Verächtern* (*On Religion: Speeches to its Cultured Despisers*) (1893 [1799]), with an apologia to a philosophical audience for the study of the Hebrew Bible. Bruch begins his foreword by acknowledging that the title of the work, particularly its subtitle, *Ein Beitrag zur Geschichte der Philosophie* (*A Contribution to the History of Philosophy*), may awake an unfavor able prejudice in the reading public, especially the philosophers, who believe the Hebrews did not take up philosophical speculation until Alexandrian Jewish philosophy, as their omission of the Hebrews from histories of philosophy demonstrates (Bruch 1851, ix).[22] However, Bruch (1851, ix–x) disputes the allegation that the Hebrew people lacked any philosophical efforts. He writes:

> It seemed to me that the non-theocratic spirit, blowing already in multiple texts of the Old Testament, ought to have made one aware that—even among the Hebrews—there was no lack of men who found no satisfaction in the religious institutions of their nation. These men therefore sought other ways—namely, the way of free thinking—to gain answers about the questions that moved them and to seek their spirit's rest.[23]

[21] The translator's foreword explains that though the work was originally written in French, it is the product of a German spirit, since the author is of German birth and education and better known in German scholarship.

[22] Bruch (1851, 2–3) quotes, e.g., Krug's declaration in the *Philosophisch-encyclopädisches Lexicon* that there is no such thing as Hebrew philosophy.

[23] "Es schien mir, als ob schon der in mehreren Schriften des Alten Testaments wehende untheokratische Geist darauf aufmerksam hätte machen sollen, daß es auch

As in Umbreit's depiction, wisdom provides an inner peace. Further, this speculative wisdom, though it communicates a rich ethical and religious conception of the world far above the normal consciousness of the Hebrews, is not separated from the divine, since all are guided by God (Bruch 1851, x, xv–xvi).

Bruch's work is divided into three parts. The first is a discussion of the "cosmogonic fragments" in Genesis, in which the essence of the Hebrew conception of God as found in their myths is discussed first in Gen. 1:1–2:4 and then in Gen. 2:4–3:24. The second part deals with Proverbs and Job, which he considers the pre-exilic products of Hebrew Wisdom, laying out in particular their views on God, the world, humanity, and human relationships. The Proverbs chapter has an extended discussion of the nature of wisdom as a concept, dividing it into divine and human wisdom, and then dividing the latter into theoretical and practical wisdom, echoing de Wette. The third part discusses postexilic Hebrew Wisdom, dealing with many of the same topics in Ecclesiastes, Ben Sira, and the Wisdom of Solomon, with a short discussion of Baruch as well.

At the beginning of the Introduction, Bruch again attempts to justify his title, this time explaining the choice of "wisdom teaching" (*Weisheitslehre*) instead of "philosophy" (*Philosophie*). He does so because, echoing Umbreit again, the speculative efforts of the Hebrews are different from those in the West, and because the term "wisdom" is concentrated in their opinions and teachings (Bruch 1851, 1). Though Bruch uses similar terminology to Vatke to describe the Wisdom books, the role he sees them playing in the development of Hebrew religion is unlike Vatke's Hegelian view and much more along the lines of de Wette and of Schleiermacher (1893 [1799], 59–60). Bruch claims Hebrew myth contains the conception of a unique, eternal, all-powerful divinity, who was essentially differentiated from nature. Though this divinity is presented anthropomorphically, he could also be conceived of in a purer form. Therefore, even though the Hebrew thinkers recognized the emptiness of the whole ceremony of their national cult and its numerous laws, rarely spoke of its theocratic institutions, and had an aversion for the narrow-minded spirit of the priesthood, they had no

unter den Hebräern nicht an Männern fehlte, deren Geist in den religiösen Instituten ihrer Nation keine Befriedigung fand, und die daher auf anderin [anderen] Wege, dem Wege nämlich des freien Denkens, sich Auffschluß über die sie bewegenden Fragen und Ruhe des Gemüthes [Gemüts] zu verschaffen suchten."

reason to separate themselves from the essence of their religion and instead held fast to the old Hebrew conception of God.

Like Kant, Bruch (1851, 65) argues this elevated thought arose at a time when the adherence to the theocracy and statutory worship had chilled and the priesthood had lost its power. However, anticipating von Rad's "Solomonic Enlightenment," he argues this occurred during Solomon's reign, when a new class of wise men began to follow his example of indifference to the theocratic institutions of the nation, aversion to its exclusive particularism, and patience with foreigners (Bruch 1851, 47–8).[24] Thus, rather than initially encountering the foreign influences that inspired the development of their wisdom in the time of the Greeks, as Kant suggested, it was in Solomon's time when the king's openness to them provided new knowledge and awakened reflection (Bruch 1851, 48). And he argues these views are not a later addition to Judaism, but a return to the true essence of its religion. It was this wisdom, elevated far above the ordinary consciousness of the Hebrews, that was deepened in Jewish Alexandrianism and contributed to Christianity (Bruch 1851, x). Like de Wette before him and Wellhausen after him, Bruch solves the problem of the continuity between Judaism and Christianity by arguing that the Jewish emphasis on theocracy, cult, and law are a distortion of the original religion. His distinct contribution is to make the wise the conduit of those essential beliefs (Bruch 1851, xvi–xvii). Bruch's view is therefore less anti-Semitic than Kant's, which participates in the broad efforts at the time to denigrate the Jewish contribution to European thought in favor of Greek philosophy.[25] He defends the essence of Hebrew religion and demonstrates the value of at least part of the Hebrew Bible, though only to the degree that it transcends its distinctively Israelite context. The "most striking characteristic" uniting the Wisdom Literature still remains "the absence of what one normally considers as typically Israelite and Jewish" (Murphy 2002, 1).

However, as Bruch (1851, 379–80) claims in his conclusion, the most important characteristic of Hebrew Wisdom, one that distinguishes it from other peoples, and the Greeks in particular, is that it never

[24] As his critics were quick to point out (Oehler 1854, 2), Bruch appears simply to ignore the conflict Bauer struggled with between Solomon's purported enlightened viewpoint and his promotion of both theocracy and cult.

[25] See Hazony 2012, 12–15. Though this anti-Semitism is now gone, he claims, it continues to shape the disciplines, research agendas, and courses of well-intentioned professors who have never considered their origins (19).

rejected the religion of the collected consciousness of the nation. Though they transcended every feature of the theocracy of their religion, all the Hebrew wise men proceeded from the doctrines that formed its true substance; their philosophy remained always a religious philosophy. Thus, neither the priests nor the prophets, nor even later the scribes contested the Hebrew sages, but the "mockers," whom Ewald mentioned, took their indifference to the law and national cult and developed it into a true unbelief (65).

Bruch's extended description of Hebrew Wisdom incorporated elements from the works that preceded it. The independence of the Wisdom Literature from the particularism of Israel's theocracy found in several of these works is prominent in Bruch's interpretation. The opposition between "wisdom" and theocracy goes back at least to Kant. For Bruch, however, the wisdom that enlightened Judaism with concepts of virtue and made it a "religion" was not a later addition to its merely statutory and national origins, as Kant argued, but the original essence of the faith. Connecting these universalistic ideas, not with a later development in Hebrew thought, but with a renewal of the essence of Hebrew theology, which was obscured by the particularism of the theocracy, links his views with de Wette, and not Vatke's progressive understanding of history. However, de Wette does not give the Wisdom Literature a prominent position in his discussion of Hebrew religion, so here Bruch is closer to Vatke. In Bruch's repeated affirmation that Wisdom is never in conflict with Hebrew religion, he repeats an idea Umbreit and Ewald had emphasized. Bruch's work is therefore not without its precedents, but he appears to be the first to draw these earlier views together into a compelling systematic and comprehensive examination of the issue. If not its father, we could at least call Bruch the Wellhausen of Wisdom.

3.4 IMPLICATIONS

The implications of the origin of Wisdom Literature must be interpreted with care, since any conclusions drawn from it run the risk of the genetic fallacy that an idea's origins can be used either to confirm or contradict its truth. Even so, the timing and location of this origin are certainly suspicious. In the nineteenth century, German Christians were struggling to reconcile the universalistic, humanistic, and philosophical aspects of their religion with its particularistic connection with a history that was becoming increasingly problematic under the intense examination of eighteenth-century rationalism and nineteenth-century historical criticism. This was fertile soil in which Wisdom Literature might sprout as the "universalistic, humanistic, philosophical" collection within the Old Testament (Delitzsch 1864, 5), independent of Israel's particularistic theocracy, cult, and law.

Oehler (1854) immediately challenged these aspects of Bruch's work. He accepted Wisdom as the section of the Old Testament with the closest relationship with philosophy, but argued it was distinctive from other cultures, and unified with Israel's theocracy, revelation, and law. He later expressed his disagreement succinctly in his Old Testament theology (Oehler 1873, 2:49; trans. 1874, 177–8):

> There is not, however, the slightest trace that the Khachamim (as Bruch especially represents the matter in his *Weisheitslehre der Hebräer*, 1831 [*sic* 1851]) set themselves in opposition to theocratic enactments, particularly those relating to worship, and occupied the position philosophers do with respect to orthodox theologians.

Further on, he adds, Old Testament Wisdom does not attempt "as Bruch very mistakenly thinks, to give out a wisdom discovered independently of revelation, and thus to place itself above revelation" (Oehler 1873, 2:277–8; trans. 1874, 433). Though he adopted the Wisdom category from Bruch, Delitzsch (1873, 38) raised the same concerns. Echoing Oehler, he claimed that Bruch was "mistaken in placing [Wisdom] in an indifferent and even hostile relation to the national law and the national cultus, which he compares to the relation of Christian philosophy to orthodox theology."[26] Schultz (1869, 2:186–7) adopts Oehler's arguments as well, taking a swipe at Bruch along the way: "Nothing can be less true than to see in those, whom the Old Testament truly marks as wise, those whom 'the people's religion [*Volksreligion*] provided no more satisfaction' (Bruch)."

Despite Bruch's attempts to affirm the religious faith of the wise in Israel, all these scholars from the "conservative quarter" (Smend 1995, 266), perceive that he has set the movement marching against Israelite religion. Though these battles would be refought in the twentieth century (see, e.g., Zimmerli 1963), the lines were already drawn in the

[26] C. L. W. Grimm (1860, 1 n. 3) was similarly concerned that Bruch had, along with Ewald, drawn "a somewhat too narrow parallel between the Israelite Wisdom teaching and philosophy."

nineteenth century. Even so, each of these scholars assume the existence of a distinct Wisdom Literature promulgated by a distinct group of *Khachamim* ("wise men") and, therefore, even in disagreement, their interpretation of these texts is framed by Bruch's association of these texts with philosophy and against theocracy. Fighting on his terms, they are destined to fail.

Bruch's attempts to carve out Wisdom as the universal philosophy of the Israelites, transcending the limited national religion, suggest that the development of Wisdom Literature was the equivalent in Old Testament theology to Schleiermacher's *On Religion*, which similarly shows an aversion to theocracy as it attempts to defend Christianity to its "cultured despisers" (e.g., Schleiermacher 1893 [1799], 24–5). The similarities between Bruch's description of the wise in Israel and Steinhoff's description of the liberals in Strasbourg are undeniable. It is difficult not to see this as another example of nineteenth-century scholars looking into the well and seeing their own reflection, though this is an interpretive tendency from which scholars of other centuries, even our own, are not immune. We have the benefit of historical and cultural distance in evaluating these early views of Wisdom Literature. Rather than hubristically believing we now see clearly, we should pursue similar distance from our current views by putting them into dialogue with others (see Part II).

After all, Crenshaw (1976, 3) observes that since its identification as a separate category, Wisdom Literature "has stood largely as a mirror image of the scholar painting her portrait." In that vein, he had earlier queried whether the current emphasis on Wisdom Literature corresponded to waning confidence in revelation (Crenshaw 1970, 395). However, his belief that study of a distinctive Wisdom category only began in 1908 means he misses the marked evidence of this phenomenon in the nineteenth century. Reflecting on the debates during that time, Smend (1995, 267) notes the frequent and ultimately inevitable involvement of scholars' theological positions "when such a close connection of religious, philosophical and ethical questions is being treated (as is the case with wisdom), or at least when such a connection quickly develops in the course of its interpretation." When Ewald, teaching in a German university and opposing the atheists of his time, envisions the Wisdom teachers in their schools in Israel opposing the atheistic "mockers" who criticized Israel's religion, it certainly appears that he is reading his own modern circumstances into the text. The same could be said for Bruch's attempts to argue to both theologians and philosophers that there was indeed a Hebrew philosophy that deserves a place in the history of the subject. He does so by abstracting a philosophy from the rest of the Hebrew Bible that is itself built on his abstraction of the essence of Hebrew religion from its particularistic qualities. This, in itself, does not mean that their interpretations are wrong. Perhaps their personal circumstances and the intellectual trends of their time enabled them to see actual features of the text that earlier interpreters had missed. The same should be said of the prominent influence of contemporary philosophy on all these interpreters; it may have offered new, valid insight into the biblical texts.

However, if the interpretive goal is to uncover what the texts meant within their original context, the contemporary cultural convenience of the conclusions that these interpreters reach, which serve apologetical purposes in the arguments of their time, does legitimate a healthy skepticism toward their results. Ideology seems to have "crippled" Wisdom scholarship at its start by predetermining its conclusions (see section 1.5 Prescribed Treatment). In the circular relationship between Wisdom Literature's definition and its contents, the early nineteenth-century development of the category suggests that the universalistic, humanistic, and philosophical definition influenced by the likes of Kant, Fries, Schleiermacher, Herder, and Hegel came first, and the contents were found and molded to fit it. The problem is not that the texts are seen to address philosophical questions, but that they are supposed to have answered them in ways so congenial to modern philosophical presuppositions and collected together precisely for this reason. These do not seem to be "extraneous assumptions" that scholars may simply set aside (Fox 2015, 76), but fundamental to the category's origin. Indeed, the birth of the Wisdom category draws into question Wellhausen's claim that "philosophy does not precede, but follows [biblical criticism]."[27]

Whether valid or not, the development of the Wisdom category with its own distinctive features within Israelite religion, presented most fully, prominently, and influentially by Bruch, has created a persistent interpretive trajectory for the so-called Wisdom texts. Though Bruch's work, after being repeatedly cited in the latter half of the

[27] Cited in Rogerson 1982, 63. Though he generally overlooks Wisdom, Rogerson provides a broader context for the development of the category amidst the pervasive influence of "philosophical-theological presuppositions" (1982, 75) on nineteenth-century biblical criticism (see also Rogerson 1984).

nineteenth century, would fade out of scholarly consciousness, its effect would live on. Ever since then, Proverbs, Ecclesiastes, and Job have been read together as both philosophical and increasingly independent from the rest of the canon and Israelite religion. The pronounced nineteenth-century tendency to read the Wisdom Literature according to a "European *Geistgeschichte*" culminates in von Rad's vision of a "Solomonic Enlightenment" (Smend 1995, 265; von Rad 2001 [1957–60], 1:48–56), which paints the wise king's reign with a palette Ewald and Bruch provided a century before. Though widely criticized, von Rad's creation "survives as a kind of disembodied datum which underpins the popular idea of a longstanding intellectual tradition in Israel and Judah" (Hunter 2006, 37). The same might be said for the Wisdom corpus as well.

Some of this may be due to the twentieth-century discovery of ancient Near Eastern parallels and preference for Israel's history, as mentioned above. Though it would be difficult to prove, Bruch's work may disappear in the early twentieth century because the soil displaced in unearthing these ancient documents was piled upon it in a scholarly enthusiasm to recreate the Wisdom Literature on a historical rather than philosophical basis. The twentieth-century desire for unifying theological concepts, which has often become united with speculations about textual *Sitze im Leben*, may have also exacerbated the tension between Wisdom and the rest of Hebrew Bible (see Weeks 2016b), though Oehler, Schultz, and Delitzsch recognized this potential at the category's origin.

But, beyond the ebbs and flows of scholarly interest, the increasing isolation of Wisdom is also likely due to the nature of categorization. In order to justify its own existence, the classification has created an echo chamber in which the similarities among the books within it are magnified and their connections with texts outside of it are muffled, so that the rest of the canon is allowed little influence on Wisdom's interpretation (see section 4.2.1 Intertextual Shorthand). When the category was developing, Job, for example, was seen as responding to the doctrine of retribution as it is represented throughout the canon (e.g., de Wette 1807, 288; Umbreit 1824, xi–xii; Oehler 1873, 2:279). Now, however, it is primarily a dispute between Proverbs and Job that drives the interpretation of the two books. Weeks provides a second example when he wonders if interpreters credit Wisdom with a creation theology in an attempt "to identify a theoretical basis for apparent differences between these texts and others." This creation-theology emphasis can lead to the neglect and marginalization of the influences of revelation or Torah within Wisdom, since they challenge that paradigm (Weeks 2010a, 116–17).

While reading the Wisdom Literature as increasingly distinct from the rest of Israelite religion, interpreters have continued to consider its contents similar to their own academic pursuits. John Rylaarsdam (1946, viii–ix), for example, writes,

> At its inception the Hebrew movement shows no religious or national particularism to inhibit its full correspondence with the more ancient traditions of wisdom in other lands. It may have arisen in imitation of these, or it may have begun as a "revolt" of a free-thinking, empirically minded element of "scientists" against the tribalistic and irrational ideas of religion characteristic of pre-Exilic Hebrews.

He then compares this movement and its later return to full acceptance of the Jewish outlook in later Wisdom texts to the modern Western conflict between science and religion. He demonstrates a notable continuity with Bruch's original self-reflective depiction of Wisdom without ever citing his work, which indicates how Bruch's views had seeped into the interpretive groundwater of the twentieth century. Even Weeks, despite his awareness of the tendency to read Wisdom according to modern concerns quite foreign to it, is not immune to this temptation. Though he denies that the Wisdom Literature "arose as the products of an academic discipline *per se*," he does claim that "we need not look far afield to find the same sort of phenomenon, in which a recognizable kinship between texts defies precise delimitation, and for which criteria of style or theme cannot be applied in isolation" (Weeks 2010a, 143; cf. 126).

The main problem is that the definition of Wisdom Literature is so vague that it invites interpreters to import their own modern presuppositions into the texts to fill it out. In fact, when scholars start with what some admit is a "presumption" (Hunter 2006, 7) or "assumption" of a "subjective nature" (Crenshaw 1976, 5) that the Wisdom category exists, and that it is primarily composed of Proverbs, Ecclesiastes, and Job, they are forced to move to a level of abstraction to justify the grouping that leaves ample room for their own views, as is evident in the category's nineteenth-century origins. Might the "mysterious ingredient" that Crenshaw (2010, 10) claims holds the category together in fact be scholarly presuppositions that originated in the nineteenth century? Because little concrete evidence exists, either literarily or historically, to confirm or deny these scholarly suppositions, it is little surprise that these vague, abstract features of Wisdom, such as "didactic emphasis" or "humanistic interest" or "focus on creation"—knowledge that is recognized as good—may be found in so many other texts, both in the Hebrew Bible and in the ancient Near East (and even in New Testament texts like James). This process enables these unfounded presuppositions to spread virus-like through the canon, transforming texts into Wisdom texts that then contribute to the definition and spread the contagion. We do not know what Wisdom is, but we see it everywhere, or, perhaps, more accurately, it is *because* we do not know what Wisdom is that we *can* see it everywhere.

Categories should be judged on their inherit merits, not their misuse, but the Wisdom category's propensity for misuse certainly counts against its merit. Given the questionable origins of the Wisdom corpus, its lack of assured results, and its potential to distort interpretation, it would be wise to consider anew the meaning that may be found between its contents and a broader range of texts. A new approach is needed. It is time to break the mirror, scattering its shards throughout the Hebrew Bible and the ancient Near East, so that in gathering them again, interpreters might see the true nature of Israelite wisdom instead of merely their own reflections. The result will not be a mirror but a mosaic, which, though it may not be as clear, will likely be more accurate, and, perhaps, more attractive as well. Indeed, in the following chapters, I argue that as selective and subjective cultural artifacts, genres are inevitably self-reflective. Rather than rejecting them for a single "objective" genre identification, however, which is just as likely to reflect readerly interests, each could be considered a reflective tessera in one of Hagia Sophia's exquisite Byzantine mosaics. Viewed in isolation, it only reflects the image of its viewer, but, viewed together, those reflections combine to create the brilliance of another image altogether.

Part II

Genre Methodology

4

The Universe of Texts

The Intertextual Network of Genres from Multiple Perspectives

> Most of the ways of conceiving a poetical world are still as primitive and childish as the old pre-Copernican ideas of astronomy. The usual classifications of poetry are mere dead pedantry designed for people with limited vision. Whatever somebody is capable of producing, or whatever happens to be in fashion, is the stationary earth at the center of all things.
>
> (Schlegel 1971 [1798], 237)

This book, so far, has described the first, metacritical factor contributing to Wisdom Literature's demise, as the field comes to terms with the weaknesses of an unwieldy scholarly category developed in mid-nineteenth-century German scholarship according to the ideological currents swirling around it at the time. In this second part of the book, I engage with the second, methodological factor. In this chapter, I develop a new approach for addressing the question of genre, before applying it to texts commonly associated with Wisdom in Part III. As I argue below, a genre should be understood as simply a group of texts gathered together due to some perceived significant affinity between them. Despite this simple definition, genres are complex concepts that respond to the complexity of texts. They also have great hermeneutical power, which must be properly conducted if they are to draw meaning out of the vast universe of texts while accounting for historical and cultural influences on interpretation. Therefore, like Michael Sinding (2011, 468), I believe we need to move beyond thinking about genres "to thinking about how we think about and use genres." To this end, I build on recent insights from the study of intertextuality, networks, emergence, and conceptual blending to analyze how genres are created and then re-envision them as constellations in three-dimensional space that gain their significance from the cultural perspectives from which they are viewed. Following its death, Wisdom will find its afterlife in the heavens.

4.1 THE TRADITIONAL TAXONOMIC APPROACH

The reigning model for genre in biblical studies has long been taxonomic. Literary genres are used to categorize texts based on lists of essential features they share. Form criticism, with its emphasis on pairing each literary genre with a specific historical *Sitz im Leben*, has reinforced the "rigidity" of approaches to genre in biblical studies (Newsom 2005, 437–9; Sneed 2015a, 60–1; see Introduction: Wisdom as a Genre). Such categorization is not performed without nuance and circumspection. As Barton (1996a, 24) puts it, "[U]nless we can read a text *as* something—unless we can assign it to some genre, however ill-defined and in need of subsequent refinement—we cannot really read it at all" (emphasis original). And yet, genre remains a taxonomical tool for classifying texts as either in or out of a limited number of potential literary categories. Barton (1996a, 16–17), for example, uses the development of the Wisdom Literature genre as an example of the way "modern critical study has made it possible to read with understanding texts which previously had to a greater or lesser extent been misread, because they were seen *as something they were not*" (emphasis added).

Recently, however, cracks in the older taxonomic approaches to genre, which reigned in the nineteenth and early twentieth centuries, have begun to show. Genre criticism has entered a new stage that is directly addressing how texts participate in multiple genres as those genres themselves combine and change (Cohen 2003). Biblical scholarship more broadly has also begun to shed its commitment to strictly separated, taxonomic approaches to genre and instead to incorporate more recent flexible developments in genre theory. Alistair Fowler's (1982, 37) dictum, "genre is much less of a pigeonhole than a pigeon," flutters through many of the recent works on the topic (e.g., Newsom 2005, 439; Zahn 2012, 276). The difficulties of solidly defining the Wisdom genre have inspired the adoption of these more pliant and permeable approaches to genre within Wisdom study. These include Sneed's (2011) general dismissal of "generic realism" in favor of "generic nominalism," and more specific approaches such as prototype (Wright 2010), family resemblance (Dell 2015), or speech-act theories (Cheung 2015). These scholars rightly acknowledge that Wisdom cannot be justified according to the traditional approaches to genre that have long ruled in biblical studies.

However, by seeking out new approaches to genre flexible enough to accommodate the category's difficulties, they have put the cart before the horse. They have not gone far enough, either in acknowledging the weaknesses of Wisdom or in appropriating the strengths of recent genre theory for biblical interpretation. They all maintain Wisdom Literature as a category, which is understandable, given the current scholarly consensus. But, in failing fully to leave taxonomy behind, they risk perpetuating many of the interpretive problems the category has inspired, if not exacerbating them by facilitating its spread across the canon through these flexible definitions. To refuse to accept someone's death, one can take a new approach to defining "life," perhaps giving it more fuzzy boundaries, but eventually the stench will become unbearable and unavoidable. If, however, the scholarly assumption of the Wisdom category is set aside, recent genre theory may actually provide a means to incorporate its fundamental insights while holding its zombie-like, pan-sapiential cravings at bay.

4.2 THE REBIRTH OF GENRE

The time may have come to say farewell to Wisdom as a generic *classification*, but genre itself will live on; it must, because, as Barton rightly observes, interpretation is impossible without it. On one hand, texts cannot be understood in isolation (Fowler 1982, 113; Beebee 1994, 251–3). In Harold Bloom's (1975, 3) provocative formulation: "There are *no* texts, but only relationships *between* texts" (emphasis original). To communicate, texts rely on an inevitable interplay with the endless network of meaning in which they exist, as each utterance "enters a dialogically agitated and tension-filled environment of alien words, value judgments and accents, weaves in and out of complex interrelationships, merges with some, recoils from others, intersects with yet a third group" (Bakhtin 1981, 276).

On the other hand, once the complex interrelatedness of texts is acknowledged, the cacophonous potential infinitude of those relations threatens to overwhelm attempts at interpretation, making the text just as indecipherable as if it were spoken into silent solitude. Thus, Clifford Geertz (1983, 20–1) observes that as interpreters recognize the relational nature of interpretation, they exchange "an array of natural kinds, fixed types divided by sharp qualitative differences" for "a vast, almost continuous field of variously intended and diversely constructed works." Genres are necessary, then, as a "constraint on semiosis" that distinguishes the types of meaning which are more relevant and appropriate in a given context and therefore more probable (Frow 2015, 110). They create a "horizon of expectations" to "orient the reader's understanding" (Jauss 2000 [1970], 131). Both these connective and isolating purposes of genre must work together, such that any text "can only be read in connection with or against other texts, which provide a grid through which it is read and structured by establishing expectations which enable one to pick out salient features and give them a structure" (Culler 1975, 147).

4.2.1 Intertextual Shorthand

Genre, therefore, is nothing more than a formalized version of intertextuality, a "shorthand" for textual comparison that offers intertextuality sorely needed "referential specificity" (Burkes 2002, 22; Snyder 1991, 210). Recognizing the intertextual nature of interpretation, however, reveals genre's way of giving with one hand while taking with the other. It guides interpretation by limiting it, channeling those connections in a particular direction, even as they constantly seek to wash over its banks. Genres should act as irrigation ditches that maximize a text's fertile potential, but they often become a dam, halting the flow of meaning and leaving it stagnant, or, occasionally, causing it to flood across the terrain. Job's complaint is fitting: "If he withholds the waters, they dry up; if he sends them out, they overwhelm the land" (12:15). As a result, the interpretive "power" of genres must be handled with care (Briggs and Bauman 1992, 163–4):

> Since intertextual relations produce disorder, heterogeneity, and textual open-endedness, as well as order, unity, and boundedness, scholarly strategies for creating generic links similarly involve arbitrary selections between competing intertextual relations and are affected by ideological,

> social, cultural, political-economic, and historical factors. Therefore, no system of genres as defined by scholars can provide a wholly systematic, empirically based, objective set of consistently applied, mutually exclusive categories.

Genre's "constraint on semiosis" represents a "*restrictive* model of intertextuality" (Duff 2000a, 17; emphasis original). Recognizing this changes the significance of Hirsch's oft-repeated dictum: "All understanding of verbal meaning is necessarily genre-*bound*" (Hirsch 1967, 76; emphasis added). The inevitable betweenness of interpretation means that genre's guidance of the textual relationships that are pursued (or overlooked) will shape hermeneutical conclusions. Genre expresses this power in various ways. Simone de Beauvoir's obituary would convey something different if moved from the "news" section of the newspaper to the Women's Pages, where her femininity would become its "salient feature" (Freadman 1988, 81). Reading Thomas Pynchon's *Gravity's Rainbow* according to various genre proposals has moved different scenes from the periphery to the center of the book's meaning (Sinding 2011, 484). *Hamlet* "has not recovered yet from its grouping with novelistic psychologically motivated literature" and "has become a difficult, even obfuscated, play" (Fowler 1982, 272).

By providing a "horizon of expectations," genre classification *is* interpretation because it determines the texts between which the meaning of a work is found: "The assignation of a text to a genre is already its reading" (Freadman 1988, 94). However, individual texts constantly press the boundaries in which they are placed, perhaps even to the point that "[e]very work deviates from any particular set of characteristics that may be attributed to its kind" (Snyder 1991, 1). Therefore, in order to bring the particularities of a specific text into line with the universal genre ideal, genres have the tendency to function like echo chambers: similarities between the texts within them are magnified, while the connections of those texts with others outside are muffled, and thus "some degree of distortion is inevitable" (Drott 2013, 9).[1]

In a seminal psychological study of the perception of similarities between objects, Amos Tversky (1977) demonstrated how changing

[1] Alan Bale (2015, 72) observes, e.g., that the quest to identify the proper genre of Acts hinders the book's interpretation by encouraging critics to "maximise some features and minimise others" to align it with particular genre proposals.

one object in a set could reverse subjects' perception of which of the other two objects in the set were most like a target object. For example, more subjects considered Austria to be like Sweden than Hungary when Poland was included, but when Norway replaced Poland, far more considered Austria to be more similar to Hungary than Sweden. Changing the membership of the set affected the criteria on which similarity was judged. He concluded that despite the general assumption that classifications are determined by similarities among the objects, the opposite might also be true, "that the similarity of objects is modified by the manner in which they are classified." Therefore, similarity may serve as "a basis for the classification of objects, but it is also influenced by the adopted classification" (Tversky 1977, 344).[2] In a recent, popular presentation of his work, Michael Lewis (2017, 115) draws out the implications of Tversky's findings:

> By changing the context in which two things are compared, you submerge certain features and force others to the surface.... A banana and an apple seem more similar than they otherwise would because we've agreed to call them both fruit. Things are grouped together for a reason, but, once they are grouped, their grouping causes them to seem more like each other than they otherwise would. That is, the mere act of classification reinforces stereotypes. If you want to weaken some stereotype, eliminate the classification.

4.2.2 The Intertextual Network

Genre-driven interpretation, therefore, constantly runs the risk of deforming a text's interpretation by illegitimately restricting its manifold significant intertextual connections, while an attempt to do without genre would leave an infinite, amorphous mass of meaning. This tension is not unique to textual interpretation. Network theory has recently been developed to explain the emergence of various complex systems from the interrelationship of smaller parts. This integrative theory takes up where the nineteenth-century quest to understand the world through reduction and classification was forced to admit its failure. For example, when the sequencing of the human genome revealed only about thirty thousand genes—far less than most had expected—it became clear that life would have to be explained through the complexity, not of its individual parts, but of their interactions (Barabási 2002,

[2] See, e.g., the different perceptions of theology in Ecclesiastes based on the context in which the book is placed (see section 6.3.4.2 Tone).

180–1; Watts 2003, 25–6). As Duncan Watts (2003, 26) puts it, "Although genes, like people, exist as identifiably individual units, they function by interacting, and the corresponding patterns of interactions can display almost unlimited complexity."

The same can be said of texts. In network parlance, the texts are nodes (or vertices), their relationships are links (or edges), and genres are patterns of interactions. This intertextual network could be envisioned as a sky sparkling with textual stars, with genres as the constellational patterns formed by the links perceived between them. Indeed, Thomas Beebee (1994, 282) observes that the constellation analogy is particularly productive for understanding genre for three reasons. First, constellations are used to subdivide the sky, just as genres are employed to create "zones of reading" in the vast textual expanse (see Barthes 1974, 14). Second, genres are to texts as constellations are to stars; both represent "an imaginary way of representing real relationships." Third, a constellation, like a genre, is more than simply a list of the features of the items it contains, but "a form...a central symbol of their relationship."

4.2.3 The Emergence of Genres

Genres, therefore, like constellations, may be patterns of interactions between nodes in a vast network, but they are also more than that. They gain an explanatory power and interpretive influence beyond merely the sum of their parts. They "emerge" from and achieve an autonomy over the basic phenomena of which they are composed (see Bedau and Humphreys 2008, 1). Steven Johnson (2001, 19) defines emergence as "a higher-level pattern arising out of parallel complex interactions between local agents." Ant colonies are a prime example of this phenomenon, since the ants work together to forage and build without a leader directing their movement, as the ancient Israelites long ago realized (Johnson 2001, 29–67; he includes Prov. 6:6–8 as an epigraph). Genres are also emergent phenomena, since they derive from texts and yet stand before them as guides or over them as judges.

Emergence theory explains this "bottom-up" system (Johnson 2001, 18). For example, an emergent explanation of consciousness transcends both the materialistic reduction of consciousness to a fiction and the dualist promotion of the phenomenon to an independent reality by arguing instead that consciousness emerges out of the way the neurons relate and are structured.[3] No neuron is sentient, and yet, somehow, through their interaction self-awareness appears, just like none of the ants knows the plans for the sophisticated colony that emerges from their collective behavior. Similarly, an emergence theory of genre would reject attempts both to reduce genres to merely heuristic fictions (e.g., Rosmarin 1985) and to promote them to independent realities, akin to Platonic Forms, to which texts conform (e.g., Hirsch 1967) (see Snyder 1991, 204). Instead, it would argue that genres emerge *between* readers and texts as readers perceive and structure "real" textual relationships.

This emergence of genres as "symbols of relationship" occurs through readers' perceptions of the patterns of affiliation between texts, just as consciousness emerges from patterns of firing neurons. Beebee compares genres to constellations by adapting Walter Benjamin's (1977 [1963], 34) statement, "Ideas are to objects as constellations are to stars."[4] According to Benjamin, only as individual phenomena interact do ideas become visible as figures that fill in the lines *between* them (DeShell 1997, 32). However, Benjamin (1977 [1963], 33) argues that this process requires a mediating step, the introduction of the "concept" to reduce phenomena in their "crude empirical state" to their "basic elements" and then configure them into constellations, since they cannot do this on their own. Rather than discard the phenomena in order to represent the idea, according to Benjamin, the concept puts them in a reciprocal relationship, in which the objects make the idea visible, while the idea gives the objects significance (DeShell 1997, 33). Each star in the Orion constellation, for example, has no significance until viewers collect them and combine them with the mythic figure of Orion, while the Orion constellation has no existence until it is projected onto a collection of stars. The constellation, like Benjamin's "idea," does not exist independently of or exclusively in any of its *individual* components, but only in their collection.

[3] See, e.g., Clayton 2004, 23. The debate documented there over whether and how consciousness may be an emergent phenomenon is extensive. I simply use the example here to demonstrate how emergence aims to overcome this dichotomy between reductionism and dualism without attempting to weigh in on the philosophical or scientific merits of its application to this particularly thorny problem.

[4] For an overview of the various uses to which Benjamin put the constellation metaphor, see Wurgaft 2014, 260–1. See also Gilloch (2002, 70–2, 238), who analyzes Benjamin's work through multiple constellations (20, 234), and Salzani 2009, esp. 21–3.

As emergent phenomena, genres are similarly "Janus faced," dependent upon and yet autonomous from more basic phenomena (see Bedau and Humphreys 2008, 6). In the creation of genres, the abstraction of shared features from the variegated textual husk may be the "concept" that draws texts together, but the definition of a genre does not exist in the texts themselves; rather, it is projected onto them from the "idea" of the genre. Genres are not properties of texts but categories imputed to them based on the circumstances in which they are read (Frow 2015, 111). Yet, they are not merely arbitrary critical creations, since they respond to properties of texts (Frow 2015, 112). In other words, though genres are meta-discursive concepts, they are "not...*simply* meta-discursive" (Todorov 2000 [1976], 198; emphasis added). Though I agree with Sneed (2015a, 39) that "genres do not exist in texts themselves," I differ with his conclusion that they therefore exist "*only* in the minds of authors and readers" (emphasis added). Instead, as genres emerge between readers and texts, the various textual affinities that readers perceive, like the stars and their relative locations, must actually exist to be perceived.[5]

"Like the stars in a constellation," therefore, the significance of any given text depends on its perceived relationship with other texts (DeShell 1997, 36). Certainly, texts are created to convey meaning in a way that stars are not, and yet, just like stars, that meaning can only be perceived relationally. It might appear, therefore, that the pattern that draws texts together is fundamentally different from the one that binds a group of stars, in that the features of a genre are presumably evident in each text within the grouping, and often intentionally so, while the pattern uniting the stars is simply projected onto them. However, both are fundamentally relational. Since genres emerge from affinities between texts, no one text can form a genre, just like no one star can be a constellation. Genre features do not exist *in* texts as much as *between* them and therefore not in their authorial creation but in their readerly comparison. They do not exist as ontological features of texts but as epistemological constructions for

[5] Hindy Najman (2012; 2014, 20–5) has also employed the constellation metaphor to discuss genre, building on Benjamin's thought. However, she refers to "a *constellation* of *features* or *elements*" that define a "non-generic class of texts" (Najman 2012, 316; emphasis original), not a constellation of texts (though see Najman 2012, 321). Following DeShell and Beebee (see above), I equate the stars, the phenomena in Benjamin's constellation metaphor, with *texts* and not *elements* within texts. In my view, the features uniting the texts would equate to Benjamin's "concept."

perceiving the features that do exist within the text and contribute to its meaning.

Therefore, I have excluded any authorial contribution to the production of genres from my discussion because an author can only intentionally create a text that participates in or defies a genre through first playing the role of reader of other texts in that genre. The author may intend to place a work in a certain textual pattern but cannot "create" a new genre without readers (including the author him- or herself) viewing that work as part of a new pattern of texts. Because no single text can originate a genre, since at least two texts are required for a genre to exist, the origin of a genre always lags behind the origins of the texts it contains and the intentions of their authors (see Fowler 1982, 130). The intent to write in a genre cannot be a necessary criterion for a text's inclusion in that genre, because it is impossible for the first text in a genre to fulfill it. An author can intend to write a text with a certain set of features, even a set that is not yet combined in any other genre, but it takes readerly comparison with another text for those features to become features of a genre. Unless that second text is exactly the same as the first, the features of the genre will be something less than the features of the first text, and they may or may not capture the features the original author intended to be prominent. Further, if applied consistently, the intentionality criterion would invalidate the existence of genres altogether, since, without a first text in a genre, a second author could not intentionally write in that genre either. Genres may therefore help identify authorial intent in the creation of texts, but a consideration of the creation of genres focuses attention on readers' intent, a factor that is often overlooked.

Interpretation should start with any genres in which the author has explicitly signaled that she intends her text to be read, either through labeling it (the subtitle "a novel") or employing genre markers recognized at the time of composition ("once upon a time").[6] However, the interpretive value of that genre must be evaluated by comparing that text to other texts both within and outside of that genre since no text perfectly corresponds to the features of a genre and authors can (and often do) violate even the genres in which they intentionally and explicitly place their texts. Whether or not a text's meaning is limited to its author's intent, rarely, if ever, does a single genre exhaust that meaning.

[6] For more "conservative" factors for corroborating a genre identification such as these, see Fishelov 1993, 11.

4.2.4 Conceptual Blending

Cognitive science offers an explanation for the process Benjamin describes in conceptual blending theory.[7] As Gilles Fauconnier and Mark Turner (2002, 40–6) explain, conceptual blends result from the integration of at least two different concepts in a mental network that contains at least four spaces: one for each concept or "input" being blended, a third "generic space" for the relevant features shared by those concepts, and a fourth for the "blend" produced by combining elements from the generic space with specific features selectively projected from the two inputs.

A constellation is a conceptual blend formed when stars and an image meld into a single entity (as is evident in the German word for "constellation," *Sternbild* or "star-image"). For example, the Orion constellation, in Figure 4.1, is a blend (space 4) of a collection of stars in an anthropomorphic arrangement (space 1) and the figure of the mythic hero Orion (space 2) built on the generic similarity between the relative location of these stars and the human form (space 3).

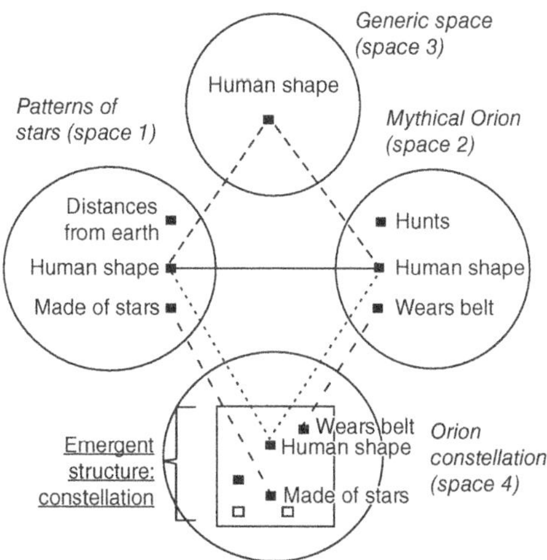

Fig. 4.1. Orion constellation conceptual blend

[7] For the application of conceptual blending to genre, see Sinding 2005, 2011, 2012, 2014, though his primary concern is with how authors mix genres together, rather than how readers create genres through conceptual blends. Recently biblical scholars have followed literary critics in applying conceptual blending theory to metaphor (Goering 2014; Wassell and Llewelyn 2014) and intertextuality (Tappenden 2010) in biblical texts.

The effect is more complex than a mere metaphor between the pattern of stars and the mythic hunter; instead, cognitive blending theorists suggest, the two items compared remain distinct in the viewer's mind even as their juxtaposition creates a new concept. Once this blend is created, the mind "runs," or explores, it, using both creative elaboration and logical restraint to test how ancillary features of each original input space fit in this new space (Hart 2006, 233–4). As a result, the emergent structure of the Orion blend has features that do not exist in either input: we can now speak of *stars* collectively wearing a belt, and of the star in *Orion's* shoulder. Other elements of the two inputs are not projected: the constellation never actually hunts, for example, nor is the stars' relative distance from earth considered relevant, but only the shape they form.

A more abstract blend proceeds and enables this one. To recognize the anthropomorphic pattern of stars that inspires the blend with Orion, one must first simultaneously evaluate the relationships between each individual star in the pattern and those surrounding them to choose the significant relationships that will form the pattern. Through pareidola, the human tendency to find meaningful patterns in random stimuli, the human form emerges from an undifferentiated array of stars (Barentine 2016, 8). Though the cognitive processes at work here are complex, they result in the blend of a group of stars with a basic human shape which gives those stars new meaning as a group.

The genre blend is also a two-stage process. First, it requires a number of individual relationships between different texts to be analyzed simultaneously in order for a pattern to emerge that associates some texts together more closely than others, differentiating them into a separate grouping with an emergent *Gestalt* significance.[8] The relationships are not spatial, but literary, involving internal affinities, such as content or form, or external ones, such as authorship or date of composition, and often some combination of both (e.g., Shakespearean tragedy). Thus, "any feature may become genre-linked" to the degree that it contributes to perceived patterns of similarity and dissimilarity (Newsom 2003, 11; see also Buss 2007, 9–10). Thus, for genres, when one text (space 1) is compared to another (space 2) (however the two

[8] Cognitive category theory offers several potential explanations for how these groupings emerge (see Sinding 2011), but I am more interested here in how they gain an emergent significance that transcends a mere list of similar texts. For more on the dynamics of "multiple blends" of this sort, see Fauconnier and Turner 2002, 279–98.

might be originally chosen), "generic" affinities may be abstracted from them (space 3). These give the genre its "shape" (Benjamin's "concept").[9] These similarities may then gain an existence independent from those two texts (generally when further texts are affiliated with that same generic space), such that other texts may be contrasted, not merely with the individual texts that share these similarities, but with the collection of affinities themselves.[10] Then a new concept, a blend of those texts, has emerged (space 4).

However, for this concept to gain the significance to create a genre, a second stage of blending must occur. That shape must be given meaning by being blended with something else to become the equivalent of Benjamin's "idea." Simply listing similar texts or the traits they share falls short of describing a genre (Beebee 1994, 258), just as a constellation is more than a shape connecting stars in the sky (of which there are infinite possibilities), but a significant symbol representing their relationship. So, once the shape has emerged through a process of conceptual blending, that shape is then blended with something else to give it *significance* and create the genre.

Weeks (2013, 19), for example, notes that, among the numerous potential links that could draw texts together, genres are a choice of specific affinities that are deemed particularly significant, such that, for instance, "the genre Epic Poetry is more meaningful than the genre Poems Starting with the Letter B." This, he observes, inevitably ties the history of generic classification to the history of literary interpretation, since "the elements that *have been deemed important* in literature have tended to constitute the elements used as the basis for genres" (emphasis added).[11] And yet, Weeks observes, this process "has not always been

[9] In the creation of a genre, the abstraction of these "basic elements" does not entirely shed the texts' "crude empirical state." Elements of the two (or more) texts being blended may still be projected into the genre blend that may not be in the generic space, just like aspects of the mythical Orion are associated with the anthropomorphic collection of stars. This explains the tendency toward chain reactions in genre definition, as aspects of any text associated with a genre may become part of the genre's defining features, even if they are not shared by every text in the genre (see Sinding 2002, 214 n. 48; Swales 1990, 51).

[10] For the progression from "like-statements" to "not-statements" as the essence of generic classification, see Freadman 1988, 77, and, similarly, Beebee 1994, 28, 263. For constellations, stating, "These stars form a pattern," is also saying, "And those stars do not fit into that pattern; if they were added, the pattern would be transformed."

[11] Michael Satlow (2005) makes a similar point about categories used in comparative study of religion. To the degree that they serve as second-order descriptors of cultural phenomena, they are inescapably circular, and yet they can still provide a valuable

self-consciously subjective." Of the numerous shapes that could be drawn on the stars, only those blended with a significant, culturally resonant symbol become constellations.

This final blend, including the content of this "something else" that transforms the "concept" into the "idea," is generally overlooked in genre analysis, and yet it is where genres have the greatest potential both to illuminate and distort the texts they interpret. The analysis of the move from texts to genre, just like that from stars to constellation, influenced by the apparent obviousness of the inherited blend, tends to overlook the injection of cultural perspective that has made that blend stick. Seeing this as a one-stage process, as in Beebee's adaptation of Benjamin's initial statement, rather than a two-stage process, as Benjamin explains that statement, occludes its subjectivity.[12] A group of texts, like a group of stars, is insignificant in itself; its significance comes from the meaning perceived in the relationship (whether literary or spatial) that inspired the grouping. But an endless number of relationships, of "webs of signification" are possible, both between texts and between stars (DeShell 1997, 38); only when that relationship resonates with something "deemed important" is it worth recognizing. Subjective significance is the electric current that transforms the inert collection of textual materials into the powerful interpretive machine of genre.

4.2.5 Cultural Influence on Conceptual Blends

Conceptual blending theory helps explain where this significance comes from, as it highlights the role of culture in the creation and preservation of concepts. Elizabeth Hart (2006, 234–5) offers a succinct summary of this process:

> A blend is a temporary construction, a product of fleeting working memory; but it always has the potential to become a more permanent one—a holding of long-term memory—if for some reason its constructed reality seems especially resonant with other aspects of experience, especially cultural experience. Thus, a blend might form a new semantic

utilitarian function as long as they are recognized not to "indicate anything 'real,'" but rather as a means to "select data to compare" (293). He claims "good" categories can be separated from "bad" ones based on whether they create "comparisons that a community of scholars find interesting" (295).

[12] Beebee (1994, 249–83) provides a thorough analysis on Benjamin's thought on genre and thus reaches a similar conclusion through a different route.

> category or contribute to the expansion or revision of existing categories, and its salience as such would be agreed upon by a group of people. However, an important thing to remember is that this process of meaning-making is entirely relative to what individual brains/minds understand.

Referring to the blend, all too common in advertising, between a beautiful woman and a sports car, Hart observes that no objective association exists between a woman's sexual availability and the commercial availability of the car for sale. "Rather," she observes, "that association is embodied, a symptom of some viewers' idiosyncratic experience and specific cultural conditioning."

The effectiveness, and even the existence, of a blend, then, "depends on where we look *from*" (Brooke 2009, 133–4; emphasis original). So, for example, a culture ignorant of Greek mythology would not blend the figure of Orion with a pattern of stars in the sky, since this would not resonate with their cultural experience, nor would stars in the shape of a desktop computer be recognized by a culture before the late twentieth century. Instead these cultures would create different constellation blends, which may incorporate some of the stars from these patterns into different shapes.[13]

Thus, when Carol Newsom (2005, 440) observes that "genre recognition involves some sort of mental grouping of texts on the basis of perceived similarity," conceptual blending theory reminds us that this similarity is perceived *from* a particular cultural perspective. Different societies, whether separated ethnologically or historically from those around them, will have different generic systems, as they "institutionalize" different recurring textual features, making genre "nothing other than the codification of discursive properties" (Todorov 2000 [1976], 198). Because "a society chooses and codifies the acts that correspond most closely to its ideology," these differing systems reveal features of that ideology (Todorov 2000 [1976], 200; see also Devitt 2004, 64). Thus, the collective hero of the epic was possible in one period, Tzvetan Todorov observes, while the individual hero of the novel was better suited for the differing ideological framework of another period.

A prototype theory of genre could also lead to the same cultural insight. It suggests categories are formed through comparison to an influential prototype. Thus, a small bird, such as a robin or sparrow, is widely considered more typically "birdy" than other birds (Rosch 1999

[13] Penprase (2011, 29–76), e.g., describes the different constellational patterns developed in various cultures ranging from the Inuit to the Incan.

[1978], 199). However, cultural location would also shape the choice of prototype: for someone raised in Antarctica, a penguin would be the prototypical bird, and the sparrow, which flies instead of swims and eats worms instead of fish, might not seem very "birdy" at all (see Williamson 2010, 345). Replace the *Iliad* as the prototypical epic with another text, and the religious aspects of other epics, such as the Epic of Gilgamesh and *Paradise Lost*, might lead the book of Genesis to be included in the genre (Frow 2015, 59; cf. Tversky 1977).

Beebee (1994, 249–50), therefore, develops a dialectical approach to genre that builds on the fact that readers may assign the same text to different genres.[14] This enables him to describe "genre's volatility and flux as a system of cultural values and as the only partly realizable possibility of 'using' any particular text" (28). What makes genre ideological, he observes, is the tendency to speak of it as a "thing" rather than as the expression of a relationship between users and texts (18). Thus, though genres reflect actual discursive properties in texts, they do not reflect all of them, but a choice amongst the "excess of generic markers to be sorted" in every text (269). This choice reveals the ideology of a culture. Thus, Beebee discusses several genre systems and concludes, "All of these genre theories have more to say about *our conceptions* of authenticity, subjectivity, and futurity than about literature itself" (269–73; emphasis added). He argues (Beebee 1994, 283; emphasis added):

> Though the way we constellate texts changes as a function of history through the *perspective of individual critics*, genres designate relations between texts that are as real as the critical language we have developed and which we can scarcely avoid using in order to describe and understand the effects texts have on us.

If properly understanding a genre necessitates a return to its sources (Bakhtin 1984, 106), then a complete analysis of the role of genre in a text's interpretation must take into account how the genres that readers apply to the text are themselves shaped by historical and ideological forces (see Duff 2000a, 18; Hitchcock 2003, 311). As such an analysis would reveal, "[g]enres emerge and survive because they meet a demand" (Frow 2015, 148). In many cases, that demand is one to which both the authors who create the texts and the readers who

[14] Beebee thereby improves on Fredric Jameson's (1981) dialectical genre criticism, which presupposes an identity between the genres of writers and those of readers and assumes the existence of genres within the texts themselves (Sinding 2004, 380, 391).

group them are responding, such as when circular letters, manuals, and forms were developed between 1850 and 1920 to meet the needs of new approaches to business management (Devitt 2004, 93–7). However, in some cases, such as the development of the four rhetorical "modes" of discourse between 1850 and 1900, the demand that inspires a certain group of texts to be gathered into a genre did not exist at the time those texts were composed (see Introduction: Part I: Historical Metacriticism). Then, the genre originates independently of the texts' authors, though not of the texts themselves.

4.2.6 Genres and the Small World Phenomenon

Network theory offers a helpful means of understanding the culturally influenced nature of this emergence of genres from intertextual networks through conceptual blending. Watts (2003) explores the powerful role groups play as patterns of interaction that increase network connectivity. Groups, he argues, can explain the "small world phenomenon," in which two people chosen at random, even on opposite sides of the world, can be connected through a small number of intermediaries, which has contributed to the popular view that any two people are within no more than six degrees of separation (the real number may be closer to eleven). Previous network models had been unable to explain this phenomenon, which appears in various types of networks, but by analyzing "affiliation networks," in which two nodes are "affiliated" if they participate in the same group, Watts (2003, 118) provides a solution. If nodes belong to multiple groups, they create affiliations between those groups and the nodes within them (120–1; cf. 58, 116). He then observes that multiple dimensions are used simultaneously to partition the world into smaller and more specific social groups. At times we think of affiliation in terms of geographical proximity, but in many cases other features of identity, such as place of employment or of education have greater influence on who a person knows. Proximity in one dimension does not necessarily imply proximity in another, but one only needs proximity in one dimension to be considered "close." This means social distance "emphasizes similarities over differences" (150). He gives the example of a colleague of his at an American research institute who was born and raised in Beijing. In terms of occupation, she is closely affiliated with Watts and distant from the people she grew up with. And yet, in terms of geography, she has close ties to people in China that Watts lacks completely (146–7).

However, through his close occupational proximity with this colleague, Watts has a connection to people on the other side of the world.

Therefore, the multiple, independent social dimensions through which individuals perceive others both draw people together across the barriers of any single group ("because only the shortest distance counts") and make the perception of proximity to others dynamic, depending on the dimension used (Watts 2003, 151). Watts concludes, "Another way to think about this property is that *while groups can be categorized easily, individuals cannot be*" (151; emphasis original). A group is categorized on the basis of a single dimension (or, at least, a quite limited number of them), whereas social identity "exhibits a multidimensioned nature—individuals spanning different social contexts" (151).

4.2.7 A Multidimensional Approach to Genre

Like social distance, the perception of textual proximity is also dynamic, with individual texts exhibiting a "multidimensioned nature" that makes them difficult to categorize. Individual texts, like individual people, can rarely be exclusively defined by one grouping to which they belong.[15] The same text may be considered a member of different genres when read from different cultural perspectives.[16] Even different people, who bring different interests and cultural assumptions to the same text, may place it in different genres. Texts participate in genres without ever belonging to them (Derrida 2000 [1980], 230).

The constellation metaphor can be further developed to envision Watts's multidimensional approach to network dynamics. Rather than picturing the nodes of a network as stars studding a two-dimensional firmament viewed from earth, they could be envisaged as the stars actually exist in the universe, scattered across three-dimensional space.[17]

[15] Wright (2010, 303) also compares genres to social groupings, but by using clubs for his analogy, he creates an overly restrictive understanding of genre, despite his references to "conflicted" or "fuzzy" genre boundaries. He envisions texts participating "fully" in one genre club and potentially as an affiliate in others, which reflects his underlying taxonomic impulse.

[16] Fowler (1982, 130–48) discusses numerous examples of how genre labels differ between cultures, though he does not discuss the hermeneutical effect of these different labels overlapping in the same text.

[17] Christopher Kilgore (2013, 51–2) proposes a different three-dimensional metaphor for the complexity of network systems that imagines networks as "texture-maps," which are images stretched across the nodes and links of the network to create "faces"

The traditional constellational scheme can locate any star in the *sky*, which is, in fact, how the International Astronomical Union uses the constellations. However, because the stars are actually spread across three dimensions of space, not two, this scheme cannot locate stars accurately within the *universe*; the dimension of depth is ignored. The map is not the territory. This limited perspective may actually distort the perception of the actual location of stars. Those that appear relatively close together from an earthly vantage point may in fact be much farther apart. For example, as illustrated in Figure 4.2, the stars in the Orion constellation are in reality quite distant from one another (see Brown 2013). This distance would make them unlikely to be grouped into the same constellation if viewed from elsewhere in the universe. The anthropomorphic relationship between the stars that form Orion would disappear and new relationships between its stars and others in the sky would inspire other constellations to emerge. Though thinking of constellations in three dimensions relativizes each constellation, multiplying perspectives like this and creating new constellations would enable the actual location of each star to be more accurately triangulated by revealing their positions relative to other stars from different angles. To determine a star's three-dimensional location, astronomers use a similar method called parallax, which compares its location relative to others from the different perspectives provided by the earth's orbit.

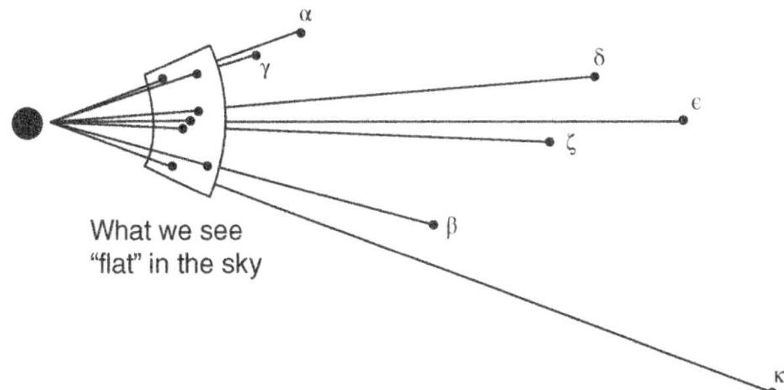

Fig. 4.2. Orion constellation in three dimensions

and "boundaries" that contribute to a "multidimensional *shape*" (emphasis original). The multiple dimensions in his model are intended to represent the extent of network connections, as they fill in the empty space between points and lines in the older metaphors. In my version, the multiple dimensions represent the effect differing perspectives have on how the links between nodes are recognized.

Like constellations, which represent the relative locations of the stars by carving up the flat, smooth sky as viewed from earth, the traditional taxonomic approach to genre is similarly "pre-Copernican" according to Friedrich Schlegel (1971, 237), who writes, "Whatever somebody is capable of producing, or whatever happens to be in fashion, is the stationary earth at the center of all things." From this fixed perspective, genres partition the textual expanse, creating a "horizon of expectation" for each group of texts and establishing a single, authoritative meaning for each text. The "law of genre" that undergirds this system declares, "Genres are not to be mixed" (Derrida 2000 [1980], 220). This interdiction must be stated forcefully to counter the generic tendency toward "miscegenation" (Beebee 1994, 264). When such situations arise, the traditional approach attempts to create a new genre or subgenre. Like the acting troupe in *Hamlet* (2.2.398–401), critics become experts in "tragedy, comedy, history, pastoral, pastorical-comical, historical-pastoral, tragical-historical, tragical-comical-historical-pastoral," and so on. Such an approach conforms with the principles of effective classification, which involves: (1) consistent, unique classificatory principles; (2) mutually exclusive categories; and (3) a complete system, that leaves nothing out (Bowker and Star 1999, 10–11).

Paul Hernadi (1972, 153) calls, instead, for a "polycentric" genre theory that triangulates texts among the numerous, non-exclusive respects in which works may be similar. He cites Karl Popper's (1959, 421) observation that "things may be similar in *different respects*, and any two things which are from one point of view similar may be dissimilar from another point of view" (emphasis original; Hernadi 1972, 4).[18] Thus, Hernadi (1972, 153) concludes, "We seem to need several systems of coordinates… lest we lose our way in the more-than-three-dimensional universe of verbal art." Similarly, reflecting on recent developments in music theory, Eric Drott (2013, 9–10) advocates "a hermeneutics that does not presume a single, undivided horizon of expectation," but acknowledges the plurality of texts, genres, *and* subject positions. Genre, as he defines it, is not a stable class defined by fixed characteristics, but "a dynamic ensemble of correlations… not so much a *group* as a *grouping*… something that must be continually produced and reproduced" (emphasis original). Therefore, he argues,

[18] Similarly, in the psychological study cited above, Tversky (1977, 349) states, "The same pair of objects… can be viewed as similar or different depending on the choice of a frame of reference."

genres "result from acts of assemblage, acts performed by specific agents in specific social and institutional settings."[19]

The dynamic, perspective-determined nature of genre in the more-than-three-dimensional universe of verbal art indicates that "most works not only can but *must* be analyzed in more than one generic way in order for their messages to have any effective meaning or value" (Beebee 1994, 265; emphasis original). Throughout his book Beebee compares potential genre classifications for texts ranging from *Oroonoko* to the lyrics of Bob Dylan, documenting "the extent to which the meaning of a literary text can depend on the play between its generic categories" (249). He works with the conviction that "critics should be less interested in generic classification than in discovering, first of all, the kinds of systems and intertextual relationships (rather than individual genres) that have given them the classifications they take for granted, and second, the tensions *within* texts between contradictory generic features" (256; emphasis original). The dialectic between the directly opposed genres of encomium and invective in a "meta-parody," such as Erasmus's *Praise of Folly*, exemplifies this tension, though Beebee claims "this same instability is implicitly at work in any literary text" (264). John Frow (2015) offers further examples. The intertextual cues in *Showboat* draw in a number of genres and sub-genres, which "coexist in a complex fusion," such that the interpretation of the film depends on making sense of their intersection (Frow 2015, 124). In the same way, Goethe's *Elect Affinities* is not reducible to any one of the distinct genres it incorporates, but the "core of its generic structure" is the way it weaves them together (133).

Fishelov (1993, 26–7) explains how this generic intersection works in interpretation: "the specific text activates our relevant knowledge and assumptions concerning various genres of whose tradition the text reminds us, and those generic frameworks contribute, on their part, to our understanding and integrating various elements of the specific text." He contrasts his approach with Fowler's vision of genres as "signal systems" that ensure correct interpretations. On this basis, Fowler disputes the Romantic interpretation of *Paradise Lost* as a classical epic with Satan as the hero by arguing that the "true" genre of the text is "Christian epic," which indicates its hero is actually the Son.

[19] Genre criticism should therefore operate with the same recognition of the contingency of how it chooses to direct and limit its field of vision that Brennan Breed (2014, 13) argues should characterize text criticism and reception criticism.

Fishelov argues, though, that Fowler lets his determination of the text's "true" genre stand in for the work of interpretation. In fact, he claims, the conflict over the true hero of the poem, the question of whether it participates more fully in the classical or Christian epic genre, contributes to the work's power.

Conceptual blending not only provides a model for how genres are formed, it can also explain how the affinities that inspire those genre designations are blended in a particular text (see Sinding 2005, 2011, 2012). Consider a two-dimensional analogy: the constellations Ursa Major and the Big Dipper (see Figure 4.3). Four of the stars in the bear's tail also serve as the dipper's handle. Thinking of them as part of the tail depends on a relationship between those stars and others, including those that make up the bear's head and legs, but for the Dipper, these relationships must be ignored. The integrity of each constellation requires viewers to choose between projecting two different images on the same pattern of stars that make up the handle/tail, as in Rubin's vase, which fills in the space between two faces. Because astronomers use constellations for classification, they only consider one of them, Ursa Major, an official constellation. However, once the two projections have been made, it is difficult, if not impossible, to avoid allowing the two images to coalesce in our minds. This creates a conceptual blend between the two constellations, a dipper-handle-tailed bear, which is a figure not envisioned in either constellation considered individually. This blend makes interpreting the position of any given star more complex even as it makes locating them easier and more precise, since it can identify a star based on where it sits in the intersection of the constellations, so that, for example, one of the stars

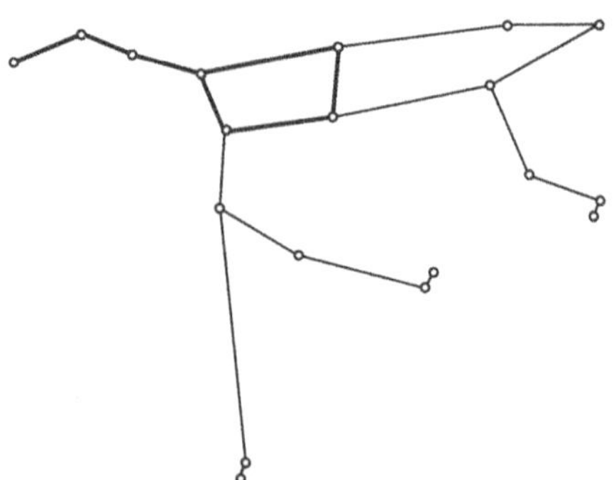

Fig. 4.3. Big Dipper and Ursa Major

in the bear's back can be identified as the one that is at the end of the dipper. Similarly, genres that overlap in a text project different meanings onto it that blend into new interpretations that are both more complex and more accurate. Features of romance and picaresque blend in *Don Quixote* to form the novel (Sinding 2012). Epic and novel are blended to make *Ulysses* a mock-epic (Sinding 2005).

This invites a reconsideration of the example Tremper Longman (2003, 178) cites from Heather Dubrow (1982, 1–3). She provides the first paragraph of an imaginary literary work titled "Murder at Maplethorpe":

> The clock on the mantelpiece said ten thirty, but someone had suggested recently that the clock was wrong. As the figure of the dead woman lay on the bed in the front room, a no less silent figure glided rapidly from the house. The only sounds to be heard were the ticking of that clock and the loud wailing of an infant.

With that title, the reader is led to assume that this is a mystery and thus that the mother was murdered, potentially by the figure gliding away, and the child was awakened by the violence. However, Dubrow argues, if the same exact text is read under the title "The Personal History of David Maplethorpe," the reader will assume that it begins the biography of Maplethorpe with the death of his mother at birth and the doctor or midwife departing. Longman therefore concludes that "the more we learn about the genre of a biblical text, the better our reading will be."

The example, however, proves slightly more than Longman intends. The introduction of a second title for the piece, which creates a second generic grouping for comparison, illuminates the features it shares with *both* biography and mystery. Even under the title signaling the biography genre, we can now see how Maplethorpe's birth is itself cloaked in mystery. Will his life be shaped by the guilt he feels as he blames himself for "murdering" his mother at his birth? Or will he never trust the medical profession or others with expertise because of the doctor's "murder" of his mother? Alternatively, if the mystery title is original and the biography title is secondary, we would now ask to what degree the murder of his mother transforms the life of the baby, causes him, in a sense, to be reborn. This textual star sits at the intersection of two genre constellations, and a comprehensive interpretation requires its relation to both to be taken into account. Thus, adapting Longman's conclusion, I would argue, "the more we learn about the *genres* of a biblical text, the better our reading will be."

Recent biblical scholarship has begun to embrace this approach and appreciate the ways genres may overlap within texts. Sean Burt (2014) argues that the Nehemiah Memoir combines two genres, the court tale and the official memorial, each representing a conflicting ideology regarding Israel's relation to Persia during rebuilding (see Burt 2014, 91–2, 144–5, 148). Similarly, Alan Bale (2015, 215) uses the continuing debate over *the* genre of Acts to question a binary taxonomic approach to the question. This "methodological error" attempts "to narrow the range of texts used to interpret Acts by first identifying its genre," and thereby "reduces the number of intertextual frames we apply to the text" and "minimises potentially important textual elements" (93). Instead, he advocates a consciously intertextual and "ecumenical" approach to the book of Acts that "makes use of any genre that suggests itself, either through similarity or difference." For Acts, these include "the Septuagint, the Jewish novella, the *Bios*, the Epic, and even the Greco-Roman Novel" (93). In the following chapters, I consider how the various "intertextual frames" applied to Job, Ecclesiastes, and Proverbs demonstrate the broader network of texts in which these books participate.

Using conceptual blending to explain how genres emerge from multidimensional networks will allow a more precise examination of *how* texts are linked into broader groupings. A conceptual blend of genres and three-dimensional constellations will encourage both a more precise examination of *why* certain groupings are favored over others in specific times and places, and of *what* these texts may fully mean.[20] Table 4.1 summarizes this theory of genre, which I have created here through conceptually blending several other theories along with a series of metaphors and examples to communicate them on a "human scale" in which they can be more easily comprehended.[21] Each theory, metaphor, or example is an input, and all are united by a

[20] Along similar lines, Buss (1974) and Kim (2003) both advocate a "multidimensional" approach to form criticism. Buss (1974, 53) writes, "OT form critics have often not seen, as others have, that genres are abstractions ('ideal forms') and that virtually all human experiences involve a combination of categories applied simultaneously." Kim (2003, 103) pictures his approach, which takes into account numerous layers of "historicality" and multiple critical methods, transforming the "face" of a text from a simple one drawn by Cézanne to a complex one drawn by Picasso that depicts the image "from many angles."

[21] For the importance of human scale in conceptual blends, see Fauconnier and Turner 2002, 322–4. Due to their complexity, networks (Kilgore 2013, 39), like genres (Fishelov 1993, 155–8), often inspire such metaphors to aid their comprehension.

Table 4.1. An intertextual network approach

Input	Generic space			Contribution to blend
	Individual	Related	Emergent	
Network theory	Nodes	Links	Patterns	Connectivity, multidimensional affiliation
Astronomy	Stars	Shape	Constellation	Human scale
Emergence theory	Local agents	Complex interactions	Higher-level pattern	Emergence
Neuroscience	Brain cells	Neural activity	Consciousness	Human scale
Philosophy	Phenomena	Concept	Idea	Interdependence, significance
Conceptual blending	Inputs	Generic space	Blend	Process of creation, role of culture, overlap
Literature	Texts	Affinities	Genre	

common generic space, which involves individual local agents participating in complex interactions to create an emergent higher-level pattern. I have added each to the argument to contribute a feature to the final understanding of genre, in which they are all blended together.

4.3 THE REBIRTH OF WISDOM

This multidimensional understanding of genre encourages new perspectives on Wisdom Literature by comparing this *grouping* to others that emerge from links between texts "deemed important" at other stages in the texts' history of interpretation. The most prominent early grouping in which some of the current Wisdom texts appeared was the collection associated with Solomon: Proverbs, Ecclesiastes, and Song of Songs. As the simplified conceptual blend in Figure 4.4 demonstrates, at a time when authority was tied to authorship (see Meade 1987, 72; Saebø 1998, 303–4), the figure of Solomon was projected onto the links between these texts, like Orion onto the stars, creating a Solomonic emergent structure for interpreting the texts. Elaborating on this structure, the rabbis associated each book with a phase of Solomon's

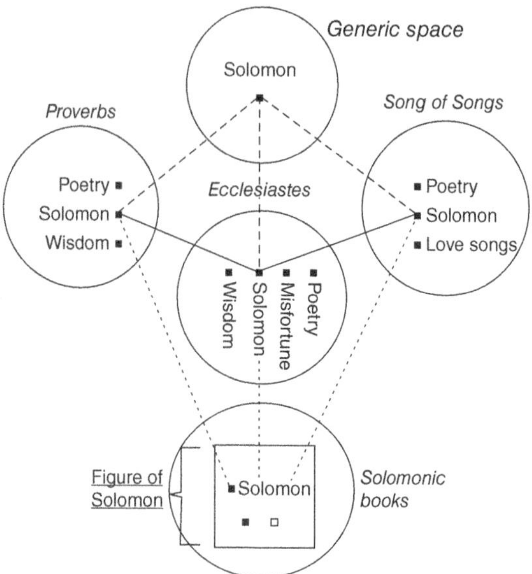

Fig. 4.4. Solomonic books conceptual blend

life, an exegetical move only possible in the blend (see section 2.2 Solomonic Association).

Before the Wisdom category emerged, de Wette (1807) grouped Job, Ecclesiastes, and the lament Psalms together in a study of the prominence of *Unglück* or "misfortune" in Israelite religion (Figure 4.5). De Wette, inspired by the philosophy of Jakob Friedrich Fries to seek out deeply felt religious experience in the Hebrew Bible, created this emergent structure for the texts by tracing a suffering Israelite onto this textual constellation.

In order to include the Israelites in the history of philosophy, Bruch then developed the Wisdom category, using Proverbs, Ecclesiastes, and Job to depict the emergent structure of an Israelite philosopher due to their common interest in wisdom (Figure 4.6).

However, the texts in all three of these constellations were also found together among the five Poetic books of the Greek tradition, which organized the canon around more formal concerns (see section 2.1.2 Greek Order). This is only a taste of the number of "fashionable ideas" that have stood as stationary earths at the center of biblical interpretation throughout its history; each providing its own perspective on how to constellate the texts. Much is also left to explore, regarding which

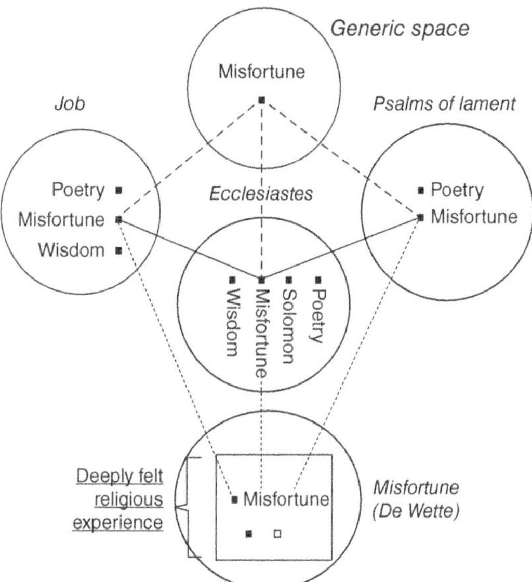

Fig. 4.5. Misfortune conceptual blend

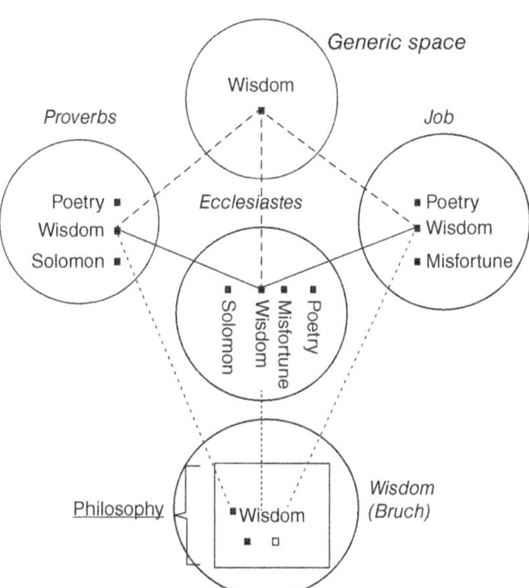

Fig. 4.6. Wisdom Literature conceptual blend

textual features are projected to each blend and how each emergent structure shapes the texts' interpretation.

One may notice, though, that Ecclesiastes, for example, appears in all four of these textual constellations, leading it, in Culler's words, to be read in connection with different groups of texts that provide different interpretive grids and reveal different salient features. Comparing the grouping of texts suggested by de Wette with the modern Wisdom category introduced by Bruch reveals that Ecclesiastes and Job share different aspects with Proverbs than they do with the lament Psalms (in conceptual blending terminology, they create a different generic space with each). This is reflected in the subdivision of Wisdom into optimistic and pessimistic collections, with Proverbs representing the former and Job and Ecclesiastes the latter. Thus, Martin Buss (2007, 12) notes, for example, that in content, purpose, and form, Ecclesiastes "represents a different genre" from Proverbs, and Sneed (2015a, 62) entertains the possibility of a collection of Ecclesiastes, Lamentations, certain psalms, and Job as "a corpus of pessimistic or lament literature."

The textual relationships above could be imagined as three different constellations, the wise king, the sufferer, and the philosopher, all sharing Ecclesiastes as one of their "stars." Like the shared stars in the Big Dipper and Ursa Major, none of these constellations exists without the recognition of Ecclesiastes's particular relationship to separate patterns of different textual stars in the literary sky, but interpreting the book fully requires these three patterns of textual meaning to be blended together.[22] Its meaning is more than any one generic grouping can comprehend, but this meaning cannot be comprehended without generic groupings. Thus Weeks (2010a, 73) observes, "For all its associations with memoirs, autobiographies, and instructions, however, it is impossible to stick any generic label on Ecclesiastes: we simply have no other work quite like it." I would prefer, however, to stick all those labels on the book to see the different features each reveals.[23]

Significantly as well, in this analysis wisdom as a concept is used to identify affiliations between texts, not defined on the basis of the texts chosen, and the concept is only one feature that contributes to the understanding of each text; each is more than merely a "Wisdom" text.

[22] The *Gestalt* effect of this blend is greater, therefore, than merely envisioning the genres as interlocking Venn diagrams with Ecclesiastes in the center (cf. Wright 2010, 303).

[23] For a fuller discussion of the genres of Ecclesiastes, see chapter 6 The Intertextual Network of Ecclesiastes and the Self-Reflective Nature of Genre.

The word wisdom has returned to the orbit of other concepts in the Israelite worldview, such as righteousness or holiness (see Conclusion: The Revitalization of Wisdom). This classification, long considered absolute and exclusive, has become relative and partial.

Given the lack of ancient evidence for the Wisdom category, current biblical scholarship should not be limited to the stationary view from a single, nineteenth-century perspective, in which a "universalistic, humanistic, philosophical" conception of Wisdom is "at the center of all things." Instead, a "polycentric" approach that demotes Wisdom from *the* to merely *a* grouping in which Proverbs, Ecclesiastes, and Job may be read offers new opportunities, not just for the interpretation of those books, but also for others across the canon and beyond and for the concept of wisdom itself. For example, the long-held association between taxonomic genres and distinct social settings in biblical scholarship has set a high bar for pursuing connections between texts. However, a lower bar, one that sees genres merely as texts grouped together because they share one or more similarities, creates less motivation for unsubstantiated historical conjecture and more freedom to explore the many ways comparing texts in the canon and beyond may illuminate their interpretation.

4.4 A MULTIDIMENSIONAL APPROACH TO THE TENSIONS OF GENRE

Any attempt to define genre is shot through with tensions. The multidimensional network approach proposed here is no different. However, it does offer a novel perspective on three of the tensions at the heart of genre theory.

4.4.1 Between Particularity and Generality

The overlapping constellations discussed above, with their differing interpretive emphases regarding the Wisdom texts, are merely a sample, since, according to Frow (2015, 52), "All texts are *relevantly* similar to some texts and *relevantly* dissimilar to others" (emphasis added). Different approaches to genre handle this potential surplus of meaning in different ways. The traditional taxonomic approach over-emphasizes both the similarity and the difference, creating echo chambers that place texts in distorting isolation (Figure 4.7). The recent pan-sapiential

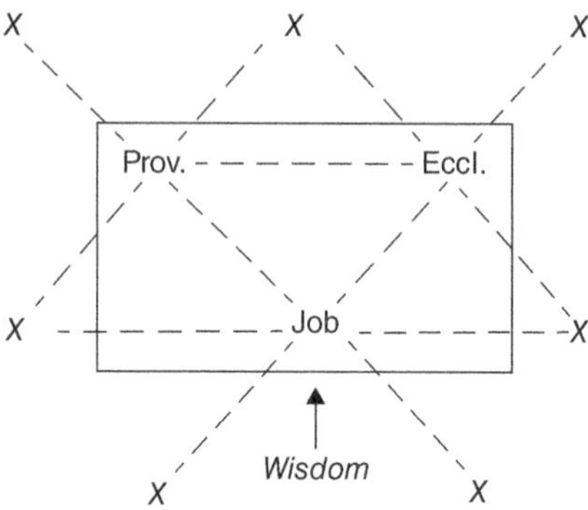

Fig. 4.7. Taxonomic approach: similarity *and* difference overemphasized

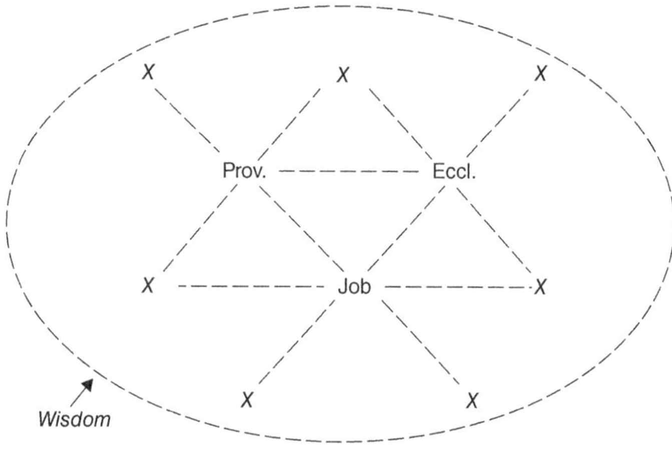

Fig. 4.8. Pan-Sapiential approach: similarity emphasized over difference

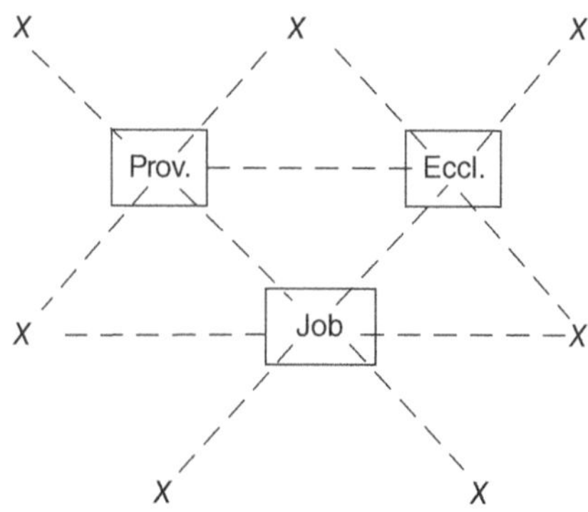

Fig. 4.9. Individualistic approach: difference emphasized over similarity

response emphasizes similarity to the detriment of difference, flattening out textual diversity (Figure 4.8). An individualistic approach (Figure 4.9), which suggests every text is unique (Croce 2000 [1902], 26–8), *sui generis* (Schlegel 1957 [1797–1801], 116), or has its own "intrinsic genre" (Hirsch 1967), would make the opposite mistake, and would actually be practically impossible, since texts cannot be understood alone. Even Benedetto Croce (2000 [1902], 28), while ardently opposing the structures of genre, acknowledged their value as a means to "draw attention to certain groups of works, in general and approximately, to which, for one reason or another, it is desired to draw attention."

Responding to the individualistic approach, Fishelov (1993, 82) argues that "no matter how fervently an author claims that his text is unique, it still has intimate links with existing types of literature, i.e., with literary genres." However, his response relies on the assumption of two-dimensional, non-overlapping genres and thus on a false disjunction: a text's unique character need not be set against its links with other types of literature, since every text will relate differently with others and involve a *unique set* of "intimate links with existing types of literature." Though there is an "inevitable tension between particularity and generality" at the heart of genre (Prince 2003, 456), this multidimensional approach overcomes it by understanding textual particularity through multiple dimensions of generality. Viewing the text from varied perspectives, each which considers different affinities "relevant," reveals how that text participates in multiple generic constellations, which will better enable readers to triangulate its distinctive location in the vast expanse of literature. Fishelov's own interpretation of *Paradise Lost* mentioned above is, in fact, an excellent example of this.

For example, if a fourth text, such as Psalms, is considered along with Proverbs, Ecclesiastes, and Job, with the three-dimensional network between them creating a pyramid shape with Psalms at the top as in Figure 4.10, it will reveal different affinities between them as their relationships are viewed from various angles. Proverbs, Ecclesiastes, and Job may share an interest in wisdom, as Bruch argued, but, looking at the canon from a different perspective, de Wette united Job, Ecclesiastes, and Psalms in their representation of *Unglück*, or misfortune. Earlier, the rabbinic *Sifrei Emet* category drew Proverbs, Job, and Psalms together. Though the reasons for this grouping are elusive, it reveals the texts' common affinity for dividing the world into the "righteous" and the "wicked" (see section 7.2.1.1 *Sifrei Emet*).

Genre is a means of recognizing that this text is like those in respect to one or more significant characteristics. Fully comprehending all the

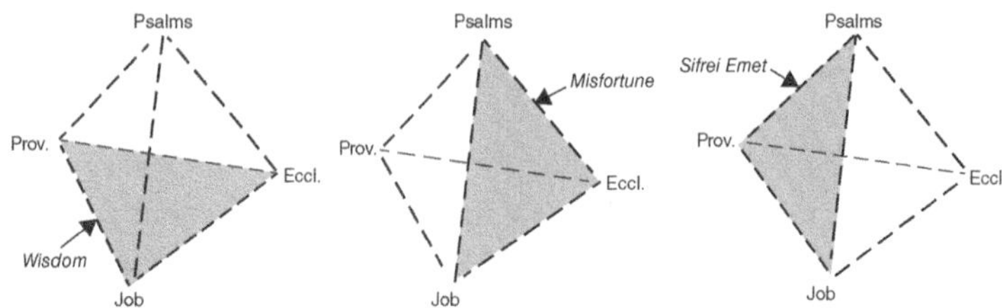

Fig. 4.10. Multidimensional approach: similarities and differences from multiple perspectives

characteristics of a text therefore involves identifying *all the genres* in which a text participates. Restricting the interpretation of Wisdom of Solomon to its connections with other Wisdom Literature, for example, has left its meaning "somewhat flattened and obscured," while placing it among apocalyptic literature as well would bring new features into focus (Burkes 2002, 43–4). Genres are treated as intrinsic and essential qualities of texts, but they are, in fact, more often extrinsic and always relational qualities, leaving genre theorists with a nagging guilt "for always being deductive while trying to appear inductive" (Snyder 1991, 203). Therefore, genres should describe not prescribe (Drott 2013, 37). They should inform, not norm, lest they deform. As Dell (2015, 157) writes:

> On the one hand, any new grouping is a fresh lens on the material and thus helpful in its own way, yet, on the other hand, it seems that any dogmatic insistence on a grouping is an ultimate dead end. Perhaps this is why the frustration with the wisdom category has emerged in recent scholarship: perhaps it has had its day, certainly in the terms in which the debate has been engaged in so far.

Reflecting on scholarly disagreement on the definition of Wisdom, Van Leeuwen (2003, 66) notes that a tree can be classified differently depending on which of its "real properties" is considered significant and thereby "belong to the classes of objects combustible, economic, aesthetic, and sacred":

> It is not simply one or another "kind" of thing, as we arbitrarily choose to name it, but potentially many things, if we rightly name the one tree in its diverse aspects. This does not mean that the tree is unreal or unknowable, just that its reality is functionally rich and complex, and that analysis may legitimately take many approaches to that reality.

The partial knowledge of the tree revealed by any one of these various classifications does not detract from the true perception of its nature unless it is presented as its definitive classification through which that nature may be comprehensively understood.[24]

4.4.2 Between Subjectivity and Objectivity

The role readers play in creating genres necessitates the analysis of the various culturally influenced perspectives those readers bring to texts as they group them together. And yet, these various groupings together testify that something does exist to be grouped "out there" beyond readers' minds. The camper may classify a tree as a source of warmth, the logger may classify it as a source of income, the artist as an object of beauty, and the animist as an object of worship, while all looking at the same tree. Similarly, comparing the different shapes traced over the stars in different cultures makes clear that constellations are subjective mental projections.[25] And yet, those constellations are inspired by an objective, transcultural reality, the locations of the stars in the sky.[26] Intertextual interpretation thus exhibits a "fundamental dualism," as it is inspired by the object but performed by the subject "who must force the object to collide with other texts," making interpretation "simultaneously objective and subjective," and subverting those categories (DeShell 1997, 46–7).[27]

Because any genre grouping is constrained by the actual features of the text, this embrace of subjectivity does not degenerate into relativism. Just like the locations of the stars constrain a viewer from including a star in the Southern Hemisphere in the Orion constellation,

[24] Breed (2014, 117–19) similarly speaks of recognizing texts' various "capacities" as they are read in different contexts, which includes various genres (see 87).

[25] Wolfgang Iser (1974, 282) makes a similar point with regard to features within a given text, which he compares to a "collection of stars" in which different readers may see different images. Though those features are fixed, he argues, the lines connecting them are variable.

[26] Here, I differ with Najman (2012, 316), who writes, "The constellation is objectively available and is not a subjective projection." Instead, the stars are objectively available, but the constellations are subjective projections. I also disagree with Nelson Goodman (1996, 156), who argues that both the constellations and the stars are constructed. For a discussion of the philosophical weaknesses of this fact-constructivist view, see Boghossian 2006, 25–41.

[27] Fox (2015, 78) reflects genre's subversion of the objective/subjective duality when he speaks of the *reality* of genre *constructs*: "Science fiction really exists—as a construct, of course."

one cannot include Proverbs in the legal or prophetic genres. However, viewed from elsewhere in the universe, where they can be seen in the same field of vision, a star in the earth's Southern Hemisphere and stars in Orion may form a meaningful pattern and could be put in the same constellation; it just will not be Orion. For example, in order to defend the traditional consensus that the Wisdom texts demonstrate a distinct worldview, Schellenberg (2015, 131–2) contrasts their view of the poor with texts from the Law and Prophets. In so doing, however, she has created a grouping of poverty texts, which reveals the range of views on the subject similar to the way that the Wisdom grouping reveals the nuances of each book's views on that concept.[28] Genre *classifications* can be wrong; genre *groupings* can only wrongly identify the textual affinity that connects a group of texts. This may occur because one of the texts does not have that attribute, or because the affinities identified are not significant enough to form an emergent pattern. Assigning a text to the wrong genre classification is a greater danger because it limits the text's meaning to that genre and distorts its interpretation. Texts will not become meaningless if they cannot be placed in a single genre. In fact, placing a text in a single genre does not reveal its meaning but obscures it by making some part of its meaning its whole meaning. Arguing that *Pilgrim's Progress* is not an allegory is a misinterpretation, but so is arguing that an allegory is all that it is.

Rejecting the notion of a single correct genre for texts—a single pattern in which they should be read that has emerged from a solitary vantage point—and instead embracing the multidimensional subjectivity of interpretation might actually enable interpreters to produce a *more objective* interpretation by triangulating the text's meaning among a broader array of subjective vantage points.[29] This interpretation transcends cultures by engaging with the interpretations of as many of them as possible, revealing and then illuminating the "blindspots" of each perspective (see Green 2000, 41). The Hebrew Bible endorses such a multidimensional approach by including within itself numerous different viewpoints (Hazony 2012, 65) as well as presenting the texts in different orders in the Greek and Hebrew traditions, which

[28] For more examples like this for Job, Ecclesiastes, and Proverbs, see chapters 5 The Intertextual Network of Job and the Selective Nature of Genre, 6 The Intertextual Network of Ecclesiastes and the Self-Reflective Nature of Genre, and 7 The Intertextual Network of Proverbs and the Subjective Nature of Genre, respectively.

[29] Edmund Husserl's phenomenology similarly develops a multiperspectival intersubjective conception of objectivity (see Hermberg 2006, 12).

encourages the books to be interpreted with different emphases. The recent enthusiasm for the history of interpretation and contextual interpretation among biblical scholars reflects this insight, as it draws more subjects into the undeniable "intersubjective" nature of genres (Fishelov 1993, 11–12; Beebee 1994, 255). Each culture, throughout time and across the globe, that reads the biblical text provides a different perspective on the relationships between the texts, just as each individual places the texts in a different intertextual network based on the texts he or she knows. Thus, Roland Barthes (1977, 148) speaks of the reader as "the space on which all the quotations that make up a writing are inscribed without any of them being lost." He, however, envisions an impersonal reader "without history, biography, psychology," while I advocate multiplying readers to transcend history through engaging it; multiple readers, each *with* history, biography, psychology.

Discovering the "true meaning" of a text is an "infinite process," argues Hans-Georg Gadamer (2004 [1960], 298): "Not only are fresh sources of error constantly excluded...but new sources of understanding are continually emerging that reveal unsuspected elements of meaning." Therefore, as Jean Grondin (2010, 196) reads Gadamer, interpreters may "indeed have a strong experience of truth, not only in spite of, but more rightly *thanks* to our historical nature" (emphasis original). Michael Sinding (2012, 165–6) similarly states, "To do justice to literary textual meaning, we must recognize the breadth and complexity of the range of possible mental networks that may have led to—and that may follow from—a text." Incorporating the history of interpretation, he claims, gives interpretation a "dimension of depth," as "there will always be more to learn, more input spaces and connections to discover and integrate."

4.4.3 Between Stability and Change

Unlike some other three-dimensional network schemas (e.g., Kilgore 2013, 54), the constellation metaphor also incorporates the fourth dimension of time. Though the stars are objective, transcultural phenomena, they are moving within their constellations. Over thousands of years some constellations will grow, others shrink, others will become distorted beyond recognition. Also, some of their stars will die and others will be born, just as new texts are constantly written, while others are lost to cultural memory. Both the stars and their viewers, therefore, are dynamically moving through both space and time.

This reflects both the elements of stability and change necessary of any analogy for genres (Fishelov 1993, 159). As Schlegel (1971 [1798], 237) observes in his criticism of "pre-Copernican" approaches to genre, "in the universe of poetry nothing stands still, everything is developing and changing and moving harmoniously." This process may alter perceptions of a text's meaning relative to other texts as new texts cause ripples to spread through the pool of literature, even affecting preceding works.[30] This will move some texts closer and others farther apart, potentially making some of the genres in which they currently participate eventually unrecognizable. In this way, genres "change, evolve, and decay" (Miller 2005, 31) and may even be pronounced "dead" (Fowler 1982, 164–7). Genre criticism, then, is the attempt to hit a moving target from a moving vehicle.

Biblical scholars are like astronomers seeking to identify the location of the stars relative to one another at a particular point in the life of the universe, but they have to acknowledge, not only that they view the text from a particular vantage point, but also that its current "place" may not be where it was then. The task is therefore "largely heuristic and highly subjective" (Sneed 2015a, 39). An understanding of ancient Israelite culture, and the Israelite understanding of the network of texts in which their writings participated may be the end goal. But, starting at this goal, particularly with a modernly imposed Wisdom class or movement, would be viciously circular. Unavoidably, as it moves into different contexts and genre systems, "what we think of as the 'same' text will change" (Frow 2015, 141). This, Frow notes, makes it all too easy for interpreters to project contemporary understandings onto ancient genres, creating essences for genres that can only have "historically changing values." The tendency of critics, therefore, to read earlier texts through the genre categories of their own time as if those genres were static and universally applicable is widespread (Fowler 1982, 51). Given that modern biblical critics inevitably place the ancient text in a different system of texts than its original readers, who were aware of a different group of texts, including ancient ones now lost, it is impossible for critics not to "move" its meaning somewhat. Just as meaning is produced between texts, it is recognized between interpreters. To adapt Bloom's axiom, then, there are *no* texts, but only relationships *between* texts *and interpreters*, as those

[30] See Eliot 1920, 49–50. For example, F. R. Leavis (1963, 5) argues that Jane Austen's work has a "retroactive effect," which unveils "potentialities and significances" in earlier works "in such a way that, for us, she creates the tradition we see leading down to her."

textual relationships are conceptualized in multiple overlapping genres shaped by various cultural perspectives. In other words, any genre on its own is selective, self-reflective, and subjective, but multiplying these hermeneutically suspect perspectives on the text offers much more reliable and powerful insight into the complexity of its meaning.

4.5 OTHER BIBLICAL CATEGORIES

The Wisdom texts, with their defiance of genre definitions, like the broader Writings, unified only in their idiosyncrasy, are like wandering stars in the canonical universe. The difficulties they pose for the old classificatory paradigm inspire a search for another that can better explain that universe as a whole. This new paradigm will also illuminate different salient features of each of the books in the other biblical categories as they are read three-dimensionally according to multiple groupings viewed from various perspectives.

In contrast to Wisdom Literature, though, from an extrinsic perspective, the labels Law and Prophets, at least, do have the strength of antiquity. They are recognized as classifications of biblical books, not only in early Judaism and Christianity, but in Second Temple texts (Sir. prol.; 2 Macc. 15:9; 4 Macc. 18:10), the New Testament (e.g., Luke 24:44), and potentially the Hebrew Bible itself (e.g., 2 Kgs. 17:13; see Chapman 2000, 286). From an intrinsic perspective, however, these categories do not fare quite as well. The Pentateuch contains a diverse mix of genres, ranging from cosmology and genealogy to law and folklore. Though debate continues over whether a single genre category, such as epic or historiography, could encapsulate this diversity (e.g., Van Seters 2004, 68–74), "Law" or "Torah" are rarely proposed (though, see Watts 1999, 158–61). Prophets, if the Latter Prophets are treated separately, has stronger intrinsic genre markers, such as association with a single prophetic personage of the past, self-presentation as YHWH's word, and the claim to convey legitimate and authoritative knowledge about YHWH (Ben Zvi 2003, 282). Even so, the diversity of the prophetic texts suggests their authors were not working under the guidance of clear generic constraints, such that the texts are unified in little more than their "self-presentation as products of prophecy" (Weeks 2010b, 27).

In the pursuit of the texts' original meaning, their antiquity indicates these categories need not be regarded with the same degree of suspicion as the Wisdom category, which was developed in the nineteenth-century and justified by an abstract definition influenced and facilitated by the philosophical interests of that time. None of these criticisms apply to Law and Prophets.[31] Yet, these categories still should be held lightly and not considered to exhaust the texts' meaning. As George Nickelsburg (2005, 37) writes (emphasis original):

> As we try to understand the functions that [ancient texts] fulfilled and the settings in which they were employed, we may discover that the similarities in texts that *we have decided* belong to different categories are not really all that strange after all, because in the wholeness of life in antiquity they were tied together in ways that we have yet to understand. In short, the problem may not be in the texts, but in the categories and methods that we have used to describe and interpret them.

CONCLUSION

The problem, then, is not only why the Wisdom texts were perceived in this one way (see chapter 3 The Birth of Wisdom Literature: The Nineteenth-Century Origin of the Wisdom Corpus), but that they are perceived in only one way at all. By taking into account the multiple perspectives through which texts are grouped together, an intertextual network approach to genre is better able to represent "the wholeness of life in antiquity" than traditional taxonomic categorization. Recognizing how the so-called Wisdom texts participate in various genres should invite further intertextual interpretation. As specific biblical examples demonstrate in the following chapters, this approach has several benefits over the Wisdom Literature categorization. It can account for the shared subject matter linking the so-called Wisdom books without confining them within externally imposed, culturally limited taxonomic boundaries that create a distorting echo chamber. It can explain connections between these texts and texts across the canon without

[31] Though similar ones may apply to "apocalyptic," a genre first proposed by Friedrich Lücke (1832). Like Bruch's definition of Wisdom Literature, Lücke's characterizations of the apocalyptic genre have continued to affect the interpretation of the texts it contains (see Sturm 1989, 18–20).

expanding Wisdom indefinitely. And it can appreciate the unique ways each so-called Wisdom text interacts with other texts and genres. Thus, it enables the appreciation, if not disentanglement, of the textual web in which every text finds itself. Each is intertwined in an intricate network of meaning as vast as the heavens above, twinkling in numerous textual constellations.

Part III

The Reintegration of Wisdom Literature

5

The Intertextual Network of Job and the Selective Nature of Genre

> All that exists, as contemplated by the human mind, forms one large system or complex fact, and this of course resolves itself into an indefinite number of particular facts, which, as being portions of a whole, have countless relations of every kind, one towards another. Knowledge is the apprehension of these facts, whether in themselves, or in their mutual positions and bearings. And, as all taken together form one integral subject for contemplation, so there are no natural or real limits between part and part; one is ever running into another; all, as viewed by the mind, are combined together, and possess a correlative character one with another, from the internal mysteries of the Divine Essence down to our own sensations and consciousness, from the most solemn appointments of the Lord of all down to what may be called the accident of the hour, from the most glorious seraph down to the vilest and most noxious of reptiles.
>
> (Newman 1891, 45)

In chapter 4 The Universe of Texts: The Intertextual Network of Genres from Multiple Perspectives, I argued that genre is simply a means of recognizing that one text is similar to a group of other texts in respect to one or more significant characteristics. The significance of these characteristics is determined by the cultural resonance of a particular conceptual blend that emerges from the infinite textual network. Adapting Bloom's provocative expression of the inescapably relational nature of textual understanding, I concluded, therefore, that there are no texts, but only relationships between texts, as those relationships are conceptualized in multiple overlapping genres shaped by various cultural perspectives. Fully comprehending all the significant characteristics of a text therefore involves identifying all the genres in which a text participates. Reading a work in this rich, complex, interlocking intertextual network transcends the limiting subjectivity of a solitary viewpoint, thereby providing a more robust and objective understanding of the text's meaning. In this final part of the book, I apply this intertextual network approach to the three books grouped together by modern interpreters due to their shared interest in wisdom: Job, Ecclesiastes, and Proverbs. Though they each demonstrate all three features of genre interpretation highlighted in chapter 4, each text is particularly helpful for communicating one of them—that genres are selective (Job), self-reflective (Ecclesiastes), and subjective (Proverbs), as interpreters create genres based on textual affinities selected for their culturally relevant significance.

Chapters 5–7 deal with the books in that order, progressing from the border of the Wisdom category to its center, increasingly challenging common assumptions about the category. I start in this chapter with Job, a text that cries out for a new approach, since the Wisdom Literature category has never been able to contain its vast intertextual potential. Its defiance of classification has already inspired multiple genre proposals for the book beyond Wisdom. Though each of those proposals similarly fails to comprehend the book fully, each reveals some facet of the book and thus together they illuminate its complex contours. Ecclesiastes, discussed in chapter 6 The Intertextual Network of Ecclesiastes and the Self-Reflective Nature of Genre, has also been associated with numerous genres, but these have consistently been subordinated to its Wisdom categorization.

An analysis of Job therefore demonstrates well the value of an intertextual network approach, but in order truly to challenge the Wisdom Literature paradigm, this approach will have to prove its merit for the other Wisdom books in the Hebrew Bible. Even those who have disputed Job's Wisdom categorization have generally been content to maintain the classification for Proverbs and Ecclesiastes (e.g., Johnson 2009, 18–19; Dell 2015, 154), even if this creates a category of two contradictory texts within the Hebrew Bible (Dell 2016). Ecclesiastes's hermeneutically generative ambiguity similarly demonstrates how mapping out these genres offers more comprehensive insight into its meaning. As the Bible's Rorschach test, the book also highlights particularly well how genre proposals, Wisdom included, tend to treat texts like Ecclesiastes as a mirror that reflects back the interests of a particular interpretive perspective. This leads to a reconsideration of the interpretation of Proverbs, the quintessential "Wisdom text," in chapter 7 The Intertextual Network of Proverbs and the Subjective Nature of Genre. If the Wisdom category is not "real," but a modern projection onto the book, then other intertextual groupings should also be explored, which conceptualize its meaning in different ways and may alter the interpretation of both the book and its conception of wisdom.

5.1 READING JOB AS WISDOM LITERATURE

The classification of Job as a Wisdom text is the development that creates the modern Wisdom corpus. Sheppard (2000, 372) argues that around the turn of the nineteenth century, "various historical, comparative, and form-critical criteria" replaced Solomonic attribution as the "obvious" starting point for "defining biblical wisdom literature." Though it is misleading to refer to the Solomonic collection as "wisdom literature," given the qualitative and quantitative differences between that category and modern Wisdom Literature (see section 2.2 Solomonic Association), the hermeneutical shift Sheppard identifies did indeed enable Job to be associated with Wisdom, creating a new category. Concurrently, reading Job as Wisdom Literature transformed the book's interpretation. Job must be made to fit the category that its inclusion creates; the case for classifying Job as Wisdom Literature is viciously circular. The fact that the classification is a modern invention is not in itself problematic, since "we see things in ancient texts that their first readers probably did not, and they are often actually there" (Good 1990, 10). However, Edwin Good continues, "The problem arises if we use the modern classification to determine our interpretation." Relying on "assumed genre context" in interpretation, he warns, can lead readers to "avoid reading the work," to "walk around" it, or to "produce another," which leads him to question Job's classification as Wisdom (11).

Several scholars have joined Good in raising objections to this genre classification for the book.[1] Though I find many of their arguments compelling, I am not going to rehearse or attempt to add to them here. Recent genre research suggests that arguments like this are unnecessary. Clearly, Job *can* be read as Wisdom Literature; it has been almost

[1] e.g., Dell 1991, 63–88; Wolfers 1995, 47–51; Johnson 2009, 15–23; Harding 2010.

universally read this way for more than a century. These recent arguments indicate, though, that it is not the case that Job *must* be read as Wisdom Literature. Though they question Job's classification as Wisdom, these studies all continue to assume to some degree the binary taxonomic approach to genre, and so dismissing Wisdom simply clears space for them to propose an alternative genre in which the book *must* be read (even if that means reading it as *sui generis*).[2] This only deposes one despot in order to enthrone another. The death of the Wisdom Literature category along with the taxonomic understanding of genre propping up its reign, however, creates the conditions for a more representative, even democratic, approach to governing the book's meaning.

Classifying Job as Wisdom Literature is not without its hermeneutical benefits, however, which have contributed to its widespread acceptance. Weeks, for example, is happy to use the classification as long as it is solely acknowledged as a reflection on the books' subject matter (see section 1.5 Prescribed Treatment), and the classification indeed highlights the prominent role of the concept of wisdom in the book. Grouping Job with Proverbs and Ecclesiastes has inspired reflection on how it compares with those works. For example, this has highlighted the challenge Job poses to the general confidence Proverbs displays in the blessings of wise living, which is a similarity Job shares with Ecclesiastes (e.g., Marböck 2006). Further, this classification has shed light on the features Job shares with both Proverbs and Ecclesiastes, such as the humanistic relevance and universal applicability of the questions with which it wrestles. By focusing attention on such features of the book, the category enables them to be seen clearly. However, because it has been employed exclusively, the Wisdom Literature classification has blurred interpreters' peripheral vision and distorted Job's interpretation in at least three ways.

5.1.1 Canonical Separation

First, the classification of Job as Wisdom Literature has discouraged scholars from pursuing literary connections between Job and books in

[2] e.g., "The book of Job *should* be classified with those works that evidence both wisdom and apocalyptic characteristics" (Johnson 2009, 180); "Whatever else the book of Job may be, it *should* be construed as 'metaprophecy'" (Harding 2010, 538); emphasis added. As these citations indicate, both these scholars acknowledge the possibility of some mixing of genres in the book, however.

the rest of the canon (see Harding 2010, 525). The history of interpretation testifies to this. In early critical study on Job, parallels between Job and other books of the Hebrew Bible were frequently addressed, though the discussion was largely limited to the question of relative dating. Thus, Hugo Grotius (1644, 398) argued that the book of Job was written after the time of David and Solomon because it quoted their works. However, in 1812, John Mason Good (1812, xlvii) claimed that Job was one of the oldest books in the canon because it "is occasionally quoted or copied by almost every Hebrew writer who had an opportunity of referring to it, from the age of Moses to that of Malachi; especially by the Psalmist, Isaiah, Jeremiah, and Ezekiel." As the nineteenth century progressed, the scholarly tide turned against such a conclusion. Bateson Wright (1883, 11), for example, suggested that Job's priority had "been too much taken for granted" and claimed that Job is an improbable "storehouse of Hebrew expression on philosophical and theological problems, to which all Hebrew poets and philosophers are indebted." Instead, Wright argued, in many of the parallels the opposite is the case (see also Cheyne 1887, 83–9; Dhorme 1967 [1926], clii–clxxiv).

However, this debate was cut short by the concurrent and interdependent development of form criticism and the Wisdom Literature category. Two examples demonstrate their effect on the interpretation of Job. First, in studies of Job in the nineteenth and early twentieth centuries, the book's airing of the doctrine of retribution draws it into conversation not merely with Proverbs' act–consequence relationship, but with the doctrine of retribution in texts across the Hebrew Bible. While discussing Job, Samuel Davidson (1862, 217) claims that retribution was "the genius of Mosaism," Davison (1894, 79) associates the doctrine with the Deuteronomic covenant, which became "the traditional teaching of law-givers, wise men, and prophets," and Edouard Dhorme (1967 [1926], cxxxvii, cxxxix) claims that retribution is "everywhere characteristic of Israelite theology." These comments would also suggest that to the degree that Proverbs presents the doctrine of retribution, it too participates in the broader biblical tradition. Thus, Job's treatment of the issue does not restrict it to the Wisdom Literature but "inevitably invites the reader to hear Job in the context of the entire Bible" (McCann 1997, 18). In that broader context, Job is clearly not the first to challenge this doctrine: "it is hard to suppose that the reader of the Bible is expected to conclude that Abel, Uriah the Hittite, and Naboth were murdered because they deserved to be" (Rowley 1976, 18).

However, as Wisdom Literature became established as a category, the genre boundary and the corresponding sapiential *Sitz im Leben* demanded by form criticism discouraged scholars from drawing these other texts into their interpretations of Job, making Proverbs into Job's main dialogue partner and limiting the book's links with retribution across Israel's law, covenant, and history. David Clines (1989, lxi–lxii), for example, acknowledges Deuteronomy as the pre-eminent exponent of retribution, but takes Job's questioning of the doctrine as a confrontation of "the ideology of Proverbs."

Second, a survey of interpretations of what is likely the strongest verbal parallel between Job and a book outside the Wisdom category shows the isolating effect of these scholarly trends. Toward the end of his thanksgiving hymn, the author of Psalm 107 writes, "He pours contempt on princes and makes them wander in a trackless waste" (v. 40). These words appear nearly verbatim, separated by two verses in Job 12:21a, 24b (see Kynes 2012a, 80–1).

Ps. 107:40

שֹׁפֵךְ בּוּז עַל־נְדִיבִים וַיַּתְעֵם בְּתֹהוּ לֹא־דָרֶךְ	He pours contempt on princes and makes them wander in trackless wastes.

Job 12:21, 24

שׁוֹפֵךְ בּוּז עַל־נְדִיבִים וּמְזִיחַ אֲפִיקִים רִפָּה 21	*He pours contempt on princes* and looses the belt of the strong…
מֵסִיר לֵב רָאשֵׁי עַם־הָאָרֶץ וַיַּתְעֵם בְּתֹהוּ לֹא־דָרֶךְ 24	He strips understanding from the leaders of the earth *and makes them wander in a pathless* *waste.*

Though not exhaustive, the overview of commentaries on Job and the Psalms in the appendix is widespread enough to reveal two troubling trends. First, the works in bold print appeared in the period between the publication of Gunkel's commentary on the Psalms in 1926, which solidified form criticism's influence on Hebrew Bible studies, and Michael Fishbane's *Biblical Interpretation in Ancient Israel* in 1985, which re-injected attention to inner-biblical allusion into study of the Hebrew Bible. In that period, attempts to determine which of the two texts is referring to the other decrease, as scholars prefer instead merely to mention that there is some similarity, usually with a "cf.," or ignore the parallel altogether, indicated by "N/A" in the table.

However, second, after 1985 there is a rise, particularly in Job studies, in the recognition of allusion, but contradicting consensus positions have developed on whether Job or Psalm 107 has priority. Psalms commentators continue to attribute the dependence to the psalm, as they had done consistently throughout history. The one exception, Rosenmüller in 1823, also wrote a commentary on Job, and he claims Job is alluding to the psalm in both commentaries. The Job commentaries do not display such unanimity. In the nineteenth century, again with the exception of Rosenmüller, and two ambiguous statements by Delitzsch and August Dillmann, commentators universally claim the psalm is dependent on Job. However, in the 1920s Driver and Gray and Dhorme defended Job's dependence on the psalm, and this view has prevailed since among those who address the issue, aided undoubtedly by the critical reevaluation of Job's date, which moved it from being one of the earliest books written in the Hebrew Bible to one of the latest.[3] More surprising than this difference in interpretation of the parallel is the general lack of acknowledgement of the opposing position. These factors together suggest that the commentary writers are not interacting with the work of those writing on the other book. Thanks to the growing specialization of biblical studies, which encourages scholars to be "Wisdom experts," few write commentaries on both books (I found only twelve who did, and only three, Samuel Terrien, Robert Alter, and Tremper Longman, in the past fifty years). Thus, two nearly independent "traditions" on the issue of dependence for the potential allusion between Job 12 and Psalm 107 have developed, with Job's Wisdom classification creating a boundary between them.[4]

5.1.2 Theological Abstraction

In addition to creating this type of canonical separation, reading Job as Wisdom Literature also leads to theological abstraction. Cordoned off with Proverbs and Ecclesiastes, Job has been increasingly read as the philosophical treatment of a "problem." Thus claims Claus Westermann

[3] Even after critical scholarship began to question the early date of Job, Psalms scholars simply adjusted the date of Job and the psalm accordingly to continue to justify Joban priority. Charles Briggs (1906–7, 2:362), for example, claims that Ps. 107:40 was added by a later glossator, while Michael Goulder (1998, 127) dates Job soon after the exile to fit an early postexilic date for the psalm, and Walter Beyerlin (1979, 84) dates the psalm extremely late (late third century) to account for the generally accepted late date of Job.

[4] Charlotte Hempel (2017, 2, 26–7) notes a similar phenomenon in Qumran studies, in which the bifurcation of scholarly expertise between Law and Wisdom has obscured the "dynamic interplay" between them that she finds evident both in Proverbs 1–9 and the Community Rule.

(1981 [1956], 1–2), who believes this classification of the book "has clearly exerted a pervasive, perhaps even controlling, influence upon nineteenth- and twentieth-century exegesis."[5] For example, Ernst Sellin and Leonard Rost argue that the book treats the problem, "How is the suffering of a just man to be reconciled with the existence of a just God?"[6] As Westermann observes, to consider the book as the treatment of a question, and to attempt to grasp that question conceptually, is to objectify its contents, and thus to make Job an object—the object of thought. This approach may correspond well with the gnomic instruction of Proverbs and the philosophical investigation of Ecclesiastes, but the interpreter must recognize the way it predetermines the meaning of Job. The book might just as well address the existential question, "Why must I suffer?" as Westermann argues, or even, "How should one speak of God in the face of chaos?,"[7] and the parallels with the psalmic laments would support this reading just as strongly.

Something similar happens if a "didactic" intent is ascribed to the book in order to justify including it in the Wisdom category. Since Job demonstrates the limits of human knowledge, the book wears this label with significant discomfort (see Dell 1991, 61; Oorschot 2007). However, it can be made to do so, if the meaning of the book is treated at an abstract enough level. Of course, beyond distorting the book's message, a didacticism defined broadly enough to include Job will also apply to every other book in the Hebrew Bible (Collins 2010, 429) and therefore add little to the understanding of Job. After all, "[n]o Hebrew writer is merely a poet or a thinker. He is always a teacher. He has men before him in their relations to God" (Davidson 1891, xxvi).

Interpreting Job as a didactic text makes its message more abstract, just as a lecture on suffering is more abstract than screams of pain, but it does not change its overall message much. Due to the limited interpretive value of this justification for including Job among the Wisdom Literature, few commentators are willing to stop here. However, Alistair Hunter (2006, 23) provides a particularly forthright example of the challenges they face when they attempt to go further. He acknowledges that his efforts to identify the Wisdom Literature on formal

[5] For earlier opposition to this philosophical reading of the book for similar reasons, see Volz 1911, 25.

[6] Cited in Westermann 1981 [1956], 1. In a later edition, Sellin and Rost (1959, 147) are more circumspect and take Westermann's argument for Job's use of the lament form into account.

[7] Paraphrasing Choon-Leong Seow (2013, 108), who also questions "Wisdom Literature" as the book's genre classification (61).

linguistic grounds has left a "glaring omission": the book of Job. Given the "effective unanimity among scholars that it belongs in this category," Hunter explains "the intuitive urge" to include Job in Wisdom Literature by considering "the underlying perspectives which emerge from a consideration in broader terms of what these books are concerned with." He summarizes these broader concerns as: "(1) a universal perspective on life, (2) a humanistic view of the problems addressed, (3) evidence of curiosity about the natural and everyday world and (4) an intellectual approach to solving them." This list fairly well summarizes the post-Enlightenment approach to reality in which Job was first associated with Wisdom Literature, and, when applied to the book, directs attention to an abstract philosophical plane. As a result, Sneed (2011, 57) argues that Wisdom should be considered a "mode" that unites the texts at a "higher level of abstraction" than genre. Arguments like these demonstrate the "historical harmonizing" in modern critical attempts to find a unity amidst the diversity of the texts identified as wisdom, which produces "a lowest common denominator of wisdom over time" rather than appreciating the differences among the texts associated with the category (Sheppard 2000, 377). This lowest common denominator floats high above the text of Job in ethereal abstraction.

5.1.3 Hermeneutical Limitation

As canonical separation leads to theological abstraction, so both together contribute to a third distorting effect: hermeneutical limitation. Read as Wisdom Literature, Job's potential meaning is severely restricted. This is the intent of categorization, to corral the multivalent text into a fenced-in pre-understanding (see section 4.2 The Rebirth of Genre). So, readers listen for genre clues, such as the opening words, "Once upon a time," and then know what to expect: the possibility of talking animals, supernatural powers, and, of course, a happy ending (Briggs and Bauman 1992, 147).[8] Though she is discussing the use of genre by authors rather than readers, Newsom's (2003, 12) observation still applies: "The power a genre possesses to focus one aspect of reality is purchased at a price, however; it cannot see things otherwise." The Wisdom Literature categorization has encouraged interpreters to treat the book like Job's friends treated him, as they use preconceptions of

[8] Some have argued that the opening words of Job serve a similar function, identifying the story as a folk tale (see Williamson 2007).

normality to stifle its claim that in its case the norms have been broken. Indeed, the book of Job intends to deconstruct pre-understanding, to undercut human claims to wisdom (e.g., chs 28, 38–41). As many scholars admit, its relationship to Wisdom is best explained as oppositional. The book "questions the wisdom tradition to such an extent that it breaks outside its bounds" (Dell 1991, 83). It seems strange to claim Job as an object-lesson within Wisdom Literature when the book is an "uninhibited parade of all that negates it" (Wolfers 1995, 49). At most, then, Job is "anti-wisdom wisdom" (Pope 1973, lxviii). But even this understanding is limiting, because it only defines the book by what it is not, instead of by what it is, which is a consistent weakness of attempts to define Wisdom Literature as a whole, as well (see section 7.3 Network Approach).

Those who argue against Job's classification as Wisdom Literature see this. They warn that due to the classification, the book's interpretation has been "hedged in" (Johnson 2009, 77) and "unduly restricted" (Harding 2010, 525). James Harding (2010, 525) points to the "inescapably circular manner" in which scholars assign Job to the category Wisdom "on the basis of a scholarly convention" and then interpret it according to the concerns of a class of sages inferred from the texts, for which, in Job's case, at least, "unequivocal evidence" is lacking. Perdue (2008, 142), for example, takes potentially prophetic features of Job and incorporates them into a sapiential social context by interpreting them as evidence of "mantic wisdom" (Harding 2010, 529).

David Wolfers (1995, 48–9) similarly complains of the way categorizing Job as Wisdom Literature "imposes an estoppal on particular lines of thought," such as the evidence of national concerns that he claims pervade the book. This despite the fact that the "relatively modern imposition" of the "*post facto*" classification that prevents such conclusions relies on "perfectly circular" reasoning. The categorization, he argues, is "arbitrary, reflecting nothing but our own decisions as to which works to place into which categories," and therefore "invalid for imposing restrictions on content or form."[9] For Wolfers there is "too much beside" to assign Job to Wisdom Literature. It bursts the bounds of the category in content and form (see Dell 1991, 64–83). Thematically,

[9] Wolfers (1995, 49) goes too far, however, when he argues, "The content of a book is to be determined from the book itself, alone and isolated from every other consideration." Such an approach is impossible, as even his interpretation of Job, inspired by comparison with other historical allegories, demonstrates (see section 5.2.1.3 History).

it presents a "whole new intellectual universe" and, formally, it borrows broadly from Hebrew literary tradition, which makes it "the realisation of the combination of forms, wisdom, prophecy, psalm, drama, contest, lament, theodicy, history, and allegory" (Dell 1991, 50–1). The Wisdom classification impoverishes this rich interpretive potential, obscuring the book's "bewildering diversity of literary genres" (Terrien 1978, 361).

5.2 THE INTERTEXTUAL NETWORK OF JOB

In light of the difficulties Job poses for attempts at classification, several interpreters have unsurprisingly thrown their hands in the air and categorized it as *sui generis*, in a class of its own (e.g., Engnell 1970, 256; Pope 1973, xxx; Seow 2013, 61). This widely accepted view goes back to Robert Lowth (Witte 2007, 107). On the basis of the book's "single and unparalleled" status in the canon, Lowth (1829 [1753], 264) concluded, "It seems to have little connexion with the other writings of the Hebrews, and no relation whatever to the affairs of the Israelites." Harold Rowley (1976, 5) similarly claims, "It is wiser to recognize the uniqueness of this book and to consider it without relation to any of these literary categories." If Job is *sui generis*, however, this results not from the book's isolation from other texts, but its connections with so many of them—its uniqueness is better recognized in its relations with so many other categories. As Crenshaw (2010, 115) says, "Like all great literary works, this one rewards readers who come to it from vastly different starting points." Along these lines, Childs (1979, 544) argues that the book's "proper interpretation depends on seeing Job in the perspective, not only of wisdom traditions, but also of Israel's liturgy and historical traditions," though, as I will argue, these traditions are only the start. The *sui generis* categorization has the advantage of not restricting Job's interpretation to one genre, but, even worse, it limits it to none, leaving the reader stumbling in interpretive darkness. Throwing up one's hands when faced with the book's complexity and opting for this "counsel of despair" only makes it "unreadable" (Longman 2012, 30).

In terms of both form and content, Job is embedded in a remarkably dense intertextual network. As a particularly bright star in the canonical universe, it shines in numerous constellations. Throughout history, readers have associated Job with other groupings of texts, and in recent scholarship these alternative genre suggestions have increased as the Wisdom Literature category has weakened. The book is unique, but appreciating its distinctiveness fully requires not reading it independently of the many literary categories in which it could be placed, but in relationship to as many of them as its content and form justify. This will create a map of the intertextual network that contributes to its meaning.

5.2.1 Genres before "Wisdom Literature"

Before the Wisdom category, Job appeared in a number of different groupings. It may be the most variably placed book in canon lists, appearing in numerous positions in both Jewish and Christian lists, ranging from the beginning of the histories (e.g., Bryennios Manuscript) to the end of the prophets (Josephus, Rufinus).

5.2.1.1 Sifrei Emet

In Jewish tradition, the primary groupings were the larger Writings collections and the *Sifrei Emet* within it (see section 2.1.1 Hebrew Order). Since the Writings are unified primarily by their distinctiveness both from the Law and Prophets and from each other, this grouping is a recognition of Job's multivalence, rather than an attempt to limit it. Though the reasoning behind the narrower *Sifrei Emet* grouping of Psalms, Job, and Proverbs is less clear, this ordering of the books, which appears in b. Baba Batra 14b and the Leningrad and Aleppo codices, does seem to capture some important features of Job,[10] such as how in many ways it stands between Psalms and Proverbs (see Kuhl 1953, 311, 312; Engnell 1970, 256) and the interpretive value of reading Job following the Psalms, given the many connections between them (Kynes 2015b). It also reveals the importance of the dichotomy of righteousness and wickedness in the book (see section 7.2.1.1 *Sifrei Emet*).

5.2.1.2 Poetry

In the Greek and later Christian tradition, Job is predominantly associated with the Poetry collection (see section 2.1.2 Greek Order).

[10] Ashkenazi manuscripts and some early printed editions have the order Psalms–Proverbs–Job (Fox 2000, 4).

Though the Wisdom associations of other books in this collection may invite an exploration of the role wisdom plays in Job, the grouping primarily acknowledges the book's undeniable poetic form, and encourages that to be taken into account in its interpretation (see Alonso Schökel 1988; Alter 1990; Van der Lugt 1995). Lowth (1829 [1753], 281), while attempting to sift through the generic categories already competing to contain Job in his time, concludes it should be considered poetry above all, and above all poetry: "It is of little consequence whether it be esteemed a didactic or an ethic, a pathetic or dramatic poem; only let it be assigned a distinct and conspicuous station in the highest rank of the Hebrew poetry." Even so, this broad, formal classification provides limited illumination. Even the division of the Poetic books in the latter nineteenth century between the lyric and the didactic,[11] with Job included with Proverbs, Ecclesiastes, and some psalms in the latter, poorly represents Job, with its emotionally personal lyric style (see section 3.1 Wisdom's Date of Birth, n. 6). This distinction neither reflects the broad range of genres included in the work, which even when poetic are not necessarily didactic, nor distinguishes the dialogic and dramatic structure of its poetry from other texts in the category (Mies 2003, 338–9). The retroactive association of this collection with instruction under the title *libri didactici* simply suggests that though Job may be read in connection with other books associated with wisdom, it need not be; it could fit just as well in other groupings. In fact, the inclusion of Psalms and Song of Songs with Job in this broad category invited comparisons that would contribute to further alternative genre proposals.

5.2.1.3 *History*

The other places Job appears in ancient canon lists further testify to the book's multivalence. In some, Job appears with the histories. In b. Baba Batra 14b, 15a–b, a number of dates for Job are considered: the time of Jacob, Moses, the judges, David, the Sabaeans (or possibly the Queen of Sheba), the Chaldeans, and Ahasuerus. This historical association is reflected in the addition to the book in the Septuagint (Job 42:17 LXX), which identifies Job and his friends with figures in

[11] Lowth (1829 [1753], 201, 204–5) once again provides a precursor, though he does not include Job among the didactic poetry.

the genealogy of Esau's descendants (Genesis 36).[12] Christian Peshitta manuscripts follow suit and often place Job directly after either the Pentateuch or Judges, as do the four canon lists recorded by Epiphanius, where Job consistently follows books from these two periods, though in two it is followed immediately by the poetic books (Beckwith 1986, 189–90). Origen, on the other hand, puts the book with Esther in a historical subgroup at the end of his list, and Job was widely considered historical in the West even into the medieval period (Beckwith 1986, 224 n. 13). Two of the three canon lists recorded in *Codex Amiatinus* and Cassiodorus's *Institutiones*, Augustine's and "the Septuagint," also include Job on the later end of the histories (the third, from Jerome, puts it with the *Hagiographa*) (see section 2.5 Medieval Interpretation). To the degree that placement in canon lists suggests literary classification, the inclusion of Job with these "historical" texts reflects the contribution of narrative to the book and its potential connections to figures in biblical history, such as Abraham or Jacob, which recent interpreters have rediscovered (e.g., Davis 1992; Boström 2000). This historical connection is even evident in the eighteenth-century definition of "sapiential" from Chambers' *Cyclopedia* (1728), which acknowledges "Historical Books" as an alternative classification for Job (see section 2.1.2 Greek Order, n. 16). Indeed, the debate over whether Job should be considered a historical figure, which goes back to the rabbis (b. B. Bat. 15a), still continues among some readers today (Longman 2012, 32–4).

Links with history need not require historicity, however. Wolfers (1995, 67–70) connects the book to Israel's history as a politico-historical allegory of the nation's trials similar to Dryden's *Absalom and Achitophel*. Though its prose-framed poetry is distinctive, he compares it to three other unified "fictional" tales: Ruth, Esther, and Jonah, the last also sharing an allegorical function. Through the story of Job, he argues, the author attempts to justify God's involvement in the historical catastrophes experienced by Israel and Judah, in particular the Assyrian invasions in the late eighth century BCE. Wolfers's allegorical reading is not unprecedented, though the book is more commonly associated with the exile (e.g., Kellett 1940; Schmid 2007, 250). Though this view had largely fallen out of favor, thanks perhaps in part to the widespread presupposition that Wisdom texts are uninterested in Israel's history, Lambert (2015, 570–1) has recently reintroduced it, though more as an

[12] For whether Job may be a "midrash" of Genesis 36, see Schmid 2007, 241–2.

explanation for the book's inclusion in the canon than as a representation of its intended meaning. In so doing, he draws parallels with allegorical readings of Song of Songs, Ruth, and Ecclesiastes.

5.2.1.4 Torah

The rabbinic tradition that Job was a contemporary of Moses, and that Moses wrote the book, may also contribute to the book's placement immediately after the Torah in canon lists. According to the logic that would associate Proverbs, Ecclesiastes, and Song of Songs with the "Wisdom tradition" due to the books' common attribution to Solomon, this Mosaic attribution would connect Job with the Law. In fact, at Qumran only copies of texts from the Torah and Job were discovered written in paleo-Hebrew script, and Targumim were only found at Qumran for Job and one of the books of the Torah, Leviticus (Tov 2008, 142). Though the book's pentateuchal association likely results from its apparent patriarchal setting rather than its content or form, reading Job along with Moses's other purported productions, particularly Deuteronomy, does yield some significant insight into the book's meaning.

Beyond the more general way Job wrestles with the Deuteronomic doctrine of retribution, more recent scholarship has begun to explore possible direct allusions to Deuteronomy itself. Despite the "paradigmatic assumptions" about the separation of Wisdom Literature from history and Torah which have discouraged study on this question, Witte argues the rabbinic association of Job with the Torah, followed by several church fathers, "is reinforced by a literary and theological relationship between the book of Job and Deuteronomy" (Witte 2013b, 82–3; Witte 2013a, 54). He builds on the work of several earlier studies that examined allusions to Deuteronomy in specific passages of Job, such as ch. 24 (Braulik 1996) or ch. 31 (Oeming 2001), to explore allusions to Deuteronomy throughout the book (Witte 2013a). Witte (2013a, 65) concludes that Job's critical interaction with Deuteronomy "seems to be a precursor, possibly even a precondition, to an identification of Torah and cosmic wisdom" in Ben Sira.

Job's parallels with and potential allusions to Deuteronomy do not end there (see, e.g., Ticciati 2005, 61–3; Schmid 2007, 49–52; Greenstein 2013), and neither do the book's connections with the Torah. Job's prologue has been seen as a "conscious adaptation" of Genesis 1–3 (Meier 1989, 183), his self-curse in ch. 3 as a "counter-cosmic incantation" reversing Gen. 1:1–2:4a (Fishbane 1971, 153) along with aspects of Exodus

(Burnight 2013), while the divine speeches (Job 38–41) rival the description of creation in Genesis (e.g., Gottlieb 2016). Beyond the numerous parallels to the Priestly creation account in the book, readers have seen connections with the broader Priestly tradition in all of its major sections (Schmid 2007, 244–8; Balentine 2013). The connections between Job and the patriarchal figures mentioned above further connect Job with the Pentateuch. In studies such as these, contemporary scholars are just beginning to unearth the hermeneutic potential of the ancient correlation between Job and the Torah.

5.2.1.5 Prophecy

Job is also grouped with Prophecy in early interpretation: in Ben Sira's Praise of the Fathers (49:8–10), in Josephus's canon list (Ag. Ap. 1.8 or 1.40), and in the rabbinic debate over Job's prophetic status (b. B. Bat. 15b–16a). This genre grouping has also experienced a modern renaissance. Bardtke (1967), for example, is inspired by this ancient evidence to explore the book's prophetic traits. Though he acknowledges that Job deviates considerably in form and content from the other prophetic books, he notes common traits extending from the heavenly council in the book's prologue to the divine speech at its end, which he considers the strongest evidence of the book's prophetic character (see also Janzen 1985, 217–25). Crenshaw (1971, 108) claims that in light of the stylistic and theological influence of prophecy on the book, "the continuity between Job and prophecy cannot be denied." Elsewhere, he explains that Job's adaptation of the ancient Near Eastern controversy dialogue (*Streitgespräch*) genre (see below) according to prophetic models explains the book's "kinship with 2 Isaiah" and demonstrates that "Job is rooted in wisdom and prophetic theology, both as to literary genre and final resolution of the problem by a theophany" (Crenshaw 1970, 389).[13]

Susannah Ticciati (2005, 59) recognizes the "indebtedness" of the book's concerns to the prophets and therefore seeks to "understand Job against the background of Israel's prophetic literature." This leads her to notice how the legal language of Job's ריב with God accords with similar lawsuit speeches in Israel's prophetic literature, the significance of Job's desire for a prophetic מוכיח, a figure who intercedes between God and humanity and calls God to account (9:33), and the way Job,

[13] For more on the close ties between Job and Isaiah 40–55, see Kynes 2013b.

like the prophets, builds his argument on the basis of the Deuteronomic Covenant (Ticciati 2005, 58, 120–37, 156–7). Others have joined her in drawing prophetic parallels into their interpretation of Job, such as those with Jeremiah (Fishbane 1971; Greenstein 2004; Dell 2013a), Ezekiel (Joyce 2013), Joel (Nogalski 2013), Amos (Marlow 2013), Habakkuk (Gowan 1986), and Jonah (Harding 2010; see below).

5.2.1.6 Drama

Though not reflected in canon lists, the association of Job with drama also boasts an ancient pedigree, apparently dating back to Theodore of Mopsuestia (d. 428 CE), to whom the Fifth General Council (553) attributed the view that Job was composed in imitation of Greek tragedy. Though the Council condemned this interpretation, the dramatic interpretation found a number of prominent supporters in the sixteenth century (Johannes Brenz, Johannes Oecolampadius, and Theodore Beza), and was widespread from the seventeenth into the nineteenth centuries (Seow 2013, 48). This often led Job to be associated with the Song of Songs, which also was interpreted as a drama during this period (e.g., Lowth 1829 [1753], 249; Delitzsch 1864, 11–13; de Wette 1869 [1817], 557; Cheyne 1887, 108; see Mies 2003, 346). Horace Kallen's (1918) reconstruction of the book according to the tragedies of Euripides, which took remarkable liberty in "restoring" the original text, was the death rattle of this approach, which virtually disappeared as Wisdom Literature gained greater prominence in the following decades. However, the book's association with tragedy has been resurrected, though the structural differences in Job, such as the book's happy ending, and the lack of evidence for the author's knowledge of the foreign genre, have prevented interpreters from embracing it fully (see Steiner 1979, 508; Hoffman 1996, 45; Dell 2007, 18).

This return to dramatic interpretation has also taken a different route with a proposal that, due to its use of incongruity and irony and the happy restoration of its hero at the end, the book is better associated with comedy, whether serious (Whedbee 1977) or humorous (Pelham 2010). However, the line between comedy and tragedy is "fluid" (Whedbee 1977, 31), and, even if a comedy, the book still has a tragic message (Pelham 2010, 93). Therefore, some reasonably avoid the difficulties of conforming Job to either subgenre by interpreting it as drama in a more general sense (e.g., Shelton 1999; Mies 2003) and suggesting that such a reading, at the least, serves heuristically to draw the audience into the impassioned "intellectual action" of the book (Alonso Schökel 1977). Terrien (1971, 506) even proposes that Job represents the invention of a new genre, a "para-cultic drama" developed for the celebration of the New Year Festival. Seow (2013, 48) counters that the unlikelihood of Greek dramatic influence, the literary devices the book employs, and its limited character development and action all militate against classifying the book as a drama (see Barr 1971–72, 40–1). Still, he acknowledges that dramatic interpretations account well for the book's dialogic character and the numerous plays it has inspired (see Newsom 2007).

5.2.1.7 Epic

At least an implicit association of Job with the epic genre is also evident in the early church as well when Jerome (mistakenly) characterizes the poetry of Job according to the dactylic hexameter commonly employed by Greek epics in his preface to the book (Jerome 1846, 1081). The epic interpretation of Job, which understood the book's protagonist as a heroic paragon of virtue in the face of crushing adversity, was prominent in Christian interpretation from Gregory the Great, Isidore of Seville, Bede, and Rabanus Maurus to no less than Milton himself. The book was compared to Homer's epics (see Witte 2007, 105), or, more often, Boethius's *Consolation of Philosophy*, which similarly wrestles with the question of theodicy (Astell 1994, 1–20). Like the *Consolation*, the text depicts not military exploits or adventures but an "epic of inner life" full of "struggles and adventures unknown to sense but real to faith" (Genung 1891, 23; see also Schlottmann 1851, 41).[14] Sarna (1957), however, sees in the prose tale an "epic substratum" with close parallels in Ugaritic epics. The epic interpretation has also reappeared in modern interpretation (Andersen 1976, 36–7), and the formalist reading of Job as a "poeticized folk tale" similarly reads the book as a narrative in poetic form (Fontaine 1987).

5.2.2 Ancient Near Eastern Genres

In addition to being the most variably placed in early canonical lists, Job may also well be the "altorientalischste" ("most ancient Near

[14] Due to their similarities, Marco Treves (1995, 264) argues Job and the *Consolation* both had the work of the Greek Cynic Menippus as their "common model."

Eastern") book in the Hebrew Bible (Uehlinger 2007, 99). In addition to Wisdom Literature, which was actually inspired by comparison with canonical rather than ancient Near Eastern texts (see section 1.4.3 Wisdom in the Ancient Near East), Job has been grouped with other collections of ancient Near Eastern works, each of which, like Job itself, breaks beyond the boundaries of Wisdom in various ways.

5.2.2.1 Exemplary-Sufferer Texts

One of these groupings includes the Babylonian texts, Ludlul Bēl Nēmeqi ("I Will Praise the Lord of Wisdom") and the Babylonian Theodicy, and two texts, one Babylonian and one Sumerian both labeled Man and His God (the latter sometimes referred to as "the Sumerian Job") (see Albertson 1983; Weinfeld 1988). Influenced by the comparison with Job, these texts are frequently labeled "righteous-sufferer literature," but their protagonists generally confess their sinfulness, so this is a misnomer (see Uehlinger 2007, 108–9, 144). The question driving the texts is the unexplained reason for the suffering rather than its injustice, so these might be better termed "unexplained-suffering literature" (e.g., Ludlul, II.33–38), or, because they focus on the experience of an individual, "exemplary-sufferer texts" (see Seow 2013, 51).

None of these texts include a frame narrative and all are hymns, except the Babylonian Theodicy, which uses an acrostic poem to recount a dialogue between the sufferer and his friend over the meaning of his misery. In fact, since these texts bear close resemblance with laments, they reinforce Job's connection with that biblical genre (see below) more than Wisdom (Roberts 1977, 112–13; Weinfeld 1988, 221–2). Thus, as he examines the ancient Near Eastern texts that have the most affinities with Job, Gray (1970, 255, 256, 263, 268) again and again notes their shared similarities with lament Psalms. Dhorme (1967 [1926], cxi) observes a similar phenomenon in Ludlul. Similarly, the alphabetic acrostic and lack of narrative frame in the Babylonian Theodicy create formal affinities with acrostic psalms and Lamentations that it lacks with Job (Mies 2003, 340–1). Though J. J. M. Roberts (1977, 113) claims the Babylonian Theodicy does not fit the lament category, he argues it integrated the "cultic tradition" with "wisdom elements," preparing the way for Job's more radical development of this approach (similarly Uehlinger 2007, 148).

5.2.2.2 Controversy Dialogue (Streitgespräch)

The Babylonian Theodicy is also less sanguine than the other texts about divine justice and is willing to question the doctrine of retribution rather than assume the sinfulness of the sufferer (Seow 2013, 55). With its debate between two friends on a single specific issue, the book conforms with numerous other *Streitgespräch* or "controversy dialogue" texts known from the ancient Near East, some of which engage similar questions as Job.[15] These include the Akkadian Dialogue of Pessimism and an Egyptian text known as Dialogue between a Man and His Ba or The Man Who Grew Tired of Life. These texts offer an apt parallel for the form of a major section of the book of Job, though not for the genre of the entire book (unless one follows Friedrich Baumgärtel [1933] and excises any part of the book that does not correspond to this genre). Though, of these texts, Job most closely parallels the Babylonian Theodicy (see Uehlinger 2007, 146–59), the differences between the two works, including Job's more vitriolic dialogue and the greater number of genres and tropes it incorporates, suggest this genre comparison fails to encapsulate the book (see Seow 2013, 56). Job's defiance of comprehensive comparison to even its closest ancient Near Eastern analogue demonstrates the limits of attempting to interpret the text within a single genre, ancient or otherwise.

5.2.2.3 Didactic Narrative

Parallels have also been suggested for the narrative features of the book. Some associate the prose tale with other "didactic narratives," such as the Joseph story, Esther, Daniel, Aḥiqar, and Tobit. These stories all attempt to inculcate virtue by depicting a virtuous individual's conquest over a test of his character and any who oppose him to earn a reward (von Rad 1972 [1970], 46–7; Müller 1977; Müller 1994; Seow 2013, 50). Donald Gowan (1992) finds a common "wisdom script" in several of these tales, which the book of Job as a whole invokes before violating its expectations. Newsom (2003, 41) argues that Job's prose narrative takes that genre to an extreme, while employing folktale style and evoking a "prophetic example story," such as Nathan's parable in

[15] See van der Toorn (1991), who prefers to label these texts "literary dialogues." Some have also drawn parallels to Greek philosophical dialogues, such as Plato's (e.g., Fries 1904), though their prose form and teacher–student relationship offer a weaker analogue (Mies 2003, 340).

2 Sam. 12:1–14 (following the rabbinic suggestion in b. B. Bat. 16b that Job is a *mashal*). Robert Alter (1981, 33) follows the same rabbinic opinion to classify the book as a "philosophic fable." However, this leads him to group the book not with the narratives mentioned above, but with Jonah, as the only other exception to the Bible's presentation of events as history. Outside of the Bible, such a genre might include philosophical novels such as *Zadig*, *Candide*, or *Robinson Crusoe* (Mies 2003, 339).

5.2.3 Adapted Genres

Rather than illuminating the definitive genre of Job, these only partially applicable ancient Near Eastern parallels reveal instead the multitudinous concatenation of genres in the book (Crenshaw 2011, 10). Not only can no known genre comprehend the book as a whole, the genres to which Job is most similar as well as those it incorporates within itself are consistently remolded and repurposed. As Norman Habel (1985, 42) observes, "It is a mark of creative genius that this author rarely appropriates literary forms or genres in their ideal traditional form. Rather, they are adapted, modified, and transformed to meet particular artistic and theological ends."

5.2.3.1 Lament

Thus, the lament, a genre that undeniably contributes to Job's speeches, is "dramatized" through the addition of the friends (Bentzen 1948–49 [1941], 1:182; Westermann 1981 [1956], 8) or "answered" with Job's restoration (Gese 1958). Murphy (1981, 17) argues that "dramatization of lament" is not a literary genre, but merely the description of the book's blending of genres. Whether the blend could be called a genre of its own would depend on whether other texts attempted to do the same, as Westermann (1981 [1956], 8), following Aage Bentzen (1948–49 [1941], 182), claims is the case with Ludlul. Even if Westermann's proposed genre designation fails to capture the entire work, Murphy (1981, 17) acknowledges his work is "helpful" in creating new exegetical sensitivity to the complaint motifs in the book. Seow (2013, 57) makes similar arguments against interpreting the book as a form of lament but also says Bentzen, Westermann, and Gese "are correct to call attention to it" given the "numerous formal, thematic, and lexical affinities between parts of the book of Job and the laments of the

Psalter and Lamentations."[16] Drawing on these affinities, Seow (2013, 58) argues that in the book the lament is "subverted" to make God, not the deliverer from enemies but the enemy himself (e.g., 13:24; 16:9; 19:11). Reading the book in that grouping provides new exegetical insight without requiring the book to be definitively classified as a "subverted lament." The same could be said for others who use a similar thematic thread to draw Job together with other texts, such as the lament psalms and Ecclesiastes, which are characterized by *Unglück* or "misfortune" (de Wette 1807), or Lamentations, the Confessions of Jeremiah, and Psalms 73 and 88, which all wrestle with the failure of divine justice (Crenshaw 2011, 22–3).

5.2.3.2 Lawsuit

According to Murphy (1981, 17), the judicial interpretation of Job similarly stretches a prominent genre within the text, evident in vocabulary, metaphors, and the judicial complaint in Job 31, to cover the whole. Heinz Richter (1959, 13, 16), who popularized this classification, argues that legal forms far outnumber wisdom forms in the book and legal language appears in 444 verses as opposed to 346 that deal with wisdom. To conform the entire book to this genre, though, these legal connections must be dramatized to make the book a "lawsuit drama" (Scholnick 1975; cf. Richter 1959, 131–2) or "trial narrative" made up of conflicting "legal stories" patterned on ancient Near Eastern models (Magdalene 2007, 263, 50; see also Hoffman 2007).[17] However, the roles of the characters, nature of the charges, and numbers of suits, counter-suits, and even parallel suits (Shveka and Van Hecke 2014) are debated (Magdalene 2007, 6–8). Murphy argues that the "mere occurrence" of the legal genre, like the lament genre, is insufficient to determine the book's genre, but he similarly acknowledges the importance of paying attention to the legal genres and motifs in the book, since they "make the reader aware of the strong claims made by Job." For Dell (1991, 89–93), despite the hermeneutical insight they offer into particular passages, Westermann's and Richter's studies fall prey to the common interpretive "pitfall" of attempting to determine the genre of Job by projecting the most predominant

[16] Indeed, there is an "inevitability" to reading Job with Lamentations (Aitken 2013).

[17] Magdalene (2007, 2–3, n. 6) argues, however, that the extensive legal metaphor is "subservient" to the book's didactic Wisdom genre.

smaller genre onto the book as a whole, though the Wisdom classification is guilty of this as well. Grouping Job with laments and lawsuits illuminates certain features of the texts and obscures others, just as reading it with texts concerned with wisdom would.

5.2.3.3 Metaprophecy

Harding (2010, 528), however, argues that the author of Job adapts the prophetic genre, not by dramatizing it, but by criticizing it, making the book, like Jonah or the Words of Agur (Prov. 30:1–4), a "metaprophecy," which "draws on themes and ideas present in the prophetical books, in order to wrestle with the assumptions underlying them."[18] In his view, the book upends the prophetic confidence in entering the divine council and hearing the word of God and inverts the prophetic ריב against Israel to take aim at God (526). Job, therefore, is a "prophet in reverse" (Wolfers 1995, 49). Combined, these criticisms threaten to break the "nexus between divine revelation and theodicy" fundamental to the prophetic message (Harding 2010, 528).

5.2.3.4 Apocalyptic

A final adapted genre proposal for Job is apocalyptic. Building on a handful of brief comments on the affinities between Job and this genre (Cross 1969, 163; Collins 1977, 140; Gruenwald 1980, 3–28; Rowland 1982, 206–7), Timothy Johnson (2009, 11) argues that the book "is marked by such core apocalyptic features as revelation, plot, heavenly conflict, perseverance in the midst of persecution, and otherworldly mediator and reward due to faithfulness." To explain the differences between Job and later apocalyptic texts (most prominently the lacking belief in immortality), Johnson goes in the opposite historical direction of these other studies that suggest the book has adapted an already established genre in some way. Instead, he argues that Job is "an early, undeveloped form of apocalypse," containing some apocalyptic features only in "very embryonic forms" (71). Thus, it is the "proto-apocalypse" Job that has been adapted by later texts (51). Though some of Johnson's conclusions are questionable, the apocalyptic comparison offers a

[18] Konrad Schmid (2007, 253–8) focuses his discussion of the book's "Prophetiekritik" on Eliphaz's trivial and relativized "prophecy" in 4:12–17. See Beuken 2007 for a contrasting interpretation.

valuable new perspective on Job's perseverance and the role of revelation in the book, which are particularly helpful for understanding its relationship with the later *Testament of Job* (see Portier-Young 2013).

5.2.4 Meta-Genres

The sheer number of genre proposals for Job, which seems to be continually expanding, proves that no single genre has yet satisfactorily comprehended the book. It also reveals the book's promiscuous genre participation. As Marvin Pope (1973, xxxi) writes, "It shares something of the characteristics of all the literary forms that have been ascribed to it, but it is impossible to classify it exclusively as didactic, dramatic, epic, or anything else." Interpreters take a number of different approaches to Job's surfeit of genres. Some emulate Procrustes and simply use text criticism to lop off the parts that do not fit the single genre they believe represents the work (e.g., Kallen 1918; Baumgärtel 1933). More commonly (and less violently), interpreters simply ignore or reinterpret the parts that fail to conform. Elihu, for example, regularly suffers one of these indignities or the other (Johnson 2009, 24–38). Others follow Dr Moreau instead, creating some novel kind of chimeric genre, such as dramatized lament or lawsuit drama. A third approach treats the book as Frankenstein's monster and attempts to identify where the different parts, belonging to disparate times and different genres, have been sewn together to form a new creature.[19] Others vivisect the book like a captured alien life form to identify the various forms that give it life with little regard for the genre of the whole.[20] Some even argue that the conglomeration of genres in the book is proof of its monstrous birth, its composition according to a genre characterized by such genre-mixing, such as Menippean satire (Treves 1995), or at least one able to incorporate it, such as drama (Mies 2003, 346-7). Still others, as Newsom (2003, 7–10) observes, simply avert their eyes from the book's monstrous form with a New Critical focus on its final form (e.g., Habel 1985) or deconstructionist disregard for genre altogether (e.g., Clines 1990; Good 1990). There are

[19] Paul Volz (1911, 2) more picturesquely describes the book as a cathedral built over multiple phases and with various building styles.

[20] Fohrer (1963, 49–50, 53), e.g., traces how the Job poet mixes forms, particularly sapiential, psalmic, and legal ones, throughout the speeches, often for purposes different from their original function. However, for the book's genre, he proposes merely "Dichtwerk mit Rahmenerzählung" ("poem with frame story").

those, however, who take the difficulty of identifying Job's genre as a starting point, not for proposing yet another genre, but for identifying a particular meta-generic literary technique, a *Textstrategie* (Köhlmoos 1999), that may have led its author to incorporate a variety of genres and create such a generic "monster" (see Sinding 2011). To the degree that these approaches associate the book with other texts that use this same technique, they could also be considered proposals for its genre.

5.2.4.1 Parody

Dell (1991, 88–107), for example, argues all previous efforts to identify Job's genre have failed either because they assume that the overall genre of the book corresponds with its most predominant smaller genre or because they decide on the overall genre on the basis of its form or content before studying the smaller genres that make up the whole. She claims that the consistent intentional "misuse" and parody of these smaller genres or "forms" throughout the book indicates that the book as a whole is a parody, and therefore "sceptical literature" (109–57).[21]

5.2.4.2 Citation

In contrast to Dell's form-critical approach, others attribute the book's affinities with a wide range of genres to its incorporation of and critical reflection on so many *texts* from the Hebrew Bible (Reed 1993, 114–38; Köhlmoos 1999; Schmid 2007). Job includes potential allusions to a broad swath of texts beyond Wisdom Literature, including Genesis, Exodus, Deuteronomy, 1 Samuel, Isaiah 40–55, Jeremiah, Amos, Psalms, and Lamentations (see, e.g., Dell and Kynes 2013). Melanie Köhlmoos (1999, 15) concludes, therefore, that the Hebrew Bible is the primary contextual and intertextual background for Job (see also Schmid 2007, 243). Many have noted the book's widespread use of citation and allusion without linking it to the book's genre,[22] while others have used certain allusions to make alternative genre proposals (e.g., Wolfers 1995, 50; Harding 2010, 526).

[21] Zuckerman (1991) employs tradition criticism to arrive at a similar conclusion, though he continues to classify the book as Wisdom Literature (104).

[22] e.g., Wright 1883, 11; Dhorme 1967 [1926], cxv; Hartley 1988, 11–13; Mettinger 1993; Pyeon 2003; Wilson 2006.

I would argue, however, that this text strategy characterizes the text to such an extent that it suggests a genre grouping in which to interpret it (though not the book's definitive genre classification). Though all texts are intertextual, some are more insistently and deliberately so than others (Weiner 1991, 246). Some texts "insist on their own intertextual composition" by calling their own deliberate allusiveness to the reader's attention (Greene 1982, 16). Job appears to be this kind of "citational text," defined as a text for which readers can "justifiably suppose its author intentionally acquired other pre-texts, counting on the public not only to be able to recognize citational connections but to interpret them as an aesthetically and semantically relevant writing strategy" (Juvan 2008, 146). Biblical examples would include Second Isaiah (see Tull Willey 1997; Sommer 1998) and Revelation (see Moyise 1995). Modern texts of this type include the poetry of T. S. Eliot and the novels of James Joyce.

5.2.4.3 Polyphony

Whereas Dell begins with form criticism and citational approaches draw on intertextuality, Newsom (2003) is inspired by text-critical questions about the book's unity to take a dialogical approach drawing on the work of Mikhail Bakhtin. Rather than allow the drastic differences in genre within the book to drive her to pursue the text's "original form," Newsom explores how these different genres contribute to the meaning of the book's final form. As readers move through one genre after another, from the narrative of the prologue to the various types of poetry in the dialogue, they are invited to see the world according to each genre's "particular nexus of values and perspectives" (Newsom 2003, 13). The author, she claims, intentionally creates a polyphonic dialogue between different genres in the book to demonstrate that the idea of piety transcends "the bounds of a single consciousness" and "can only be grasped at the point of intersection of unmerged perspectives" (30). Newsom claims her polyphonic approach enables Job to be conceptualized "as an unified composition without sacrificing the hermeneutical significance of the many genres that comprise the book" (261). Her approach is ultimately unable to achieve this admirable goal, however, since it limits each genre to a single section of the book and restricts each section of the book to a single predominant genre.

Like the *sui generis* classification, these meta-generic proposals recognize Job's connections with texts from a broad range of other genres, but they draw those other texts into the interpretation of Job rather than isolating the book from them. For Dell, this involves a debate with forms found in earlier texts. For those who read Job as what I have called a "citational text," the book incorporates a discourse with the earlier texts themselves. For Newsom, the dialogue is primarily between genres within the book, though identifying and interpreting each of those genres depends on comparisons with similar texts outside of it.

5.3 NETWORK APPROACH

After surveying many of the genres discussed above, Seow (2013, 61) concludes that there is "no precise parallel anywhere" for Job; it is "one of a kind in form, though it employs a rich variety of genres, which together contribute to the theological conversation encapsulated in the book." Job, then, is an ideal text to analyze as the unique intersection of multiple generic groupings in a complex intertextual network, since "[n]o single genre can explain all the facets of the book, and several have certainly contributed to it" (Crenshaw 1974, 253). The pressing interpretive question is how far its "theological conversation" extends. Given the multiperspectival nature of genre, this conversation is not "encapsulated *in* the book," but spills out to include readers who have gazed on it from different perspectives across history and the other texts with which they have compared it.

Newsom's work moves in this direction. She forthrightly acknowledges that her attribution of the book's polyphonic juxtaposition of genres to its author's intention is hypothetical, a "heuristic fiction" (Newsom 2003, 16–17). The book's internal dialogue between genres draws in the various reading communities that encounter it, including her own, as its "complex and elusive nature allows interpreters to see mirrored in it perspectives congenial to the tenor of their own age" (3). Job's hermeneutical openness requires readers' judgment (Marböck 2006, 207), and in so doing involves their presuppositions to an unparalleled degree; what they believe about God, justice, humanity—even, I would add, hermeneutics—is what they are likely to find it teaching (Gowan 1986, 86).

As she concludes her book, Newsom (2003, 261) acknowledges that her interpretation is motivated by "the desire to read Job as a book of our own age," in accord with the inescapable postmodern, multicultural reality of "the multiplicity of differently situated consciousnesses that continually engage one another over questions of meaning and value." She reads this into the book itself, imagining it as the author's intention, but I would rather read it *onto* the book as simply the nature of interpretation.[23] After all, her concluding advice is to "go and reread the book in the company of others who will contest your reading" (264). Rather than being a mere embrace of relativism, she argues, such a polyphonic pursuit of truth "engages in the discipline of seeing how one's position appears from the perspective of another, listening to the objections that one must answer, seeing what one's own position hides from itself, and being open to the possibility of modification in light of dialogical engagement" (262).

An intertextual network approach to genre offers precisely this. It treats the genre of a text as a dialogic truth, one that is plural, embodied, relational, and unfinalizable (Newsom 2003, 22–3). By juxtaposing genres applied to a text (rather than those deployed within one, as Newsom suggests), this approach makes readers aware of the situated and selective nature of their genre proposals, enabling them to overcome their naiveté (see Bakhtin 1984, 271). *Genre* designations ("*Gattungs*zuweisungen") are also *reading* instructions ("*Lese*anweisungen") that restrict the reading horizon (Witte 2007, 123; emphasis original). The texts that various genre designations draw into comparison with the book depict its essence and cultural profile differently; a drama reads differently than a philosophical dialogue, a lament differently than a sapiential disputation (Witte 2007, 122). Therefore, interpreters must take into account, not merely questions of *Sitz im Leben* and *Sitz im Buch* when evaluating Job's genre, but *Sitz in der Welt des Lesers* as well (122). By finding a book's meaning in the place where the perspectives of the various genres applied to it intersect, an intertextual network approach creates, therefore, a richer understanding of both the book *and* its readers. This is the full dialogical engagement that Job invites, and that, to a greater or lesser degree, each significant text requires.

Read this way, Job appears as a text which raises important philosophical questions of universal significance, yes, but also one that tackles those questions with the language of worship, expressing itself

[23] Jon Levenson (2004, 272) criticizes Newsom for not distinguishing clearly enough between the implied reader of Job and her own study of it, which judges the book according to her own modern perspective.

with poetic power, drawing history within itself even as it explodes out of it, wrestling with divine covenant and law, meeting the deity in the prophetic realm to accuse him for his absence, dramatically embodying this conflict, narrating an epic conquest over unexplained and unjust suffering, teaching in story and in vitriolic debate, living out lament, initiating a trial between humanity and God, contemplating divine revelation as it cites and parodies it, and placing this all in polyphonic dialogue. Though many of these features of the book would be considered contradictory in the old taxonomic genre paradigm, that reveals more about the limitations of that paradigm than the accuracy of this interpretation.

For example, when Lambert (2015) argues for a ritual reading of Job, he challenges the common assumption of modern Wisdom interpretation that Job stands in opposition to Israelite religion, including its ceremonial practices. This interpretation sets over against the book's endorsement of ritual conformity, he claims, the "modern impulse to canonize revolution, to embed a certain myth of individual innovation and defiance within Scripture itself" (575). Putting his ritual interpretation into dialogue with the traditional Wisdom reading comprehends the complexity of the book better than either would alone, highlighting its tensive presentation of Job as both an internally conflicted individual sufferer and a performer of external, communal ritual (573). Along similar lines, Harding (2010, 526) concludes that "the book of Job is best read as a critical exploration, through the juxtaposition of an array of genres, voices, and theological ideas, of the implicit assumptions of Israel's sacred traditions in all their variety." If "critical" is not solely understood as "skeptical," I would agree with him, though I would not want to limit the book's aim to Israel. The connections to the various genres made in the history of Job's interpretation support his conclusion. This variety also suggests that the book encourages a critical interpretation of the implicit assumptions of its interpreters in all their variety as well.

The numerous genre constellations between which the meaning of Job is found reveal together how brilliantly this star blazes in the Hebrew Bible and world literature. Wisdom is certainly an important concept in the debate between Job and his friends, and the book as a whole engages many of the issues central to Proverbs and Ecclesiastes. However, Job is far more than a Wisdom book, and it defies selective attempts to restrict it to this or any other single genre. A taxonomic approach to genre has inspired the proposal of a succession of insufficient genres like waves crashing on a rocky shore. And yet each partial insight has worn away at the book's craggy inscrutability. Rather than deny the value of previous genre proposals in order to justify their own, recent meta-generic approaches have sought to incorporate them into their interpretation. The multiperspectival depiction of Job's intertextual network here takes this a step further by considering such interpretations as yet more incomplete perspectives on the book that contribute to a comprehensive understanding of its meaning. After all, "[a] work like Job is too fertile for one mind. Indeed, its greatness lies in the fact that it is as complex and many sided as life itself" (Patrick 1977, 63).

6

The Intertextual Network of Ecclesiastes and the Self-Reflective Nature of Genre

> What he had to say was beyond his resources, and probably beyond the resources of language, to say once for all through any one medium of expression. Hence, probably, the variety of forms in which he wrote....Much of his work may appear to realize its form only imperfectly; but it is also true in a measure to say that...no form, if he had obeyed all its conventional laws, could have been satisfactory for what he wanted to say. What it is, essentially, that he had to say, comes near to defying definition. It was not simply a philosophy, a theology, or a set of ideas: it was primarily something imaginative.
>
> (Eliot 2016, xi, xiii)

T. S. Eliot's description of Charles Williams's literary efforts above could apply just as well to those of Qoheleth,[1] though their struggles produced radically different results. Eliot (2016, xv) believed Williams groped unsuccessfully for an appropriate genre in which to express his thoughts because he was not merely attempting to persuade but to communicate his experience, and this could describe Qoheleth as well. The two authors' divergent experiences explain the contrast between the worlds each imagines, with the eerie immanence of the supernatural in Williams's work at odds with Qoheleth's distant yet domineering deity. Yet the common desire to express their personal experience

[1] For ease of reading, in this chapter I use Ecclesiastes to refer to the book and Qoheleth to refer to its author, at least in 1:12–12:8. Though convenient, the drawbacks of this convention should not be overlooked. In particular, Ecclesiastes is a foreign imposition on the book (being late, Latin, and Christian). Referring to the book's author as Qoheleth could also obscure the debates over whether or not the book is the product of a single author and whether Qoheleth is intended to be perceived as the book's author or a persona the author has invented.

drives both to forego the comfort of generally recognized forms and grasp at disparate means of expression. Eliot, who interacted frequently with Ecclesiastes in his work (see Christianson 2007, 68–9, 137–8, 168–9), may well have noticed the similarity.

Biblical scholars have certainly recognized the intensely personal and experiential nature of Ecclesiastes. Many have also noted the difficulty of putting the book in a single genre category, as it seems to adapt, distort, or discredit so many. However, this struggle has only extended to a certain point, since all agree that the book should be classified as Wisdom Literature. Scholars have also broadly recognized to an even greater degree than for Job that the difficulties of interpreting Ecclesiastes invite readers to shape its meaning in their own image. However, here again, they have not extended that metacritical awareness to its Wisdom classification.

As with Job, then, Ecclesiastes's genre defiance invites a new approach that takes into account both the complex intertextual network in which the book finds its meaning and the situated perspectives from which it is grouped with other texts in that network, including the Wisdom corpus. This multiperspectival analysis is not intended to claim that any perspective is wrong simply because it approaches the text subjectively but that all are in some way inadequate because, viewing the text from a limited, subjective perspective, each sees it incompletely, and thus each would distort its meaning if applied exclusively. Though finally unattainable, a complete understanding of the book will incorporate the insights from as many of these genres as possible. The survey of those genres that follows reveals that many of these alternative genres have been considered both before and after the development of the Wisdom category. Once it arrived, though, the category has subsumed these alternatives, both shaping them into its image and limiting their interpretive potential. However, if "every disagreement about an interpretation is usually a disagreement about genre" (Hirsch 1967, 98), then the disputed interpretation of Ecclesiastes suggests that the book's genre is far from settled.

6.1 THE BIBLE'S RORSCHACH TEST

Ecclesiastes prompts disagreement by its very nature, and hardly a feature of the book has escaped it, from its date and authorship to its structure and message. The confusion is so pervasive that readers may wonder if perhaps Qoheleth "forgot" to include some crucial clue to the book's meaning (Miller 2000). Gary Salyer (2001, 397) blames the book's "vain rhetoric," its failure to clearly communicate, on its first-person presentation, the debate between Qoheleth's first-person reflections and the Epilogist's evaluation of his message (12:9–14), and the widespread use of ambiguity to offer an experience of life's absurdity. Fox (1977, 105) similarly highlights the ambiguity created by the contrast between the "orthodox affirmations" of the epilogue at the end of a "profoundly unorthodox book." This, however, is only one of many apparent contradictions that pervade Ecclesiastes. The history of the book's interpretation, from early Jewish and Christian interpreters to modern scholars, is a parade of different approaches to resolving these contradictions, from harmonization to the proposal of purported additions or quotations (see Fox 1989, 19–28). However, recent interpreters, including Fox (1989, 11) and Salyer (2001, 396), have come to appreciate the contradictions as part of the book's "didactic purpose" (Brown 2000, 12), in which "ambiguity is an integral part by design," reflecting the ambiguous nature of life under the sun (Ingram 2006, 271).

Amongst the various attempts to resolve the book's ambiguity, a few common underlying tendencies stand out. First, throughout history, interpreters have selectively emphasized some features of the book over others (Murphy 1992a, lv), even as they have disagreed over which features should be "centred" or "marginalised" (Ingram 2006, 50). The epilogue is a prime example, with pre-critical interpreters generally using its orthodox perspective to temper Qoheleth's unorthodoxy and source critics using its purported later addition to dismiss it and allow Qoheleth to speak uninhibited (Bartholomew 2009, 37). Second, as this example demonstrates, before one can emphasize one aspect of the book over another, one must first identify those aspects. This requires some element of classification, whether that is grouping some parts of the text together as "positive" and others as "negative," as "optimistic" or "pessimistic," "conservative" or "radical." This, however, involves a modern imposition on the text that frequently exaggerates the dissonance between its various features (Seow 1997, 39). Using one of these categories to encompass the text's message further risks oversimplifying its profundity as much as would an attempt to classify Stravinksky's *The Rite of Spring* as happy or sad (Brown 2000, 10).

Since at least the early church, interpreters have employed a more nuanced approach by diffusing the ambiguity of the whole into a series of coherent voices or authors (see Bolin 2017, 74–5 and section 6.3.4.1

Form). Fox (1977, 105), for example, claims that the author "has allowed the reader to choose which voice to identify most closely with," whether Qoheleth's or the Epilogist's (similarly, Perry 1993, xii). Others hear a dialogue of different voices continuing throughout the text. Though these readings claim the interaction of different voices contributes significantly to the book's message (similar to Newsom's dialogical reading of Job; see section 5.2.4.3 Polyphony), rarely do readers refrain from privileging one voice over the others.[2] Thus, selective emphasis, whether associated with an assumed dialogical structure or not, has enabled interpreters to come to conflicting and even diametrically opposed interpretations of the text. Doug Ingram (2006, 44–9) offers an extensive collection of these opposing views, including Heinrich Heine's classification of Ecclesiastes as "Das Hohelied der Skepsis" ("the quintessence of skepticism") and Delitzsch's characterization of the book as "Das Hohelied der Gottesfurcht" ("the quintessence of piety").

Watching the "interpretive sweat" break out as interpreters wrestle with Ecclesiastes's iconoclastic contradictoriness, Newsom (1995, 190–1) notes the book's "uncanny ability to mirror and to resist the interpreter." Like Wisdom Literature as a whole (see section 3.4 Implications), Crenshaw (1983, 51) similarly calls Ecclesiastes "a mirror which reflects the soul of the interpreter." Gazing into that mirror himself, Crenshaw (1987, 53) credits his fascination with Ecclesiastes to the way it provides a "solidly biblical" foundation for his own skepticism. In so doing, he forthrightly admits the interplay between author and reader in the book that de Pury (1999, 187) poetically describes: "The reader is challenged by the author's ploy; he is first, victim, next, partner, and finally, accomplice. Of all the biblical books, Qoheleth is the one closest to his readers: he says aloud things that everyone else is thinking." As Ecclesiastes embodies life's ambiguity, then, the different presuppositions brought to "reading" the world are reflected in readers' various responses to the text (Ingram 2006, 263).

In rabbinic interpretation, Qoheleth becomes a "rabbinic sage" who puts supreme value on Torah study, while Christians for a millennium after Jerome envisioned him as an ascetic putting his hope in the world to come until Luther and his fellow Reformers recreated him as an

[2] Perry (1993) may be an exception here, though he frequently sides with the voice of his "Presenter" (see 33–42). Contrast Kyle Greenwood's (2012, 491) clear preference for the voice of the "Preacher."

advocate of worldly pleasures.[3] Luther even envisions the book as a Solomonic *Tischreden* like his own *Table Talk* (Bolin 2017, 90). The rise of the modern age found an eager compatriot in a empirical, skeptical, humanistic, and rationalistic Qoheleth (Christianson 2007, 41). As Edward Plumptre wrote in 1881, Ecclesiastes was fitting "to meet the special tendencies of modern philosophical thought, and the problems of life which it discusses are those with which our own daily experience brings us into contact" (quoted in Bartholomew 2009, 34). A few decades later, Morris Jastrow (1919) described Qoheleth as a "gentle cynic" who suffered from the misunderstanding of "uncritical" pious readers, just as Jastrow himself had (Bolin 2017, 91–2). Qoheleth has been held up as a model for a canon-critical and more "enlightened" contact with Israel's religious traditions (Krüger 1997, 322). And now, Qoheleth the Deconstructionist has arrived, questioning the validity of religious knowledge, the possibility of determinate meaning, and reflecting cynically on life's vicissitudes (Miller 2000, 218; Salyer 2001, 16, 19, 398; see section 6.3.4.2 Tone).

Murphy (1992a, lv) claims that the various conflicting interpretations of the book that appear time and again across its history of interpretation are inevitable due to the tensions both within the book and amongst its interpreters. Ecclesiastes's rough terrain creates "a tremendous interpretive pressure to raise the valleys and lower the hills, to make the way straight and level before the reader," but, to produce "a reading faithful to this book," Fox (1989, 28) argues that one must attempt "to describe the territory with all its bumps and clefts, for they are not mere flaws, but the essence of the landscape." Santiago Bretón (1973, 25, 48) concludes his survey of scholarship on the enigmatic book with a call to pursue objectivity, lest "the personal categories of the interpreter blur the evidence and cast misleading shadows on the text being studied." The theological and ideological commitments of readers, however, inevitably inform their interpretations of such an open text (Schwienhorst-Schönberger 1997a, 6). Ecclesiastes has inspired readers throughout its history either to "sit together with Qohelet in sameness—or stand apart in otherness," such that, in recent times, "European academics can view Qohelet as a fellow wise man" (Mills 2003, 158).[4]

[3] For the history of interpretation of Ecclesiastes, see Ginsburg 1861, 27–243; Holm-Nielsen 1974; Holm-Nielsen 1975; Murphy 1982; Christianson 2007.

[4] Bolin (2017, 80–1), for example, warns of the theological biases that may have crept into the interpretation of Ecclesiastes due to the fact that most critical biblical scholarship on the book in the twentieth century was carried out at seminaries, theological schools,

Therefore, a more objective interpretation is not likely to be found by setting aside one's presuppositions but by appreciating the insights into the book of those who come to its interpretation from different places. The book's interpretive history, therefore, helps modern readers examine their own presuppositions (Murphy 1982, 335–6). But it can do more than that. As Johannes Pedersen (1931, 20) observes, even if interpreters have tended to see only "what was most fitting for themselves and their age," the diverse aspects in the book allow divergent interpretations that still have some foundation in the text. These readings can illuminate one face of the mountainous terrain of Ecclesiastes, but they will cast "misleading shadows" into its valleys if applied exclusively. Only by shining lights from multiple directions will the darkness be dispelled.

Every interpretive stance is "partial and selective," allowing readers to see some things more clearly while also rendering others invisible. This, Thomas Bolin (2017, 3) argues, puts an obligation on readers to be aware of and responsible for their chosen perspective on the text. He warns particularly of the tendency of modern biblical scholars to be ignorant of their own ideological standpoints and thereby "mistake their limited horizon for an Archimedean point of view from which they mistakenly believe they can see everything." Tracing how readers throughout history and across traditions have "created" the author of Ecclesiastes in various forms (Solomon, king, sinner, saint, philosopher), he catalogues both what readers have seen from certain perspectives and what has been obscured from their vision. Given the link between the taxonomic role of the author function and genre (Bolin 2017, 9), the survey of genre proposals for the book here will serve a similar function.

6.2 READING ECCLESIASTES AS WISDOM LITERATURE

In the widespread and often forthright acknowledgement of the subjectively influenced nature of the interpretation of Ecclesiastes, one presupposition has gone unexamined: that Ecclesiastes is best read as

or religious institutions, but he fails to consider that all this scholarship was also carried out in a post-Enlightenment and primarily Western academic context and took on many of those assumptions as well, which the Wisdom classification reinforces.

Wisdom Literature. Oswald Loretz (1964, 208–12), for example, claims that the nature of Ecclesiastes defies any scholarly attempts to project upon it modern rational categories in order to discern its message or structure. However, when he attempts to relate the various *topoi* of the book to other literature, he focuses almost exclusively on parallels within Wisdom Literature (197–208). He notes, for instance, that Qoheleth's reflection on "envy" (קנאה) in 4:4 and 9:6 is paralleled in Job 5:2 and Prov. 6:34; 14:30; 27:4 (201). In a footnote he makes one of his few mentions of texts outside the category (Isa. 11:13: Ezek. 35:11), but he could have referred to numerous texts across the Hebrew Bible, including Numbers 5, where the description of the ritual for "cases of jealousy (קנאה)" has the greatest concentration of the term in the Hebrew Bible, as well as narratives that describe envy without using the term, including Sarah's behavior toward Hagar (Genesis 16), Jacob's sons' treatment of their brother Joseph (Genesis 37), and Saul's pursuit of David (e.g., 1 Sam. 18:6–9).

This does not, of course, mean that comparing Ecclesiastes to other texts concerned with wisdom is without its merits. The book undoubtedly shares a number of features with Proverbs and Job, including similar vocabulary (חכם and its derivatives appear fifty-two times), forms (such as proverbs, admonitions, example stories, and didactic poems), and topics (such as the seventy-one listed by Loretz). Some even argue that the book's epilogue identifies Qoheleth's words among the collected sayings of the "the wise" (12:13; see section 2.4 The Title "Wisdom"). As with Job, classifying Ecclesiastes as Wisdom has encouraged reflection on how Ecclesiastes compares with other books so classified, offering a more nuanced view of how each conceives of wisdom, and revealing, for example, how the book incorporates the didactically oriented form of Proverbs with the reflective, problem-oriented content of Job (Krüger 2004, 11).

Also similarly to Job, comparing Ecclesiastes with other Wisdom texts has introduced a significant tension into attempts to identify a unified school or movement behind the texts. Though "wisdom" is indeed a key word for Qoheleth, he denigrates it as הבל (2:15)[5] while criticizing a supposedly fundamental thesis of the purported Wisdom

[5] Rather than attempt to contribute to the extensive debate surrounding the precise meaning of this Hebrew word, I will leave it untranslated with the understanding that it has a negative connotation in keeping with the many translations that have been proposed for it, such as "vanity," "futility," "illusion," and "absurdity" (see Weeks 2012, 14–20).

movement: that wisdom, and not wickedness, leads to life (Eccl. 8:12; cf. Prov. 8:35) (Hertzberg 1963, 233–4). He thereby "strikes at the foundation of the sages' universe" (Crenshaw 1987, 23). Thus, even within the "heterogenous mix" of Wisdom texts, Ecclesiastes "stands out" with its focus on human fragility and insecurity, divine inscrutability, and call to *carpe diem*, and thus demonstrates a theological and ethical orientation "unlike anything that is encountered elsewhere in the biblical wisdom, much less throughout the Old Testament" (Brown 2000, 12). If Ecclesiastes is Wisdom, then it is "wisdom at its limits," outside of the tradition both before it in Proverbs and after it in Ben Sira and Wisdom of Solomon (Dell 2013b, 11–12). The book may even be the "reverse of 'wisdom'" (Holm-Nielsen 1975, 51), representing a "crisis" within the movement (e.g., Schmid 1966, 186–96), and perhaps the "end" of the movement altogether (Michel 1988, 67; Shields 2006, 6).

Since Ecclesiastes resides at the borderland of the purported Wisdom tradition, questioning or even rejecting many of its tenets, how much interpretive guidance can the Wisdom classification provide? As Thomas Krüger (2004, 11) observes, "The expectations of readers awakened by the form of the book of Qoheleth as a work of instructive wisdom literature are, however, systematically disappointed by its contents." It is indeed somewhat strange that the near unanimous classification of Ecclesiastes as Wisdom Literature coexists with vastly divergent interpretations of its meaning (Holm-Nielsen 1975, 40). And yet, not only does the category fail to provide adequate interpretive guidance, but, applied exclusively, it also distorts the book's interpretation in the same ways it does for Job, separating it from the rest of the canon, encouraging abstract theological interpretations, and limiting its hermeneutical potential. Having established the dynamics of these effects with Job, I will merely provide a few brief examples of these phenomena for Ecclesiastes.

6.2.1 Canonical Separation

Craig Bartholomew (2009, 84) states the problematic working assumption of current scholarship explicitly: "Since Ecclesiastes is an OT wisdom text, Proverbs and Job provide the immediate intertextual context for reading it." If the book's interpretation starts from this presupposition that Ecclesiastes is part of Wisdom, a "third strand of Hebrew culture" next to Torah and Prophecy (Gordis 1968, 16), it will inevitably (and circularly) reinforce it, as the interplay of those three books circumscribe and determine its meaning. Starting by separating Ecclesiastes from the rest of the canon is sure to fortify its perceived distinctiveness from the broader interests and theology of the Hebrew Bible. Diethelm Michel (1988, 67–73) rejects attempts to find connections to the rest of the canon in Ecclesiastes by, in part, claiming they are "postulates of the commentators" that do not actually exist. However, his affirmation of the book's independence from the canon could just as well be a postulate, informed by the Wisdom category.

As with Job, the questions Ecclesiastes raises for the retribution principle were put in the broader context of the Hebrew Bible in the nineteenth century before the Wisdom category gained hermeneutical hegemony (e.g., Ginsburg 1861, 21–2). Now, however, the conflict is presented as one within Wisdom, contributing to the perceived "crisis" within the movement. Murphy (1992a, lxi, lxvi) demonstrates how widespread this view is through his efforts to counter it and prove that the alleged "crisis" of Wisdom is "no less a crisis for the rest of the Bible." He argues that Proverbs shares its purported optimistic view of retribution with Deuteronomy and the Deuteronomistic History, while the psalms of lament and "confessions" of Jeremiah challenge this view just as radically as Job and Qoheleth. This separate and unsubtle sapiential presentation of retribution as the backdrop for Ecclesiastes is one instance of the broader tendency to judge Ecclesiastes as "unorthodox" in contrast to a biblical orthodoxy defined by some other part of the canon. Bolin (2017, 96–7) finds this phenomena across the history of interpretation. He notes, however, that the characterization of Wisdom texts as outliers from "normative," covenantal, revelatory, and historical biblical theology in twentieth-century scholarship has exacerbated it, such that if Wisdom is at the "edge" of biblical theology, then Ecclesiastes is "at the very edge" (Brueggemann 1997, 393).

6.2.2 Theological Abstraction

Ecclesiastes's Wisdom classification shapes interpretations of its theology as well. As with Job, it encourages a philosophical characterization of the book's message. The reflective nature of Ecclesiastes, however, leads to an even closer association with philosophy, which tends to overshadow its theological character, despite its frequent mention of and reflection on God. Ecclesiastes does present a more abstract view of God than most other biblical texts, emphasizing the distance of the transcendent deity from humanity (e.g., Eccl. 5:1 [ET 2]). But the Wisdom classification magnifies that abstraction.

In line with conceptions of the Wisdom tradition, Qoheleth's work is conceived as philosophical in its inception and execution. Seow (1997, 54), for example, observes that Qoheleth's skepticism toward wisdom makes labeling it "philosophy" (etymologically, "love of wisdom") rather ironic, and that the "the deity's presence is pervasive in the book." However, even he proceeds to read Qoheleth's thought according to a sapiential approach that is hardly distinguishable from philosophy: "True to the tendency of the wisdom tradition, the sage's starting point in his reflection is not God, but the cosmos, society, and humanity." After all, the distinction between philosophy and theology is not whether God is discussed (as in philosophy of religion), but whether God is the "starting point" of the discussion. Murphy (1992a, lxiii) similarly describes wisdom as "a methodology that implies an analytical approach to life's situations" and then argues that Qoheleth "trusts in the methodology of wisdom, experience and observation, throughout his investigation" (see, similarly, Michel 1988, 66–7). At the extreme, by grounding Qoheleth's thought in natural philosophy rather than Yahwism, Hans-Peter Müller (1978) claims that the sage operates according to a different religion with a distinct, impersonal God (similarly, Michel 1989, 274–89).

6.2.3 Hermeneutical Limitation

Jacques Ellul (1990, 27) warns against reading Qoheleth as a philosopher simply because he deals with "philosophers' favorite subjects," such as life, death, God, and happiness. He also raises concerns about how "almost all scholars limit themselves to seeing it as a reflection within the limitations of the wisdom genre," which can occlude its meaning by stripping the book of "the essential distinctives of Israel's belief" (25). Murphy (1992a, lv–lvi), for example, argues that the common selective emphasis of all previous periods of the history of the book's interpretation should encourage modern readers to examine their own presuppositions, lest they be "locked up in their own crippling presuppositions." Even so, he fails to recognize that the Wisdom category is itself an unexamined and severely limiting, if not crippling, modern presupposition. He describes Wisdom as the tradition within which Qoheleth thought and wrote and claims, therefore, that "his work is intelligible only in this perspective" (Murphy 1992a, lxiv). And yet, the Wisdom tradition as it is now understood may not have been the way it was understood then, if it even existed at all. This single perspective is just as liable to selective emphasis, as Murphy demonstrates by proceeding to define Qoheleth's goal, methodology, practical focus, and the limits of his conclusions according to those associated with the purported Wisdom tradition. He concludes that, "for Qoheleth the road of the wise leads nowhere, but it was the only one he could walk." Who, however, is constraining his steps?

The interpretation of the epilogue is the prime example of Wisdom's hermeneutical limitations. Fox (1999, 374) cites the common view that "obedience to God's commands is not a factor in Wisdom Literature prior to Ben Sira." This, he argues, leads many commentators to understand the epilogue's admonition to keep God's commandments (12:13) as irreconcilable with the body of the book and even an interpretation of Qoheleth's words "according to the alien criterion of orthodox legal piety" (Zimmerli 1962, 250–1). Fox will not go that far. Instead, he argues that the body of the book, like Proverbs, "simply does not deal with this aspect of religion."[6] Though Fox (1999, 374–5) claims that Qoheleth does not contradict "legal piety," he still proceeds to set up an opposition between the epilogue's ultimate endorsement of the obedient fear of God and "all the words of the sages" (cf. 12:11) such that, instead of summing up Qoheleth's words, the epilogue relegates them to "a place of secondary importance," and sets "a boundary to wisdom . . . circumscribing wisdom's scope."

The Wisdom classification similarly drives Fox's (1977, 102) interpretation of the mention of the "shepherd" who gives wise sayings earlier in the epilogue (12:11). He argues against those who see God as the intended referent because "the epilogist is speaking within the tradition of didactic wisdom," and in that tradition across the ancient Near East, God is not called "shepherd," metaphorical epithets are almost never used for the divine, and the words of the wise are never considered God's gift. This argument from as careful a scholar as Fox demonstrates the hermeneutical influence of two problematic yet widespread assumptions: that didactic Wisdom Literature is a consistent genre across the ancient Near East and that Ecclesiastes conforms to its practices.

[6] For an alternative view on the relationship between Proverbs and the Law, see section 7.2.2.2 Ethical Paraenesis.

Though Bartholomew reads Ecclesiastes primarily in the intertextual context of Wisdom, he recognizes some of the problems the category causes, including the failure of modern scholarship to recognize the moral and religious significance of terms in the book, such as משׁפט ("judgement"; 11:9; cf. 3:17) and חטיא ("sin"; 5:5 [6]; cf. 2:26; 7:26; 8:12). In his view, assumptions about the category, such as its development from secular to religious and separation from the Torah and Prophets, contribute to the illegitimate restriction of these terms' meanings. To the contrary, Bartholomew (2009, 90) argues that Ecclesiastes's links to Genesis and Deuteronomy draw into question the modern construction of a strong distinction between Law and Wisdom. Once the hermeneutical limitation of the Wisdom category is set aside, in fact, multiple connections between Ecclesiastes and texts across the canon emerge, suggesting, as Bartholomew (2013, 380) writes elsewhere, "a more organic interdependence of the various genres of OT literature" than traditional historical criticism has allowed. Viewing Ecclesiastes from the multiple perspectives of genre groupings across history rather than the single Wisdom perspective may open up new meaning in the book and retrieve features long ignored. Perhaps it is not the book's epilogue, but the Wisdom category that has truly circumscribed Qoheleth's wisdom.

6.3 THE INTERTEXTUAL NETWORK OF ECCLESIASTES

As Dell (2013b, 5) observes and then demonstrates, both old and new, pre-critical and post-critical approaches provide new perspectives that can enliven critical interpretation of Ecclesiastes. As for Job, I seek here to map out the intertextual network of Ecclesiastes by looking at the book with the perspectives of genre groupings in which it has been placed across history, both before and after the Wisdom category imposed its hermeneutical hegemony on the book's interpretation.

6.3.1 Genres before "Wisdom Literature"

Unlike Job, Ecclesiastes's location in canon lists is fairly consistent, thanks undoubtedly to its strong association with Solomon. However, before the Wisdom Literature category develops, it only appears with Job in the broad Poetry category.

6.3.1.1 Megilloth

The date and reasoning behind the collection and liturgical associations of the five books of the Megilloth (Song of Songs, Ruth, Lamentations, Ecclesiastes, and Esther) is debated (see Stone 2013, 105–11). Some of the texts fit naturally with the festivals at which they are read (Lamentations on the Ninth of Ab, Esther on Purim), but Ecclesiastes's connection with Sukkot, the Feast of Tabernacles, is not so obvious. However, inspired by this grouping of festival-associated texts, several interpreters have sought to uncover the logic behind the association, which goes back at least to the eleventh century (see Seow 1997, 5; Fox 2004, xv; Birnbaum and Schwienhorst-Schönberger 2012, 12). Ellul (1990, 42–6) claims that the choice of Ecclesiastes to accompany this festival is not the result of "chance or historical accident," but a confirmation of the book's "ritual nature." He therefore provides an extensive attempt to read the entire book in light of the festival's various meanings and thus, "as the royal book of Solomon; the book of the dedication of the temple; the book of an astonishing covenant; the book of the fragility of human shelter (the thatched hut); the book of the vanity of everything people possess (the desert); the book of God's absolute kingship." It also communicates, he argues, the vain joy of a week of festivities as winter approaches, and combines all this in a complexity of symbols that reminds the people of God's inscrutable mysteries. Ellul then takes the festival's complex thematic amalgam as support for a similar mixture in Ecclesiastes, with no need to posit orthodox additions.

It seems unlikely that Qoheleth wrote with this multivalent festival in mind, and we cannot even be sure that the Jewish community that connected the two was motivated by the depth of resonance Ellul sees between them. However, they did see something linking the two, which modern interpreters have tended to overlook, often suggesting that the association was simply a marriage of convenience between the remaining festival and book that lacked clear connections after the others were matched up. The failure of comprehension may be in part due to assumptions about the book's meaning based on its Wisdom classification that obscure the associations by submerging joy under skepticism, the temple and covenant under universalism, the law under rationalism, and God under humanism.

Ecclesiastes's inclusion in the Megilloth does not merely offer an occasion to consider why it, like the other texts in the collection, has been associated with a specific festival. It also encourages comparison with the other texts in the category. Previously put off by the lateness and fluidity of the corpus, biblical scholarship has recently begun to take an interest in the Megilloth as a "coherent collection," recognizing the "insights to be gained from a critical examination of the individual books in relation to one another and to the whole" (Erickson and Davis 2016, 300–1).[7] Little research, however, has been done on Ecclesiastes in this regard.[8] The even later and more fluid Wisdom category has stood in the way.

6.3.1.2 Poetry

The Poetry collection in which Ecclesiastes appeared in the Greek and later Christian tradition has similarly had little effect on the book's interpretation (see section 2.1.2 Greek Order). This reticence to read Ecclesiastes as poetry may be influenced by an opposition between philosophy and poetry that goes back to Plato, who banned poets from his Republic (Hobbins 2013, 163, 191). When Weeks (2012, 147–50) discusses poetry in the book, he occasionally sets it against argumentation.[9] John Hobbins (2013, 163), however, argues that the two are not mutually exclusive, primarily because both rely heavily on metaphor. Qoheleth's poetic use of הבל as a "master metaphor" is a natural feature of his philosophical argument, one that in itself earns him the title poet (163, 166). Robert Gordis (1968, 16–17) offers biblical support for this integrated view by arguing that חכמה ("wisdom") refers "above all...to the arts of poetry and song" based on 1 Kgs. 5:10–12 [ET 4:30–32], where Solomon demonstrates his חכמה by writing proverbs and songs, and where the term is associated with Heman and Ethan, heads of musical guilds (1 Chr. 15:19), to whom are attributed Psalms 88 and 89, respectively. Hobbins (2013, 191), who argues

[7] Erickson and Davis (2016, 300) credit the recent interest in the interpretive value of the category to a new program unit on the topic at the Society of Biblical Literature, which they claim is a reminder that "elite readers with vested interests have always created and advocated for inscribing boundaries around texts in particular ways and in the service of particular ideologies."

[8] As I argued above (section 2.1.1 Hebrew Order, n. 10), Stone's attempt to uncover the intertextual significance of the Megilloth actually reads Ecclesiastes out of the grouping, and instead in a Wisdom grouping, primarily with Proverbs.

[9] A form of this opposition is also evident in Loretz's (1993, 188–9) attempt to distinguish Qoheleth's emulation of the "high-flown prose" of Hellenistic-Greek philosophy from the verse later inserted into his work by later "traditionalists" in order to curb its radical, alien character.

that Qoheleth incorporates poetic verse throughout the book, concludes, "The poetry of the book of Qohelet, far from being a concession to irrational methods of knowing, is one of the book's most compelling features." His work is an encouragement to pay more attention to the book's poetic character, particularly since he does not discuss at any length how recognizing stretches of poetry in the book helps interpret its meaning.

At the least, appreciating Ecclesiastes's poetic nature should inspire further reflection on its similarities with other poetic texts, such as those included in the Poetry collection. Though Weeks (2012, 149–50) warns against speaking of Qoheleth as a poet simply because he uses poetic language, he notes that "key themes in Qohelet's monologue are best attested elsewhere in Hebrew poetry," particularly Job, which is "primarily poetic," and the Psalms, especially Psalms 39, 49, and 73 (see, e.g., Krüger 2004, 26). Thus, Weeks argues, "Poetry and poetic language have to be considered not only as a component of our book but as a significant characteristic of the works which seem to stand closest to it in Hebrew literature." This should include the other members of the Poetry grouping; not only Proverbs, Job, and Psalms, but also Song of Songs (see below) and Lamentations, which appears there when not appended to Jeremiah.

6.3.1.3 Solomonic Collection

Though Solomon's name is never mentioned, interpreters have traditionally followed Qoheleth's clear intention that his words be associated with the wise king of Israel. This creates two intertextual contexts in which to interpret the book: first, the other texts attributed to Solomon in the Hebrew Bible, and, second, the account of Solomon's reign narrated in 1 Kings 1–11 (cf. 1 Chr. 29:21–2 Chr. 9:31). However, when scholarship set aside the book's Solomonic authorship in the nineteenth century as a thinly veiled fiction, it displaced the book from these contexts and began to read it in a new one, the Wisdom category, with its differing contents and defining characteristics. The contexts provided by the Solomonic collection are worth retrieving, though, not only because, like the other groupings discussed so far, they have been applied to the text for centuries, but also because, unlike those groupings, this one may very well have been intended by the author himself.

Though ancient interpreters proposed theories for how Proverbs, Ecclesiastes, and Song of Songs may be related to the sequence of life experiences or philosophical reflections of Solomon (see section 2.2 Solomonic Association), discussion of the interpretive significance of the *Corpus Salomonicum* is largely lacking in modern commentaries. Krüger (2004, 27–8) provides a rare exception, as he argues that the juxtaposition of the three books creates "threads of meaning that span the whole corpus." According to the sequence in which the books often appear in ancient lists (Proverbs, Ecclesiastes, Song of Songs), Krüger argues that Ecclesiastes offers critical reflection on the wisdom of Proverbs (e.g., Eccl. 1:12–2:26), while Song of Songs realizes Qoheleth's call to enjoy life, including "with the wife whom you love" (Eccl. 9:9) (similarly, Birnbaum and Schwienhorst-Schönberger 2012, 13). Drawing further connections between the texts, such as the common theme of "seeking" (בקשׁ) and "finding" (מצא), Krüger argues that, whatever the history behind the corpus, it "shows an early reception of the book of Qoheleth that takes its essential concerns seriously and agrees with them."

Within this corpus, the intertextual interplay between Ecclesiastes and Proverbs, which, according to Gerald Wilson (1984), was endorsed by allusions to the prologue of Proverbs in the epilogue of Ecclesiastes, has been thoroughly discussed, thanks in large part to their shared membership in the Wisdom category (see, recently, Saur forthcoming; Estes 2014; Horne 2014). The connections between Ecclesiastes and Song of Songs, the odd book out when Wisdom supplanted the Solomonic corpus, have received less attention. The rabbis' struggle to reconcile both with the rest of the canon (see m. Yad. 3:5) invites their comparison, however (Hirschman 2001, 87–89). Brittany Melton (2014) traces a number of "resonances" between them, grouped around the Solomonic attribution, the pursuit of wisdom, and the enjoyment of love (see also Müller 1978, 252–3, 259–60).

Longman (2014, 46–52) describes how Ecclesiastes both associates itself with and distances itself from the Solomon of 1 Kings 1–11 with the purpose of substantiating its claim that the king's failure to find meaning in his impressive work, wisdom, pleasure, status, and wealth means that doing so is impossible, "for what can the one do who comes after the king?" (Eccl. 2:12). Indeed the "fictional autobiography" early in the book relies for its force on knowledge of Solomon's accomplishments, if not the actual text in 1 Kings (Seow 1995, 87–8).[10] The title

[10] Most commentators argue that the royal fiction is dropped after the first few chapters, but thanks perhaps to the diminishing influence of form criticism, interpreters

דברי קהלת ("words of Qoheleth") in Eccl. 1:1 may even be an allusion to the "Acts of Solomon" (דברי שלמה), where further accomplishments and wisdom of the King not mentioned in 1 Kings 1–11 are said to be recorded (1 Kgs. 11:41), though the erasure of the king's name further undercuts the memorializing purpose of royal autobiographies (Vayntrub forthcoming b). Many argue that the book's canonical status also depends on its association with Solomon's authority; however, the record of Solomon's downfall into idolatry due to his love of foreign women may actually mean that the canonicity of both Ecclesiastes and Song of Songs was accepted "despite their attribution to Solomon and not because of it" (Hirschman 2001, 88).[11] In both Jewish and Christian tradition, this connection between Ecclesiastes and the account of Solomon's reign led readers to suppose that an elderly Solomon may have written the book after repenting of his idolatry (see Christianson 2007, 91–3). The conflicted presentation of Solomon's wisdom in both texts forces readers to reconsider the complexity of the figure of Solomon and the wisdom with which he is associated, overcoming the false boundary between Wisdom and historical narrative to develop a more nuanced view of both (Bartholomew 2013, 383; similarly, Perry 1993, 190).

6.3.2 Other Canonical Genre Groupings

This nuanced view can be applied within the Wisdom interpretation. Childs (1979, 584) claims that reading the book as Solomon's "final reflections" authorized the book as "an official corrective from within the wisdom tradition itself." However, it can also connect Ecclesiastes with other groups of texts, such as the Historical Books and the Prophets.[12] Other features of the book associate it with Torah and apocalyptic texts. Though early interpreters do not group Ecclesiastes with texts from these genres in canon lists, they do note connections between the book and each of them and read them together in various ways.

have more recently begun to argue that the royal associations continue throughout the book, beyond the boundaries of the royal autobiography form (e.g., Christianson 1998, 143–5; Koh 2006, 38–9; Barbour 2012).

[11] For further evidence against Solomonic authorship playing a decisive factor in Ecclesiastes's canonization, see Christianson (1998, 148–54).

[12] See section 7.2.2 The Genres of Solomon's Wisdom, where I develop further the multivalent presentation of wisdom in 1 Kings 1–11 and trace how its connections with political narratives, law, cult, and prophecy are also evident in Proverbs.

Modern interpreters have done the same, though always within Wisdom's hermeneutical influence, providing further evidence of the resilience of certain interpretive trends across the (imagined) divide between pre-critical and critical exegesis of Ecclesiastes (see Murphy 1982a, 331–2; Bolin 2017, 75). If the persistent identification of the same main ideas in the book demonstrates that "the essential themes of the book are clear" (Fox 1999, 349), then the recurrence of these links beyond the Wisdom boundaries suggests that they deserve further exploration.

The degree to which Ecclesiastes alludes to earlier texts in the Hebrew Bible is, like nearly everything else in the book, unclear and debated. Some envision Qoheleth writing with the scrolls of Genesis (Hertzberg 1963, 230) or Chronicles (Kamenetzky 1921, col. 13) laying before him, while Carr (2011, 451) claims that the book "shows a remarkable lack of explicit awareness of Hebrew biblical texts." As threads to weave texts together into genres, authorial quotations and allusions may be sufficient but are not necessary. Few attempt to justify the Wisdom category on this basis. The *sine qua non* for a genre grouping is merely a shared significant feature (such as interest in wisdom), though echoes of other texts, whether actual allusions or not, may bring such features to light.

Some interpreters have argued that inner-biblical allusions contribute substantially to Ecclesiastes's message, despite their elusiveness. Weeks (2014) discusses the vital rhetorical role of "inner-textual" allusions within Ecclesiastes, as Qoheleth constantly refers back to and modifies earlier statements, returning time and again to an idea like a dog with a bone (e.g., the question of human profit in 1:3; 3:9; 5:15 [ET 16]). Weeks claims this pervasive self-reference contributes to Qoheleth's depiction as intellectually self-reliant. His expectation that his readers would recognize allusions within the book, comparing texts to discern his thought, suggests, though, that he may have expected them to uncover allusions to other texts as well, even with the types of modifications Qoheleth applies to his own earlier words. A high degree of reliance on the reader to recognize references to traditional concepts, codified traditions, and even texts in the book may be part of its text strategy (Krüger 1990, 51).[13] Perhaps Qoheleth could have such trust because, writing one of the latest books in the Hebrew Bible, he could take for granted that his readers were familiar with the Torah

[13] Compare the intertextual and even "citational" text strategy of Job (see section 5.2.4 Meta-Genres).

and Prophets and other older works of wisdom, enabling him to "so clearly play upon the opening chapters of Genesis, adopt proposals from Deuteronomy, and skip over so much that is well expressed, as is, in Proverbs" (Lohfink 2003, 13).[14] However, in so doing, Qoheleth employs a distinctively personal and idiosyncratic style, in which he draws on existing religious traditions and language while transcending it (Loretz 1964, 196–7) or introducing into it "sharp differences or 'swerves' of meaning" (Fisch 1988, 162). Just as in Ecclesiastes's relationship with Proverbs, these differences do not negate the interpretive value of reading Ecclesiastes in dialogue with these texts. The contrast, which in some cases may be invited by allusions, similarly illumines the meaning of the work.

6.3.2.1 Torah

Just as the downfall of the wise king concludes the narrative in 1 Kings 1–11 with an implicit exhortation to obey the law (Parker 1992), Ecclesiastes similarly concludes with an admonition to "fear God, and keep his commandments" (12:13). Wilson (1984, 175) argues that this "canonical statement" is appended as an interpretive instruction. It primarily ties the book with other "words of the wise" (12:11), particularly Proverbs 1–9, though the implicit connections with Deuteronomy there resonate with the emphasis on God's commandments in Ecclesiastes's epilogue. This "inextricably" binds the wisdom of Proverbs and Ecclesiastes with the Torah, such that the "words of the wise" cannot be rightly understood apart from the "commandments of God/YHWH" (Wilson 1984, 192). Since the epilogue is widely believed to be a later addition to the book, this ligature with law is broadly considered a "new element in the wisdom tradition" (Dell 2013b, 17). Instead, since few would argue that Deuteronomy, which links the law with wisdom in 4:6, was composed before the epilogue of Ecclesiastes, wisdom could instead be considered a pre-existing element in the Torah tradition (see section 7.2.2.2 Ethical Paraenesis).

Whether or not the epilogue was added to the book as an interpretive guide, early readers followed its encouragement to understand the

[14] Similarly, Whybray 1982b, 28–30; Murphy 1992a, xlii. Gordis (1968, 43–50) notes parallels to several books, including Genesis, Deuteronomy, 1 Samuel, and 1 Kings, and concludes that Ecclesiastes is "in the mainstream of Jewish literature, drawing upon the past and contributing to the future." For similar lists, see Hertzberg 1963, 46; Birnbaum and Schwienhorst-Schönberger 2012, 13–14.

book in light of the Torah. Dell (2013b, 23) observes the "often overlooked" fact that during the canonization process Ecclesiastes "was not only mentioned in connection with Solomonic wisdom but was interpreted in relation to the law." The Targum of Ecclesiastes understands the book in this way.[15] Despite some initial consternation at apparent contradictions, the rabbis also harmonize the book with the Torah, which Dell (2013b, 36) argues was the decisive factor in its canonization. The Talmudic tract b. Shabbat 30b claims that Ecclesiastes's beginning and ending with the Torah (thanks to a creative reading of Eccl. 1:3, along with 12:13) overcomes its internal inconsistencies (see Dell 2013b, 23). Just as Jewish interpreters read the book as an endorsement of the study of the Torah, early Protestant interpreters similarly understood Ecclesiastes through their distinctive perspective on the Law. John Brentius, who wrote the first Protestant commentary on the book, called it an "appendix to the Law of Moses," which underscored the Law's indictment of human inability to act virtuously (see Ginsburg 1861, 111–12).

Viewing Ecclesiastes from the perspective of the epilogue and the Jewish and Christian interpreters who followed it in setting Qoheleth's words in the context of the Torah reveals more clearly the numerous links between the book and the other points in this textual constellation. Qoheleth appears to allude to texts from at least Genesis,[16] Numbers,[17] and Deuteronomy.[18] These allusions across the Pentateuch and the likely late date at which Ecclesiastes was written make it reasonable to conclude that the author had access to the collection in something like its final form (Hertzberg 1963, 46; Gordis 1968, 43). As with his interactions with the wisdom of Proverbs, or even his own earlier words, Qoheleth engages with the texts to which he alludes, often critically. However, just as with Proverbs, knowing the texts with which he wrestles—not just the individual verses, but their broader context as well—illuminates his message (see Kynes 2014). The close

[15] e.g., "What profit does a man have after he dies from all his labor which he labors under the sun in this world unless he occupies himself with Torah in order to receive a complete reward in the world to come before the Master of the world" (1:3). Targum translations from Knobel 1991.

[16] e.g., Eccl. 3:20; 12:7; cf. Gen. 2:7; 3:19. Dell (2014) discusses several more possible allusions, though she thinks arguments for diachronic intertextuality between the texts frequently exceeds the evidence.

[17] Eccl. 11:9; cf. Num. 15:39 and Eccl. 5:5 [ET 6]; cf. Num. 15:22–31 (see Kynes 2014).

[18] e.g., Eccl. 5:1 [2]; cf. Deut. 4:39 and Eccl. 5:3–4 [4–5]; cf. Deut. 23:22–4 [21–23] (see, e.g., Seow 1997, 56; Levinson 2014).

connection between Torah and wisdom in texts like Deuteronomy 4 and Ben Sira 24 indicates that at the time Ecclesiastes was written, an understanding of the Torah had developed that saw it "as a rational foundation for an orientation to life," and thus shifted the focus to "the Torah as a whole with its basic lines of ethical orientation, not as a collection of individual commandments and prohibitions" (Krüger 2004, 24–5). Qoheleth could be "indebted to the essence of the Torah" in his theology while engaging it critically (Krüger 2004, 24), just as is often assumed of his relationship with Wisdom. Like the Torah, Ecclesiastes combines narrative and instruction to reflect on how life should be lived between the boundaries of creation (Genesis 1–2; Ecclesiastes 1–2) and death (Gen. 49:29–50:26; Deut. 34; Eccl. 12:1–7).

6.3.2.2 History

Just as the Targum follows the lead of the epilogue in relating Ecclesiastes to the Torah, it follows the superscription in binding the book with history. After adding the word "Solomon" to the book's first verse to explicitly identify the king as the speaker, the Targum continues to read the second verse through a historical lens, with Solomon lamenting the "vanity" of his and David's work, having seen "through prophetical spirit" the division of the kingdom, the destruction of Jerusalem and the temple, and the exile. Israel's history reappears throughout the Targum, including references to the reigns of Hezekiah and Manasseh (3:11, 14; 4:15; 9:7, 10). Other rabbinic sources share this historical understanding (e.g., Tg. 1 Kgs. 5:13; Sifre on Deut. 1:1; b. Sot. 48b; see Knobel 1991, 5). Jerome also reports that the rabbis apply the poem on time (3:2–8) to events in Israel's history (Ginsburg 1861, 34). The Greek translation may even recognize allusions to Israel's kings in the book and create more allusions of its own, making it a "critical relecture of the royal history" (Vinel 1998, 296–301).

Early interpreters are not alone in hearing echoes of Israel's history in Ecclesiastes. During Wisdom's early nineteenth-century gestation, Gottlieb Kaiser reads Ecclesiastes as "an allegorico-historico-didactic poem," which provides a veiled, chronological chronicle of each of Israel's twenty kings from Solomon to Zedekiah (see Ginsburg 1861, 200–5). More recent and less radical attempts to integrate Ecclesiastes with Israel's history include Graham Ogden's (1980) proposal that Eccl. 4:13–16 alludes to the Joseph and David traditions and Jennie Barbour's (2012) efforts to uncover the ways Israel's historical traditions flow beneath the surface of the entire book, as it creates a stereotyped "pastiche king" of Israel, judging the monarchy through "a palimpsest of all Israel's history" (29). In contrast to earlier historical readings, however, Ogden and Barbour both characterize the allusions and echoes they find as "wisdom at work reading history" (Barbour 2012, 171; cf. Ogden 1980, 315). For Ogden (1980, 309–10) this means Qoheleth refers to people and events "honoured by the wisdom tradition" to illustrate his counsel, referring to them obliquely because that is all that "the generalized form of the wisdom statement" will allow. For Barbour (2012, 172–3), however, the category's hermeneutical influence is less limiting. She takes the epilogue's linkage of wisdom and law seriously, arguing, for example, that Qoheleth combines allusions to Saul's and Solomon's failures with an allusion to Deuteronomy to reinforce the "Deuteronomistic" rebuke of Israel's kings for Jerusalem's downfall (Eccl. 4:17–5:6; cf. Deut. 23:22–4).

Holm-Nielsen (1975, 64) remarks with apparent consternation that the "historical analysis" the targumist provides of the book removes the "universal character of *Koheleth's* sayings" by restricting their validity to certain situations in Israel's history. This opposition between the universal and the nationalistic is an effect of the Wisdom category, which has contributed to the view that Qoheleth "denationalizes" the concept of God (Hengel 1974, 1:117).[19] Even Aarre Lauha (1981, 394), who discusses several apparent allusions to Israel's history in the book, claims that Qoheleth follows the general line of the Wisdom Literature in similarly disregarding history, though the sage is motivated less by universalism than by his view of history as meaningless. Similarly, Whybray (1989, 29) notes that the election of Israel is missing in the book, but that this omission is consistent with other Wisdom texts, which "always have the characteristic of being concerned with the individual member of society rather than with the nation as a whole." Ogden demonstrates, however, that Israel's national history may illustrate universal truths with individual application. Similarly, Barbour (2012, 169) hears "national consciousness . . . everywhere in the book," as she tunes her ear for the "Israelite voice" in which "Qohelet speaks of a universalized God," in keeping with later texts associated with the Wisdom tradition, Ben Sira and Wisdom of Solomon.

[19] Barbour (2012, 1–2) begins her book with a catena of quotations from scholars representing the widespread view that Ecclesiastes is "abstracted from history" (Fox 1999, 137).

Whether Barbour, Ogden, and earlier interpreters are hearing intended historical resonances or the echoes of their own interests, their arguments should not be rejected *a priori* simply on the basis of a categorical imposition (see Ogden 1980, 310). Barbour notes that general trends in scholarship have obstructed the full critical analysis of the historical character of the book. She claims the interpretation of Ecclesiastes is a prime example that "[t]he quest to place Wisdom in the traditions of Judaism of the Second Temple Period has not been pursued as aggressively, nor with as clear a focus, as that for its Hellenistic philosophical placement" (Barbour 2012, 169; citing Mack and Murphy 1986, 383). However, she does not attempt to identify what changed interpreters' focus from one to the other. The development of the Wisdom Literature category, however, undoubtedly played a large role.

6.3.2.3 Prophecy and Apocalyptic

To find Israel's later history foreshadowed in words attributed to Solomon, the Targum depicts the king as a prophet, who foresees the monarchy's future failure (Tg. Qoh. 1:12). Gregory of Thaumaturgos also refers to Solomon as a prophet in his paraphrase of Ecclesiastes (see 1:1; Jarick 1990, 7). Though modern critics who address the issue prefer instead to understand an implicitly pseudonymous Solomon looking back on that history and so do not need to impute prophetic vision to this author, some still recognize other prophetic features in the book. Richard Schultz (2014), for example, reads Ecclesiastes in dialogue with Isaiah and finds "striking" parallels, such as that between Eccl. 10:16–17 and Isa. 5:11–12, 22–23, which may indicate Ecclesiastes's authorial dependence on Isaiah. He also finds a number of shared motifs, such as הבל and the brevity of life, including the servant's lament at laboring in vain (Isa. 49:4) that "easily could have come from the mouth of Qoheleth" (63, 64). Others note parallels with the prophetic concern for social justice, such as Eccl. 4:1; cf. Isa. 51:19; Jer. 15:5 (Christianson 1998, 136 n. 30); Eccl. 5:7 [ET 8]; cf. Isa. 10:2; Ezek. 18:18 (Seow 1997, 202); Eccl. 6:12; cf. Mic. 6:8 (Fisch 1988, 163). Qoheleth's criticism of the social conditions of his time put him "in a line with the old prophets" (Hertzberg 1963, 62), as he decried the powers behind societal ills "with a bluntness greater than the prophets" (Crüsemann 1984, 57), even if, unlike the prophets, he did not plead for social transformation (Seow 1997, 58).

The prophets combine a concern for social justice with a passion for proper worship, and Qoheleth joins these causes as well. In Eccl. 4:17–5:6; 9:2, Qoheleth takes up the cult criticism shared by Proverbs and the prophets (Krüger 2004, 27; see section 7.2.2.4 Inspired Instruction). The prophets also frequently take up Ecclesiastes's key term, הבל, to denigrate the "vanity" of idolatry (e.g., Isa. 57:13; Jer. 2:5; 8:19; 10:3, 8, 15; 14:22; Jon. 2:9 [ET 8]; Zech. 10:2).[20] Holm-Nielsen (1975, 52) finds Qoheleth's polemic "against all falsifiers of genuine fear of God, against false piety, against all who honour God with their mouth and believe that thus he will leave them in peace and neglect their way of living" reminiscent of the prophets. He parallels the prophetic polemic against the false prophets, who promulgated "a false opinion of life" and "a self-invented picture of God" with Qoheleth's opposition toward popular wisdom.

Krüger (1996) argues that Qoheleth is responding to both sapiential and prophetic views, critically deconstructing prophetic expectations of eschatological judgment, particularly in 1:9–11 (cf. Isa. 43:16–21; 65:17) and 12:1–8 (cf. Isa. 13:10; Joel 2:10; Jer. 13:16), and then reconstructing them according to an anthropology developed from Genesis 1–11. The Targum expands the eschatological imagery of the book (see Holm-Nielsen 1975, 64–5). In Tg. Qoh. 9:7, for example, Solomon speaks "by the spirit of prophecy" of the righteous eating and drinking in the Garden of Eden (cf. Isa. 65:13).

The end of Ecclesiastes has fittingly received the most attention for its eschatological and apocalyptic features. Gregory Thaumaturgos recognized (and amplified) the apocalyptic aspects of Ecclesiastes's final poem (12:1–7) in the third century (Jarick 1990, 289–99). Here Qoheleth draws on the imagery and language of other "proto-apocalyptic" prophetic texts, such as Joel 2, Ezekiel 32, and Isaiah 24 (Beal 1998; similarly Seow 1997, 376–82), setting the stage for the "eschatological tone" of the epilogue as it links human behavior with God's judgment (Dell 2013b, 17–18).

Some also argue that apocalyptic thought plays a role throughout the book as Qoheleth develops an anti-apocalyptic polemic. Perdue (2003) argues that Qoheleth is representing and rejecting the ideas of apocalyptic sages in 2:1–26; 3:10–15, 18–22; 4:1–5:19; 6:10–7:14; 9:1–10; 11:1–9.

[20] Ellul (1990, 20) uses the equivalence between הבל and idolatry to further associate the Solomon of Kings, who falls into idolatry, with Qoheleth, though the Hebrew term is not used in 1 Kings 11.

Krüger (2004, 30–1), similarly, claims that Qoheleth makes critical reference to early apocalyptic texts (Daniel 2–7, 1 Enoch 1–36; 72–82) in passages such as 1:3–11 and ch. 3, with the issue of time drawing them together. Building on this work, Jerome Douglas (2014, 1–2) argues that the book employs an "anti-apocalyptic genre," which is a hybrid of apocalyptic and Wisdom.

It would be as difficult to argue that Ecclesiastes is a prophetic or apocalyptic book as it would be to argue that it was Torah or history, but, as with those other genres of biblical literature, the text demonstrates more affinities than a narrow taxonomic conception would allow. Rather than discounting them as impossible for a Wisdom book, recognizing them encourages further similarities and significant contrasts to come into view. For example, after a superscription similar to that of Jeremiah and Amos[21] and first-person narrative describing Qoheleth's "calling" to pursue meaning in life, Ecclesiastes, like prophetic texts, mixes together genres and topics, such as justice, the fear of God, divine judgment, and the limits of human wisdom, with little apparent logical coherence before concluding with an eschatological vision. Despite these similarities, the book could be considered a metaprophecy like Job or Jonah,[22] because, in its deliberate avoidance of divine speech, it presents the vanity of life if God is silent and social injustice is lamented but not challenged. Qoheleth sets out to "see" (ראה) what is good in life (2:3), but when he has "seen everything" (7:15), he still has not received a "vision" (חזון), and therefore illustrates the proverbial insight, "Where there is no prophecy (חזון), the people cast off restraint" (Prov. 29:18).

6.3.3 Genres from the Ancient World

Interpreters are not restricted to the Hebrew Bible when proposing textual groupings around significant features of Ecclesiastes, and thus the book has been associated with genres from across the ancient

[21] Rashi sees דברי ("words") in the superscription as a clue to the book's message. On the basis of Deut. 1:1; Amos 1:1; Jer. 1:1; and 2 Sam. 23:1, he claims, "Wherever דברי is used at the beginning of a book, it shews that it is full of reproof" (cited in Ginsburg 1861, 39). The similarity between Ecclesiastes's superscription and those of multiple prophetic books undercuts one argument that the book is imitating Egyptian royal testaments (Bolin 2017, 47).

[22] For the common use of "polyphonic narration" in Jonah and Ecclesiastes, see Mills 2014.

world in which it was composed, ranging from Hellenistic diatribe and Egyptian royal testament to Akkadian royal autobiography (for summaries, see, e.g., Schwienhorst-Schönberger 1997a, 25–6; Weeks 2012, 134–52; Anderson 2014). I will not attempt to detail the proposals here. Since they draw on a similar taxonomic mentality, these efforts to identify *the* genre of Ecclesiastes share many of the weaknesses of the Wisdom category.

First, since their purported historicity is touted over other genre proposals, these genres face the problem of historical probability. If we are to read Ecclesiastes according to an ancient genre *because* that genre was known to its author, then both the existence of that genre and its likely recognition by both the author and his readers has to be proven. Attempts to do so raise more questions than they answer for the book's interpretation (see Hertzberg 1963, 62–3; Murphy 1992a, xlv; Weeks 2015, 170–1; Bolin 2017, 47, 108–9). How would these genres cross linguistic and cultural barriers and geographical and chronological distances to make it to Qoheleth and his audience?[23] Further, if the genres are defined broadly across a wide range of dates, places, and contexts or distinguished by ideas of universal significance that transcend a single genre (or often both), would they even be recognized as a distinct genre?

Second, the difficulty of proving that Qoheleth is deliberately employing a known ancient genre rather than modern scholars inventing and applying it to his work encounters the unavoidable danger of circularity in genre identification. The disputed nature of Ecclesiastes's message makes this threat particularly acute (see Bartholomew 2009, 67–73). For example, Perdue's (1994, 194–205) comparison of Ecclesiastes to grave biographies depends on his pessimistic reading of the book and then serves to reinforce it. His reading, as well as Longman's argument that the book is a fictional royal autobiography following an Akkadian model, both search for parallels on the basis of the diachronic assumption that the book's first-person narration defines its genre, leaving the frame narrative as an afterthought. Fox, however, starts from the final form of the text, which he argues is a frame narrative on the basis of a different set of ancient parallels. The diachronic impetus for ancient

[23] e.g., responding to Longman's view that Ecclesiastes takes up the Akkadian fictional autobiography genre, Weeks (2015, 170) wonders "how probable it is that either the author or the readers of the book would have been sufficiently aware of an Akkadian genre, which is attested principally in texts that were written several hundred years before the dates normally considered probable for Ecclesiastes, to make that connection."

comparative studies may also circularly influence a text's date. The text must be later than the inception of the proposed genre, but not so late that the genre has become irrelevant, and yet, the use of a particular genre may become a factor in dating a text. Martin Shields (2013, 135), for example, argues that Ecclesiastes is a royal autobiography and then claims that because the ancient Near Eastern royal autobiographies were from the first half of the first millennium, Ecclesiastes must be from around that time in order for the genre to be effective for the book's audience.

Third, these purportedly ancient genres impose particularly strong hermeneutical limitations because the diachronic arguments made for them encourage the exclusive application of a single intended genre to the text. The form-critical tendency to treat shared textual conventions as indications of the fixed structures or style of a particular text-type is still strong in biblical studies, encouraging the recognition of a common ancient convention, such as fictional autobiography, to drag broader assumptions about form and context in its train and "squeeze out other ways of reading material" (Weeks 2015, 172–3). If Ecclesiastes *is* a royal testament according to an Egyptian model, can it also be a Greek diatribe? Features of the text that do not correspond to the genre proposed tend to be minimized, overlooked, or declared secondary, while those that do are magnified.

Fourth, thanks to their historical nature, the hermeneutical limitations of these ancient genres goes even further. Not only do they restrict Ecclesiastes to the context of other texts of that type, but, since each type was produced in a particular culture, they encourage the book to be read primarily against that cultural backdrop. Thus, Christoph Uehlinger (1997, 155) argues that scholarship has primarily read Ecclesiastes in two contexts, biblical Wisdom Literature and Greek philosophy. Sometimes interpreters debate over which of these is the more appropriate context for the book or relate the two dialectically. For example, Lohfink (2003, 6) declares, "The book of Qoheleth can only be understood as an attempt to profit as much as possible from the Greek understanding of the world, without forcing Israel's wisdom to give up that status" (similarly Whybray 1998b). Uehlinger (1997, 156) counters that, historically considered, Ecclesiastes is part of ancient Levantine literary history and therefore should primarily be studied in the context of Mesopotamian, Egyptian, and Levantine Wisdom Literature of the Persian and Hellenistic period in its complete breadth, rather than only Israelite Wisdom Literature and Hellenistic popular philosophy.

Uehlinger's characterization of Ecclesiastes studies is somewhat overstated given the increased attention to ancient Near Eastern parallels in the latter half of the twentieth century and his exhortation to overcome modern restraints and understand the book in its broader context ironically still restricts it to a Wisdom context. He is right, though, that most interpreters still create a single primary cultural context of texts and ideas for the book in light of the single ancient genre they see it employing, whatever that might be.

For Ecclesiastes, this limitation is particularly distorting because the book challenges any context in which it is placed, whether of culture or literary genre. Even if, as Whybray (1998b, 245) argues, Qoheleth was a "conservative" in his own Jewish culture, as he must admit, in some sense he was also a "radical." We should expect nothing more, or less, when attempting to relocate his thought into a foreign cultural context.[24] Even interpreters who claim that the book's author is consciously using an ancient genre are frequently forced to acknowledge his intentional violation of its features. Qoheleth's imitation of fictional royal autobiographies is "poignant in its irony," as the book depicts the meaninglessness of the deeds they memorialize (Seow 1995). It shares multiple features with the Greek diatribe (see Birnbaum and Schwienhorst-Schönberger 2012, 18–19), but internalizes its dialogue (Crenshaw 1987, 29). If Ecclesiastes "draws upon the settings, tones and formulas" of genres like these "for its own purposes" (Fox 1999, 155), then recognizing those genres can illuminate various features of the texts but cannot define the text exclusively; an excess always exists.

This excess has led Ecclesiastes to be associated with texts and genres from across the ancient world both chronologically and geographically, from the Mesopotamian Epic of Gilgamesh to Greek popular philosophy. The diversity of proposals draws them all into question. If Qoheleth truly intended to write in one of the genres proposed, he must have done so fairly poorly if readers can read his work as something completely different as well. One response is to claim that each genre only applies to one section of the book, with, for example, the royal autobiography, limited to the first two chapters, incorporated into a diatribe. Writing in Israel, at "the crossroads of various civilizations,"

[24] See, e.g., Pedersen (1931, 26–8), for the contrasts between Qoheleth and Greek thought, which he attributes to differences between Jewish and Greek thought on humans, their relationship with divine power, with nature, and with life and its struggles.

Qoheleth may have conceivably become familiar with genres and even texts from across a wide range of cultures, (Ellul 1990, 16; similarly Anderson 2014, 173), but is it reasonable to impute such a widespread and eclectic knowledge of ancient literature to the book's author?

This diversity also demonstrates the interdependence of diachronic and synchronic approaches to intertextuality (see Kynes 2012a, 17–60). Some distinguish, for example, between the encyclopedia of production, the texts known to the author, and the encyclopedia of reception, those known to its readers, with the former contributing to diachronic, author-oriented, intertextual analysis and the latter to synchronic, reader-oriented approaches (see Alkier 2009). The various theories on Qoheleth's use of ancient Near Eastern genres are attempts to identify the ancient author's encyclopedia of production, but the only texts that may be considered are the ones that are in the modern interpreters' encyclopedia of reception. Initially the "philhellenic" philological interests of modern scholarship primarily related biblical texts to classical Greek parallels (see Legaspi 2010, e.g., 158–9), and this trend is evident in philosophical genre proposals for Ecclesiastes. However, as other ancient Near Eastern texts were discovered, biblical scholars' encyclopedia of reception expanded to include Egyptian and Mesopotamian texts, and Qoheleth's purported encyclopedia of production expanded with it.

Bartholomew (2009, 73) notes, for example, that in their genre proposals, Perdue and Longman associate the book with two distinct cultures and completely different groups of texts than Fox. Though this leads Bartholomew to conclude that each approach is in some sense circularly dependent on initial decisions about the nature of the book and only partially able to capture its meaning, he does not reject the value of comparative studies. Though their insights are partial, they are still "real" and "need not be antithetical," as each foregrounds some aspect of the text: its dialogical nature (diatribe), first-person narrative from a royal perspective (royal autobiography), pessimism and ethos of death (grave autobiography), and narratival features (frame narrative). Bartholomew proposes, therefore, a genre for the book that combines features of each: "a developed wisdom form of the royal testament or fictional autobiography cast in a frame narrative" (74). Others propose similar amalgamated genres.[25] Uehlinger (1997, 234)

[25] See, e.g., Fox 1999, 155; Brown 2000, 17; Birnbaum and Schwienhorst-Schönberger 2012, 17.

even proposes an ancient genre, the symposium, defined by its juxtaposition of other smaller genres.

Bartholomew (2009, 70) argues, "Comparative genre analysis must be based on literary analyses that, initially at least, are performed independently of studies of comparative genre" because "priority has to be given to the individuality of the text in the form we receive it." Though I agree with his concern to avoid "reading comparative genres into Ecclesiastes at the outset," I doubt that his proposed approach is possible. Rather, as Bartholomew himself models, multiple comparative studies should be taken into account *in order to* recognize the unique individual features of the text by relativizing the genres imposed upon it. One (or more) of these genres may have been intended by the author; without explicit indications, it is difficult to know (if the evidence were clear, the debate would neither be so long-running or wide-ranging). The interpretation of Ecclesiastes's genre should take advantage of ancient comparative studies, but it should not be limited by them.

6.3.4 Literary Features

Despite the widespread practice in biblical studies, genre groupings do not need to be intended by the author to illuminate a text's meaning (see section 4.2.3 The Emergence of Genres). Going "far afield" for literary models, such as comparing Ecclesiastes to Joel Chandler Harris's *Uncle Remus*, may serve "to illustrate and bring to our attention phenomena we might otherwise be unaware of and to help us break out of unjustified assumptions that may arise when working with a restricted body of texts" (Fox 1977, 94 n. 26). Even when an author intends to write in a genre, texts added to that genre later can also highlight its generic features, despite the author's ignorance of them (see section 4.4.3 Between Stability and Change). This happens even within the Wisdom category, as Job and Ecclesiastes focus interest on various features of Proverbs 10–29, even though it was likely collected before their composition. Few texts in the Hebrew Bible have profited from synchronic comparison as much as Ecclesiastes. Rather than attempt to provide an exhaustive list of the various textual groupings into which the book has been placed, I offer a few examples of the way affinities in form, tone, and content have drawn texts across both the canon and literary history into its intertextual network.

6.3.4.1 Form

Fox (1977) compares Ecclesiastes to several Egyptian texts, Deuteronomy and Tobit, and the modern parallels *Uncle Remus* and *Gulliver's Travels* to argue that the editorial frame that encases Qoheleth's words is not from a later hand but a formal convention used by the author to distance himself from them while still according them respect. By reading the book as a frame narrative, Fox encouraged future scholars to take not only its final form seriously, but also its narrative features, such as plot and characterization (e.g., Christianson 1998; Bartholomew 2009, 74–82).

The dominance of Qoheleth's first-person presentation makes his narrative autobiographical. Yee-Von Koh (2006, 154–5), drawing on studies of autobiography as a genre, and especially the examples from Augustine and Rousseau, sees in Ecclesiastes further common autobiographical features, including "the author's retrospective assessment of his life and personality, the presence of a coherent story which expresses a certain consistency of relationship between the author's self and the outside world, and the presence of a self-searching quest," along with a didactic purpose (see also Brown 2000, 7–8). It is a small step from autobiography to monologue. Harold Fisch (1988, 158–9, 172), who claims, "Ecclesiastes is indeed the nearest the Hebrew Bible gets to pure monologue," compares Qoheleth to Seneca and Montaigne, and observes that he could have said with the latter, "It is my portrait I draw…I am myself the subject of my book."[26] Salyer (2001, 237) argues that the book's reliance on first-person discourse pulls everything into "the gravitational field of Qoheleth's 'I'…inviting the reader to argue with both Qoheleth and the Epilogist in a way which is unparalleled in scripture."

This argument is already raging within the monologue, as Qoheleth debates with his own heart (Eccl. 1:16; 2:1, 15; 3:17). Ancient Near Eastern texts also employ debate and dialogue, even internal dialogue (most notably in the Dispute between a Man and His Ba; see Seow 1997, 41). Readers throughout the history of its interpretation, such as Gregory the Great, Herder, and Eichhorn (Hertzberg 1963, 39), and, more recently, Anthony Perry (1993) and Kyle Greenwood (2012) have heard different voices debating in Ecclesiastes. For others, these voices

[26] For an extensive study of the monologue genre across the Hebrew Bible, which finds the closest parallels for Ecclesiastes in the Psalms, see Bratsiotis 1961, esp. 35, 39 n. 73, 41.

are the result of Qoheleth citing views with which he disagrees (Gordis 1968, 95–108; Michel 1989, 246). Still others attribute voices to multiple layers of redaction, projecting the book's dialogue onto its redactors.[27]

The text's cacophony of genres and voices inspire it to be considered Qoheleth's *cahier* or notebook "into which the author jotted down his reflections during the enforced leisure of old age," unified only by his "mood and world-view" (Gordis 1968, 110; similarly Brown 2000, 17). As a disjointed Wisdom collection, Fox (1999, 149–50) compares Qoheleth's "journey of consciousness over the landscape of experience" to Wittgenstein's philosophical investigations, as well as Egyptian and Mesopotamian instructions, Proverbs, and Ben Sira, though, he argues, Qoheleth distinctively unifies his reflections around a single concept: the absurdity of life (1:3; 12:7). Perry (2015, 203–6), in a later work, also proposes "wisdom collection" for the book's genre, though he compares it to La Rochefoucauld's *Maximes*, Cioran's gnomic writings, Marcus Aurelius's *Thoughts*, and Montaigne's *Essais* in addition to Proverbs.

Qoheleth's name is indeed derived from a word meaning "to collect" (קהל), and the epilogue describes him "weighing, studying, and arranging many proverbs [משלים]" (12:9). Seventy or so proverbs may be found in the book along with other smaller forms associated with Wisdom (Birnbaum and Schwienhorst-Schönberger 2012, 19–20). Given the broad meaning of משל in the Hebrew Bible, which encompasses proverbs and extended allegories (see section 7.2.3 Ancient Near Eastern Genres), Friedrich Ellermeier (1967, 49–50, 89–92) briefly considers it for the genre of Ecclesiastes as a whole before eventually opting for reflection.[28] Christian Klein (1994, 166–7) also ultimately concludes that the book is not a משל, but claims that both its parts and its depiction of Qoheleth can function as משלים for readers, since, in keeping with his definition of the term (38), they attempt to persuade readers of a message by an image.

For Klein, then, the smallest genre in Ecclesiastes takes us back to the literary form of the entire book. The proverbs do this in a second sense because Qoheleth often employs them to challenge the easy assumptions of proverbial wisdom, attacking his opponents with their

[27] Siegfried (1898, 10–12) offers an explicit example, proposing that an original work by a pessimistic philosopher was adapted by a series of glossators, which he characterizes as an epicurean Sadducee, a wise man, and a pious *Chasid*. See Murphy 1992a, xxxiii, lv; Bolin 2017, 65.

[28] For discussion of Ecclesiastes as reflection, a genre that is "easier to recognize than to describe," see Murphy 1992a, xxxi–xxxii.

own weapons (Birnbaum and Schwienhorst-Schönberger 2012, 19–20). If Qoheleth indeed engages with Mesopotamian royal inscriptions or Egyptian royal testaments, his use is also ironic, since the former memorialize the king's accomplishments, while Qoheleth declares his "vanity and a chasing after wind" (2:11), and the latter are addressed to a successor, while Qoheleth hates the thought of handing on the fruit of his efforts (2:18–19) (Birnbaum and Schwienhorst-Schönberger 2012, 21–22; cf. Seow 1995). This ironic self-presentation encourages the entire text to be read as a parody, which "stands at the end of the biblical wisdom tradition and... uses the characteristic forms and genres of that tradition in order to criticize it" (Dell 1991, 147). However, even the recognition of Qoheleth's parodistic criticism of Wisdom is constrained within the distorting limitations of the category itself, such that he "makes use predominantly of short wisdom forms, rather than drawing on a wider range of genres from other areas of Israelite thought" (Dell 2013b, 12).[29] This overlooks the evidence presented above for Qoheleth's interaction with other genres from the canon. He quotes the Torah along with proverbs and parodies historical narrative, prophetic speech, and apocalyptic expectation.[30] Arguing that he critiques these other genres from the perspective of Wisdom seems like special pleading given the criticism he is widely considered to level against that purported tradition itself.

Just as the Wisdom category limits the genres with which Qoheleth is seen to engage, it also shapes the perception of those that are recognized. Most of the genres proposed above are presented as forms of Wisdom Literature. However, this classification does not come from the literary forms themselves. Narratives, autobiographies, monologues, dialogues, collections, and reflections can deal with a wide range of topics for just as many purposes. Even the term משל is used to label texts that are difficult to rein into the Wisdom classification (e.g., Ezek. 17:1–10). The classification is imposed upon these genres based on other assumptions about Ecclesiastes's meaning.

[29] Similarly, Crenshaw 1987, 38; Brown 2000, 11; Miller 2000, 229–30. Given that some of the forms in Ecclesiastes are designated Wisdom forms primarily because they appear in the book or conform to characteristics of the tradition abstracted from comparing Ecclesiastes to the other Wisdom books, and that a number of forms, such as the monologue, appear in non-Wisdom texts as well, such a statement is problematically circular.

[30] For a brief example of what this sort of analysis of the book could look like, though one that still embraces an overarching Wisdom perspective, see Krüger 2004, 24–7; cf. Krüger 1996, 1997.

6.3.4.2 Tone

The text's tone is another literary feature that could indicate its genre. Since the parody genre can engage any literary form, for example, tone defines it as much as form. Indeed, some have argued that Ecclesiastes revels in the ironic tone that frequently accompanies parody to such a degree that it becomes the book's defining feature (Good 1965, 168–95; Fisch 1988, 158–78; Sharp 2009, 196–220). Both Fisch (1988, 175) and Carolyn Sharp (2009, 220) argue that the epilogue is integral to the book's message, such that after everything, including wisdom, wilts under Qoheleth's piercing ironic gaze, only fear and obedience of God are left, while Edwin Good (1965) largely ignores the epilogue and claims the gift of joy is the remaining hope for meaning (see 194). Its use of irony links Ecclesiastes to texts across the Hebrew Bible, such as Jonah, the story of Saul, Genesis, Isaiah, and Job (Good 1965), as well as presentations of foreign kings and prostitutes, prophetic performance, and Psalm 73 (Sharp 2009).

Such a sweeping rejection of human endeavor could just as easily lead to pessimism as piety. In this vein, both William Anderson (1998) and Sneed (2012, 234–40) identify the book's genre as pessimistic literature, a genre that they both claim is defined primarily by a work's "mood." Pessimistic works, they claim, could be found across the ancient Near East, such as the Dispute between a Man and His Ba and the Babylonian Theodicy. Within the Bible, pessimism is not distinctive to Wisdom Literature. Lament psalms can have a similar cathartic effect (Sneed 2012, 236). The two laments virtually devoid of praise, Psalm 39, the "Qohelet-Psalm" (Seybold 1996, 162), and Psalm 88 are the closest parallels. Perdue (2013, 103) also compares Qoheleth's skepticism to Job, Habakkuk, and the Psalms of Imprecation (e.g., Psalms 13, 94).

As is often the case for Ecclesiastes, a diametrically opposed interpretation has been proposed that claims the book is fundamentally optimistic, with its author a "preacher of joy" (Whybray 1982b; cf. Lee 2005; Perry 2015). If Whybray (1982b, 92) is right that Qoheleth looks squarely at the inscrutable evils of the world and yet provides answers that transcend them, then the book would resonate with a recurrent theme across the Hebrew Bible, not only in Job and Jeremiah, whom Whybray mentions (93), but in the many lament psalms that end in praise or the prophetic hope on the other side of doom.

A similar opposition is evident in conceptions of the metaphysical tone of Qoheleth's reflections. Fox (2004, 12) represents a common view when he claims, "Ecclesiastes is the closest the Bible comes to philosophy, which is the intellectual, rational contemplation of fundamental human issues, with no recourse to revelation or tradition." Already by the sixth century, Olympiodorus read Ecclesiastes as Qoheleth's attempt to fill in the lack of natural philosophy in the canon (Ginsburg 1861, 105–6), but it was only in the modern period that this interpretive perspective became dominant (see section 6.1 The Bible's Rorschach Test), and Qoheleth became a "philosopher" (see, e.g., Michel 1988, 103–7; Bolin 2017, 103–23). Whybray (1998b, 239), however, characterizes Qoheleth instead as a "theologian." Seow (1997, 54–60) similarly finds the philosophical categorization of the book discordant with its widespread concern with God and critical stance toward the human pursuit of wisdom Qoheleth puts in theological terms (7:16–18), even if the philosophical approach's legacy of theological abstraction is still evident in his interpretation (see section 6.2.2 Theological Abstraction).

These conflicting interpretations result from a phenomenon that Tversky (1977, 342) labels the "diagnosticity principle" in his broader study of the effect of classification on interpretation (see section 4.2.1 Intertextual Shorthand). He observes that the classificatory significance of particular features is related to the set in which they are placed, which tends to obscure features shared by all objects in a set. In the set of actual animals, for example, the shared feature "real" is without diagnostic value because it cannot be used to distinguish some objects from others. However, if legendary animals, such as centaurs, mermaids, and phoenixes, are added to the set, then the "reality" of an object becomes diagnostically significant. Similarly, in the context of the Hebrew Bible, Qoheleth's theological commitments have minimal classificatory significance, since they are shared with every text in the canon (except, perhaps, Esther and Song of Songs). In that context, the book's affinities with philosophy set it apart. However, when Whybray (1998b, 239, 254) sets the book in the context of contemporary Hellenistic philosophy, Qoheleth's dependence on the divine comes into relief, such that he becomes a "defender of the Jewish faith" whose "primary aim" was to counsel his readers to "fear God" (3:14; 5:6 [ET 7]; 7:18; 8:12, 13).

Genre's context-creating influence on interpretation is also evident in the characterization of Qoheleth's tone as "existential," which is widespread (see Christianson 2007, 86). Fox (1989, 14–15, 31–3) offers an influential example. While arguing that הבל is best understood as "absurd" in the sense that Camus uses the term, he notes a "fundamental congruency" between the French existential thinker and Qoheleth as both "insist on the value of knowledge, understanding, and experience in a world whose irrationality seems to confound all values." Though he also acknowledges significant differences between the two, he believes that their deep "kinship" justifies using similarities with Camus's thought to illuminate features of Qoheleth's. The comparison is illuminating, but also inevitably influenced by modern commitments that are foreign to the Israelite author. Any attempt to find in an ancient text a "forerunner" (Gordis 1968, 114) or "precursor" (James 1984) for influential modern ideas such as existentialism, must, by definition, read back through the concerns of the later texts to the earlier text. Though this comparison can clarify features of the ancient text, it also "allows contemporary readers to situate the ancient literary artifacts in their own world of social discourse" (Mills 2003, 125). It should not, therefore, be the exclusive grouping through which to understand the text, as both Fox and Gordis rightly emphasize.

Postmodernism has provided a new opportunity to situate Ecclesiastes in the contemporary world of social discourse. The potential of postmodern approaches to suggest alternative ways to think about Ecclesiastes's heterogeneity in light of the book's persistent thwarting of modernist attempts to organize and control its meaning, recognized in the 1990s (Newsom 1995, 187; Bartholomew 1998, 203), has since borne fruit in numerous studies (see Bartholomew 2009, 41). Salyer (2001, 398), for example, focuses on the book's self-deconstructing first-person discourse, which "becomes a rhetorical mirror for the postmodern reader who sees something of himself or herself in the protagonist's epistemological use of the self." Ingram (2006) claims, however, that its many "voices" create its postmodern appeal. Contrary to modern and "scientific" attempts to discern consistent meaning in Ecclesiastes by privileging one voice and pushing the others to the margins, he argues that the book's ambiguity is intentional, creating a plurality, discord, lack of consistent meaning, and unstructuredness that "accords well with the world seen through postmodern eyes" (272). Just like Newsom's polyphonic approach to Job (see section 5.2.4.3 Polyphony), these postmodern readings valuably draw multiple viewpoints together into the book's interpretation, and yet they can fall prey to the temptation to restrict the book's meaning according to contemporary interests if projected onto the book's author or applied exclusively. Ecclesiastes certainly lends itself to postmodern readings, but Qoheleth was not a postmodernist (see Sneed 2002).

6.3.4.3 Content

As with his use of literary forms, Qoheleth is eclectic in the topics to which he refers, which offers a third mode for generating literary contexts in which to interpret the book. Ecclesiastes has been read as the biblical equivalent to Alexander Pope's "Essay on Man" (Fisch 1988, 172) and a "theological anthropology" (Seow 1997, 54–60). Its political character led Luther to dub its author the "doctor politicus" of the Old Testament (see Dell 2013b, 32–3) and Jacobi to claim in the eighteenth century that the book was intended exclusively for courtiers (Ginsburg 1861, 186). In keeping with the optimistic tone some perceive in the book, it has been characterized as "Lehre vom guten Leben" ("instruction on the good life") (Birnbaum and Schwienhorst-Schönberger 2012, 9), while others consider the "problem of death" the book's driving theme and main concern (Burkes 1999, 1, similarly Kutschera 1997; Lo 2008). As "a story of Man and Thanatos," Marc Hirschman (2001, 88–9, 96) suggests that Ecclesiastes's confrontation with death as an elemental theme of human existence, developed from psalms such as Psalm 144, was the reason for its inclusion in the canon, and a prominent theme in its rabbinic exegesis. In Qoheleth's struggle with passing on knowledge beyond the limit of his own mortality, the book may also be compared to deathbed testaments, such as Genesis 49 and Deuteronomy, a genre that the book subverts, like so many others (Vayntrub forthcoming b).

Wisdom is vague and abstract enough to encompass these topics, but it does not exhaust their significance. Each cuts across the canon in various ways, including other so-called Wisdom books to greater or lesser degrees, but is hardly restricted by that boundary. Beyond the canon, they spread Ecclesiastes's intertextual network in a variety of directions as well. For example, in a later study, Shannon Burkes (2003) considers the encounter between God, self, and death in Second Temple literature, where she finds it to be a prominent theme that unites Job, Ecclesiastes, Daniel, Ben Sira, Wisdom of Solomon, and 4 Ezra across traditional genre barriers, in particular Wisdom and apocalyptic (see 253–61).

6.4 NETWORK APPROACH

As with Job, this abundance of potential genres for Ecclesiastes has forced many interpreters to concede that the book is *sui generis* (e.g., Murphy 1981, 129; Crenshaw 1987, 28), put the question of its genre aside (Klein 1994, 163), and focus instead on the genres of its parts (Longman 1998, 15). Qoheleth, the collector, becomes an assembler, not merely of wise sayings (12:9–10), but of genres (Murphy 1981, 131; Perry 2015, 203–4). As a unique text in the Hebrew literary tradition, interpreters may be tempted to conclude that Ecclesiastes "can only be interpreted in its own terms" (Whybray 1998b, 239). The distinctive nature of the book should be credited, however, not to its distance from all Israelite traditions, but to its high degree of critical reflection on them (Krüger 1996, 129). Klein (1994, 163) therefore argues, just as Eliot had for Williams, that Qoheleth could not find adequate resources in the existing ancient Near Eastern genres, and so had to modify them in order to express his thoughts.

However, despite acknowledging Qoheleth's "höchst eigenartiger, durchaus selbständiger Stil" ("extremely idiosyncratic, thoroughly independent style") with Hans Hertzberg (1963, 32, 55), most also follow him in still classifying the book as a product of Wisdom Literature. After affirming the book's uniqueness, Whybray (1998b, 239) immediately adds, "This is not, of course, to deny or belittle its origins in the so-called 'wisdom tradition' and its affinities with that tradition." Fox (1999, 153) goes even further. First, he declares, "A literary work does not have a single genre," but may belong to several because "[g]enres are sets defined by criterial features." Then, after denying that Qoheleth's genre has any "close parallel," he concludes, "The broad genre of Qohelet is Wisdom Instruction," based on its combination of elements from other genres associated with Wisdom Literature and the book's attempt to provide guidance for living on the basis of human reflection rather than divine revelation or specific traditions (see also Perry 1993, xi–xii).

There is something incongruous about declaring Ecclesiastes's defiance of any genre categorization and then ensconcing it neatly in the Wisdom category. What, after all, is Wisdom Literature if not a genre, a group of texts designated on the basis of one or more significant affinities? After his extensive survey of the history of interpretation of Ecclesiastes, Ginsburg (1861, 242–3) summarizes the many conflicting views that have been proposed for its meaning and draws, perhaps, precisely the conclusion Qoheleth was hoping for: "What a solemn lesson for the pious and for the learned to abstain from dogmatism, and what an admonition not to urge one's own pious emotions or ingenious conceits as the meaning of the Word of God!" Whether considered the Word of God or not, Ecclesiastes has proven over two millennia of interpretation its capacity to expose the self-reflective nature of genre while escaping the restraints of any single interpretation.

Bartholomew (2009, 43) claims that research into Ecclesiastes is "in a condition of pluralism and fragmentation." The book's interpretation would profit, however, from an approach that combines pluralism with integration. Dell's (2013b, 95) insight that different interpretive methodologies illuminate different features and sections of the book applies just as well to the different genre groupings in which it could be placed, which themselves often result from different methodologies. Ellul (1990, 36–8) imagines the book as a "complex variegated piece of cloth" in which various themes are woven together. Reading the book as *sui generis* blinds readers to the colors Qoheleth weaves into his tapestry. Teasing out the separate generic threads as independent "parts" destroys their interwoven beauty. Limiting one's vision to the textures Ecclesiastes shares with the other Wisdom books obscures the whole. Skepticism, wisdom, and piety may be in tension in the book, but the depiction of each is dependent on the other (see Pedersen 1931, 46). Emphasizing one of these themes (or any of the many others) to the detriment of the others will distort the meaning of both that theme and the entire book. And yet, without analyzing these separate features, the whole will not be recognized for what it is. Ecclesiastes is eclectic, not merely in its theology (Whybray 1982b, 29), but also in its expression, drawing on ideas and genres from across the Hebrew Bible, and, likely from the ancient world in which it was written. Comparison with later compositions brings further significant aspects of Ecclesiastes into focus. A multiperspectival network approach to the book's genre will enable readers to see these diverse features more clearly, while still appreciating the unique way the author of Ecclesiastes weaves them together.

7

The Intertextual Network of Proverbs and the Subjective Nature of Genre

> A century ago the Swiss historian Jacob Burckhardt foresaw that ours would be the age of "the great simplifiers," and that the essence of tyranny was the denial of complexity. He was right. This is the single greatest temptation of the time. It is the great corrupter, and must be resisted with purpose and with energy.
>
> (Moynihan 1970, 1731)

Unlike Job, which appears to chafe at the restrictions of any classification, and Ecclesiastes, which seeps like a vapor through the grasp of any category, Proverbs seems stable and content in the place it has been given. However, despite the undeniable importance of the concept of wisdom to Proverbs, reading the book as Wisdom Literature creates similar problems for its interpretation as it does for Job and Ecclesiastes. Though the network of texts surrounding Proverbs may not be as dense, the book's interpretation will still profit from better appreciating its complexity, perhaps more so because the obviousness of its Wisdom classification has previously discouraged such efforts.

Though fewer genre groupings tug at the meaning of Proverbs, it does not sit as solidly in the modern conception of the Wisdom category as is often assumed. In fact, that widespread assumption may have contributed to the lack of intertextual study of the work. The similarities between Proverbs and texts outside the category may not have previously been widely recognized, not because they are not there, but because few thought to look. However, taking into account even the limited links interpreters have recognized provides new depth to the book's interpretation and opens up new avenues of research into its place in the canon and the ancient Near East. More than that, given the close association between Proverbs and Israelite conceptions of wisdom, a new approach to the book's interpretation will inevitably affect the understanding of wisdom as a concept.

7.1 READING PROVERBS AS WISDOM LITERATURE

Proverbs makes clear its interest in wisdom early and often. The word "wisdom" (חכמה) appears in its pages more than in any other book in the Hebrew Bible. After the attribution to Solomon (Prov. 1:1), the king renowned for his wisdom (1 Kgs. 5:10 [ET 4:30]), the prologue (Prov. 1:2–7) expresses the book's purpose, which begins with providing wisdom (v. 2). More than that, the "first interpretation" of the book offered there reads its sayings "as *text* that must be studied and interpreted, not just heard and obeyed," presenting the book, therefore, "as Wisdom *literature*, not just wisdom" (Fox 2000, 571, 76; emphasis original). Fittingly, then, Fox (2000, 17) makes similarity to Proverbs the primary criterion for his family resemblance approach to defining Wisdom Literature. Proverbs, Dell (2015, 146–7) agrees, is "universally acknowledged as the supreme example of traditional Israelite wisdom" and "the head of the family of wisdom books." In support, she points to its use of the proverb form, which is "at the heart of wisdom," its pervasive use of the word "wisdom," and the prominence of personified Wisdom in Proverbs 1–9.

Proverbs, as Wisdom Literature's *paterfamilias*, naturally demonstrates the traits that interpreters associate with the category, unlike the wayward son, Ecclesiastes, or the black sheep, Job. Even Zoltan Schwáb (2013), in his canonical and theological reading of Proverbs, questions the Wisdom "tradition" but not the Wisdom Literature category, and can only qualify, not fully reject, the secularism, universalism, eudaemonism, and individualism applied to it (see, e.g., 66–7, 176, 209, 241). In fact, he employs the distinctiveness of Wisdom as a "mode of discourse," with its interests in the individual and "abstract level of discussion," to explain away potential theological contrasts between Proverbs and the rest of the canon, such as its lack of interest in Israel's history (Schwáb 2013, 67; similarly, Delkurt 1993, 146; Van Leeuwen 1997, 21).

The Wisdom Literature category was tailored to fit Proverbs, so its restriction of the book's hermeneutical movement is less noticeable than the way it tears at the seams when Job, in particular, wears it second-hand. As with Ecclesiastes, less effort has been devoted, therefore, to demonstrating how reading Proverbs as Wisdom Literature limits its interpretation than for Job. Yet, the same issues arise.

7.1.1 Canonical Separation

Along with the other Wisdom books, Proverbs is singled out from the canon as uniquely concerned with reason or philosophy (Hazony 2012, 284–5 n. 26) and participating in "a different world of thought" (Crenshaw 2010, 24–5). Preuss (1970, 414–17) famously took this distinction, the way the Wisdom Literature "stands outside all that is specific to the Old Testament," as an indication of its theological and homiletical deficiency (see Fox 2009, 948). In accord with Wisdom generally, which is "human in its particulars and in its workings" and "offers itself as a complete and self-contained moral system," Fox (2009, 946, 947) claims that Proverbs "shows no interest in Yahweh's revealed Torah" and has little regard for prophetic revelation. The pervasiveness of Wisdom's canonical marginalization in scholarship inspired Dell (2006, 155–87) to attempt to demonstrate its integration with the rest of the Hebrew Bible by documenting "echoes" in Proverbs of texts from prophecy, Deuteronomy, cultic texts, and Psalms. Whether or not one agrees with her conclusion that "in the book of Proverbs the wisdom tradition is truly integrated with its canonical bedfellows" (199), her work demonstrates how the Wisdom category has previously forced Proverbs to sleep on the floor.

7.1.2 Theological Abstraction

Even Dell (2006, 125–54), however, when she turns to the theology of Proverbs, maintains the central value of the abstract concepts creation and order. Schwáb (2013, 63–4, 66), in his theological interpretation of the book, observes how the concept of order "stands between the text and the interpreter," leading away from the text itself to reconstructions of the abstract ideas it utilizes, and creation tends to "silence the plurality of theological themes offered by Proverbs" (see Weeks 2010a, 108–17). And yet, Schwáb (2013, 241) explains the differences between Proverbs and the rest of the Hebrew Bible as, in part, due to its being written on a "more abstract, theoretical level," a view he admits "has some parallels with the nineteenth-century understanding of wisdom as 'philosophical.'"

The Wisdom category encourages theological abstraction, not merely by emphasizing differences from the rest of the Hebrew Bible, but also by magnifying contrasts between Proverbs and the other books in the category. Proverbs becomes optimistic, traditional wisdom in contrast to Job and Ecclesiastes as products of a pessimistic "crisis" in Wisdom. This leads scholars to characterize the sages responsible for Proverbs as "dogmatic, rigid, or removed from the human condition," as they present "a wisdom that is removed from reality and is more theoretical than practical" (Stewart 2016b, 352–3).[1] As a result, Proverbs has been "marginalized" in scholarship (Hatton 2008, 17–45). The "neatness" of this scholarly consensus "obscures complexities, not only in Proverbs, but also in all biblical wisdom," though attention to the book's "contradictions" can uncover them once again and may actually demonstrate a similar indeterminate dialogical clash of voices as in Job (Hatton 2008, 20, 170; see also Van Leeuwen 1992; Yoder 2005).

7.1.3 Hermeneutical Limitation

Given that Proverbs is widely considered "the fountainhead of the wisdom movement," Murphy (1998, xix) naturally concludes, "However singular the profile of the book of Proverbs may be, it should not be viewed apart from the other books of wisdom." Murphy likely means those other books should be considered in any interpretation of Proverbs. But, in practice, the Wisdom category has encouraged interpreters to follow the second possible meaning of his ambiguous directive, not interpreting Proverbs outside of the narrow set of concerns it shares with those "other books of wisdom." Even when additional texts are considered, the category restricts the meaning of Proverbs to a separate domain.

This hermeneutical limitation is evident even in the interpretation of specific words and phrases, like "torah" (תורה) or "fear of the Lord," which are given a distinct meaning in Proverbs, reflecting a "false separation" between Proverbs and the rest of the canon (Dell 2006, 174–6; see also Schwáb 2013, 79).[2] For example, Clifford (1999, 5) argues that "law" and "command" in Proverbs "lack concreteness and specificity,"

[1] For Stewart's use of Proverbs' poetic nature to respond to the "mistaken assumption" of the "simplicity" of Proverbs' wisdom (355), see section 7.2.1.2 Poetry.

[2] Dell (2006, 174) does include a "proviso" that when Proverbs was composed, *torah* was not yet a formal description of the Pentateuch or its law codes.

and yet he specifically denies that they refer to the Mosaic Torah (see Brown 2005b, 253). Attempts to restrict words like these to a secular meaning (e.g., Fox 2000, 79), despite the religiously allusive context in which they are placed in Proverbs 1–9, give the impression that interpreters are allowing the assumption that Wisdom Literature must be distinct to exclude "almost *a priori*" the possibility of such resonances (Weeks 2016a, 14; see also Weeks 2007, 106–7). For example, when interpreting the word "land" (ארץ) in Prov. 2:21–2, Fox (2000, 123) demonstrates the category's interpretive sway by arguing that, despite the Deuteronomic resonance, it refers to "this world" and not the land of Israel, supporting his conclusion, in part, with the circular argument, "Concern for the Land of Israel is absent from biblical Wisdom literature."[3]

7.2 THE INTERTEXTUAL NETWORK OF PROVERBS

Unlike Job or even Ecclesiastes, where different genre identifications lead to different conclusions about the nature of the book's message, the emphasis on wisdom in Proverbs guarantees that this topic will play a prominent role in any interpretation of the book. However, the other texts included in that grouping will affect how that wisdom is understood. Through canonical separation, theological abstraction, and hermeneutical limitation, the Wisdom classification paints the whole book of Proverbs with one of its most prominent hues, directing readers' attention away from, rather than toward the nuance and complexity of both the text and the wisdom it describes. Mapping Proverbs' intertextual network will retrieve some of the meaning that the Wisdom classification has obscured.

7.2.1 Genres before "Wisdom Literature"

Before the nineteenth century, Proverbs was not classified exclusively with Ecclesiastes and Job as part of Israel's Wisdom Literature. Instead,

[3] For a mediating view that later readers would inevitably hear the echo of Deuteronomy here no matter the text's original intent, see Dell 2006, 170. Similarly, on the comparable passage in Prov. 10:30, see Weeks 2010a, 110. Rylaarsdam (1946, 23) sees this "Deuteronomic flavor" across the book, in these passages as well as 4:21, 38; 15:4; 19:10; 21:23; 24:4; 25:19; 26:1.

it appears in multiple groupings, each of which illuminates different features of the book.

7.2.1.1 Sifrei Emet

For example, whatever the reason Proverbs was grouped with Psalms and Job in the *Sifrei Emet* grouping, the relevant hermeneutical point is that reading Proverbs along with those two texts would not highlight the secular, universalistic, international, empirical, or rationalistic aspects of the book. Instead, it would focus attention on the features Proverbs shares with Job and the Psalms, such as their disproportionate use of the word רשע ("wicked") compared to the rest of the Hebrew Bible, which indicates "a relationship of these three complexes to one another" (Westermann 1995 [1990], 81). צדק ("righteous") and its cognates, the common antonyms of רשע, are also used at a disproportionately high rate in these books (along with Isaiah),[4] and the 117 proverbs depicting an antithesis between the righteous and the wicked are the largest grouping in the book (Westermann 1995 [1990], 83). Further, the words חכם and צדיק are "co-referential," designating the same person (Fox 2009, 928; see also Heim 2001, 77–108), and righteousness is repeatedly paired with wisdom in Proverbs (Prov. 9:9; 10:31; 11:30; 23:24). Reading Proverbs in this way could redefine both the emphasis of the book and the definition it supplies for wisdom. Grouped with Job and Ecclesiastes, wisdom receives more emphasis, but combined with Psalms and Job, righteousness becomes more prominent. Thus, after exploring the interest Psalms shares in righteousness with Proverbs, Sun Myung Lyu (2012, 115–33, 135) notes, "Proverbs chooses the righteous person—rather than the wise person—as the most fundamental and overarching appellation for the ideal human type" (see also Steiert 1990, 156).

Though he does not mention the *Sifrei Emet* category, William Brown (forthcoming) takes the close proximity of Psalms and Proverbs

[4] Psalms and Job use the nominal and verbal forms of צדק more often per word than any other books in the Hebrew Bible (fifty-four and twenty-four times, respectively, or 1.81 and 1.91 times every 1,000 words). Isaiah and Proverbs are the only other books to use the word more than once every 1,000 words. Psalms and Proverbs, however, use the term צדיק ("righteous one") far more than any other books (fifty-two and sixty-six times, respectively). When these words are combined with צדקה ("righteousness"), the order is Psalms (140), Proverbs (94), Isaiah (81), Ezekiel (45), and Job (35), though relative to length, Job comes ahead of Ezekiel. The next book in the list, Deuteronomy, uses the terms eighteen times.

in both the Jewish and Christian canons as inspiration to read the two texts dialogically. In so doing, he finds a counterpart for sapiential rebuke in psalmic complaint/petition and resonance with psalmic lament and praise in Proverbs, particularly its final two chapters. These features contribute to the books' intracanonical dialogue over the rugged road to happiness *coram deo*, and, as such, Brown concludes, "It is no accident that the accolade 'happy' (*ʾašrê*) concludes Proverbs (Prov 31:28) and opens the Psalter (Ps. 1:1), a designation that commends the kind of person who seeks what is good and righteous, including God."

7.2.1.2 Poetry

Though the inclusion of Proverbs in the Poetry section of the canon in the Greek tradition certainly contributed to the eventual characterization of that collection as the *libri didactici* or "didactic books" of the Hebrew Bible, the effect could also work in the other direction to shape the interpretation of Proverbs. The fact that the text could be included among the "books written in verse" (see section 2.1.2 Greek Order) testifies to its commonly overlooked poetic form. Even when the book's poetry is addressed, the tendency is to separate a number of poetic sections from the rest of the book (e.g., Westermann 1995 [1990], 95–9). Though generally treated as incidental, the text's poetic form, as Anne Stewart (2016a, 2–3) argues, is "central to the book's content and its didactic purpose"; it is the honey with which it dispenses its medicine, even part of the prescription (see von Rad 1972 [1970], 24; Hatton 2008). Through its poetry, it appeals, not merely to the rational capacities, but to the whole human person: emotions, motivations, desires, and imagination. For example, Stewart (2016a, 61–9) compares Proverbs 1–9 to Song of Songs, another book in the Poetry collection, and argues that it employs similar poetic techniques to cultivate desire for wisdom.[5] Her study, therefore, reveals the "porous bounds of genre" when applied to Proverbs (69).

7.2.1.3 Solomonic Collection

Finally, in both Jewish and Christian traditions, the association of Proverbs with Solomon (1:1; 10:1; 25:1) inspires the book to be grouped

[5] Carol Fontaine (1993, 113) also speaks of the "rich, lyric language of erotic poetry" employed to engender desire for wisdom in the book.

with Ecclesiastes and Song of Songs in a "Solomonic Collection" in the Hebrew Bible (see section 2.2 Solomonic Association). Even those who argue that this grouping is a precursor to the modern Wisdom category must acknowledge that it makes an appeal to the authority of the figure of Solomon, which would counter many of the modern assumptions about the nature of Israelite wisdom. This is not wisdom that is available to anyone or that can be gained merely by rational and objective analysis of the natural world, but Solomon's divinely inspired wisdom.[6]

As a member of the Solomonic collection, Proverbs is read in a different constellation of texts than the modern Wisdom category, which inevitably affects the interpretation of all of them. It provides an alternative "equally valid" and "helpful" lens through which to focus on the material (Dell 2015, 157; Dell 2016, 51–2). The Song of Songs may have been attributed to Solomon, who appears five more times in the text (1:5; 3:7, 9, 11; 8:11–12), not due to the book's wisdom, but due to the king's notorious womanizing (1 Kgs. 11:1–5) (Jastrow 1921, 49–50; Murphy 1981, 103–4; van der Toorn 2007a, 37), or as "a way of bringing it within the sapiential tradition and bestowing on it a special authority" (Blenkinsopp 1995, 3). Either way, reading Proverbs as a member of the same Solomonic collection invites comparison between the two texts, both in modern interpretation (e.g., Dell 2005; Imray 2013; Hauge 2015; Hagedorn forthcoming) and in ancient attempts to connect both in a series with Ecclesiastes in some meaningful way (see section 2.2 Solomonic Association).

The Solomonic collection also binds Proverbs with the depiction of Solomon in 1 Kings 1–11.[7] Indeed, given the numerous connections between them, "it is hard to imagine ancient readers interpreting these

[6] Sneed (2015b, 235) argues, therefore, that the book presents itself as a book of aphorisms rather than of proverbs, since the former are associated with a famous person, while the latter are general folk knowledge.

[7] Mathias Winkler (2017, 63; cf. 68–70; 340–4) argues that the use of the name "Solomon" creates "an inner-biblical encyclopedia of privileged intertexts" composed of 1 Kings 1–11, Proverbs, Ecclesiastes, Song of Songs, 2 Chronicles 1–9, Nehemiah 13, Psalms 72 and 127, Wisdom of Solomon, and Ben Sira 47, that takes interpretive priority over broader canonical intertextual connections. He focuses on the affinities between 1 Kings 1–11 and Proverbs, particularly, the attribution of "proverbs" (משל) to Solomon (1 Kgs. 5:12 [ET 4:32]; cf. Prov. 1:1; 10:1; 25:1), foreign women (1 Kgs. 11:1–8; cf. Prov. 2; 5; 6:20–35; 7), the בן חכם ("wise son"; 1 Kgs. 5:21 [ET 5:7]; cf. Prov. 10:1; 13:1; 15:20), and the blessing of עשר ("riches"), כבד ("honor"), and יארך+מים ("long life"; 1 Kgs. 3:13–14; cf. Prov. 3:16).

two texts independently of each other" (Camp 2000, 150).[8] This ties Proverbs into Israel's history and, because 1 Kings emphasizes the divine endowment of Solomon's wisdom (3:12, 28; 10:24) (Sneed 2015b, 254–5), into the involvement of a particular god, YHWH, with a particular people, Israel. Associated with Solomon, Proverbs does not offer merely an unspecified wisdom, but one oriented toward YHWH, the Torah, and righteousness (Winkler 2017, 357). Though 1 Kings does set Solomon's wisdom in a broader international context (1 Kgs. 5:9–11 [ET 4:29–31]), the comparison is intended to proclaim the superiority of the Israelite king's YHWH-bestowed wisdom (Cogan 2001, 223–4).

Childs (1979, 552), however, sets the international context of Solomon's wisdom in Kings against his participation in Israel's sacred history. Carrying on the contrast between the Solomon of Proverbs and the one depicted in Kings that goes back at least to Bauer at the turn of the nineteenth century, he argues that the Solomonic superscription of Proverbs only connects the book with the "sapiential material" in Kings, thereby preserving "the uniqueness of the sapiential witness against the attempts to merge it with more dominant biblical themes" (see section 3.2 Bruch's Influences). Zimmerli (1964 [1963], 147) also acknowledges that the report of the divine gift of wisdom to the king of God's covenant people (1 Kgs. 3:14–15) might well lead one to deduce a relationship between history and Wisdom. And yet, he argues, Proverbs and Ecclesiastes make no attempt to incorporate "this way of thinking." He even argues that though both books speak of the king, this king "is never the anointed king of God's people Israel and the son of David, who received God's special promise," despite the fact that Solomon is explicitly identified in Prov. 1:1; 10:1; 25:1 and strongly implied in Eccl. 1:1, 12. Similarly, Scott (1960, 269–71) identifies several types of wisdom in the Solomonic account, but argues that only Solomon's superior knowledge and intellect (1 Kgs. 5:9–14 [ET 4:29–34]; 10:1–10, 13, 23–4) earns him his reputation for founding the Wisdom Literature.

7.2.2 The Genres of Solomon's Wisdom

Instead of perpetuating this Wisdom-inspired canonical separation and projecting the modern definition of Wisdom back onto the description

[8] Schwáb (2013, 203–4), building on the work of Van Leeuwen (2000) and Camp (2000), lists thirteen parallels, including the repetition of the triad of "wisdom" (חכמה), "understanding" (תבונה), and "knowledge" (דעת) in both texts in the same order (1 Kgs. 7:14; cf. Prov. 3:19–20; 24:3–4).

of Solomon in Kings, I propose allowing the text's presentation of wisdom to shape our understanding of the concept. The account of Solomon and his reign then provides a personified, narrative definition of the term's semantic range, including its antonyms (1 Kgs. 11:1–8). If mention of the word "wisdom" (חכמה and its derivatives), which appears twenty-one times, or interest in the topic are the main criteria for the category, then 1 Kings 1–11 should be chief among the Wisdom texts (Whybray 1974, 91; Lemaire 1995, 106–7). Rather than the widely debated historical value of the depiction of Solomon in 1 Kings 1–11 (e.g., Crenshaw 2010, 42–50; Dell 2010), I will pursue its commonly overlooked hermeneutical significance. The material in 1 Kings 1–11 may be late and legendary, as Crenshaw (2010, 50) argues, but even he acknowledges that the Solomonic connection must tell us something about how wisdom was understood, and thus he claims Solomon exemplifies the success that wisdom promises.

To this end, the other types of wisdom Scott recognizes in the text, skillful and successful rule (1 Kgs. 2:1–2, 5-9; 5:15–26 [ET 5:1–12]) and discernment to render true justice (3:4–15, 16–28), deserve more attention. He also observes that the Deuteronomist glorifies Solomon as builder of the temple, which the text presents as a further expression of wisdom.[9] The account incorporates prophetic elements as well. Just as Proverbs' superscription invites the book to be read according to the wisdom attributed to Solomon in 1 Kings, so the variegated presentation of wisdom in that account draws other texts across the canon into the interpretation of Proverbs and reveals that the intersection of genre groupings in 1 Kings 1–11 is also evident in Proverbs.[10] A modern definition of Wisdom Literature, as enlightened, universalistic, scholarly reflection, distinct from Israel's history and cult, has been projected back onto the description of Solomon in Kings, sundering it from the Solomon of Proverbs and the wisdom attributed to him there. Interpreters have ignored, excluded, or denigrated several of the

[9] Taking all the references to wisdom in the Bible into account, including those in 1 Kings, Stéphanie Anthonioz (2016, 56) creates a similar list of types of sapiential knowledge: building and manufacturing (including of the tabernacle and temple), governance, and scribal concerns about writing, singing, or praying.

[10] For a detailed analysis of the complex image of Solomon presented in 1 Kings 3 in particular, see Nitsche 2015. Reading the text in its broader canonical context, and with particular attention to its connections with Proverbs, he notes, among other features, the king's relationship with the cult and his multifaceted wisdom, which involves distinguishing between good and evil, fearing God (cf. Prov. 1:1–7), and being loved by God (cf. Prov. 3:12), competent to rule (cf. Prov. 20:26), and young (153–88).

features of wisdom mentioned in 1 Kings, employing a definition of wisdom that Dell (2010, 35–6) argues is "too narrow." Instead, this reading will use those features to uncover a broader definition of wisdom in Proverbs, recognizing that it, as Dell writes, "is not a monochrome concept but has different manifestations."

7.2.2.1 Political Education

The first definition of wisdom in 1 Kings 1–11 is education for good governance. Solomon receives his wisdom in 1 Kings 3 after asking, "Give your servant therefore an understanding mind to *govern your people*" (1 Kgs. 3:9).[11] Even so, Crenshaw (2010, 44) declares that, in fact, "the putative 'wisdom' language [in 1 Kgs. 3:4–15] belongs to royal ceremony," and Scott (1960, 270) claims that this political type of wisdom "has nothing to do with the making of proverbs." However, those who argue significant sections of Proverbs, such as chs. 28–9 (Malchow 1985; Tavares 2007), if not the entire composition, commonly deal with the topic, were produced in a court setting, and were intended primarily to train courtiers would disagree with the disjunction Crenshaw and Scott create between the proverbial and the political (e.g., McKane 1970; Ansberry 2010). Passages such as Prov. 4:7–9; 8:14–16, 23 reflect the common ancient Near Eastern conviction that "wisdom was required in quite a special way by those who were charged with the duty of government" (Porteous 1960, 253–4; cf. von Rad 1972 [1970], 15–16; Ansberry 2010, 11–35).[12]

Along these lines, Whybray (1968, 95) argues that the records of political intrigue in the Succession Narrative (2 Samuel 9–20; 1 Kings 1–2) result from a deliberate effort "to illustrate specific proverbial teaching" for school pupils. Solomon's execution of his political rivals in 1 Kings 2, for example, demonstrates the "royal wisdom" of Prov. 20:26: "A wise king winnows the wicked, and drives the wheel over them" (Whybray 1968, 90). However, Crenshaw (1969, 138) counters, "It is difficult to see how any story could fail to 'illustrate' themes in Proverbs, for this book covers the whole gamut of human existence." Crenshaw's point is well taken, but it would work just as well to argue

[11] In 2 Chr. 1:10–11, the connection between wisdom and governance is even more pronounced.

[12] This does not exclude the contribution of other contexts, such as the family, tribe, or school to the composition of the book (see Fontaine 1993).

either that Job should not be considered Wisdom Literature, since it simply illustrates yet another theme from Proverbs (see Job 1:1, 8; 2:3; cf. Prov. 16:6; Saur 2011b, 239) or that Proverbs should not be cordoned off from the rest of the canon as distinct in its interests, since biblical stories abound in which proverbs are "writ large" (Van Leeuwen 1997, 24).[13]

Putting aside the problematic concept of Wisdom influence, Whybray has, in effect, created a grouping of historico-political texts consisting of Proverbs and the Succession Narrative, according to their common interest in wise government. The narrative in 1 Kings 3–11 could be added to this collection, removing the artificial boundary erected between the purported conclusion of the Succession Narrative in 1 Kings 2, where Solomon's "wisdom" is mentioned in vv. 6 and 9, and the account of his reign beginning in 1 Kings 3 (Gordon 1995, 104; see also Parker 1988). Though it must be acknowledged that the presentation of wisdom in these historical texts is rather ambiguous and even "divided" (Gordon 1995, 98), the same could be said of Job and Ecclesiastes. Like the Wisdom corpus, which incorporates a wide variety of smaller genres, interest in a common theme, in this case political training, ties these texts together, not formal similarity.[14] Reading Proverbs in this group of texts reveals the importance of that political theme in the book, and invites connections to other political texts, such as the Joseph narrative (von Rad 1953), the birth story of Moses (Childs 1965, 119–22), Esther (Talmon 1963), and the accounts of the courtly "sages" in the prophetic literature (Van Leeuwen 1990, 301).[15] Maurice Gilbert (2003, 17) draws this conclusion when he argues that Genesis 2–3, the Joseph story, the Succession Narrative, Solomon's Reign, the prophetic critique of the royal counselors in Isaiah and Jeremiah discussed below, and Ezekiel's criticism of the king of Tyre

[13] Abraham, for example, may be considered the "parent idéal" according to the proverbial model (Ska 2014) and the stories of Abigail and Nabal, Joseph and Potiphar's wife, and Tamar and Judah provide examples of the difference between wisdom and folly (Sneed 2011, 70). Wolff (1973, 120–3) includes the "edifying stories" of Jonah, Ruth, and Esther among the texts dedicated to wisdom and instruction.

[14] Murphy (1992b, 928) claims that von Rad's and Whybray's interpretations are mistaken because in both "one is dealing with a genre of history, not wisdom." Clearly, however, a genre can include multiple literary forms; otherwise, how could the Wisdom genre to which Murphy refers, with its aphorisms, narrative-framed dialogue, and so on, be justified?

[15] Thus Whedbee (1971, 122–6) argues that Isaiah's view of YHWH's counsel, through which he counters the court sages, is derived from "the older court wisdom" found in Proverbs, the Joseph Story, and the Court History of David (see, e.g., Gen. 50:20; 2 Sam. 17:14; Prov. 19:21; Isa. 14:24–27).

(Ezek. 28:1–19) form a group of texts that disputes a certain conception of power, which pretends to be wise without really practicing the teaching of the Wisdom sages. In 1 Kings 3–11, for example, Gilbert claims that even the wisdom of Solomon fails because of his political and religious extravagances. Whether or not a separate class of sages was responsible for teaching wisdom, Gilbert rightly observes that just political power was a crucial application of the concept. He claims, though, that these denouncements of false wisdom fail to make these texts sapiential. They maintain their narrative or oracular genres, he argues, even though he earlier acknowledged that the Wisdom texts do not themselves all share the same literary form (see Introduction: Wisdom as a Genre). If the classificatory paradigm is set aside, however, these texts could validly be collected as something else: political education, with Proverbs included among them.

7.2.2.2 Ethical Paraenesis

Second, 1 Kings 1–11 defines wisdom as ethical paraenesis. When Solomon asks for skill in governance, he requests forensic wisdom, the ability "to discern between good and evil" (1 Kgs. 3:9). The text puts this discernment in the context of the law, perhaps even beginning the association of Wisdom and Torah (Knauf 2016, 170), if the two were ever separate. Solomon's dream ends with the divine proclamation, "If you will walk in my ways, keeping my statutes and my commandments, as your father David walked, then I will lengthen your life" (1 Kgs. 3:14) (see Weinfeld 1972, 257). The broader account is widely considered to have a strong Deuteronomic cast, thereby creating "a textual conversation between wisdom and Torah" (Camp 2000, 147). When Solomon defies the Law in 1 Kings 9–11, his wisdom becomes folly, which suggests that efficacious wisdom must be subservient to the Law, at least as presented in Deuteronomy (Parker 1992). Solomon's behavior in Kings therefore violates the wisdom attributed to him in Prov. 3:7; wise in his own eyes, he fails to "fear the Lord and turn away from evil."[16]

While Deuteronomy equates wisdom with observance of the commandments (Deut. 4:6), the broader context of these words in Proverbs

[16] Compare Deut. 16:19–20, which, like Prov. 21:21, warns Israel's judicial authorities against relying on their self-acquired wisdom and instead implies that only pursuing a "righteousness" guided by the written Deuteronomic Torah will lead to judicial justice (Müller 2013, 30).

3 identifies wisdom, in effect, with observing the law (Blenkinsopp 1995, 156). Deuteronomy reverberates throughout Proverbs 3, in the emphasis on choosing life (3:8; cf. Deut. 4:40; 5:16; 11:9, 21), the mention of offering first fruits (3:9; cf. Deut. 14:22–9; 26:1–2), and allusions to the *Shema* (e.g., Prov. 3:3, 5; cf. Deut. 6:4–9) (see Overland 2000, 440; Anthonioz 2016, 45–6), which recur in Prov. 6:20–24 and 7:1–5 (Dell 2006, 170–6; Schipper 2013; Winkler 2017, 144–7). These features contribute to the widespread Deuteronomic flavor of Proverbs 1–9 (Delitzsch 1873, 29),[17] in which "instruction" may even refer to Deuteronomy itself (Weeks 2007, 103, 126, 172). Collectively, these allusions equate parental instruction with the will of YHWH and continue the parental transmission of the law initiated by Deuteronomy (see Prov. 3:12; Deut. 8:5; Brown 2005b, 272–8; Weeks 2007, 102–3; Schipper 2013, 60).

Further "echoes" of Deuteronomy also ring out across the rest of Proverbs. These include common references to the falsification of weights (Deut. 25:13–16; cf. Prov. 11:1; 20:23), moving property boundaries (Deut. 19:14; cf. Prov. 22:28; 23:10), treatment of slaves (Deut. 23:16; cf. Prov. 30:10), partiality in judgment (Deut. 1:17; cf. Prov. 24:23), and pursuit of righteousness (Deut. 16:20; cf. Prov. 21:21; see Weinfeld 1972, 265–74; Brown 2005b, 268–72; Dell 2006, 176–8). The repeated references to *torah* in 28:4–9 suggest a Deuteronomic background to the Hezekian collection (Prov. 25:1–29:27; Brown 2005b, 268–72), and allusions to Deuteronomy also appear in the Words of Agur in Proverbs 30 (e.g., Prov. 30:6; cf. Deut. 4:2; 13:1 [ET 12:32]; Fox 2009, 956–7; Saur 2014, 579).

These resonances between the two texts have contributed to the debate over whether Wisdom is derived from Law or vice versa (see Crenshaw 1992, 115–19). Diachronic speculation aside, Law and Wisdom clearly share similar ethical obligations (Scott 1961, 4), including a common concern for the welfare of society in general (Gerstenberger 1965, 49). This shared content is matched with formal similarities both between the casuistic case law and popular proverbial sayings and between apodictic commandments and sapiential instruction (Weeks 2010a, 138; see also Blenkinsopp 1995, 92, 151). Just as the proverb, the smallest and most basic sapiential form, may unite the Wisdom Literature, the admonitions, which are "essentially commands," associate Proverbs with the fundamental form of the legal material in the

[17] Accordingly, the scholarly work on the connections between the two texts is extensive. For bibliography, see Overland 2000, 425 n. 6.

Pentateuch (Sneed 2015b, 309).[18] Whether or not this "congruence in form and content" means "a common background for wisdom maxims and legal commandments can no longer be denied" (Gerstenberger 1965, 50), it certainly legitimates reading Proverbs together with legal texts such as Deuteronomy in a common literary grouping.

If wisdom and law are "two great rivers which eventually flow together and find their outlet in rabbinic writings and early Christian theology," then the "confluence" of those streams in Deuteronomy appears to be matched by a "comparable convergence" in Proverbs (Blenkinsopp 1995, 151, 118; Brown 2005b, 254). Deuteronomy equates wisdom with observance of the commandments (Deut. 4:6), just as Proverbs 1–9 identifies the law with wisdom (Prov. 3:5–8).[19] For Ronald Clements (1995, 283–4), the axiom "The Fear of the Lord is the beginning of wisdom" channels the two streams together, such that "*Torah* could be understood as a corpus of wisdom and, conversely, there could be no true apprehension of wisdom without the religious dimension contributed by *torah*." This is matched by a "sufficient overlap in instructional scope" between the two books to allow Brown (2005b, 253) to argue that they share a common conception of *torah*. Beyond Proverbs and Deuteronomy, indications of the confluence of wisdom and law are evident in the "Torah Psalms" (1; 19; 119), which mix affinities with Proverbs with torah piety, and the depiction of Daniel as a sage dedicated to the obedience of God's Law (Dan. 1; 2; 4–5) (Gilbert 2003, 17–18). This conjunction also appears in the identification of torah and wisdom in Ben Sira (15:1; 24:23), Baruch (3:9–4:4), and rabbinic Judaism (Schafer 2003).

Appropriately, then, a recent move toward reading the Law as ethical paraenesis has drawn it closer to the Wisdom Literature (Barton 2014, 21–2). Along these lines, Gammie (1990, 66, 51) argues that "the *entirety* of the books of Deuteronomy, Proverbs and Sirach may be assigned without any hesitation" to the genre "Paraenetic Literature," given

[18] Berend Gemser (1976 [1968], 144–6) counters Zimmerli's (1964 [1963], 152–3) view that, unlike the Law, Wisdom's "counsel" is not authoritative, but must rely on motive clauses to persuade. Philip Nel (1982) notes numerous similarities between the admonitions in Proverbs and Deuteronomistic law, particularly in their motivation clauses. See, e.g., Prov. 20:22; cf. Deut. 32:35 and Prov. 3:1–2; cf. Deut. 8:1; 30:16 (and 1 Kgs. 3:14!) (Nel 1982, 52, 59).

[19] Fox (2009, 952–3) argues, however, that Deut. 4:6 testifies to a conflict between Wisdom and Torah, in which Deuteronomy "effectively *subordinates*" Wisdom to Torah (emphasis original) and Proverbs "marginalizes" the Law. Either way, competition between the traditions only serves as further testimony to their overlapping aims.

their pervasive use of paraenesis, "a form of address which not only commends, but actually enumerates precepts or maxims which pertain to moral aspiration and the regulation of human conduct" (emphasis original). In his view, the Holiness Code (Leviticus 17–26) and Wisdom of Solomon could be included in this genre as well (55, 66). For Gammie, Proverbs has a closer generic affiliation to these other paraenetic texts than the rest of the Wisdom Literature, which he places in a different subdivision of "Reflective Essays."[20] Though Gammie's proposed genre is only one of many ways texts could be grouped in the Hebrew Bible, it does highlight a significant affinity between wisdom in Proverbs and legal texts.

7.2.2.3 Cultic Guidance

Providing a third definition of wisdom as cultic fidelity, 1 Kings also associates the concept with the building of the temple by presenting Solomon as "the wise master-builder" of God's house (Gordon 1995, 100; similarly, Nitsche 2015, 190–2). Hiram, king of Tyre, responds to Solomon's plan to build a house for the Lord by praising his wisdom (1 Kgs. 5:21 [ET 5:7]), potentially in recognition of his cultic piety (Winkler 2017, 334), and Hiram, the Tyrian craftsman, is filled with wisdom for the task of doing the building (1 Kgs. 7:14). Chronicles accentuates this cultic characterization of Solomon's wisdom (e.g., 2 Chr. 2:12; see Abadie 2008, 348–50).

This accords with the broader sapiential significance of architecture indicated by the close parallels between the descriptions of YHWH's foundation and filling of the earth (Prov. 3:19–20), the building and stocking of a house (Prov. 24:3–4), Hiram's construction of the temple (1 Kgs. 7:13–14), and Bezalel's crafting of the tabernacle (Exod. 31:1–3) (Van Leeuwen 2010). All these passages include the parallel terms "wisdom" (חכמה), "skill" (תבונה), and "knowledge" (דעת) in the same order in similar architectural contexts. Van Leeuwen argues that in the wider ancient Near Eastern conception of wisdom, all these types of construction were considered of a piece, interlocked like Russian dolls.[21] The "Western separation of theoretical and practical wisdom,"

[20] Similarly, Ryan O'Dowd (2010, 166) sees the presentation of "general admonitions for the conduct of the good life" uniting Proverbs with Deuteronomy over against the other "Wisdom" books, Job and Ecclesiastes.

[21] Markus Saur (2011b, 242) similarly traces how the personification of Wisdom develops chronologically across the repetitions of house-building imagery from Prov. 24:3 to 14:1 and then 9:1.

which contributes to the scholarly distinction between Wisdom Literature and the historical traditions of Israel, he contends, has fragmented this integrated presentation of reality and action "grounded in a creation suffused with the wisdom of God" (418–19).[22] Bálint Károly Zabán (2012), then, claims that the three speeches of Wisdom in Proverbs 1–9 (1:20-33; 8:1–36; 9:1–6) integrate the imagery of path, house, and treasure with the ancient Near Eastern imagery of building and filling a house to build these chapters into a cohesive argument around these pillars of the house of Wisdom.

Schwáb (2013, 190) takes this argument a step further and claims that the book of Proverbs as a whole "understands wise living as living in a temple." He is appropriately circumspect about whether this meaning was intended and skeptical of the attempt to find a replica of the architecture of Solomon's temple in the structure of the unified book (Skehan 1967). Nevertheless, he maintains that the temple-universe-wisdom topos found throughout the ancient Near East and across the Bible, from Genesis 1 onward, combined with the close connections between Proverbs and 1 Kings 1–11, suggest that the temple is the "hermeneutical key" for the book (Schwáb 2013, 202). Read together in the canon, the two texts suggest, "living wisely is like building a temple" (205).[23]

Schwáb (2013, 205–8) draws on similarities between Proverbs and a number of psalms to support his cultic interpretation of Proverbs.[24] Psalm 15, his prime example, is generally not considered a "Wisdom psalm," likely because it appears to be a cultic entrance liturgy. However, the qualifications it requires for the one who may abide in YHWH's tent and dwell on his holy hill (v. 1) are all ethical behaviors endorsed by Proverbs. These include "walking blamelessly" (הולך תמים; Ps. 15:2; Prov. 28:18) and not "doing harm" (רעה) to one's "neighbor" (רע) (Ps. 15:5; Prov. 3:29), both phrases uniquely used in these pairs of passages. According to

[22] For example, when Whybray (1974, 10–11) notes the common attribution of "wisdom" to God in the context of creation, which may be inspired by the concept's connection with building, he takes it simply as "a particular example of the use of a superior intelligence."

[23] Similarly, Camp (2000, 183) speaks of a shift in Proverbs "to the temple *as* the book that, in turn, is Wisdom's house" (emphasis original).

[24] Dell (2006, 181–5) likewise notes a broad range of connections between Proverbs and the Psalms and takes the existence of "wisdom psalms" as "[p]erhaps the most compelling evidence of mutual influence" between sapiential and cultic traditions (see also Dell 2000, 368–9).

Schwáb, therefore, as Proverbs advocates temple-worthy behavior, it sanctifies secular, everyday life, transforming it into liturgy, such that "[m]aking wise decisions becomes worship of Yahweh" (211–12).

Given the use in Proverbs of "the language of the priestly world," such as תועבה ("abomination"; 17:15; 20:10), divine רצון ("pleasure"; 11:1, 20; 12:22), and טהור ("clean"; 15:26) (Zimmerli 1964 [1963], 154), and the references to a range of cultic practices in the book, including sacrifice (15:8; 21:3; 21:27), prayer (15:29; 28:9), vows (20:25; 31:2), sacred lots (16:33), feasts (17:1), and the offering of first fruits (3:9–10), one might also argue that in Proverbs properly worshipping YHWH becomes a wise decision.[25] Solomon's extended prayer (1 Kgs. 8:22–53), his extravagant sacrifices (1 Kgs. 8:63), and the judgment levied against his idolatry (1 Kgs. 11:11) in the narrative suggest the same. Comparing these texts indicates wisdom and worship, creation and cult are more intertwined than modern conceptions of Wisdom Literature may lead one to believe.

7.2.2.4 Inspired Instruction

Finally, 1 Kings 1–11 defines wisdom as inspired instruction. Though Solomon's dream at Gibeon may have been originally intended to give temple-building instructions (Weinfeld 1972, 247–54; Hurowitz 1992, 165–6), as it now stands, it resonates with a prophetic call (1 Kgs. 3:7; cf. Jer. 1:5–6; Weinfeld 1972, 252). Moreover, Solomon's prayer at the dedication of the temple (1 Kgs. 8:22–53) is "prophetic" in its presentation of history (Ben Zvi 2013, 86). Early Jewish and Christian interpreters frequently refer to Solomon as a "prophet," which, Sheppard (2000, 389) argues, "confirms his appointment by God to 'write' and to 'testify,' like Moses (cf. Deut. 31:24–30)."

Through its attribution to this Solomon, who received his wisdom from God (1 Kgs. 3:12, 28; 4:29; 10:24), the book of Proverbs claims for itself an authority that comes not from human reason, but divine inspiration (Sneed 2015b, 254–5). As Prov. 2:6 declares, "The LORD gives wisdom; from his mouth come knowledge and understanding" (cf. 21:30). While affirming that true wisdom comes from God, Proverbs, like the prophets, is skeptical of autonomous human insight (Prov. 3:5–7;

[25] Perdue 1977, 145–6, 155–65; Brown 2005b, 262–3; Dell 2006, 178–80. Perdue (1977, 160) claims, "The wise were quite aware of cultic theology and were in accord with it," to which Brown (2005b, 263) adds, "[T]he sages drew from *cultic legislation* and actively endorsed cultic participation" (emphasis original).

9:10; 15:33; cf. Isa. 11:2–4; 33:5–6; Jer. 8:8–9; Whedbee 1971, 126; Van Leeuwen 1990, 300, 306; see Introduction: Wisdom Schools). This means that the sages cannot be distinguished from the prophets by the former's reliance purely on human reason (*contra* Rylaarsdam 1946, 70–2; Gilbert 2003, 14). In fact, this concern, repeated across the book's various sections, with establishing Proverbs' "divine backing" (*contra* Crenshaw 2010, 13) is consistent with ancient Near Eastern texts before Proverbs (Rylaarsdam 1946, 70–1; Clifford 1999, 9),[26] later texts associated with Wisdom, such as Ben Sira (1:1–10), which draws a parallel between prophecy and wise instruction (24:33; cf. 39:6; Blenkinsopp 1995, 163–4), and rabbinic interpretation.[27] The "suspiciously modern" separation of secular from theological thought, even if applied only to the earliest strata of Proverbs, would leave it radically distinct from this broader "Wisdom tradition" (Boström 1990, 36; see also Weeks 2010a, 115).

Though the Solomon to whom Proverbs is attributed may be a divinely called and inspired prophetic figure and the book may oppose autonomous human wisdom like the prophetic books, Proverbs lacks explicit verbal revelation (Fox 2009, 950). Proverbs never declares, "Thus says the Lord." Lady Wisdom, however, does cry out as a "bearer of revelation" (*Offenbarungsträger*) (von Rad 1972 [1970], 163). The "extensive prophetic portrayal" of this figure (Dell 2006, 161), both in Proverbs 8 and 1:20–33, where words from Jeremiah 7 and 20 are recontextualized (Harris 1995, 95), points to the authors' intent to enhance the authority of their teaching through presenting it prophetically (though calling it a "take-over" may be going too far; cf. Blenkinsopp 1995, 158–9).[28] Wisdom, as they present her, takes on the "mantel of the prophetess" and the authority that goes with it (Baumann 1996, 289).[29]

[26] The father in the Egyptian instruction Ptahhotep, for example, describes his teaching as the transmission across generations of a body of knowledge taught by the gods (Weeks 2016b, 15).

[27] Midrash Proverbs identifies "my instruction (*torah*)" and "my words" in Proverbs with divine speech (Fox 2009, 948) and b. Baba Batra 12a declares that prophecy has been transferred from the prophets to the sages (Blenkinsopp 1995, 159).

[28] Wise counsel could apparently rival the word of the prophet and the torah of the priest in divine authority. See, e.g., 2 Sam. 16:23; Jer. 18:18 (Kovacs 1974, 184–5; Gemser 1976 [1968], 214–16; Sneed 2011, 58). The contrast in authority between empirical observation and prophetic vision is a modern one (Whedbee 1971, 152–3; Weeks 2010a, 115–16).

[29] Given that, as Fox (2009, 949) acknowledges, Lady Wisdom "does have certain features of a prophet" (cf. Fox 2000, 104, 334), and her depiction in 1:20–33 is influenced by prophetic texts (Fox 2000, 105), he is overstating his case when he claims,

Whether the focus is on how Proverbs provides a practical outworking of prophetic instruction, as was often the case before the 1930s (Schwáb 2013, 14, 30), or on potential "Wisdom influence" on the prophets, as has tended to be the case since (Whybray 1982a, 195),[30] the similarities between Proverbs and the prophets are notable. In addition to their shared conviction that true wisdom comes from God, Proverbs also shares with the prophetic books a similar range of ethical concerns, including care for the poor (e.g., Prov. 14:21, 31; 29:7; cf. Amos 5:11–12; Jer. 5:28; Isa. 10:2) and the dangers of drunkenness (e.g., Prov. 23:29–35; cf. Isa. 5:11–13) (Delkurt 1993, 88–92, 114–22).[31] Like the prophets, Proverbs intertwines religion and morality by repeatedly critiquing "cold" cultic practices separated from such ethical behavior (Prov. 15:8, 29; 17:1; 21:3, 27; 28:9; cf. Amos 4:4–5; 5:4–7, 10, 21–27; Hos. 6:6; Isa. 1:10–17; Jeremiah 7; Murphy 1998, 274; Ernst 1994). This unity of piety and morality is evident in Proverbs' emphasis on righteousness (see section 7.2.1.1 *Sifrei Emet*), which it communicates by pairing "righteousness" (צדק), along with "justice" (1:3) (משפט), "key terms in the prophetic corpus," with "wisdom," "instruction," and "understanding" in its opening verses (Dell 2006, 162; see also Steiert 1990, 129–30; cf. 85–95).[32] Warnings against the "strange woman" in Proverbs 1–9 bring to mind the prominent prophetic use of adultery as a metaphor for idolatry, indicating that this image may be intended to enjoin both marital and religious fidelity.[33] Further, Proverbs shares with the prophets an emphasis on retribution (e.g., Isaiah 24), even individual retribution (e.g., Prov. 3:33; 10:3; cf. Ezekiel 18; Jer. 31:29–30; Rylaarsdam 1946, 56; Boström 1990, 153–4), order (e.g., Prov. 30:21–3;

"There is, however, no implication that her words are a message from God" (Fox 2009, 949). How better to imply that she is speaking a message from God than to intersperse prophetic allusions into her speech?

[30] For a recent survey of studies on this question, see Meek forthcoming.

[31] Delkurt's comparisons could profit from some more nuance, such as that offered by David Pleins (1987), though the opposition Pleins depicts between the two traditions is itself overstated (see Sandoval 2006, 187 n. 72; Lucas 2015, 291–311).

[32] William McKane (1970, 265) attributes this language to his proposed "prophetic reinterpretation of old wisdom" (cf. 10–22).

[33] Blenkinsopp 1995, 159; see also Marcus 1950–51, 165; Perdue 1977, 154–5; Camp 2000, 42. The strange woman also links Proverbs 1–9 with 1 Kings 1–11, since Solomon's fall there results from "his addiction to foreign women," and therefore invites Proverbs to be read as "a cautionary instruction of Solomon based on his own experience" (Blenkinsopp 1991, 457). Winkler (2017, 169–282) explores the connections between the two texts at length, drawing the prophetic parallels between adultery and idolatry into his discussion (e.g., 196–7, 231–3).

cf. Isa. 3:1–2; 5:8–10, 20; 29:15–16; Barton 2014, 95, 115–16), and the internalization of the Law (Prov. 2:10; cf. Jer. 31:33–4; Ezek. 11:19–20; 36:26–7; Weeks 2007, 112). Finally, the pronounced prophetic aspects of the Words of Agur (30:1–9), including its prophetic superscription (cf. Jer. 1:1; Amos 1:1) and designation as a משא ("oracle"; cf. Nah. 1:1; Hab. 1:1; Zech. 9:1; 12:1; Mal. 1:1), suggests a theological convergence between prophetic and sapiential circles (Saur 2014, 573–4; see also Sneed 2015b, 313).

Proverbs could be characterized along with the prophetic texts in the Hebrew Bible as divinely inspired instruction for righteous living. If the difference between inspired sage and prophet is "one of degree, not category" (Sneed 2015b, 56), then the same could certainly be said for the texts these groups purportedly produced. Proverbs itself acknowledges that "prophecy" (חזון) provides important "restraint" on behavior (Prov. 29:18).[34] If passages such as Prov. 11:4 ("Riches do not profit in the day of wrath, but righteousness delivers from death") or Prov. 21:3 ("To do righteousness and justice is more acceptable to the LORD than sacrifice") sound like they could be uttered by the prophets, and other passages such as Prov. 3:7 ("Do not be wise in your own eyes") actually are (Isa. 5:21), then further literary and theological connections between the texts are worth pursuing, whether or not historical influence can be demonstrated.[35]

7.2.3 Ancient Near Eastern Genres

Like Job and Ecclesiastes, Proverbs has also been placed in genres based on its affinities with ancient Near Eastern texts, which have likewise contributed to the eclipse of the book's canonical connections (Dell 2006, 14). Like Job, as well, the most prominent of these genre proposals only apply to parts of the book. However, Proverbs differs from Job in the ancient Near Eastern texts to which it has been compared, which draws into question the use of these comparisons to

[34] חזון appears in several instances (Isa. 1:1; Obad. 1; Nah. 1:1) as a label, not merely for the "visions" the prophets receive (e.g., Hos. 12:10), but also the texts associated with them (cf. Hab. 2:2).

[35] Von Rad (2001 [1957–60], 2:301–8) argued that the apocalyptic genre descended not from prophecy but Wisdom. The links between Proverbs and prophecy may suggest that this is a false dichotomy (see Blenkinsopp 1995, 174), but, nonetheless, there are still a number of profitable links between Proverbs and texts grouped together for their apocalyptic features, particularly in early Judaism. Space prevents exploring them here, but see Nickelsburg 2005.

justify a unified Wisdom genre.[36] Thus Prov. 10:1–22:16; 24:23–34; 25–29 are associated with "sayings collections" or "sentence literature," which were more common in Mesopotamia (e.g., the Sumerian proverb collections in Alster 1997), while Prov. 1–9; 22:17–24:22; 31:1–9 are linked with father–son instructions, more popular in Egypt (e.g., Instruction of Amenemope, Instruction of Any).[37] Though comparing Proverbs to texts like these has opened new vistas on its meaning (see, e.g., Shupak 2015), these two types cannot be clearly delineated; direct, parental address occasionally appears in the "sayings" (e.g., Prov. 19:27), as do collections of aphorisms in the "instructions" (e.g., Prov. 3:32–35) (Weeks 2010a, 24–5).[38] Demotic advice literature and Aḥiqar have a similar mix, and so, as for these texts, Weeks (2010a, 25) concludes that the original editors of Proverbs collected these materials because they perceived them to be closely related. He, therefore, opts for a more general genre label: "advice literature." The use of a broader classification such as this to justify collecting together the diverse material in the book suggests to Weeks (2010a, 47) that the modern Wisdom Literature category "may not be wholly a later imposition on the texts," even if it does not correspond to it.

Proverbs can profitably be compared to other advice literature as long as its content and convictions are not simply limited to what those texts contain. This grouping is less helpful if that "advice" is understood broadly enough to include Job, since its field of vision would be so wide, potentially including every book in the Hebrew Bible, that it would bring little into focus (see section 5.1.2 Theological Abstraction). Similarly, classifying Proverbs simply as a "collection" (Murphy 1981, 50) would put it in a category that includes texts as diverse as the Epic of Gilgamesh, Atrahasis, and Enuma Elish in the ancient Near East, along with the Pentateuch, the Deuteronomic History, and Isaiah (Clifford 1999, 2). Even if not an especially helpful genre designation, the collected

[36] Aḥiqar is compared to both Job and Proverbs, but only partially in each case, with the similar parts not overlapping.

[37] Proverbs may not fit the instruction genre as well as scholars widely assume (Vayntrub 2016). Weeks (2007, 176) argues that comparisons with foreign instructions offer, at most, a very shallow basis for understanding Proverbs 1–9, while the work's "Jewish roots" provide a hermeneutical key to its interpretation.

[38] Clifford (1997, 44–5) claims that *mashal* (משל), the first Hebrew word of the book, identifies its genre. However, due to its broad use in the Hebrew Bible, from Balaam's "oracle" (Num. 23:7) to Isaiah's "taunt" against the king of Babylon (Isa. 14:4) and Ezekiel's eagle "allegory" (Ezek. 17:2), the term does not likely designate "a single genre or category" (Fox 2000, 54).

nature of Proverbs has hermeneutical effects that must be taken into account (Hatton 2008, 47–82). Proverbs 1–9 at the beginning and the Words of Agur toward the end together draw the book as a whole into the broader theological discourse of the canon (Schwáb 2013, 84–5; Saur 2014, 582–3).

7.3 NETWORK APPROACH

Fox (2009, 948) observes that interpreters respond to the apparent silence of Proverbs in regard to specifically Israelite doctrines found elsewhere in the Hebrew Bible "by appealing to allusions, intertextuality, and allegory in order to uncover the expected beliefs." Though I have drawn on such arguments above, my approach is different. I agree with Bruce Waltke (2004, 1:64–5) that Proverbs' lack of integration with the rest of the Hebrew Bible is "more superficial than real," but not because of the common appeal to the "fear of the Lord" or the list of parallels he provides between the attributes and actions ascribed to God in Proverbs and in the Pentateuch. I also concur with Scott Harris (1995, 24–5) when he opposes "comparative models for interpretation into which Proverbs is made to fit" that locate the book "primarily as a wisdom text in an international context," but not because "numerous internal markings," including the attribution to Solomon and a number of inner-biblical allusions "scattered throughout" Proverbs 1–9 indicate the book's "intended location within the canon." I agree with Dell (2006, 185), too, that the proverbs should be freed from the "contextual straitjacket in which they have been traditionally confined" by scholars "trying to match a social context to a genre of material." In my estimation, she also rightly claims, "Proverbs is more unified with other parts of the Old Testament . . . than scholars have generally allowed" (188). However, my agreement is not primarily inspired by the "echoes" of and "interconnections" with texts associated with different social contexts that she discovers throughout the book.[39]

Each of these interpreters attempts to counter the separation and marginalization of Proverbs, but does not question its cause, the

[39] Dell's work does effectively address the "old idea that needs to be laid to rest" that "the 'professions' of priest, prophet and sage were not only clearly distinct but fundamentally opposed to one another" (Grabbe 1993, 60; see also Sneed 2011).

invention of the Wisdom Literature category itself. Instead, the division between Proverbs, as a Wisdom book, and the rest of the Hebrew Bible is not "real" because the very distinction is a scholarly construct, one subjective way of construing the book's similarities with one group of texts and its differences with others. The dichotomy between reading Proverbs in an international or canonical context is a false one, which relies on an outmoded approach to genre, in which Proverbs must be "made to fit" into one group of comparative texts or another. Proverbs' sapiential "straitjacket" only exists when a commitment to matching genre with social context does not "allow" interpretive connections across those boundaries. "False problems are raised by a rigid plotting of genres" (Murphy 1981, 3), and the marginalization of Proverbs and the rest of the Wisdom Literature from the remainder of the Hebrew Bible is one of them. "Ultimately the alleged incompatibility of wisdom and Yahwism is a logical creation (and Western logic, at that), and it is not real" (Murphy 1975, 118). Rather than gathering new weapons (or dusting off old ones) to defeat the monster in the closet, one can simply open the door and turn on the light.

Faced with attempts like those of Waltke, Harris, and Dell to sew Proverbs back into the fabric of biblical theology, Fox (2009, 948) wonders why "one would expect every book in the Bible to have everything." After all, he writes, "A canon ... is more than the sum of its parts. In it, the parts work together to create and convey religious ideas in a new synthesis that would have been foreign to the original authors." Van Leeuwen (1997, 21), on the other hand, argues, "Like most books, Proverbs does not reveal the full range of its authors' concerns." As a result, the silence on redemptive history in this and other Wisdom writings is "a function of their genre and purpose, and too much should not be concluded concerning the isolation of the sages from Israel's historical traditions." Whether Proverbs can be reconciled with the rest of the canon in the minds of its readers or in the minds of its authors, its distinction from that canon as part of Wisdom Literature only exists in the minds of its critics—it is "a new synthesis that would have been foreign to the original authors." Old Testament theology understood exclusively from the perspective of the history, institutions, and cult of Israel (e.g., Zimmerli 1964 [1963], 151) excludes the Wisdom books by definition (Toombs 1955, 195–6; see also Murphy 1975, 123). Similarly, definitions of Wisdom Literature based on how it differs from other types of biblical literature (e.g., Sneed 2015b, 212), circularly forestall any attempt at *rapprochement* between them from the outset. The longer these definitions influence the interpretation of the so-called Wisdom books, the more distinct they are going to appear, along with any tradition or movement associated with them.

I am not arguing that the entire Hebrew Bible is saying the same thing, breaking down all genre boundaries, or enveloping everything within Wisdom, Deuteronomism, or anything else. I am proposing that the texts can be grouped in a number of different ways, which has the effect, not of removing those boundaries as much as revealing that they are imaginary. Conceptual "borderlines" like these are contingent and transient (Breed 2014, 12). This actually encourages the drawing of more boundaries, though temporary and permeable ones, noting the affinities Proverbs has with other groups of texts, such as the "paraenetic literature," which sets it apart from Ecclesiastes and Job. This is not an attempt to flatten out the diverse terrain of the Hebrew Bible, but to tear down the neat terraces into which scholars have sculpted it. Once the critical presupposition of a separate, self-encompassing Wisdom genre is recognized for what it is—one of many textual groupings in which Proverbs may be read—then the interlocking network of "genres" in the book begins to emerge.

According to the reigning consensus, Proverbs is Wisdom Literature. And yet, Proverbs does not merely invite comparison with Ecclesiastes and Job, but political, legal, cultic, and prophetic texts as well. Weeks (2007, 174), for example, argues that Proverbs 1–9 participates in a broader Persian and early Hellenistic Jewish milieu, in which Deuteronomy associates wisdom with law (Deut. 4:6), Isaiah connects it to the knowledge and fear of YHWH (Isa. 11:2; 33:6), and Jeremiah sets it in the context of divine creation (Jer. 10:12; 51:15). Understanding Proverbs and the wisdom it seeks to communicate through such connections shines new light on both, so that facets obscured by the Wisdom Literature category can sparkle again. Given the diversity of genres already included in the Wisdom category, such as dialogue and fictional autobiography, refusing to group Proverbs with other texts due to formal differences would be special pleading. The category's formal diversity indicates its ultimately thematic foundation, which invites other thematic comparisons like those briefly explored above. Also, since the concerns of a purported class of ancient sages are derived from the contents of the category, using those commitments to exclude further texts would be circular (see Van Leeuwen 2003, 73). The Solomonic attribution does not cordon Proverbs off from the rest of the canon (*contra* Childs), but instead draws the book into the complex intertextual network represented in the description of the wise king in 1 Kings, which provides a definition of wisdom in which politics and prophecy, intellect and piety, the secular and the sacred intersect. As interpreters have noted some of these features in Proverbs, they have pointed to the potential of reading the book in multiple intertextual groupings rather than solely as Wisdom. They have also demonstrated the variegated nature of Proverbs and the wisdom it describes. The compilers of 1 Kings 1–11 were a step ahead of them.

Conclusion

> What the specialization of our age suggests, in one example after another, is not only that fragmentation is a disease, but that the diseases of the disconnected parts are similar or analogous to one another. Thus they memorialize their lost unity, their relation persisting in their disconnection. Any severance produces two wounds that are, among other things, the record of how the severed parts once fitted together.
>
> (Berry 2002, 106)

The Wisdom Literature category is dead. But this book is not its *coup de grâce*. It could not be. A culturally resonant collective construct is too large and amorphous to be dispensed with in a single blow. The moment can never be clearly identified, but at some point the construct loses its explanatory power and thus its vitality, inhibiting thought rather than inspiring understanding. The transition from one paradigm to another is painful, so the death rattle of a construct is often long and loud, but it should not be mistaken for the breath of life.

This book is closer to a coroner's report but is not quite that either. A coroner focuses on the moment of death. The search for a cause may lead somewhat earlier, but rarely to the subject's birth, unless the deceased has fallen victim to some genetic abnormality. I have argued that the Wisdom category has finally succumbed to weaknesses inherent in its very nature, bequeathed by those who gave it birth, but, unlike a coroner's report, I have sought to tell more of Wisdom's life-story. But this has not been a biography either. A biography recounts the life of its subject; death is often incidental, an afterthought, even absent when the subject is still living. My purpose, however, has not been to understand Wisdom's life, but its death.

Coroners are not asked to reflect on what follows the deceased's departure. Their concern is the dead, not those who live on. Biographers may address the state of the world that their subjects leave behind, but in so doing risk pressing beyond their purview. A eulogist's purpose, however, is explicitly to address those who survive, who have loved and lost. Though death creates the occasion for a eulogy, the topic is often studiously avoided, along with the faults of the departed. Though in the second half of this book I have shared the eulogist's aim to create new life out of loss, lacking a casket to gesture toward, I have had to focus without pity on the category's failures and death. To avoid perpetuating the hermeneutical distortions Wisdom has created, the field must recognize that the taxonomic category has been detrimental and is now dead.

Though this study shares certain salient affinities with each of those genres (and several other more traditional academic ones as well), I envision it primarily as an obituary. It tells the story of the Wisdom Literature category from the perspective of its death. In so doing, it sets Wisdom in the context of its ancestors and descendants and recounts some of its most influential accomplishments. Of course, it diverts from the genre in various ways (as every text does), not least in its length and subject matter. The account of its subject's birth and the illness that plagued its final days also receives more attention than most obituaries would allow, but these factors contribute crucially to the current impact of Wisdom. As Peter Utley, obituary editor for *The Times of London*, declares, "An obituary should be an exercise in contemporary history, not a funeral oration" (quoted in Clines 1987). The new approach to genre in Part II and its application to the three so-called Wisdom books in Part III admittedly fit rather uncomfortably into the obituary genre. However, their purpose, in part, is to encourage readers finally to let the category go, since old paradigms are more difficult to discard when nothing is available to take their place, even if, as I anticipate, this initial venture into a new mode of interpretation will be in need of further refinement.

THE OBITUARY

This obituary for Wisdom Literature began in chapter 1 The Rise and Impending Demise of Wisdom Literature: The Modern Scholarly Wisdom Tradition and the Threat of Pan-Sapientialism with the category as it has now become familiar—a confounding collection of weakness and strength, of foreignness and familiarity. Due to the category's conflicted character, scholarly interest in Wisdom Literature has waxed and waned over the past century. The debate over the category's limits focuses the question of its definition. Wisdom's expansion across the canon reached an initial peak in the proliferation of "Wisdom influence" studies in the 1960s. Despite efforts to limit its spread, in recent scholarship, Wisdom, once marginalized as a "foreign body," has extended both across the Hebrew Bible and to the "heart of the Israelite experience of God." Despite providing the appearance of health, this expansive defiance of definitional limitations threatens the meaningfulness of the category itself. As in the similar expansion of Wisdom in scholarship on the Dead Sea Scrolls, ancient Near Eastern texts, and the Psalter, attempts to define and delimit Wisdom resort eventually to the scholarly consensus on which texts make up the category's core. This pan-sapiential tendency shares a number of the struggles that contributed to the pan-Deuteronomic epidemic identified nearly two decades ago. For Wisdom Literature, this reliance on an unexamined consensus presented the most pressing problem, since this scholarly construct serves as the category's foundation.

Something was not right with Wisdom Literature, and diagnosing its malady required identifying the construct's origin. To do so, the category had to be distinguished from its ancient ancestors, with which it is often confused. Chapter 2 The Ancestry of Wisdom Literature: Ancient Tradition or Modern Invention?, therefore, evaluated the purported early "vestiges" of the category in Patristic, rabbinic, and medieval interpretation. However, the ancient literary collections often associated with the modern Wisdom category contain different groups of texts, which reflects the differing criteria used to form them. None of the evidence to which scholars appeal, whether Hebrew or Greek structures of the canon, the association of texts with Solomon, the ancient recognition of common traits between them, or the title "Wisdom," corresponds quantitatively or qualitatively to Wisdom Literature as it is now understood. This indicated that the category is a modern invention, and the accuracy of its depiction of ancient phenomena therefore merited more careful scrutiny than it had yet received.

When, where, and to whom the subject is born are questions every obituary inevitably addresses. For Wisdom Literature, answering these questions in chapter 3 The Birth of Wisdom Literature: The Nineteenth-Century Origin of the Wisdom Corpus also offered insight into why the category appeared. Johann Bruch's *Weisheits-Lehre der Hebräer* (1851) was the first work to draw together a developing concept of a Wisdom genre and present it systematically and comprehensively. However, the scholars who influenced his views demonstrate their own philosophical influences from the likes of Kant, Herder, Fries, Schleiermacher, and Hegel. If biblical scholarship, in the form of Johann Bruch, was Wisdom's father, then post-Enlightenment continental philosophy was her mother. The "non-theocratic spirit" of "free thought" that Bruch argued could be found in the Wisdom texts combines many of the philosophical ideas that the biblical scholars who influenced Bruch had themselves imbibed as they served as a collective womb for Wisdom's gestation. As the "universalistic, humanistic, philosophical" collection within the Old Testament, the Wisdom corpus addressed the Christian struggle that Kant had identified to extract "a purely moral religion" out of the "old worship" of Judaism, which he characterized as dogmatic, theocratic, legalistic, and particularistic. The abstraction necessary to justify a category that included texts as diverse as Proverbs, Ecclesiastes, and Job enabled scholars to import their own presuppositions into their interpretation.

Those presuppositions were only reinforced by the existence of the category itself. This, as chapter 4 The Universe of Texts: The Intertextual Network of Genres from Multiple Perspectives argued, is one of the hermeneutical dangers of a taxonomic approach to genre. Once a text is defined as a member of a particular genre, that genre creates a "horizon of expectation" for its interpretation that excludes other potential intertextual connections. Therefore, I proposed a new nominalist approach for addressing the question of genre, setting aside the long-reigning realist, taxonomic understanding in biblical scholarship. I defined genres simply as groups of texts gathered together due to some perceived significant affinity between them. However, to understand the complex process through which genres develop, I drew on theories of intertextuality, networks, emergence, and conceptual blending. I then re-envisioned genres as constellations in three-dimensional space, which gain their significance from culturally situated viewpoints, as readers group texts according to culturally resonant affinities. Any given text may therefore contribute to multiple genres, and only through recognizing those genres is its full meaning, its true location in the vast textual network, evident. Seen this way, genres still illuminate similarities and differences between texts, but they do not restrict them to a single horizon of expectation.

The Wisdom Literature category, then, is only one of the ways that texts may be grouped together within the Hebrew Bible. It recognizes certain salient affinities between its three core texts, most prominently their shared interest in חכמה ("wisdom"), but it hardly exhausts their meaning. Grouping each text with other texts, as was done before the category appeared, would reveal other significant features of each that transcend the boundaries set by the Wisdom category. What made the characteristics that define Wisdom Literature significant enough to generate a separate genre category in the nineteenth century appear not to have had the same significance in earlier interpretation and may not even have stood out to the texts' original authors and readers. They need not restrict the textual connections that readers in different cultural contexts make today.

The final three chapters of the book sought, therefore, to map the intertextual networks in which Job, Ecclesiastes, and Proverbs may be interpreted when they are viewed from multiple perspectives, rather than exclusively treating Wisdom Literature as the "stationary earth" from which to view the universe of texts. Though comparing Proverbs, Ecclesiastes, and Job to one another reveals important features they all share, exclusively reading them this way as members of the Wisdom Literature category restricts their meaning through canonical separation, theological abstraction, and hermeneutical limitation. Considering these texts independently of that category allows the numerous other genre groupings that respond to their unique mix of literary features to be seen. Each text is particularly helpful for communicating one of the three features of genres highlighted in the genre theory of chapter 4—that genres are selective, self-reflective, and subjective—while all demonstrate how multiplying genre perspectives transforms these weaknesses into hermeneutical strengths.

Job is embedded in a particularly dense intertextual network. Throughout history, readers have associated the book with other textual groupings. Appreciating fully Job's distinctiveness requires not reading it as *sui generis* and therefore independently of the many literary categories in which it could be placed, but as *plurium generum* and in relationship with as many genres as its content and form justify. These include genre designations applied before the Wisdom category's development, such as poetry, prophecy, and drama, as well as those produced by ancient Near Eastern parallels, such as exemplary-sufferer texts. In recent scholarship, some earlier genres have been resurrected, along with proposed adapted genres, such as dramatized lament or lawsuit drama, and meta-genres, such as parody, citational text, and polyphony. Each of these textual groupings reveals some salient feature of the book and thus combining them reveals the complexity and nuance of its meaning.

While Job demonstrates particularly well how texts are best understood in terms of their manifold genres, the numerous, often contrasting interpretations Ecclesiastes has inspired across history provide a clear example of the mirrored character of genres. Readers have consistently looked into the ambiguous and contradictory book to admire their own reflections or repudiate those of their opponents. It is easy to look back on some of these proposals—the rabbinic view that Qoheleth is actually praising the joy of studying Torah, for example—and reject them as self-interested eisegesis. But what defends the Wisdom interpretation from a similar charge? Rather than dismissing these readings completely, Wisdom included, because of their subjectivity, it is more profitable to understand each as a partial and selective perspective responding to some potential of the text. Whether inspired by the traditional collections before Wisdom Literature, intertextual links to other canonical genres, parallels to texts from across the ancient Near East, or comparisons based on the book's literary features, such as form, tone, or content, each genre proposal reveals something about the nature of the text while falling short of comprehending the whole. Illuminating all the contours of the text's rugged terrain while dispelling the "misleading shadows" of self-interested exegesis will require engaging with more rather than less of the subjective perspectives on its meaning.

The selective and self-reflective nature of genres as demonstrated with Job and Ecclesiastes clear the ground to appreciate the subjective nature of Wisdom even for Proverbs. Despite the undeniable importance of the concept of wisdom to Proverbs, reading the book as Wisdom Literature is still limiting. The obviousness of its Wisdom classification has discouraged attempts to explore alternative textual groupings, however. Recognizing that it is a modern projection onto the text encourages the potential hermeneutical value of other genre groupings to be reconsidered. Though, like Ecclesiastes, the pre-modern groupings for the book are more stable and limited than they were for Job, each provides forgotten nuances, such as its focus on righteousness or poetic presentation. Proverbs' widespread inclusion in a Solomonic collection invites comparison with the account of his reign in 1 Kings 1–11, which offers another pre-modern perspective on

Proverbs' intertextual potential. The variegated presentation of wisdom in the account of Solomon's reign associates the concept with political, legal, cultic, and prophetic texts, matching the intersection of potential genre groupings evident in Proverbs as well. The Wisdom Literature category has contributed to the muted discussion of these features in the book. Realizing that it is a modern construct and therefore not "real," however, invites the interpretive value of further genre groupings such as these to be resurrected and reconsidered.

Though I endeavored to map the intertextual networks in which each of these books has been read as comprehensively as possible, I could not hope to exhaust the semantic capacities recognized in each by readers across history. Much future research remains to be done, particularly into non-Western readings of these texts.[1] Given my comprehensive aim, I was also unable to engage in thorough criticism of these various views. Like Wisdom, each reveals something about the nature of the text but is also limited in its vision and should be evaluated to determine where the limits lie. I also have not investigated deeply into the viewpoint from which those genre constellations were created, as I did for Wisdom. As long as the subjectivity of all these proposals is recognized (which has not often been the case for Wisdom), what each perspective sees in the text is more important than where it views the text from and why, though these questions are also worth pursuing.

THE REVITALIZATION OF WISDOM

This relativization of Wisdom could lead to the revitalization of both its contents and the concept of wisdom itself. Reading all three so-called Wisdom texts in their intertextual networks offers new opportunities to reconsider not only the interpretation of those texts, but the concept that has united them for more than a century. Job's invitation of the concept of wisdom into its wide-ranging debate, Ecclesiastes's own relativization of wisdom, and the diverse network in which Proverbs, along with 1 Kings 1–11, puts the concept all challenge its

[1] See, e.g., the discussion of Proverbs in dialogue with the Confucian classics (Hancock forthcoming) or African proverbs (Masenya and Olojede forthcoming) in *Reading Proverbs Intertextually* (Dell and Kynes forthcoming).

limited characterization. Just as the category was unable to encompass these texts, Wisdom Literature could never hope to contain the conception of wisdom. It attempted to do so by closely associating the texts with the concept, so that controlling one was controlling the other, but both were too dynamic for this approach to be sustainable. Instead interpreters were forced to stretch Wisdom more broadly, but as they did so its weaknesses became increasingly evident until it could no longer be sustained.

If Proverbs is primarily about wisdom, and the way Proverbs, like any text, is interpreted is dependent on the group of texts between which its meaning is found, then, as Proverbs' meaning in different groupings is explored, new facets of the concept at the heart of its message will be revealed. For example, the "theological discourse" on the "fear of the Lord" with which Proverbs associates wisdom among the Wisdom texts (see Saur 2011b, 238–42) gains new significance if Mount Sinai (Exod. 20:20; Deut. 4:10) or the doom threatened by the prophets (e.g., Isa. 8:13; Jer. 5:22) contributes to it. The "multiperspectivity" Saur (2011b, 249) documents among and even within the Wisdom books should not be circumscribed to the category (as the Words of Agur indicate; Saur 2014), but include texts across the Hebrew Bible and, due to the texts' open nature (Saur 2011b, 248), their interpreters as well.

The Wisdom books are not grouped together on the basis of purported authorship, date of composition, common literary form, or even ancient tradition: they must be grouped together on the basis of shared subject matter as perceived by modern readers. But the content of a text is always interpreted, and could be interpreted otherwise. Is wisdom really the primary topic with which Job or even Ecclesiastes is concerned? Though the attempt is made to transform this subjective judgment into an objective one by pointing to the incidence of the word "wisdom," why is that word exclusively chosen? What about "righteousness" or "wickedness" or הבל? Though comparisons are made with ancient Near Eastern texts to distance these decisions from the modern perspective, the comparative choices are modern ones made according to modern criteria as well. Appeals are also made to the shared lack of reference to Israel's history and cult, but why is this criterion chosen? Once it is, it circularly guarantees that this will be a characteristic of the category. Why, though, are other texts that are similar in this regard (e.g., Genesis 1–11, Song of Songs, Esther) left out? Weeks (2010a, 140) warns against "making a lazy assumption that all wisdom is essentially one phenomenon" and thereby constructing an "artificial bridge" between Wisdom and apocalyptic due to their limited affinities. However, the assumption that Israelite wisdom conforms to our modern definition involves a similar indolence.[2] Having gathered together texts that would reflect their modern ideals, it is little surprise that biblical scholars have faced serious difficulties defining them on another basis or integrating them into the ancient theology of the Hebrew Bible.

An intertextual network approach would, in effect, involve a reversal of the current approach to Wisdom and its influence. Currently, scholars operate with a narrow (yet unclear) definition of Wisdom Literature based on the shared traits of Proverbs, Ecclesiastes, and Job, to which has been added a broad understanding of Wisdom's influence, in which this narrow understanding is discovered in texts across the Hebrew Bible. Even attempts to investigate afresh the term's meaning across the canon end up restricting it to an Israelite "intellectual tradition" (see Introduction: Wisdom as a Concept). Because the Wisdom category, even if not jettisoned, must be admitted to stand on quite shaky foundations, the interpretations of texts across the Hebrew Bible built upon it are sure to totter.

However, as von Rad (2001 [1957–60], 1:428) argues, "Any sound discussion of Israel's wisdom means taking the concept as broadly as it was indeed taken." He laments that wisdom, which "has to do with the whole of life and had to be occupied with all its departments," has been "thought of more or less as the product of an exclusive theological school." Therefore, I propose understanding the definition of wisdom as a concept broadly, based on the role of the concept and the diverse traits associated with it in the variety of texts in which they appear, and not necessarily united in a singular distinct worldview. Though broad and diffuse, this definition would be tied closely to the text instead of sitting high in abstraction on a wobbly scaffolding of scholarly presupposition. In this reversal, our understanding of the concept's "influence" (to the degree that influence could be attributed to a concept rather than a hypothetical "movement") would become narrow.[3] It would not even encompass the entirety of texts in which it appears

[2] Interpreters do, of course, attempt to contrast the biblical understanding of the concept wisdom from modern views and the Hebrew word חכמה from the English word "wisdom" (e.g., Fox 2000, 28–38), but they do so in the context of a Wisdom category built on modern assumptions about the nature of wisdom.

[3] Murphy (1992b, 928) makes a similar proposal that "wisdom influence be narrowly conceived," though I would not merely argue, as he does, that "the sapiential

prominently but only contribute, along with other factors in the Israelite conception of reality, to the interpretation of those texts. This, in effect, would treat wisdom (now with a lowercase "W") as a concept, similar to "holiness" or "righteousness," instead of as a genre, movement, or tradition. Thus, instead of starting with the ill-defined, circularly justified, modernly developed, and extrinsically imposed corpus of Wisdom Literature for the definition of the concept and then extending the search across the canon, this would involve beginning with the concepts now associated with Wisdom as they appear across the canon, and even throughout the ancient Near East, and then investigating how they contribute to the so-called Wisdom Literature and other texts as well.

This would be more like the interpretation of wisdom and the so-called Wisdom books before the Wisdom category developed (see chapter 2 The Ancestry of Wisdom Literature: Ancient Tradition or Modern Invention?). This approach would also solve many of the problems that Weeks notes with the current understanding of Wisdom Literature. It would reflect the fact that arguments for Wisdom influence generally find that influence in texts written before the Wisdom Literature (Weeks 2010a, 136). The relatively late date of the Wisdom texts makes it all the more "odd" that "wisdom might have had influence outside, but never itself been influenced from outside" (Dell 2006, 14). Beginning the study of the Israelite conception of wisdom with its appearance in earlier texts, and then seeing how these ideas have influenced the so-called Wisdom books would better represent the chronology of the composition of the Hebrew Bible.

Treating wisdom as a concept instead of a genre would also avoid vexing questions regarding the point at which content associated with wisdom in a text tips the balance and makes something a "Wisdom text," since this taxonomic classification would no longer exist.[4] This approach would also reflect the fact that, as Weeks (2010a, 142) says, it is "difficult to find anything in the wisdom literature as a whole which is not found elsewhere as well." Additionally, it would fit well the integrated scribal setting he posits for Wisdom on the basis of comparison with ancient Near Eastern cultures (130).

understanding of reality" was widespread in Israel, but that the Israelite conception of wisdom was broader than modern characterizations of the movement allow.

[4] Weeks (2010a, 85) asks this question in regard to the instructions in Tobit 4, but it could be asked for many other texts, including the so-called "Wisdom psalms" (see section 1.4.1 Wisdom in the Psalter).

Finally, taking this approach avoids the speculation that over a century of biblical scholarship has not been able to support with evidence definitive enough to provide scholarly consensus. It would admittedly limit our ability to draw conclusions about the historical setting of conceptions of wisdom, since the placement of texts into discrete genres is a primary contributing factor to current investigations into that issue, but it is far better to be able to say a few things that can be justified by the evidence we have than a great deal that cannot. The new theological and literary potential of this approach would account for the historical loss until either new historical evidence arises or a new method is developed for drawing it from the texts.[5]

Wisdom Literature takes with it to its grave an extensive conceptual and paratextual apparatus—a purported ancient Israelite movement and current scholarly and publishing conventions that cordon off from the rest of the canon the so-called Wisdom books and those who wrote them and continue to write about them. Its jealous efforts at canonical separation, theological abstraction, and hermeneutical limitation need no longer constrain the texts that became entangled with it. Wisdom is just one of many genre groupings responding to shared affinities between these texts and others. It may be *a* genre but it is not *the* genre of these texts. They are not "Wisdom Literature" in any definitive, categorical sense that would justify the assumption that they were composed in a separate school with a distinctive theology that requires its own introductions, specialists, or conference sessions any more than grouping texts on their interest in other concepts, such as righteousness or holiness, would. Even as constructs, genres can have these types of real effects in the world as they shape readers' expectations (Fox 2015, 78), which makes their uncritical use hermeneutically dangerous (see section 5.1.1 Canonical Separation). As the Wisdom corpus is laid to rest in the dust, the network of canonical constitutive elements from which it came, it will reintegrate, as bodies do, into those same elements. From canon it was and to canon it will return. After the death of the Wisdom Literature category, it is through this intertextual reintegration that both the concept of wisdom and the texts associated with it will be reborn.

[5] For a recent effort along these lines, see Vayntrub forthcoming a.

APPENDIX

Ps. 107:40 and Job 12:21, 24 in Commentaries on the Psalms and Job

The table below provides an overview of the discussion of the close lexical parallel between Ps. 107:40 and Job 12:21, 24 throughout interpretive history. The works in bold print appeared in the period between the publication of Gunkel's commentary on the Psalms in 1926, which solidified form criticism's influence on Hebrew Bible studies, and Fishbane's *Biblical Interpretation in Ancient Israel* in 1985, which re-injected attention to inner-biblical allusion into study of the Hebrew Bible. "Cf." denotes a comparison made without a view expressed on dependence. Italics indicate works that address Psalm 107 or parallel texts in Job but are not strictly commentaries. Dates in brackets are the edition referenced if significantly later than the original. Due to space constraints, these works are not included in the bibliography unless they are cited in the main text of this book.

Psalms			Job		
Date	Commentary	Alluding text	Date	Commentary	Alluding text
5th c.	Augustine [1993]	N/A	4th c.	Chrysostom [1990]	N/A
5th c.	Theodoret [2001]	N/A	6th c.	Olympiodor [1984]	N/A
6th c.	Cassiodorus [1991]	N/A	13th c.	Aquinas [1989]	N/A
16th c.	Calvin [1993]	N/A	16th c.	Calvin [1993]	Cf.
1766	Hare	Psalm	*1685*	*Le Clerc*	Job
1789	*Schnurrer*	N/A	1752	Chappelow	Cf.
1823	Rosenmüller	Job	1812	Good, J.	Psalm
1839	Ewald	Psalm	1824	Rosenmüller	Job
1845	Hengstenberg	Psalm	1836	Ewald	N/A
1850	Alexander	Cf.	1839	Wemyss	Cf.
1860	Delitzsch	Psalm	1849	Barnes	Cf.
1868	Barnes	N/A	1851	Schlottmann	Psalm
1869	Moll	Psalm	1864	Delitzsch	Cf. "repeated verbatim, Ps. cvii. 40"
1880	Johnson	Psalm	1866	Fausset	Psalm
1901	Kirkpatrick	Psalm	1867	Noyes	Cf.

(*Continued*)

Psalms			Job		
Date	Commentary	Alluding text	Date	Commentary	Alluding text
1904	MacLaren	Psalm	1874	Zöckler	Cf.
1904	Cheyne	Psalm	1874	Hitzig	Psalm
1907	Briggs	Psalm	1878	*Barth, J.*	Psalm
1925	Wutz	Psalm	1887	*Cheyne*	Psalm
1926	**Gunkel**	**Psalm**	1889	Davidson, A.	Cf.
1927	**König**	**Psalm**	1891	Dillmann	Cf. "wiederholt Ps. 107:40"
1934	**Schmidt**	**N/A**	1896	Budde	N/A
1945	**Cohen**	**Psalm**	1897	Duhm	Cf.
1953	**Kissane**	**Psalm**	1904	Peake	Cf.
1950	**Weiser [1955]**	**N/A**	1911	Barton	Psalm
1959	**Leupold**	**Psalm**	1913	Strahan	Cf.
1967	**Becker**	**N/A**	1919	Gibson	Cf.
1970	**Dahood**	**N/A**	1920	Torczyner	Psalm
1971	**Durham**	**N/A**	1921	Driver, Gray	Job
1975	**Mejia**	**N/A**	1922	Buttenwieser	N/A
1975	**Kidner**	**N/A**	1922	Ball	Cf.
1977	**Rogerson and McKay**	**N/A**	**1926**	**Dhorme [1967]**	**Job**
1979	**Beyerlin**	**Psalm**	**1931**	**Szczygiel**	**Cf.**
1979	**Jacquet**	**Cf.**	**1939**	**Kissane**	**Cf.**
1981	**Anderson**	**Psalm "(or vice versa?)"**	**1946**	**Reichert [1985]**	**Cf.**
1991	Van Gemeren	Cf.	**1951**	**Weiser [1988]**	**N/A**
1994	Mays	N/A	**1955**	**Lamparter**	**N/A**
1996	McCann	N/A	**1957**	**Tur-Sinai [1967]**	**Cf. (Common Source)**
1996	Seybold	Psalm	**1963**	**Fohrer**	**Cf.**
1997	*Roffey*	N/A	**1963**	**Terrien [2005]**	**N/A**
1998	*Goulder*	Psalm	**1968**	**Horst**	**Cf. (Common source)**
1999	Broyles	N/A	**1971**	**Watts, et al.**	**N/A**
2001	Schaefer	Cf.	**1973**	**Pope**	**Cf.**
2001	Gerstenberger	Cf.	**1976**	**Andersen**	**N/A**
2002	Allen	Psalm	**1976**	**Rowley**	**Cf.**
2003	Clifford	N/A	**1978**	**Gordis**	**N/A**
2003	Terrien	N/A	**1978**	**Hesse**	**N/A**
2003	Eaton	N/A	**1985**	**Habel**	**Cf. (Common source)**
2003	Weber	Psalm	**1985**	**Janzen**	**Job**
2007	Alter	Cf.	1989	Clines	Job
2007	Futato	N/A	1990	Good, E.	N/A
2008	Goldingay	Psalm	1993	Alden	Cf.
2008	Hossfeld and Zenger	Psalm	1996	Newsom	Job

Psalms			Job		
Date	Commentary	Alluding text	Date	Commentary	Alluding text
2014	deClaisse-Walford	N/A	1998	Hartley	Job
2014	Longman	N/A	1998	*Whybray*	N/A
2014	Brueggemann and Bellinger	N/A	2006	Balentine	N/A
			2006	Konkel	N/A
			2010	Alter	N/A
			2012	Longman	Cf.
			2012	Walton	N/A
			2013	Seow	Job? "alluding to such a doxological tradition"
			2015	Wilson	Cf.

Bibliography

1. Early Jewish and Christian Texts

The Acts of the Council of Constantinople of 553. 2009. 2 vols. Translated by Richard Price. TTH 51. Liverpool: Liverpool University Press.

Amphilochius of Iconium. 1969. *Amphilochii Iconiensis: Iambi ad Seleucum*. Edited by Eberhard Oberg. Berlin: de Gruyter.

Aquinas, Thomas. 1989. *The Literal Exposition on Job: A Scriptural Commentary concerning Providence*. Translated by Anthony Damico. Classics in Religious Studies 7. Atlanta: Scholars Press.

Augustine. 1904. *S. Aureli Augustini Operum Sectio II: S. Augustini Epistulae*. Edited by A. Golbacher. CSEL 44. Vienna: F. Tempsky.

Augustine. 1953. *Letters Volume III (131–164)*. Translated by Sister Wilfred Parsons. FC 20. Washington, DC: Catholic University of America Press.

Augustine. 1954. *The City of God, Books XVII–XXII*. Translated by Gerald G. Walsh and Daniel J. Honan. FC 24. Washington, DC: Catholic University of America Press.

Augustine. 1968. *The Retractions*. Translated by M. Inez Bogan. FC 60. Washington, DC: Catholic University of America Press.

Augustine. 1995. *De Doctrina Christiana*. Translated by R. P. H. Green. Oxford Early Christian Texts. Oxford: Clarendon.

Cassian, John. 1997. *The Conferences*. Translated by Boniface Ramsey. ACW 57. New York: Newman.

Cassiodorus. 2004. *Institutions of Divine and Secular Learning and On the Soul*. Translated by James W. Halporn and Mark Vessey. TTH 42. Liverpool: Liverpool University Press.

Chrysostom, John. 1859. *Synopsis Scripturae sacrae*. Pages 313–86 in vol. 56 of Patrologia Graeca. Edited by J.-P. Migne. 162 vols. Paris: Garnier, 1857–1886.

Constitutions of the Holy Apostles. 1886. In *Fathers of the Third and Fourth Centuries: Lactantius, Venantius, Asterius, Victorinus, Dionysius, Apostolic Teaching and Constitutions, Homily, and Liturgies*. Translated by A. Roberts, J. Donaldson, and A. C. Coxe. Buffalo, NY: Christian Literature Company.

Cyprian. 1972. *Sancti Cypriani Episcopi: Opera*. Edited by R. Weber and M. Bévenot. CCSL 3.1. Turnhout: Brepols.

Cyril of Jerusalem. 1968. *Works*. Translated by Leo P. McCauley and Anthony A. Stephenson. FC 61. Washington, DC: Catholic University of America Press.

Eusebius Pamphili. 1953. *Ecclesiastical History*. Translated by Roy J. Deferrari. 2 vols. FC 19, 29. Washington, DC: Catholic University of America Press.

Isidore of Seville. 2006. *The Etymologies of Isidore of Seville*. Translated by Stephen A. Barney, W. J. Lewis, J. A. Beach, and Oliver Berghof. Cambridge: Cambridge University Press.

Jerome. 1846. Praefatio S. Hieronymi in Librum Job. Pages 1079–84 in vol. 28 of Patrologia Latina. Edited by J.-P. Migne. 217 vols. Paris: Garnier, 1844–1864.

Jerome. 1965. *Dogmatic and Polemical Works*. Translated by John N. Hritzu. FC 53. Washington, DC: Catholic University of America Press.

John of Damascus. 1958. *Writings*. Translated by Frederic H. Chase, Jr. FC 37. Washington, DC: Catholic University of America Press.

Josephus. 2007. *Against Apion*. Translated by John M. G. Barclay. Flavius Josephus: Translation and Commentary 10. Leiden: Brill.

Origen. 1957. *The Song of Songs: Commentary and Homilies*. Translated by R. P. Lawson. ACW 26. Westminster, MD: Newman.

Philo of Alexandria. 1981. *Philo of Alexandria: The Contemplative Life, The Giants, and Selections*. Translated by David Winston. The Classics of Western Spirituality. New York: Paulist.

Rufinus. 1955. *A Commentary on the Apostles' Creed*. Translated by J. N. D. Kelly. ACW 20. Westminster, MD: Newman.

2. Other Works Cited

Abadie, Phillipe. 2008. Du roi sage au roi bâtisseur du Temple: Un autre visage de Salomon dans le livre des Chroniques. Pages 339–55 in *Le roi Salomon, un héritage en question: Hommage à Jacques Vermeylen*. Edited by C. Lichtert and D. Nocquet. Brussels: Lessius.

Aitken, James K. 2013. The Inevitability of Reading Job through Lamentations. Pages 204–15 in Dell and Kynes 2013.

Albertson, R. G. 1983. Job and Ancient Near Eastern Wisdom Literature. Pages 213–30 in *Scripture in Context II: More Essays on the Comparative Method*. Edited by William W. Hallo, James C. Moyer, and Leo G. Perdue. Winona Lake, IN: Eisenbrauns.

Alkier, Stefan. 2009. Intertextuality and the Semiotics of Biblical Texts. Pages 3–21 in *Reading the Bible Intertextually*. Edited by Richard B. Hays, Stefan Alkier, and Leroy A. Huizenga. Waco, TX: Baylor University Press.

Alonso Schökel, Luis. 1977. Toward a Dramatic Reading of the Book of Job. *Semeia* 7:45–61.

Alonso Schökel, Luis. 1988. *A Manual of Biblical Poetics*. Subsidia biblica 11. Rome: Pontifical Biblical Institute.

Alster, Bendt. 1997. *Proverbs of Ancient Sumer: The World's Earliest Proverb Collection*. 2 vols. Bethesda, MD: CDL.

Alter, Robert. 1981. *The Art of Biblical Narrative*. New York: Basic Books.

Alter, Robert. 1990. *The Art of Biblical Poetry*. Edinburgh: T&T Clark.

Andersen, Francis I. 1976. *Job*. London: Inter-Varsity.

Anderson, William H. U. 1998. Philosophical Considerations in a Genre Analysis of Qoheleth. *VT* 48:289–300.

Anderson, William H. U. 2014. Ecclesiastes in the Intertextual Matrix of Ancient Near Eastern Literature. Pages 157–75 in Dell and Kynes 2014.

Ansberry, Christopher B. 2010. *Be Wise, My Son, and Make My Heart Glad: An Exploration of the Courtly Nature of the Book of Proverbs*. BZAW 422. Berlin: de Gruyter.

Anthonioz, Stéphanie. 2016. A Reflection on the Nature of Wisdom: From Psalm 1 to Mesopotamian Traditions. Pages 43–56 in *Tracing Sapiential Traditions in Ancient Judaism*. JSJSup 174. Edited by Hindy Najman, Jean-Sébastien Rey, and Eibert J. C. Tigchelaar. Brill: Leiden.

Astell, Ann W. 1994. *Job, Boethius, and Epic Truth*. Ithaca, NY: Cornell University Press.

Avalos, Hector. 2007. *The End of Biblical Studies*. Amherst, NY: Prometheus.

Bakhtin, Mikhail. 1981. Discourse in the Novel. Pages 259–422 in *Dialogic Imagination: Four Essays*. Edited by Michael Holquist. Translated by Michael Holquist and Caryl Emerson. Austin, TX: University of Texas Press.

Bakhtin, Mikhail. 1984. *Problems of Dostoevsky's Poetics*. Translated by Caryl Emerson. THL 8. Manchester: Manchester University Press.

Bale, Alan. 2015. *Genre and Narrative Coherence in the Acts of the Apostles*. LNTS 514. London: Bloomsbury T&T Clark.

Balentine, Samuel E. 2013. Job and the Priests: "He Leads Priests Away Stripped" (Job 12:19). Pages 42–53 in Dell and Kynes 2013.

Banks, Diane. 2006. *Writing the History of Israel*. LHBOTS 438. New York: T&T Clark.

Barabási, Albert-László. 2002. *Linked: The New Science of Networks*. Cambridge, MA: Perseus.

Barbour, Jennie. 2012. *The Story of Israel in the Book of Qohelet: Ecclesiastes as Cultural Memory*. OTM. Oxford: Oxford University Press.

Barclay, John M. G. 2007. *Against Apion*. Flavius Josephus: Translation and Commentary 10. Leiden: Brill.

Bardtke, Hans. 1967. Profetische Zuge im Buche Hiob. Pages 1–10 in *Das Ferne und Nahe Wort: Festschrift Leonhard Rost*. BZAW 105. Edited by Fritz Maass. Berlin: Töpelmann.

Barentine, John C. 2016. *The Lost Constellations: A History of Obsolete, Extinct, or Forgotten Star Lore*. Cham: Springer.

Barney, Stephen A., W. J. Lewis, J. A. Beach, and Oliver Berghof. 2006. *The Etymologies of Isidore of Seville*. Cambridge: Cambridge University Press.

Barr, James. 1971–1972. The Book of Job and Its Modern Interpreters. *BJRL* 54:28–46.

Barth, J. 1878. *Beiträge zur Erklärung des Buches Hiob*. Leipzig: J. C. Hinrichs'sche Buchhandlung.

Barthes, Roland. 1974. *S/Z: An Essay*. Translated by Richard Miller. New York: Hill and Wang.

Barthes, Roland. 1977. The Death of the Author. Pages 142–8 in *Image–Music–Text*. Translated by Stephen Heath. New York: Hill and Wang.

Bartholomew, Craig G. 1998. *Reading Ecclesiastes: Old Testament Exegesis and Hermeneutical Theory*. AnBib 139. Rome: Pontifical Biblical Institute.

Bartholomew, Craig G. 2009. *Ecclesiastes*. BCOTWP. Grand Rapids: Baker Academic.

Bartholomew, Craig G. 2013. The Theology of Ecclesiastes. Pages 367–86 in Boda, Longman, and Rata 2013.

Barton, Carlin A., and Daniel Boyarin. 2016. *Imagine No Religion: How Modern Abstractions Hide Ancient Realities*. New York: Fordham University Press.

Barton, John. 1996a. *Reading the Old Testament: Method in Biblical Study*. Rev. and enl. ed. Louisville: Westminster John Knox.

Barton, John. 1996b. The Significance of a Fixed Canon of the Hebrew Bible. Pages 67–83 in vol. 1.1 of *Hebrew Bible, Old Testament: The History of Its Interpretation*. Edited by Sæbø Magne. Göttingen: Vandenhoeck & Ruprecht.

Barton, John. 2007a. *Oracles of God: Perceptions of Ancient Prophecy in Israel after the Exile*. Oxford: Oxford University Press.

Barton, John. 2007b. *The Nature of Biblical Criticism*. Louisville: Westminster John Knox.

Barton, John. 2014. *Ethics in Ancient Israel*. Oxford: Oxford University Press.

Bauer, Georg Lorenz. 1801. *Beylagen zur Theologie des alten Testaments*. Leipzig: Weygand.

Baumann, Gerlinde. 1996. *Die Weisheitsgestalt in Proverbien 1–9: Traditions-geschichtliche und theologische Studien*. FAT 16. Tübingen: Mohr-Siebeck.

Baumgärtel, Friedrich. 1933. *Der Hiobdialog: Aufriss und Deutung*. BWANT 61. Stuttgart: W. Kohlhammer.

Baumgartner, Walter. 1933. Die israelitische Weisheitsliteratur. *TRu* 5:259–8.

Baumgartner, Walter. 1951. The Wisdom Literature. Pages 210–37 in *The Old Testament and Modern Study: A Generation of Discovery and Research*. Edited by H. H. Rowley. Oxford: Clarendon.

Beal, Timothy K. 1998. C(ha)osmopolis: Qohelet's Last Words. Pages 290–304 in *God in the Fray: A Tribute to Walter Brueggemann*. Edited by Tod Linafelt, and Timothy K. Beal. Minneapolis: Fortress.

Beaulieu, Paul-Alain. 2007. The Social and Intellectual Setting of Babylonian Wisdom Literature. Pages 3–19 in *Wisdom Literature in Mesopotamia and Israel*. Edited by Richard J. Clifford. Atlanta: SBL.

Becker, Joachim. 1967. *Israel deutet seine Psalmen: Urform and Neuinterpretation in den Psalmen*. SBS 18. Stuttgart: Katholisches Bibelwerk.

Beckwith, Roger T. 1986. *The Old Testament Canon of the New Testament Church and Its Background in Early Judaism*. Grand Rapids: Eerdmans.

Beckwith, Roger T. 2004. Formation of the Hebrew Bible. Pages 39–86 in *Mikra: Text, Translation, Reading and Interpretation of the Hebrew Bible in Ancient Judaism and Early Christianity*. Edited by Martin Jan Mulder. Peabody, MA: Hendrickson.

Bedau, Mark A., and Paul Humphreys. 2008. Introduction. Pages 1–6 in *Emergence: Contemporary Readings in Philosophy and Science*. Edited by Mark A. Bedau and Paul Humphreys. Cambridge, MA: MIT Press.

Beebee, Thomas O. 1994. *The Ideology of Genre: A Comparative Study of Generic Instability*. University Park: Pennsylvania State University Press.

Ben Zvi, Ehud. 2003. The Prophetic Book: A Key Form of Prophetic Literature. Pages 276–97 in Sweeney and Ben Zvi 2003.

Ben Zvi, Ehud. 2013. Prophetic Memories in the Deuteronomistic Historical and the Prophetic Collections of Books. Pages 75–102 in *Israelite Prophecy and the Deuteronomistic History: Portrait, Reality, and the Formation of a History*. AIL 14. Edited by Mignon R. Jacobs and Raymond F. Person. Atlanta: SBL.

Benjamin, Walter. 1977. *The Origin of German Tragic Drama*. Translated by John Osborne. London: NLB. Translation of *Ursprung des deutschen Trauerspiels*. Frankfurt: Suhrkamp, 1963.

Bentzen, Aage. 1948–1949. *Introduction to the Old Testament*. 2 vols. Copenhagen: Gad. Translation of *Indledning til det gamle Testamente*. Copenhagen: Gad, 1941.

Berry, Donald K. 1995. *An Introduction to Wisdom and Poetry of the Old Testament*. Nashville: Broadman & Holman.

Berry, Wendell. 2002. The Body and the Earth. Pages 93–134 in *The Art of the Common-place: The Agrarian Essays of Wendell Berry*. Edited by Norman Wirzba. Berkeley: Counterpoint.

Beuken, Willem A. M. 2007. Eliphaz: One among the Prophets or Ironist Spokesman? The Enigma of Being a Wise Man in One's Own Right (Job 4–5). Pages 293–313 in Krüger et al. 2007.

Beyerlin, Walter. 1979. *Werden und Wesen des 107. Psalms*. BZAW 151. Berlin: de Gruyter.

Birnbaum, Elisabeth, and Ludger Schwienhorst-Schönberger. 2012. *Das Buch Kohelet*. NSKAT 14/2. Stuttgart: Katholisches Bibelwerk.

Bissell, Edwin Cone. 1880. *The Apocrypha of the Old Testament*. New York: Charles Scribner's Sons.

Blanton, Ward. 2007. *Displacing Christian Origins: Philosophy, Secularity, and the New Testament*. Chicago: University of Chicago Press.

Blenkinsopp, Joseph. 1991. The Social Context of the "Outsider Woman" in Proverbs 1–9. *Bib* 72:457–73

Blenkinsopp, Joseph. 1995. *Wisdom and Law in the Old Testament: The Ordering of Life in Israel and Early Judaism*. rev. ed. Oxford: Oxford University Press.

Blessig, Johann Lorenz. 1810. Foreword to *Denk- und Sittensprüche Salomo's: Nebst den Abweichungen der Alexandrinischen Uebersetzung ins Teutsche übersetzt*, by Johann Georg Dahler. Strasbourg: Amand König.

Bloom, Harold. 1975. *A Map of Misreading*. Oxford: Oxford University Press.

Blum, Erhard. 2003. Formgeschichte—A Misleading Category? Some Critical Remarks. Pages 32–45 in Sweeney and Ben Zvi 2003.

Boda, Mark J., Tremper Longman, and Cristian G. Rata, eds. 2013. *Words like Goads: Engaging Qohelet in the Twenty-First Century*. Winona Lake, IN: Eisenbrauns.

Boghossian, Paul A. 2006. *Fear of Knowledge: Against Relativism and Constructivism*. Oxford: Clarendon.

Bolin, Thomas M. 2017. *Ecclesiastes and the Riddle of Authorship*. New York: Routledge.

Boström, Lennart. 1990. *The God of the Sages: The Portrayal of God in the Book of Proverbs*. ConBOT 29. Stockholm: Almqvist & Wiksell International.

Boström, Lennart. 2000. Patriarchal Models for Piety. Pages 57–72 in *Shall Not the Judge of All the Earth Do What Is Right? Studies on the Nature of God*. Edited by David Penchansky and Paul L. Redditt. Winona Lake, IN: Eisenbrauns.

Bowker, Geoffrey C., and Susan Leigh Star. 1999. *Sorting Things Out: Classification and Its Consequences*. Cambridge, MA: MIT Press.

Brakke, David. 2010. A New Fragment of Athanasius's Thirty-Ninth Festal Letter: Heresy, Apocrypha, and the Canon. *HTR* 103:47–66.

Brakmann, Heinzgerd. 1997. Der christlichen Bibel erster Teil in den gottesdienstlichen Traditionen des Ostens und Westens: Liturgiehistorische Anmerkungen zum sog. Stellenwert des Alten/Ersten Testaments im Christentum. Pages 565–604 in *Streit am Tisch des Wortes? Zur Deutung und Bedeutung des Alten Testaments und seiner Verwendung in der Liturgie*. Edited by Ansgar Franz. St. Ottilien: EOS Verlag.

Brandt, Peter. 2001. *Endgestalten des Kanons: Das Arrangement der Schriften Israels in der jüdischen und christlichen Bibel*. BBB 131. Berlin: Philo.

Bratsiotis, Nikolaus. 1961. Der Monolog im Alten Testament. *ZAW* 73:30–70.

Braulik, Georg. 1996. Das Deuteronomium und die Bücher Ijob, Sprichwörter, Rut: Zur Frage früher Kanonizität des Deuteronomiums. Pages 61–138 in *Die Tora als Kanon für Juden und Christen*. HBS 10. Edited by Erich Zenger. Freiburg: Herder.

Breed, Brennan W. 2014. *Nomadic Text: A Theory of Biblical Reception History*. Indiana Studies in Biblical Literature. Bloomington: Indiana University Press.

Bretón, Santiago. 1973. Qoheleth Studies. *BTB* 3:22–50.

Briggs, Charles Augustus, and Emily Grace Briggs. 1906–1907. *The Book of Psalms*. 2 vols. ICC. Edinburgh: T&T Clark.

Briggs, Charles L., and Richard Bauman. 1992. Genre, Intertextuality, and Social Power. *Journal of Linguistic Anthropology* 2:131–72.

Brooke, Collin Gifford. 2009. *Lingua Fracta: Toward a Rhetoric of New Media*. Cresskill, NJ: Hampton.

Brown, Daniel. 2013. The Orion Constellation as an Installation: An Innovative Three-Dimensional Teaching and Learning Environment. *The Physics Teacher* 51:160.

Brown, William P. 2000. *Ecclesiastes*. Louisville: Westminster John Knox.

Brown, William P. 2005a. "Come, O Children . . . I Will Teach You the Fear of the Lord" (Psalm 34:12): Comparing Psalms and Proverbs. Pages 85–102 in Troxel, Friebel, and Magary 2005.

Brown, William P. 2005b. The Law and the Sages: A Reexamination of *Tôrâ* in Proverbs. Pages 251–80 in *Constituting the Community: Studies on the Polity of Ancient Israel in Honor of S. Dean McBride, Jr.* Edited by John T. Strong, and Steven S. Tuell. Winona Lake, IN: Eisenbrauns.

Brown, William P. Forthcoming. Rebuke, Complaint, Lament, and Praise: Reading Proverbs and Psalms Together. In Dell and Kynes forthcoming.

Bruch, Johann Friedrich. 1839. *Études philosophiques sur le christianisme*. Paris: Pitois-Levrault. German translation: *Philosophische Studien über das Christenthum*. Translated by Thomas Frantz. Mannheim: Hoff, 1847.

Bruch, Johann Friedrich. 1851. *Weisheits-Lehre der Hebräer: Ein Beitrag zur Geschichte der Philosophie*. Strasbourg: Treuttel & Würtz.

Brueggemann, Walter. 1997. *Theology of the Old Testament: Testimony, Dispute, Advocacy*. Minneapolis: Fortress.

Buccellati, Giorgio. 1981. Wisdom and Not: The Case of Mesopotamia. *JAOS* 101:35–47.

Buddeus, Johann Franz. 1702. *Introductio ad historiam philosophiae ebraeorum*. Halle: Orphanotrophii Glaucha-Halensis.

Burkes, Shannon. 1999. *Death in Qoheleth and Egyptian Biographies of the Late Period*. SBLDS 170. Atlanta: SBL.

Burkes, Shannon. 2002. Wisdom and Apocalypticism in the Wisdom of Solomon. *HTR* 95:21–44.

Burkes, Shannon. 2003. *God, Self, and Death: The Shape of Religious Transformation in the Second Temple Period*. JSJSup 79. Leiden: Brill.

Burnight, John Walton. 2013. The "Reversal" of *Heilsgeschichte* in Job 3. Pages 30–41 in Dell and Kynes 2013.

Burt, Sean. 2014. *The Courtier and the Governor: Transformations of Genre in the Nehemiah Memoir*. JAJSup 17. Göttingen: Vandenhoeck & Ruprecht.

Buss, Martin J. 1974. The Study of Forms. Pages 1–56 in *Old Testament Form Criticism*. Edited by John H. Hayes. San Antonio, TX: Trinity University Press.

Buss, Martin J. 2007. Dialogue in and among Genres. Pages 9–18 in *Bakhtin and Genre Theory in Biblical Studies*. Edited by Roland Boer. Atlanta: SBL.

Camp, Claudia V. 2000. *Wise, Strange and Holy: The Strange Woman and the Making of the Bible*. JSOTSup 320. Sheffield: Sheffield Academic.

Campbell, Anthony F. 2003. Form Criticism's Future. Pages 13–31 in Sweeney and Ben Zvi 2003.

Carr, David McLain. 2005. *Writing on the Tablet of the Heart: Origins of Scripture and Literature*. Oxford: Oxford University Press.

Carr, David McLain. 2011. *The Formation of the Hebrew Bible: A New Reconstruction*. New York: Oxford University Press.

Ceresko, Anthony R. 1990. The Sage in the Psalms. Pages 217–30 in Gammie and Perdue 1990.

Chambers, Ephraim. 1728. Sapiential. In vol. 2 of *Cyclopædia: Or, an Universal Dictionary of Arts and Sciences*. London: printed for James and John Knapton *et al.*

Chapman, Stephen B. 2000. *The Law and the Prophets: A Study in Old Testament Canon Formation*. FAT 27. Tübingen: Mohr Siebeck.

Cheung, Simon Chi-Chung. 2015. *Wisdom Intoned: A Reappraisal of the Genre "Wisdom Psalms."* LHBOTS 613. London: Bloomsbury T&T Clark.

Cheyne, T. K. 1887. *Job and Solomon: Or, The Wisdom of the Old Testament*. New York: Whittaker.

Childs, Brevard. 1965. The Birth of Moses. *JBL* 84:109–22.

Childs, Brevard. 1979. *Introduction to the Old Testament as Scripture*. Philadelphia: Fortress.

Childs, Brevard. 2000. Foreword. Pages xv–xvii in *Renewing Biblical Interpretation*. Edited by Craig Bartholomew, Collin Greene, and Karl Köller. Grand Rapids: Zondervan.

Christianson, Eric S. 1998. *A Time to Tell: Narrative Strategies in Ecclesiastes*. JSOTSup 280. Sheffield: Sheffield Academic.

Christianson, Eric S. 2007. *Ecclesiastes through the Centuries*. Oxford: Blackwell.

Clayton, Philip. 2004. *Mind and Emergence: From Quantum to Consciousness*. Oxford: Oxford University Press.

Clements, R. E. 1995. Wisdom and Old Testament Theology. Pages 269–86 in Day, Gordon, and Williamson 1995.

Clifford, Richard J. 1997. Introduction to the Wisdom Literature. Pages 1–16 in *Introduction to Wisdom Literature, Proverbs, Ecclesiastes, Song of Songs, Book of Wisdom, Sirach*. NIB 5. Nashville: Abingdon.

Clifford, Richard J. 1998. *The Wisdom Literature*. Nashville: Abingdon.

Clifford, Richard J. 1999. *Proverbs: A Commentary*. OTL. Louisville: Westminster John Knox.

Clines, David J. A. 1989. *Job 1–20*. WBC 17. Nashville: Nelson.

Clines, David J. A. 1990. Deconstructing the Book of Job. Pages 106–23 in *What Does Eve Do to Help? and Other Readerly Questions to the Old Testament*. JSOTSup 94. Edited by David J. A. Clines. Sheffied: Sheffield Academic.

Clines, Francis X. 1987. British Paper Adding Sting to Death Notices. *The New York Times*. 15 March.

Cogan, Mordechai. 2001. *1 Kings*. AB 10. New Haven: Yale University Press.

Coggins, Richard. 1999. What Does "Deuteronomistic" Mean? Pages 22–35 in McKenzie and Schearing 1999.

Cohen, Ralph. 2003. Introduction. *NLH* 34:v–xv.

Cohen, Yoram. 2013. *Wisdom from the Late Bronze Age*. Writing from the Ancient World 29. Atlanta: SBL.

Collins, John J. 1977. Cosmos and Salvation: Jewish Wisdom and Apocalyptic in the Hellenistic Age. *HR* 17:121–42.

Collins, John J. 1994. Response to George Nickelsburg. Paper presented at the annual meeting of the Society of Biblical Literature. Chicago, IL. 21 November.

Collins, John J. 1997. Wisdom Reconsidered, in Light of the Dead Sea Scrolls. *DSD* 4:265–81.

Collins, John J. 2010. Epilogue: Genre Analysis and the Dead Sea Scrolls. *DSD* 17:418–30.

Connors, Robert J. 1981. The Rise and Fall of the Modes of Discourse. *College Composition and Communication* 32:444–55.

Cornill, Carl Heinrich. 1891. *Einleitung in das Alte Testament*. Freiburg: J. C. B. Mohr. English translation: *Introduction to the Canonical Books of the Old Testament*. Translated by G. H. Box. London: Williams and Norgate, 1907.

Crenshaw, James L. 1969. Method in Determining Wisdom Influence upon "Historical" Literature. *JBL* 88:129–42.

Crenshaw, James L. 1970. Popular Questioning of the Justice of God in Ancient Israel. *ZAW* 82:380–95.

Crenshaw, James L. 1971. *Prophetic Conflict: Its Effect upon Israelite Religion*. BZAW 124. Berlin: de Gruyter.

Crenshaw, James L. 1974. Wisdom. Pages 225–64 in *Old Testament Form Criticism*. Edited by J. Hayes. San Antonio, TX: Trinity University Press.

Crenshaw, James L. 1976. Prolegomenon. Pages 1–60 in *Studies in Ancient Israelite Wisdom*. LBS. Edited by James L. Crenshaw. New York: Ktav.

Crenshaw, James L. 1983. Qoheleth in Current Research. *HAR* 7:41–56.

Crenshaw, James L. 1985. Education in Ancient Israel. *JBL* 104:601–15.

Crenshaw, James L. 1987. *Ecclesiastes: A Commentary*. OTL. Philadelphia: Westminster.

Crenshaw, James L. 1992. Prohibitions in Proverbs and Qoheleth. Pages 115–24 in *Priests, Prophets, and Scribes*. Edited by E. Ulrich, J. W. Wright, R. P. Carroll, and P. R. Davies. Sheffield: JSOT Press.

Crenshaw, James L. 1993. Wisdom Literature: Retrospect and Prospect. Pages 161–78 in McKay and Clines 1993.

Crenshaw, James L. 1999. The Deuteronomists and the Writings. Pages 145–58 in McKenzie and Schearing 1999.

Crenshaw, James L. 2000. Wisdom Psalms? *CurBS* 8:9–17.

Crenshaw, James L. 2010. *Old Testament Wisdom: An Introduction*. 3rd ed. Louisville: Westminster John Knox.

Crenshaw, James L. 2011. *Reading Job: A Literary and Theological Commentary*. Macon, GA: Smyth & Helwys.

Croce, Benedetto. 2000. Criticism of the Theory of Artistic and Literary Kinds. Pages 25–8 in Duff 2000b. Translation of *Estetica come scienza dell'espressione e linguitica generale: teoria e storia*. Bari: Laterza, 1902.

Cross, Frank Moore. 1969. New Directions in the Study of Apocalyptic. *JTC* 6:157–65.

Crüsemann, Frank. 1984. The Unchangeable World: The "Crisis of Wisdom" in Koheleth. Pages 57–77 in *God of the Lowly: Socio-Historical Interpretations of the Bible*. Edited by Willy Schottroff, and Wolfgang Stegemann. Translated by Matthew J. O'Connell. Maryknoll, NY: Orbis Books.

Cuddihy, John Murray. 1974. *The Ordeal of Civility: Freud, Marx, Lévi-Strauss, and the Jewish Struggle with Modernity*. New York: Basic Books.

Culler, Jonathan D. 1975. *Structuralist Poetics: Structuralism, Linguistics and the Study of Literature*. London: Routledge & Kegan Paul.

D'Angelo, Frank. 1984. Nineteenth-Century Forms/Modes of Discourse: A Critical Inquiry. *College Composition and Communication* 35:31–42.

Davidson, A. B. 1891. *The Book of Job*. Cambridge: Cambridge University Press.

Davidson, Samuel. 1862. *An Introduction to the Old Testament: Critical, Historical, Theological*. 2 vols. London: Williams and Norgate.

Davis, Ellen F. 1992. Job and Jacob: The Integrity of Faith. Pages 203–24 in *Reading between Texts: Intertextuality and the Hebrew Bible*. Edited by Danna Nolan Fewell. Louisville: Westminster/John Knox.

Davison, W. T. 1894. *The Wisdom-Literature of the Old Testament*. London: Charles H. Kelly.

Day, John, Robert P. Gordon, and H. G. M. Williamson, eds. 1995. *Wisdom in Ancient Israel*. Cambridge: Cambridge University Press.

Delitzsch, Franz. 1864. *Das Buch Iob*. Leipzig: Dörfling & Franke.

Delitzsch, Franz. 1873. *Salomonisches Spruchbuch*. Leipzig: Dörfling & Franke. English translation: *Biblical Commentary on the Proverbs of Solomon*. 2 vols. Translated by M. G. Easton. CFThL 43, 47. Edinburgh: T&T Clark, 1874–75.

Delkurt, Holger. 1993. *Ethische Einsichten in der alttestamentlichen Spruchweisheit*. BThSt 21. Neukirchen-Vluyn: Neukirchener.

Dell, Katharine J. 1991. *The Book of Job as Sceptical Literature*. BZAW 197. Berlin: de Gruyter.

Dell, Katharine J. 2000. Wisdom in Israel. Pages 348–76 in *Text in Context: Essays by Members of the Society for Old Testament Study*. Edited by A. D. H. Mayes. Oxford: Oxford University Press.

Dell, Katharine J. 2005. Does the Song of Songs Have Any Connections to Wisdom? Pages 8–26 in *Perspectives on the Song of Songs*. BZAW. Edited by Anselm C. Hagedorn. Berlin: de Gruyter.

Dell, Katharine J. 2006. *The Book of Proverbs in Social and Theological Context*. Cambridge: Cambridge University Press.

Dell, Katharine J. 2007. Job: Sceptics, Philosophers and Tragedians. Pages 1–19 in Krüger et al. 2007.

Dell, Katharine J. 2010. Solomon's Wisdom and the Egyptian Connection. Pages 21–36 in *The Centre and the Periphery: A European Tribute to Walter Brueggemann*. Edited by Jill Middlemas, David J. A. Clines, and Else Holt. Sheffied: Sheffield Phoenix.

Dell, Katharine J. 2012. Review of *An Introduction to the Study of Wisdom Literature*, by Stuart Weeks. *JTS* 63:225–7.

Dell, Katharine J. 2013a. "Cursed be the day I was born!" Job and Jeremiah Revisted. Pages 106–17 in Dell and Kynes 2013.

Dell, Katharine J. 2013b. *Interpreting Ecclesiastes: Readers Old and New*. Winona Lake, IN: Eisenbrauns.

Dell, Katharine J. 2013c. Studies of the Didactical Books of the Hebrew Bible / Old Testament. Pages 603–24 in vol. 3.1 of *Hebrew Bible, Old Testament: The History of Its Interpretation*. Edited by Magne Sæbø. Göttingen: Vandenhoeck & Ruprecht.

Dell, Katharine J. 2014. Exploring Intertextual Links between Ecclesiastes and Genesis 1–11. Pages 3–14 in Dell and Kynes 2014.

Dell, Katharine J. 2015. Deciding the Boundaries of "Wisdom": Applying the Concept of Family Resemblance. Pages 145–60 in Sneed 2015c.

Dell, Katharine J. 2016. Ecclesiastes as Mainstream Wisdom (without Job). Pages 43–52 in *Goochem in Mokum: Wisdom in Amsterdam*. Edited by George J. Brooke and Pierre Van Hecke. Leiden: Brill.

Dell, Katharine J., and Will Kynes, eds. 2013. *Reading Job Intertextually*. LHBOTS 574. New York: Bloomsbury T&T Clark.

Dell, Katharine J., and Will Kynes, eds. 2014. *Reading Ecclesiastes Intertextually*. LHBOTS 587. London: Bloomsbury T&T Clark.

Dell, Katharine J., and Will Kynes, eds. Forthcoming. *Reading Proverbs Intertextually*. LHBOTS 629. New York: Bloomsbury T&T Clark.

Dempster, Stephen G. 2008. Torah, Torah, Torah: The Emergence of the Tripartite Canon. Pages 87–127 in *Exploring the Origins of the Bible: Canon Formation in Historical, Literary, and Theological Perspective*. Edited by Craig A. Evans and Emmaneul Tov. Grand Rapids: Baker Academic.

Derrida, Jacques. 2000. The Law of Genre. *Glyph* 7 (1980): 202–13. Repr., pages 219–31 in Duff 2000b.

DeShell, Jeffrey. 1997. *The Peculiarity of Literature: An Allegorical Approach to Poe's Fiction*. Madison, NJ: Fairleigh Dickinson University Press.

Devitt, Amy J. 2004. *Writing Genres*. Carbondale: Southern Illinois University Press.

Dhorme, Edouard. 1967. *A Commentary on the Book of Job*. Translated by Harold Knight. London: Thomas Nelson and Sons. Translation of *Le livre de Job*. Paris: V. Lecoffre, 1926.

Dillmann, August. 1891. *Hiob*. 4th ed. KeH 2. Leipzig: Hirzel.

Douglas, Jerome N. 2014. *A Polemical Preacher of Joy: An Anti-Apocalyptic Genre for Qoheleth's Message of Joy*. Eugene, OR: Pickwick Publications.

Driver, Samuel Rolles. 1891. *An Introduction to the Literature of the Old Testament*. New York: Scribner's Sons.

Driver, Samuel Rolles and George Buchanan Gray. 1921. *A Critical and Exegetical Commentary on the Book of Job*. ICC. Edinburgh: T&T Clark.

Drott, Eric. 2013. The End(s) of Genre. *Journal of Music Theory* 57:1–45.

Dubrow, Heather. 1982. *Genre*. New York: Methuen.

Duff, David. 2000a. Introduction. Pages 1–24 in Duff 2000b.

Duff, David, ed. 2000b. *Modern Genre Theory*. London: Longman.

Eissfeldt, Otto. 1938. Modern Criticism. Pages 74–109 in *Record and Revelation*. Edited by H. Wheeler Robinson. Oxford: Clarendon.

Eliot, T. S. 1920. Tradition and the Individual Talent. Pages 47–59 in *The Sacred Wood: Essays on Poetry and Criticism*. Edited by T. S. Eliot. London: Methuen.

Eliot, T. S. 2016. Introduction to *All Hallows' Eve*, by Charles Williams. Eugene, OR: Wipf & Stock.

Ellermeier, Friedrich. 1967. *Qohelet I/1: Untersuchungen zum Buche Qohelet*. Herzberg: Jungfer.

Ellis, E. Earle. 1992. *The Old Testament in Early Christianity: Canon and Interpretation in the Light of Modern Research*. Grand Rapids: Baker.

Ellis, E. Earle. 2004. The Old Testament Canon in the Early Church. Pages 653–90 in *Mikra: Text, Translation, Reading and Interpretation of the Hebrew Bible in Ancient Judaism and Early Christianity*. Edited by M. Mulder. Peabody, MA: Hendrickson.

Ellul, Jacques. 1990. *The Reason for Being: A Meditation on Ecclesiastes*. Grand Rapids: Eerdmans.

Engnell, Ivan. 1970. The Figurative Language of the Old Testament. Pages 242–90 in *Critical Essays on the Old Testament*. Edited and translated by John T. Willis. London: SPCK.

Erickson, Amy, and Andrew R. Davis. 2016. Recent Research on the Megilloth (Song of Songs, Ruth, Lamentations, Ecclesiastes, Esther). *CBR* 14:298–318.

Erman, A. 1924a. Das Weisheitsbuch des Amen-em-ope. *OLZ* 27:241–52.

Erman, A. 1924b. Eine ägyptische Quelle der "Sprüche Salomos." *Sitzungsberichte der Preussischen Akademie der Wissenschaften*, XV:86–92.

Ernst, Alexander B. 1994. *Weisheitliche Kultkritik: Zu Theologie und Ethik des Sprüchbuchs und der Prophetie des 8. Jahrhunderts*. BThSt 23. Neukirchen-Vluyn: Neukirchener.

Estes, Daniel J. 2014. Seeking and Finding in Ecclesiastes and Proverbs. Pages 118–30 in Dell and Kynes 2014.

Ewald, Heinrich A. 1836. *Das Buch Iob*. Die poetischen Bücher des Alten Bundes 3. Göttingen: Vandenhoeck & Ruprecht. English translation: *Commentary on the Book of Job*. Translated by J. Frederick Smith. TTFL 28. London: Williams & Norgate, 1882.

Ewald, Heinrich A. 1839. *Allegemeines über die hebräische Poesie und über das Psalmenbuch*. Die poetischen Bücher des Alten Bundes 1. Göttingen: Vandenhoeck & Ruprecht.

Ewald, Heinrich A. 1843–55. *Geschichte des Volkes Israel bis Christus*. 5 vols. Göttingen: Dietrich.

Ewald, Heinrich A. 1848. Über die Volks- und Geistesfreiheit Israel's [*sic*] zur Zeit der großen Propheten bis zur ersten Zerstörung Jerusalems. *Jahrbücher der biblischen Wissenschaft* 1:95–113.

Fauconnier, Gilles, and Mark Turner. 2002. *The Way We Think: Conceptual Blending and the Mind's Hidden Complexities*. New York: Basic Books.

Fichtner, Johannes. 1949. Jesaja unter den Weisen. *TLZ* 74:75–80.

Fiddes, Paul S. 2013. *Seeing the World and Knowing God: Hebrew Wisdom and Christian Doctrine in a Late-Modern Context*. Oxford: Oxford University Press.

Fisch, Harold. 1988. *Poetry with a Purpose: Biblical Poetics and Interpretation*. Bloomington: Indiana University Press.

Fishbane, Michael. 1971. Jeremiah IV 23–6 and Job III 3–13: A Recovered Use of the Creation Pattern. *VT* 21:151–67.

Fishbane, Michael. 1985. *Biblical Interpretation in Ancient Israel*. Oxford: Clarendon.

Fishelov, David. 1993. *Metaphors of Genre: The Role of Analogies in Genre Theory*. University Park: Pennsylvania State University Press.

Fohrer, Georg. 1963. *Das Buch Hiob*. KAT 16. Gütersloh: Gütersloher Verlagshaus Gerd Mohn.

Fontaine, Carole R. 1987. Folktale Structure in the Book of Job. Pages 205–32 in *Directions in Biblical Hebrew Poetry*. JSOTSup 40. Edited by Elaine R. Follis. Sheffield: Sheffield Academic.

Fontaine, Carole R. 1993. Wisdom in Proverbs. Pages 99–114 in *In Search of Wisdom: Essays in Memory of John G. Gammie*. Edited by Leo G. Perdue, Bernard Brandon Scott, and William Johnston Wiseman. Louisville: Westminster John Knox.

Ford, David. 2007. *Christian Wisdom: Desiring God and Learning in Love*. Cambridge Studies in Christian Doctrine 16. Cambridge: Cambridge University Press.

Fowler, Alastair. 1982. *Kinds of Literature: An Introduction to the Theory of Genres and Modes*. Oxford: Clarendon.

Fox, Michael V. 1977. Frame-Narrative and Composition in the Book of Qohelet. *HUCA* 48:83–106.

Fox, Michael V. 1989. *Qohelet and His Contradictions*. JSOTSup 71. Sheffield: Almond.

Fox, Michael V. 1996. The Social Location of the Book of Proverbs. Pages 227–39 in *Texts, Temples, and Traditions: A Tribute to Menahem Haran*. Edited by Michael V. Fox. Winona Lake, IN: Eisenbrauns.

Fox, Michael V. 1999. *A Time to Tear Down and a Time to Build Up: A Rereading of Ecclesiastes*. Grand Rapids: Eerdmans.

Fox, Michael V. 2000. *Proverbs 1–9*. AB 18A. New York: Doubleday.

Fox, Michael V. 2004. *Ecclesiastes*. JPS Bible Commentary. Philadelphia: Jewish Publication Society.

Fox, Michael V. 2009. *Proverbs 10–31*. AB 18B. New Haven: Yale University Press.

Fox, Michael V. 2012. Joseph and Wisdom. Pages 231–62 in *The Book of Genesis: Composition, Reception, and Interpretation*. Edited by Craig A. Evans, Joel N. Lohr, and David L. Petersen. Leiden: Brill.

Fox, Michael V. 2015. Three Theses on Wisdom. Pages 69–86 in Sneed 2015c.

Freadman, Anne. 1988. Untitled: (On Genre). *Cultural Studies* 2:67–99.

Freese, John Henry. 1926. *Aristotle: The Art of Rhetoric*. Cambridge, MA: Harvard University Press.

Frei, Hans W. 1974. *The Eclipse of Biblical Narrative: A Study in Eighteenth and Nineteenth Century Hermeneutics*. New Haven: Yale University Press.

Fries, C. 1904. *Das philosophische Gespräch von Hiob bis Plato*. Tübingen: Mohr.

Frow, John. 2015. *Genre*. 2nd ed. London: Routledge.

Fukuyama, Francis. 1989. The End of History? *National Interest* 16:3–18.

Gadamer, Hans-Georg. 2004. *Truth and Method*. 2nd ed. Translated by Joel Weinsheimer and Donald G. Marshall. London: Continuum. Translation of *Wahrheit und Methode*. Tübingen: Mohr, 1960.

Gammie, John G. 1990. Paraenetic Literature: Toward a Morphology of a Secondary Genre. *Semeia* 50:41–77.

Gammie, John G., and Leo G. Perdue, eds. 1990. *The Sage in Israel and the Ancient Near East*. Winona Lake, IN: Eisenbrauns.

Geertz, Clifford. 1983. *Local Knowledge: Further Essays in Interpretive Anthropology*. New York: Basic Books.

Gemser, Berend. 1976. The Spiritual Structure of Biblical Aphoristic Wisdom. Pages 138–49 in *Adhuc Loquitur: Collected Essays of Dr B. Gemser*. Edited by A. van Selms and A. S. van der Woude. Leiden: Brill, 1968. Repr., pages 208–19 in *Studies in Ancient Israelite Wisdom*. Edited by James L. Crenshaw. New York: Ktav.

Genung, John F. 1891. *The Epic of the Inner Life Being the Book of Job*. Boston: Houghton Mifflin.

Genung, John F. 1906. *The Hebrew Literature of Wisdom in the Light of To-Day: A Synthesis*. Boston: Houghton Mifflin.

Gerber, Harry. 1955. Bruch, Johann Friedrich. Page 641 in vol. 2 of *Neue Deutsche Biographie*. Edited by Otto zu Stolberg-Wernigerode. Berlin: Duncker & Humblot.

Gerstenberger, Erhard. 1965. Covenant and Commandment. *JBL* 84:38–51.

Gese, Hartmut. 1958. *Lehre und Wirklichkeit in der alten Weisheit*. Tübingen: Mohr Siebeck.

Gibson, Edgar C. S. 1919. *The Book of Job*. 3rd ed. London: Methuen.

Gilbert, Maurice. 1984. Wisdom Literature. Pages 283–324 in *Jewish Writings of the Second Temple Period: Apocrypha, Pseudepigrapha, Qumran Sectarian Writings, Philo, Josephus*. Edited by M. E. Stone. Assen: Van Gorcum.

Gilbert, Maurice. 2003. *Les cinq livres des sages: Proverbes, Job, Qohélet, Ben Sira, Sagesse*. Paris: Cerf.

Gilloch, Graeme. 2002. *Walter Benjamin: Critical Constellations*. Oxford: Blackwell.

Ginsburg, Christian D. 1861. *Coheleth, Commonly Called the Book of Ecclesiastes*. London: Longman, Green, Longman, and Roberts.

Goering, Greg Schmidt. 2014. Sapiential Synesthesia: The Conceptual Blending of Light and Word in Ben Sira's Wisdom Instruction. Pages 121–43 in *Cognitive Linguistic Explorations in Biblical Studies*. Edited by Bonnie Howe and Joel B. Green. Berlin: de Gruyter.

Goff, Matthew. 2009. Recent Trends in the Study of Early Jewish Wisdom Literature: The Contribution of 4QInstruction and Other Qumran Texts. *CBR* 7:376–416.

Goff, Matthew. 2010. Qumran Wisdom Literature and the Problem of Genre. *DSD* 17:315–35.

Good, Edwin M. 1965. *Irony in the Old Testament*. London: SPCK

Good, Edwin M. 1990. *In Turns of Tempest: A Reading of Job*. Stanford, CA: Stanford University Press.

Good, John Mason. 1812. *The Book of Job*. London: Black, Parry & Co.

Goodman, Nelson. 1996. Notes on the Well-Made World. Pages 151–60 in *Starmaking: Realism, Anti-Realism, and Irrealism*. Edited by Peter McCormick. Cambridge, MA: MIT Press.

Gordis, Robert. 1968. *Koheleth—the Man and His World: A Study of Ecclesiastes*. 3rd ed. New York: Schocken.

Gordon, Robert P. 1995. A House Divided: Wisdom in Old Testament Narrative Traditions. Pages 94–105 in Day, Gordon, and Williamson 1995.

Gottlieb, Fred. 2016. The Creation Theme in Genesis 1, Psalm 104 and Job 38–42. *JBQ* 44:29–36.

Goulder, Michael D. 1998. *The Psalms of the Return: Book 5, Psalms 107–150*. JSOTSup 258. Sheffield: Sheffield Academic.

Gowan, Donald E. 1986. God's Answer to Job: How Is It an Answer? *HBT* 8:85–102.

Gowan, Donald E. 1992. Reading Job as a "Wisdom Script". *JSOT* 17:85–95.

Grabbe, Lester L. 1993. Prophets, Priests, Diviners and Sages in Ancient Israel. Pages 43–62 in McKay and Clines 1993.

Gray, J. 1970. The Book of Job in the Context of Near Eastern Literature. *ZAW* 82:251–69.

Green, Barbara. 2000. *Mikhail Bakhtin and Biblical Scholarship: An Introduction*. Atlanta: SBL.

Greene, Thomas M. 1982. *The Light in Troy: Imitation and Discovery in Renaissance Poetry*. New Haven: Yale University Press.

Greenstein, Edward L. 2004. Jeremiah as an Inspiration to the Poet of Job. Pages 98–110 in *Inspired Speech: Prophecy in the Ancient Near East*. JSOTSup 378. Edited by John Kaltner and Louis Stulman. London: T&T Clark International.

Greenstein, Edward L. 2013. The Parody as a Challenge to Tradition: The Use of Deuteronomy in the Book of Job. Pages 66–78 in Dell and Kynes 2013.

Greenwood, Kyle R. 2012. Debating Wisdom: The Role of Voice in Ecclesiastes. *CBQ* 74:476–91.

Grimm, Carl Ludwig Wilibald. 1860. *Das Buch der Weisheit*. Kurzgefasstes exegetisches Handbuch zu den Aprokryphen des Alten Testamentes 6. Leipzig: S. Hirzel.

Grondin, Jean. 2010. Nihilistic or Metaphysical Consequences of Hermeneutics? Pages 190–201 in *Consequences of Hermeneutics: Fifty Years after Gadamer's Truth and Method*. Edited by Jeff Malpas and Santiago Zabala. Evanston, IL: Northwestern University Press.

Grotius, Hugo. 1644. *Hugonis Grotii Annotata ad Vetus Testamentum*. Paris: Sebastiani Cramoisy, Regis & Reginae Architypographi, et Gabrielis Cramoisy.

Gruenwald, Ithmar. 1980. *Apocalyptic and Merkavah Mysticism*. Leiden: Brill.

Gunkel, Hermann. 1901. *Genesis*. Göttingen: Vandenhoeck & Ruprecht.

Gunkel, Hermann. 1926. *Die Psalmen*. Göttingen: Vandenhoeck & Ruprecht.

Habel, Norman C. 1985. *The Book of Job: A Commentary*. OTL. Philadelphia: Westminster.

Hagedorn, Anselm. Forthcoming. Erotic Wisdom for a More Independent Youth: Is There a Debate between Song of Songs and Proverbs? In Dell and Kynes forthcoming.

Halporn, James W., and Mark Vessey. 2004. *Cassiodorus: Institutions of Divine and Secular Learning and On the Soul*. TTH 42. Liverpool: Liverpool University Press.

Hancock, Christopher D. Forthcoming. Proverbs and the Confucian Classics. In Dell and Kynes forthcoming.

Haran, Menahem. 1993. Archives, Libraries, and the Order of the Biblical Books. *JANESCU* 63:51–61.

Harding, James Edward. 2010. The Book of Job as Metaprophecy. *SR* 39:523–47.

Harris, Scott L. 1995. *Proverbs 1–9: A Study of Inner-Biblical Interpretation*. SBLDS 150. Atlanta: Scholars Press.
Harrison, Peter. 2015. *The Territories of Science and Religion*. Chicago: University of Chicago Press.
Hart, F. Elizabeth. 2006. The View of Where We've Been and Where We'd Like to Go. *College Literature* 33:225–37.
Hartley, John E. 1988. *The Book of Job*. NICOT. Grand Rapids: Eerdmans.
Hatton, Peter T. H. 2008. *Contradiction in the Book of Proverbs: The Deep Waters of Counsel*. Aldershot: Ashgate.
Hauge, Martin Ravndal. 2015. *Solomon the Lover and the Shape of the Song of Songs*. HBM 77. Sheffield: Sheffield Phoenix.
Hazony, Yoram. 2012. *The Philosophy of Hebrew Scripture*. New York: Cambridge University Press.
Heim, Knut M. 2001. *Like Grapes of Gold Set in Silver: An Interpretation of Proverbial Clusters in Proverbs 10:1–22:16*. BZAW 273. Berlin: de Gruyter.
Helmer, Christine. 2014. *Theology and the End of Doctrine*. Louisville: Westminster John Knox.
Hempel, Charlotte. 2017. Wisdom and Law in the Hebrew Bible and at Qumran. *JSJ* 48:1–27.
Hendel, Ronald S. 2013. *The Book of Genesis: A Biography*. LGRB. Princeton: Princeton University Press.
Hengel, Martin. 1974. *Judaism and Hellenism: Studies in Their Encounter in Palestine during the Early Hellenistic Period*. Translated by John Bowden. London: SCM.
Hermberg, Kevin. 2006. *Husserl's Phenomenology: Knowledge, Objectivity and Others*. London: Continuum.
Hernadi, Paul. 1972. *Beyond Genre: New Directions in Literary Classification*. Ithaca, NY: Cornell University Press.
Hertzberg, Hans Wilhelm. 1963. *Der Prediger*. KAT 17/4–5. Gütersloh: G. Mohn.
Hirsch, E. D. 1967. *Validity in Interpretation*. New Haven: Yale University Press.
Hirschman, Marc. 2001. Qohelet's Reception and Interpretation in Early Rabbinic Literature. Pages 87–99 in *Studies in Ancient Midrash*. Edited by James L. Kugel. Cambridge, MA: Harvard University Center for Jewish Studies.
Hitchcock, Peter. 2003. The Genre of Postcoloniality. *NLH* 34:299–330.
Hobbins, John F. 2013. The Poetry of Qohelet. Pages 163–92 in Boda, Longman, and Rata 2013.
Hoffman, Yair. 1996. *A Blemished Perfection: The Book of Job in Context*. JSOTSup 213. Sheffield: Sheffield Academic.
Hoffman, Yair. 2007. The Book of Job as a Trial: A Perspective from a Comparison to Some Relevant Ancient Near Eastern Texts. Pages 21–31 in Krüger et al. 2007.

Høgenhaven, Jesper. 1987. *Problems and Prospects of Old Testament Theology*. Sheffield: JSOT Press.

Holm-Nielsen, Svend. 1974. On the Interpretation of Qoheleth in Early Christianity. *VT* 24:168–77.

Holm-Nielsen, Svend. 1975. The Book of Ecclesiastes and the Interpretation of It in Jewish and Christian Theology. *ASTI* 10:38–96.

Horne, Milton P. 2014. Intertextuality and Economics: Reading Ecclesiastes with Proverbs. Pages 106–17 in Dell and Kynes 2014.

Hossfeld, Frank-Lothar, and Erich Zenger. 2005. *Psalms 2: A Commentary on Psalms 51–100*. Translated by Linda M. Maloney. Hermeneia. Minneapolis: Fortress.

Hunter, Alastair. 2006. *Wisdom Literature*. London: SCM.

Hurowitz, Victor. 1992. *I Have Built You an Exalted House: Temple Building in the Bible in the Light of Mesopotamian and North-West Semitic Writings*. JSOTSup 115. Sheffield: Sheffield Academic.

Hurvitz, Avi. 1988. Wisdom Vocabulary in the Hebrew Psalter: A Contribution to the Study of "Wisdom Psalms." *VT* 38:41–51.

Imray, Kathryn. 2013. Love Is (Strong as) Death: Reading the Song of Songs through Proverbs 1–9. *CBQ* 75:649–65.

Ingram, Doug. 2006. *Ambiguity in Ecclesiastes*. LHBOTS 431. New York: T&T Clark.

Iser, Wolfgang. 1974. *The Implied Reader: Patterns of Communication in Prose Fiction from Bunyan to Beckett*. Baltimore: Johns Hopkins University Press.

Jacobs, Alan. 2013. *The Book of Common Prayer: A Biography*. LGRB. Princeton: Princeton University Press.

Jacquet, Louis. 1975–79. *Les Psaumes et le coeur de l'homme: Etude textuelle, littéraire et doctrinale*. 3 vols. Gembloux: Duculot.

James, Kenneth W. 1984. Ecclesiastes: Precursor of Existentialists. *TBT* 22:85–90.

Jameson, Fredric. 1981. *The Political Unconscious: Narrative as a Socially Symbolic Act*. Ithaca, NY: Cornell University Press.

Janzen, J. Gerald. 1985. *Job*. Interpretation. Atlanta: John Knox.

Jarick, John. 1990. *Gregory Thaumaturgos' Paraphrase of Ecclesiastes*. Atlanta: Scholars Press.

Jastrow, Morris. 1919. *A Gentle Cynic, Being a Translation of the Book of Koheleth, Commonly Known as Ecclesiastes, Stripped of Later Additions, also Its Origin, Growth, and Interpretation*. Philadelphia: J. B. Lippincott.

Jastrow, Morris. 1921. *The Song of Songs, Being a Collection of Love Lyrics of Ancient Palestine*. Philadelphia: J. B. Lippincott.

Jauss, Hans Robert. 2000. Theory of Genres and Medieval Literature. Pages 127–47 in Duff 2000b. Translation of "Littérature médiévale et théorie des genres." *Poetique* 1 (1970):79–101.

Johnson, Steven. 2001. *Emergence: The Connected Lives of Ants, Brains, Cities, and Software*. New York: Scribner.

Johnson, Timothy Jay. 2009. *Now My Eye Sees You: Unveiling an Apocalyptic Job*. HBM 24. Sheffield: Sheffield Phoenix.

Joyce, Paul M. 2013. "Even if Noah, Daniel, and Job were in it . . ." (Ezekiel 14:14): The Case of Job and Ezekiel. Pages 118–28 in Dell and Kynes 2013.

Juvan, Marko. 2008. *History and Poetics of Intertextuality*. Translated by Timothy Pogačar. Comparative Cultural Studies. Indianapolis, IN: Purdue University Press.

Kallen, Horace Meyer. 1918. *The Book of Job as a Greek Tragedy*. New York: Moffat, Yard and Company.

Kamenetzky, Abraham S. 1921. Die ursprünglich beabsichtigte Aussprache der Pseudonyms QHLT. *OLZ* 24:11–15.

Kant, Immanuel. 1960. *Religion within the Limits of Reason Alone*. 2nd ed. Translated by Theodore M. Greene and Hoyt H. Hudson. New York: Harper & Row. Translation of *Die Religion innerhalb der Grenzen der blossen Vernunft*. Königsberg: Friedrich Nicolovius, 1793.

Kautzsch, Emil. 1894. *Die Heilige Schrift des Alten Testaments: Beilagen*. Freiburg: J. C. B. Mohr. English translation: *An Outline of the History of the Literature of the Old Testament*. Translated by John Taylor. London: Williams & Norgate, 1899.

Keil, Carl Friedrich. 1859. *Lehrbuch der historisch-kritischen Einleitung in die kanonischen Schriften des Alten Testamentes* [sic]. 2nd ed. Frankfurt: Heyder & Zimmer.

Kellett, E. E. 1940. "Job": An Allegory? *ExpTim* 51:250–1.

Kilgore, Christopher D. 2013. Rhetoric of the Network: Toward a New Metaphor. *Mosaic* 46:37–58.

Kim, Hyun Chul Paul. 2003. Form Criticism in Dialogue with Other Criticisms: Building the Multidimensional Structures of Texts and Concepts. Pages 85–104 in Sweeney and Ben Zvi 2003.

Kister, Menahem. 2004. Wisdom Literature and Its Relation to Other Genres: From Ben Sira to Mysteries. Pages 13–47 in *Sapiential Perspectives: Wisdom Literature in Light of the Dead Sea Scrolls*. STDJ 51. Edited by John J. Collins, Gregory E. Sterling, and Ruth A. Clements. Leiden: Brill.

Kitzhaber, Albert R. 1990. *Rhetoric in American Colleges, 1850–1900*. Dallas: Southern Methodist University Press.

Klein, Christian. 1994. *Kohelet und die Weisheit Israels: Eine formgeschichtliche Studie*. BWANT 132. Stuttgart: Kohlhammer.

Knauf, Ernst-Axel. 2016. *1 Könige 1–14*. HTKAT. Freiburg: Herder.

Knobel, Peter S. 1991. *The Targum of Qohelet*. ArBib 15. Collegeville, MN: Liturgical Press.

Koch, Klaus. 1969. *The Growth of the Biblical Tradition: The Form Critical Method*. London: Black. Translation of *Was ist Formgeschichte? Neue Wege der Exegese*. Neukirchen-Vluyn: Neukirchner, 1964.

Koh, Y. V. 2006. *Royal Autobiography in the Book of Qoheleth*. BZAW 369. Berlin: de Gruyter.

Köhlmoos, Melanie. 1999. *Das Auge Gottes: Textstrategie im Hiobbuch*. FAT 25. Tübingen: Mohr Siebeck.

Kooij, Arie van der. 1998. The Canonization of Ancient Books Kept in the Temple of Jerusalem. Pages 17–40 in *Canonization and Decanonization*. SHR 82. Edited by Arie van der Kooij and Karel van der Toorn. Leiden: Brill.

Kovacs, Brian. 1974. Is There a Class-Ethic in Proverbs? Pages 173–89 in *Essays in Old Testament Ethics*. Edited by James L. Crenshaw and John T. Willis. New York: Ktav.

Kraus, Hans-Joachim. 1982. *Geschicte der historisch-kritischen Erforschung des Alten Testaments*. 3rd ed. Neukirchen-Vluyn: Neukirchener.

Krüger, Thomas. 1990. Theologische Gegenwartsdeutung im Kohelet-Buch. Habil. Theol., Universtiy of Munich.

Krüger, Thomas. 1996. Dekonstruction und Rekonstruction prophetischer Eschatologie im Qohelet-Buch. Pages 107–29 in *"Jedes Ding hat seine Zeit": Studien zur israelitischen und altorientalischen Weisheit*. BZAW 241. Edited by Anja Angela Diesel et al. Berlin: de Gruyter.

Krüger, Thomas. 1997. Die Rezeption der Tora im Buch Kohelet. Pages 303–25 in Schwienhorst-Schönberger 1997b.

Krüger, Thomas. 2004. *Qoheleth: A Commentary*. Translated by O. C. Dean. Hermeneia. Minneapolis: Fortress.

Krüger, T., M. Oeming, K. Schmid, and C. Uehlinger, eds. 2007. *Das Buch Hiob und seine Interpretationen*. ATANT 88. Zurich: Theologischer Verlag.

Kuhl, Curt. 1953. Neuere Literarkritik des Buches Hiob. *TRu* 21:163–204; 257–317.

Kurtz, Paul Michael. 2016. Waiting at Nemi: Wellhausen, Gunkel, and the World behind Their Work. *HTR* 109:567–85.

Kutschera, Franz. 1997. Kohelet: Leben im Angesicht des Todes. Pages 363–76 in Schwienhorst-Schönberger 1997b.

Kynes, Will. 2012a. *My Psalm Has Turned into Weeping: Job's Dialogue with the Psalms*. BZAW 437. Berlin: de Gruyter.

Kynes, Will. 2012b. The Nineteenth-Century Beginnings of "Wisdom Literature," and Its Twenty-First-Century End? Paper presented at the Senior Old Testament Seminar. University of Oxford. 21 May.

Kynes, Will. 2013a. Intertextuality: Method and Theory in Job and Psalm 119. in *Biblical Interpretation and Method*. Edited by K. J. Dell and P. M. Joyce. Oxford: Oxford University Press.

Kynes, Will. 2013b. Job and Isaiah 40–55: Intertextualities in Dialogue. Pages 94–105 in Dell and Kynes 2013.

Kynes, Will. 2014. Follow Your Heart and Do Not Say It Was a Mistake: Qoheleth's Allusions to Numbers 15 and the Story of the Spies. Pages 15–27 in Dell and Kynes 2014.

Kynes, Will. 2015a. The Modern Scholarly Wisdom Tradition and the Threat of Pan-sapientialism: A Case Report. Pages 11–38 in Sneed 2015c.

Kynes, Will. 2015b. Reading Job Following the Psalms. Pages 131–45 in *The Shape of the Ketuvim: History, Contoured Intertextuality, and Canon*. Siphrut 16. Edited by Julius Steinberg and Tim Stone. Winona Lake, IN: Eisenbrauns.

Kynes, Will. 2016. The Nineteenth-Century Beginnings of "Wisdom Literature," and Its Twenty-First-Century End? Pages 83–108 in *Perspectives on Israelite Wisdom: Proceedings of the Oxford Old Testament Seminar*. LHBOTS 618. Edited by John Jarick. London: Bloomsbury T&T Clark.

Lambert, David A. 2015. The Book of Job in Ritual Perspective. *JBL* 134:557–75.

Lambert, W. G. 1960. *Babylonian Wisdom Literature*. Oxford: Clarendon.

Lang, Bernhard. 1998. The "Writings": A Hellenistic Literary Canon in the Hebrew Bible. Pages 41–65 in *Canonization and Decanonization*. SHR 82. Edited by Arie van der Kooij and Karel van der Toorn. Leiden: Brill.

Larrimore, Mark J. 2013. *The Book of Job: A Biography*. LGRB. Princeton: Princeton University Press.

Lash, Nicholas. 1996. *The Beginning and the End of "Religion."* Cambridge: Cambridge University Press.

Lauha, Aarre. 1981. Kohelets Verhältnis zur Geschichte. Pages 393–401 in *Die Botschaft und die Boten*. Edited by Jörg Jeremias and Lothar Perlitt. Neukirchen: Neukirchener.

Le Clerc, Jean. 1685. *Sentimens de quelques theologiens de Hollande sur l'Histoire critique du Vieux Testament*. Amsterdam: Chez Henri Desbordes.

Leavis, F. R. 1963. *The Great Tradition: George Eliot, Henry James, Joseph Conrad*. New York: New York University Press.

Lebram, J. C. H. 1968. Aspekte der alttestamentlichen Kanonbildung. *VT* 18:173–89.

Lee, Eunny P. 2005. *The Vitality of Enjoyment in Qohelet's Theological Rhetoric*. BZAW 353. Berlin: de Gruyter.

Legaspi, Michael C. 2010. *The Death of Scripture and the Rise of Biblical Studies*. Oxford Studies in Historical Theology. Oxford: Oxford University Press.

Leiman, Sid (Shnayer) Z. 1989. Josephus and the Canon of the Bible. Pages 50–8 in *Josephus, the Bible, and History*. Edited by Louis H. Feldman and Gohei Hata. Leiden: Brill.

Leiman, Sid (Shnayer) Z. 1991. *The Canonization of Hebrew Scripture: The Talmudic and Midrashic Evidence*. 2nd ed. New Haven: Connecticut Academy of Arts and Sciences.

Leithart, Peter J. 2016. *The End of Protestantism: Pursuing Unity in a Fragmented Church*. Grand Rapids: Baker Academic.

Lemaire, André. 1984. Sagesse et ecoles. *VT* 34:271–81.

Lemaire, André. 1990. The Sage in School and Temple. Pages 165–81 in Gammie and Perdue 1990.

Lemaire, André. 1995. Wisdom in Solomonic Historiography. Pages 106–18 in Day, Gordon, and Williamson 1995.

Lemche, Niels Peter. 2008. *The Old Testament between Theology and History: A Critical Survey*. Louisville: Westminster John Knox.

Levenson, Jon D. 2004. Review of *The Book of Job: A Contest of Moral Imaginations*, by Carol A. Newsom. *JR* 84:271–2.

Levinson, Bernard M. 2014. "Better That You Should Not Vow than That You Vow and Not Fulfill": Qoheleth's Use of Textual Allusion and the Transformation of Deuteronomy's Law of Vows. Pages 28–41 in Dell and Kynes 2014.

Levitin, Dmitri. 2015. *Ancient Wisdom in the Age of the New Science: Histories of Philosophy in England, c. 1640–1700*. Cambridge: Cambridge University Press.

Lewis, Michael. 2017. *The Undoing Project: A Friendship that Changed Our Minds*. New York: Norton.

Lichtheim, Miriam. 1996. Didactic Literature. Pages 243–62 in *Ancient Egyptian Literature: History and Forms*. Probleme der Ägyptologie 10. Edited by Antonio Loprieno. Leiden: Brill.

Liere, Frans van. 2014. *An Introduction to the Medieval Bible*. New York: Cambridge University Press.

Lo, Alison. 2008. Death in Qohelet. *JANESCU* 31:85–98.

Lohfink, Norbert F. 1999. Was There a Deuteronomistic Movement? Pages 36–66 in McKenzie and Schearing 1999.

Lohfink, Norbert F. 2003. *Qoheleth: A Continental Commentary*. Translated by Sean E. McEvenue. Minneapolis: Fortress.

Longman, Tremper, III. 1998. *The Book of Ecclesiastes*. NICOT. Grand Rapids: Eerdmans.

Longman, Tremper, III. 2003. Israelite Genres in Their Ancient Near Eastern Context. Pages 177–95 in Sweeney and Ben Zvi 2003.

Longman, Tremper, III. 2012. *Job*. BCOTWP. Grand Rapids: Baker Academic.

Longman, Tremper, III. 2014. Qoheleth as Solomon: "For What Can Anyone Who Comes after the King Do?" (Ecclesiastes 2:12). Pages 42–56 in Dell and Kynes 2014.

Loretz, Oswald. 1964. *Qohelet und der alte Orient: Untersuchungen zu Stil und theologischer Thematik des Buches Qohelet*. Freiburg: Herder.

Loretz, Oswald. 1993. Poetry and Prose in the Book of Qoheleth (1:1–3:22; 7:23–8:1; 9:6–10; 12:8–14). Pages 155–89 in *Verse in Ancient Near Eastern Prose*. Edited by Johannes C. de Moor, and Wilfred G. E. Watson. Neukirchen-Vluyn: Neukirchener.

Lowth, Robert. 1829. *Lectures on the Sacred Poetry of the Hebrews*. Translated by G. Gregory. Boston: Crocker & Brewster J. Leavitt. Translation of *De Sacra Poesi Hebraeorum: Praelectiones Academicae*. Oxford: Clarendon, 1753.

Lozada, Carlos. 2013. The End of Everything. *The Washington Post*. 5 April.

Lucas, Ernest C. 2015. *Proverbs*. THOTC. Grand Rapids: Eerdmans.

Lücke, Friedrich. 1832. *Versuch einer vollständigen Einleitung in die Offenbarung Johannis und in die gesamte apokalyptische Literatur*. Bonn: Weber.

Lyu, Sun Myung. 2012. *Righteousness in the Book of Proverbs*. FAT II 55. Tübingen: Mohr Siebeck.

Maas, Michael. 2003. *Exegesis and Empire in the Early Byzantine Mediterranean: Junillus Africanus and the Instituta regularia divinae legis*. Studien und Texte zu Antike und Christentum 17. Tübingen: Siebeck.

MacDonald, Nathan. 2003. *Deuteronomy and the Meaning of "Monotheism."* FAT II 1. Tübingen: Mohr Siebeck.

Mack, Burton L., and Roland E. Murphy. 1986. Wisdom Literature. Pages 371–410 in *Early Judaism and Its Modern Interpreters*. Edited by Robert A. Kraft and George W. E. Nickelsburg. Philadelphia: Fortress.

Magdalene, F. Rachel. 2007. *On the Scales of Righteousness: Neo-Babylonian Trial Law and the Book of Job*. BJS 348. Providence, RI: Brown University.

Mahlev, Haim. 2014. Kabbalah as Philosophia Perennis? The Image of Judaism in the German Early Enlightenment: Three Studies. *JQR* 104:234–57.

Malchow, B. V. 1985. A Manual for Future Monarchs: Proverbs 27:23–29:27. *CBQ* 47:238–45.

Marböck, Johannes. 2006. Zwischen Erfahrung, Systematik und Bekenntnis: Zu Eigenart und Bedeutung der alttestamentlichen Weisheitsliteratur. Pages 201–14 in *Weisheit und Frömmigkeit: Studien zur alttestamentlichen Literatur der Spätzeit*. Österreichische biblische Studien. Edited by Johannes Marböck. Frankfurt: Peter Lang.

Marcus, Ralph. 1950–1951. On Biblical Hypostases of Wisdom. *HUCA* 23:157–71.

Marlow, Hilary. 2013. Creation Themes in Job and Amos: An Intertextual Relationship? Pages 142–54 in Dell and Kynes 2013.

Masenya, Madipoane, and Funlola Olojede. Forthcoming. Sex and Power(lessness) in Selected Northern Sotho and Yorùbá Proverbs: An Intertextual Reading of Proverbs 5–7. In Dell and Kynes forthcoming.

Mason, Steve, and Robert A. Kraft. 1996. Josephus on Canon and Scriptures. Pages 217–35 in vol. 1.1 of *Hebrew Bible, Old Testament: The History of Its Interpretation*. Göttingen: Vandenhoeck & Ruprecht.

McCann, J. Clinton, Jr. 1987. Psalm 73: A Microcosm of Old Testament Theology. Pages 247–57 in *The Listening Heart*. JSOTSup 58. Edited by Kenneth G. Hoglund et al. Sheffield: JSOT Press.

McCann, J. Clinton, Jr. 1997. Wisdom's Dilemma: The Book of Job, the Final Form of the Book of Psalms, and the Entire Bible. Pages 18–30 in *Wisdom, You Are My Sister: Studies in Honor of Roland E. Murphy, O. Carm., on the Occasion of His Eightieth Birthday*. CBQMS 29. Edited by Michael L. Barré. Washington, DC: Catholic Biblical Association of America.

McDonald, Lee Martin. 2007. *The Biblical Canon: Its Origin, Transmission, and Authority*. Peabody, MA: Hendrickson.

McDonald, Lee Martin. 2013. Hellenism and the Biblical Canons: Is There a Connection? Pages 13–50 in *Christian Origins and Hellenistic Judaism: Social and Literary Contexts for the New Testament*. Edited by Stanley E. Porter and Andrew W. Pitts. Leiden: Brill.

McKane, William. 1970. *Proverbs: A New Approach*. OTL. London: SCM.

McKay, Heather A., and D. J. A. Clines. 1993. *Of Prophets' Visions and the Wisdom of Sages*. JSOTSup 162. Sheffield: Sheffield Academic.

McKenzie, John L. 1967. Reflections on Wisdom. *JBL* 86:1–9.

McKenzie, Steven L. 1999. Postscript: The Laws of Physics and Pan-Deuteronomism. Pages 262–71 in McKenzie and Schearing 1999.

McKenzie, Steven L., and Linda S. Schearing, eds. 1999. *Those Elusive Deuteronomists: The Phenomenon of Pan-Deuteronomism*. JSOTSup 268. Sheffield: Sheffield Academic.

Meade, David G. 1987. *Pseudonymity and Canon: An Investigation into the Relationship of Authorship and Authority in Jewish and Earliest Christian Tradition*. Grand Rapids: Eerdmans.

Meek, Russell L. Forthcoming. Prophet and Sage in Dialogue: History and Methodology. In *Riddles and Revelations: Explorations into the Relationship between Wisdom and Prophecy in the Hebrew Bible*. LHBOTS. Edited by Mark J. Boda, Russel L. Meek, and Rusty Osborne. London: Bloomsbury T&T Clark.

Meier, Sam. 1989. Job I-II: A Reflection of Genesis I-III. *VT* 39:183–93.

Meinhold, Johannes. 1908. *Die Weisheit Israels in Spruch, Sage und Dichtung*. Leipzig: Quelle & Meyer.

Mejía, J. 1975. Some Observations on Psalm 107. *BTB* 5:56–66.

Melton, Brittany N. 2014. Solomon, Wisdom, and Love: Intertextual Resonance between Ecclesiastes and Song of Songs. Pages 130–41 in Dell and Kynes 2014.

Mettinger, Tryggve N. D. 1983. *A Farewell to the Servant Songs: A Critical Examination of an Exegetical Axiom*. Lund: CWK Gleerup.

Mettinger, Tryggve N. D. 1993. Intertextuality: Allusion and Vertical Context Systems in Some Job Passages. Pages 257–80 in McKay and Clines 1993.

Meyvaert, Paul. 1996. Bede, Cassiodorus, and the Codex Amiatinus. *Spec* 71:827–83.

Michel, Diethelm. 1988. *Qohelet*. ErFor 258. Darmstadt: Wissenschaftliche Buchgesellschaft.

Michel, Diethelm. 1989. *Untersuchungen zur Eigenart des Buches Qohelet*. BZAW 183. Berlin: de Gruyter.

Mies, Françoise. 2003. Le genre littéraire du livre de Job. *RB* 110:336–69.

Miller, Carolyn R. 2005. Genre as Social Action. Pages 20–36 in *Genre and the New Rhetoric*. Edited by Aviva Freedman and Peter Medway. London: Taylor & Francis.

Miller, Douglas B. 2000. What the Preacher Forgot: The Rhetoric of Ecclesiastes. *CBQ* 62:215–35.

Miller, Douglas B. 2015. Wisdom in the Canon: Discerning the Early Intuition. Pages 87–113 in Sneed 2015c.

Mills, Mary E. 2003. *Reading Ecclesiastes: A Literary and Cultural Exegesis*. Aldershot: Ashgate.

Mills, Mary E. 2014. Polyphonic Narration in Ecclesiastes and Jonah. Pages 71–83 in Dell and Kynes 2014.

Moore, Stephen D., and Yvonne Sherwood. 2011. *The Invention of the Biblical Scholar: A Critical Manifesto*. Minneapolis: Fortress.

Morgan, Donn F. 1981. *Wisdom in the Old Testament Traditions*. Atlanta: John Knox.

Moyise, Steve. 1995. *The Old Testament in the Book of Revelation*. JSNTSup 115. Sheffield: Sheffield Academic.

Moynihan, Daniel Patrick. 1970. Dr Moynihan's Remarks at a Cabinet Meeting Prior to His Return to Private Life. December 21, 1970. *Weekly Compilation of Presidential Documents* 6:1729–31.

Müller, Hans-Peter. 1977. Die weisheitliche Lehrerzählung im Alten Testament und seiner Umwelt. *WO* 9:77–98.

Müller, Hans-Peter. 1978. Neige der althebräishcen "Weisheit": Zum Denken Qohäläts. *ZAW* 90:238–64.

Müller, Hans-Peter. 1994. Die Hiobrahmenerzahlung und ihre altorientalischen Parallelen als Paradigmen einer weisheitlichen Wirklichkeitswahrnahme. Pages 21–39 in *The Book of Job*. BETL 114. Edited by W. A. M. Beuken. Leuven: Leuven University Press.

Müller, Reinhard. 2013. The Blinded Eyes of the Wise: Sapiential Tradition and Mosaic Commandment in Deut 16:19–20. Pages 9–33 in Schipper and Teeter 2013.

Mullins, R. T. 2016. *The End of the Timeless God*. Oxford: Oxford University Press.

Murphy, Roland E. 1967. Assumptions and Problems in Old Testament Wisdom Research. *CBQ* 29:101–12.

Murphy, Roland E. 1969. The Interpretation of Old Testament Wisdom Literature. *Int* 23:289–301.

Murphy, Roland E. 1975. Wisdom and Yahwism. Pages 117–26 in *No Famine in the Land*. Edited by James W. Flanagan and Anita Weisbrod Robinson. Missoula, MT: Scholars Press.

Murphy, Roland E. 1978. Wisdom—Theses and Hypothesis. Pages 35–42 in *Israelite Wisdom: Theological and Literary Essays in Honor of Samuel Terrien*. Edited by John G. Gammie, Walter A. Brueggemann, W. Lee Humphreys, and James M. Ward. Missoula, MT: Scholars Press.

Murphy, Roland E. 1981. *Wisdom Literature: Job, Proverbs, Ruth, Canticles, Ecclesiastes, and Esther*. FOTL 13. Grand Rapids: Eerdmans.

Murphy, Roland E. 1982. Qohelet Interpreted: The Bearing of the Past on the Present. *VT* 32:331–37.

Murphy, Roland E. 1992a. *Ecclesiastes*. WBC 23A. Dallas: Word Books.

Murphy, Roland E. 1992b. Wisdom in the OT. Pages 920–31 in vol. 6 of *Anchor Bible Dictionary*. Edited by David Noel Freedman. New York: Doubleday.

Murphy, Roland E. 1998. *Proverbs*. WBC 22. Nashville: Nelson.

Murphy, Roland E. 2000. Wisdom and Yahwism Revisited. Pages 191–200 in *Shall Not the Judge of All the Earth Do What Is Right? Studies in the Nature of God in Tribute to James L. Crenshaw*. Edited by D. Penchansky and P. L. Redditt. Winona Lake, IN: Eisenbrauns.

Murphy, Roland E. 2002. *The Tree of Life: An Exploration of Biblical Wisdom Literature*. 3rd ed. Grand Rapids: Eerdmans.

Najman, Hindy. 2012. The Idea of Biblical Genre: From Discourse to Constellation. Pages 307–21 in *Prayer and Poetry in the Dead Sea Scrolls and Related Literature*. Edited by Jeremy Penner, Ken M. Penner, and Cecilia Wassen. Leiden: Brill.

Najman, Hindy. 2014. *Losing the Temple and Recovering the Future: An Analysis of* 4 Ezra. New York: Cambridge University Press.

Nel, Philip Johannes. 1982. *The Structure and Ethos of the Wisdom Admonitions in Proverbs*. BZAW 158. Berlin: de Gruyter.

Newman, John Henry. 1891. *The Idea of a University Defined and Illustrated*. London: Longmans, Green, and Co.

Newsom, Carol A. 1995. Job and Ecclesiastes. Pages 177–94 in *Old Testament Interpretation: Past, Present, and Future: Essays in Honor of Gene M. Tucker*. Edited by James Luther Mays, David L. Petersen, and Kent H. Richards. Nashville: Abingdon.

Newsom, Carol A. 2003. *The Book of Job: A Contest of Moral Imaginations*. Oxford: Oxford University Press.

Newsom, Carol A. 2005. Spying out the Land: A Report from Genology. Pages 437–50 in Troxel, Friebel, and Magary 2005.

Newsom, Carol A. 2007. Dramaturgy and the Book of Job. Pages 375–93 in Krüger et al. 2007.

Newsom, Carol A. 2010. Pairing Research Questions and Theories of Genre: A Case Study of the Hodayot. *DSD* 17:270–88.

Nickelsburg, George W. E. 2005. Wisdom and Apocalypticism in Early Judaism: Some Points for Discussion. Pages 17–37 in *Conflicted Boundaries in Wisdom and Apocalypticism*. SBLSymS 35. Edited by B. G. Wright and L. Wills. Atlanta: SBL.

Nitsche, Martin. 2015. *"Und das Königtum war fest in der Hand Salomos": Untersuchungen zu 1 Kön 3*. BWANT 205. Stuttgart: Kohlhammer.

Nogalski, James D. 2013. Job and Joel: Divergent Voices on a Common Theme. Pages 129–41 in Dell and Kynes 2013.

Nöldeke, Theodor. 1868. *Die alttestamentliche Literatur in einer Reihe von Aufsätzen dargestellt*. Leipzig: Quandt & Händel.

Nongbri, Brent. 2013. *Before Religion: A History of a Modern Concept*. New Haven: Yale University Press.

O'Dowd, Ryan. 2010. *The Wisdom of Torah: Epistemology in Deuteronomy and the Wisdom Literature*. FRLANT 225. Göttingen: Vandenhoeck & Ruprecht.

Oehler, Gustav Friedrich. 1854. *Die Grundzüge der alttestamentlichen Weisheit*. Tübingen: Ludwig Friedrich Fues.

Oehler, Gustav Friedrich. 1873–74. *Theologie des Alten Testaments*. 2 vols. Tübingen: Heckenhauer. English translation: *Theology of the Old Testament*. 2 vols. Translated by Sophia Taylor. CFThL 44, 48. Edinburgh: T&T Clark, 1874–75.

Oeming, Manfred. 2001. Hiobs Monolog—der Weg nach innen. Pages 57–75 in *Hiobs Weg: Stationen von Menschen im Leid*. BThSt 45. Edited by Manfred Oeming and Konrad Schmid. Neukirchen-Vluyn: Neukirchener.

Oeming, Manfred. 2008. Wisdom as a Hermeneutical Key to the Book of Psalms. Pages 154–62 in *Scribes, Sages, and Seers: The Sage in the Eastern Mediterranean World*. FRLANT 219. Edited by Leo G. Perdue. Göttingen: Vandenhoeck & Ruprecht.

Ogden, Graham S. 1980. Historical Allusion in Qoheleth IV 13-16? *VT* 30:309–15.

Oorschot, Jürgen van. 2007. Grenzen der Erkenntnis als Quellen der Erkenntnis: Ein alttestamentlicher Beitrag zu Weisheit und Wissenschaft. *TLZ* 132:1277–92.

Orlinsky, Harry M. 1974. Prolegomenon. Pages 833–69 in *The Canon and the Masorah of the Hebrew Bible*. Edited by Sid Z. Leiman. New York: Ktav.

Overland, Paul. 2000. Did the Sage Draw from the Shema? A Study of Proverbs 3:1–12. *CBQ* 62:424–40.

Parker, K. I. 1988. Repetition as a Structuring Device in 1 Kings 1–11. *JSOT* 42:19–27.

Parker, K. I. 1992. Solomon as Philosopher King? The Nexus of Law and Wisdom in 1 Kings 1–11. *JSOT* 53:75–91.

Patrick, Dale. 1977. *Arguing with God: The Angry Prayers of Job*. St. Louis: Bethany Press.

Peake, Arthur S., ed. 1925. *The People and the Book: Essays on the Old Testament*. Oxford: Clarendon.

Pedersen, Johannes. 1931. *Scepticisme Israélite*. Paris: F. Alcan.

Pelham, Abigail. 2010. Job as Comedy, Revisited. *JSOT* 35:89–112.

Penprase, Bryan E. 2011. *The Power of Stars: How Celestial Observations Have Shaped Civilization*. New York: Springer.

Perdue, Leo G. 1977. *Wisdom and Cult: A Critical Analysis of the Views of Cult in the Wisdom Literatures of Israel and the Ancient Near East*. SBLDS 30. Missoula, MT: Scholars Press.

Perdue, Leo G. 1994. *Wisdom and Creation: The Theology of Wisdom Literature*. Nashville: Abingdon.

Perdue, Leo G. 2003. Wisdom and Apocalyptic: The Case of Qoheleth. Pages 231–58 in *Wisdom and Apocalypticism in the Dead Sea Scrolls and in the*

Biblical Tradition. BETL 168. Edited by García Martínez. Leuven: Leuven University Press.

Perdue, Leo G. 2008. *The Sword and the Stylus: An Introduction to Wisdom in the Age of Empires*. Grand Rapids: Eerdmans.

Perdue, Leo G. 2013. The Book of Qohelet "Has the Smell of the Tomb about It": Mortality in Qohelet and Hellenistic Skepticism. Pages 103–16 in Boda, Longman, and Rata 2013.

Perry, T. Anthony. 1993. *Dialogues with Kohelet: The Book of Ecclesiastes*. University Park: Pennsylvania State University Press.

Perry, T. Anthony. 2015. *The Book of Ecclesiastes (Qohelet) and the Path to Joyous Living*. Cambridge: Cambridge University Press.

Pleins, J. David. 1987. Poverty in the Social World of the Wise. *JSOT* 37:61–78.

Pope, Marvin H. 1973. *Job*. 3rd ed. AB 15. Garden City, NY: Doubleday.

Popper, Karl R. 1959. *The Logic of Scientific Discovery*. New York: Basic Books.

Porteous, N. W. 1960. Royal Wisdom. Pages 247–61 in *Wisdom in Israel and in the Ancient Near East*. VTSup 3. Edited by M. Noth and D. Winton Thomas. Leiden: Brill.

Portier-Young, Anathea. 2013. Through the Dung-Heap to the Chariot: Intertextual Transformations in the *Testament of Job*. Pages 234–45 in Dell and Kynes 2013.

Preuss, Horst Dietrich. 1970. Erwägungen zum theologischen Ort alttestamentlicher Weisheitsliteratur. *EvT* 30:393–417.

Prince, Michael B. 2003. Mauvais Genres. *NLH* 34:453–79.

Purvis, Zachary. 2016. *Theology and the University in Nineteenth-Century Germany*. Oxford Theology and Religion Monographs. Oxford: Oxford University Press.

Pury, Albert de. 1999. Qohéleth et le canon des *Ketubim*. *RTP* 131:163–98.

Pury, Albert de. 2003. Zwischen Sophokles und Ijob: Die Schriften (Ketubim): Ein jüdischer Literature-Kanon. *Welt und Umwelt der Bibel* 28:25–7.

Pyeon, Yohan. 2003. *You Have Not Spoken What Is Right about Me: Intertextuality and the Book of Job*. Studies in Biblical Literature 45. New York: Lang.

Rad, Gerhard von. 1953. Josephsgeschichte und ältere Chokma. Pages 120–27 in *Congress Volume: Copenhagen, 1953*. VTSup 1. Leiden: Brill.

Rad, Gerhard von. 1972. *Wisdom in Israel*. Translated by James D. Martin. Harrisburg, PA: Trinity Press International. Translation of *Weisheit in Israel*. Neukirchen-Vluyn: Neukirchener Verlag, 1970.

Rad, Gerhard von. 2001. *Old Testament Theology*. 2 vols. OTL. Louisville: Westminster John Knox. Translation of *Theologie des Alten Testaments*. Munich: C. Kaiser, 1957–60.

Reed, Walter L. 1993. *Dialogues of the Word: The Bible as Literature according to Bakhtin*. Oxford: Oxford University Press.

Reuss, Eduard. 1881. *Die Geschichte der heiligen Schriften alten Testaments*. Braunschweig: Schwetschke & Sohn.

Rice, Eugene, Jr. 1958. *The Renaissance Idea of Wisdom*. Cambridge, MA: Harvard University Press.

Richter, Heinz. 1959. *Studien zu Hiob: Der Aufbau des Hiobbuches, dargestellt an den Gattungen des Rechtslebens*. Theologische Arbeiten 11. Berlin: Evanglische Verlagsanstat.

Roberts, J. J. M. 1977. Job and the Israelite Religious Tradition. *ZAW* 89:107–14.

Roffey, J. W. 1997. Beyond Reality: Poetic Discourse and Psalm 107. Pages 60–76 in *A Biblical Itinerary: In Search of Method, Form and Content*. JSOTSup 240. Sheffield: Sheffield Academic.

Rogerson, J. W. 1982. Philosophy and the Rise of Biblical Criticism: England and Germany. Pages 63–79 in *England and Germany: Studies in Theological Diplomacy*. Edited by S. W. Sykes. Frankfurt: Lang.

Rogerson, J. W. 1984. *Old Testament Criticism in the Nineteenth Century: England and Germany*. London: SPCK.

Rollston, Chris A. 2010. *Writing and Literacy in the World of Ancient Israel: Epigraphic Evidence from the Iron Age*. Archaeology and Biblical Studies 11. Atlanta: SBL.

Römer, Thomas. 2003. The Form-Critical Problem of the So-Called Deuteronomistic History. Pages 240–52 in Sweeney and Ben Zvi 2003.

Rosch, Eleanor. 1999. Principles of Categorization. Pages 189–206 in *Concepts: Core Readings*. Edited by Eric Margolis and Stephen Laurence. Cambridge, MA: MIT Press. Orig. ed., 1978.

Rosenmüller, C. 1821–1823. *Psalmi*. 3 vols. Scholia in Vetus Testamentum 4. Leipzig: Ioh. Ambros. Barthii.

Rosenmüller, C. 1824. *Iobus*. Scholia in Vetus Testamentum 5. Edited by C. Rosenmüller. 2nd ed. Leipzig: Ioh. Ambros. Barthii.

Rosmarin, Adena. 1985. *The Power of Genre*. Minneapolis: University of Minnesota Press.

Ross, James F. 1978. Psalm 73. Pages 161–75 in *Israelite Wisdom: Theological and Literary Essays in Honor of Samuel Terrien*. Edited by John G. Gammie et al. Missoula, MT: Scholars Press.

Rowland, Christopher. 1982. *The Open Heaven: A Study of Apocalyptic in Judaism and Early Christianity*. New York: Crossroad.

Rowley, Harold Henry. 1976. *Job*. 2nd ed. NCB. Grand Rapids: Eerdmans.

Rylaarsdam, John Coert. 1946. *Revelation in Jewish Wisdom Literature*. Chicago: University of Chicago Press.

Saebø, Magne. 1998. *On the Way to Canon: Creative Tradition History in the Old Testament*. Sheffied: Sheffield Academic.

Salyer, Gary D. 2001. *Vain Rhetoric: Private Insight and Public Debate in Ecclesiastes*. JSOTSup 327. Sheffield: Sheffield Academic.

Salzani, Carlo. 2009. *Constellations of Reading: Walter Benjamin in Figures of Actuality*. Oxford: Peter Lang.

Sandoval, Timothy J. 2006. *The Discourse of Wealth and Poverty in the Book of Proverbs*. Leiden: Brill.

Sarna, Nahum M. 1957. Epic Substratum in the Prose of Job. *JBL* 76:13–25.

Sarna, Nahum M. 1971. The Order of the Books. Pages 407–13 in *Studies in Jewish Bibliography, History, and Literature in Honor of I. Edward Kiev*. Edited by C. Berlin. New York: Ktav.

Sarna, Nahum M. 2007. Bible: The Canon, Text, and Editions. Pages 572–86 in vol. 3 of *Encyclopedia Judaica*. Edited by Fred Skolnik and Michael Berenbaum. Jerusalem: Keter.

Satlow, Michael L. 2005. Disappearing Categories: Using Categories in the Study of Religion. *Method & Theory in the Study of Religion* 17:287–98.

Saur, Markus. 2011a. Die literarishe Funktion und die theologische Intention der Weishetsreden des Sprüchebuches. *VT* 61:447–60.

Saur, Markus. 2011b. Sapientia discursiva: Die alttestamentliche Weisheitsliteratur als theologischer Diskurs. *ZAW* 123:236–49.

Saur, Markus. 2014. Prophetie, Weisheit und Gebet. *ZAW* 126:570–83.

Saur, Markus. 2015. Where Can Wisdom Be Found? New Perspectives on the Wisdom Psalms. Pages 181–204 in Sneed 2015c.

Saur, Markus. Forthcoming. Qohelet as a Reader of Proverbs. In Dell and Kynes forthcoming.

Schafer, Peter. 2003. Wisdom Finds a Home: Torah as Wisdom. Pages 26–44 in *Light in a Spotless Mirror: Reflections on Wisdom Traditions in Judaism and Early Christianity*. Edited by James H. Charlesworth and M. A. Daise. Harrisburg, PA: Trinity Press International.

Schearing, Linda S. 1999. Introduction. Pages 13–19 in McKenzie and Schearing 1999.

Schellenberg, Annette. 2015. Don't Throw the Baby out with the Bathwater: On the Distinctness of the Sapiential Understanding of the World. Pages 115–43 in Sneed 2015c.

Schipper, Bernd. 2013. When Wisdom Is Not Enough! The Discourse on Wisdom and Torah and the Composition of the Book of Proverbs. Pages 55–80 in Schipper and Teeter 2013.

Schipper, Bernd, and D. Andrew Teeter, eds. 2013. *Wisdom and Torah: The Reception of "Torah" in the Wisdom Literature of the Second Temple Period*. JSJSup 163. Leiden: Brill.

Schlegel, Friedrich. 1957. *Literary Notebooks 1797–1801*. Edited by H. Eichner. London: Athlone.

Schlegel, Friedrich. 1968. *Dialogue on Poetry and Literary Aphorisms*. Translated by Ernst Behler and Roman Struc. University Park: Pennsylvania State University Press. Translation of Gespräch über die Poesie. *Athenaeum* 3 (1800): 58–121.

Schlegel, Friedrich. 1971. Athenaeum Fragments. Pages 161–240 in *Friedrich Schlegel's* Lucinde *and the Fragments*. Translated by Peter Firchow. Minneapolis: University of Minnesota Press. Orig. ed., 1798.

Schleiermacher, Friedrich. 1893. *On Religion: Speeches to Its Cultured Despisers*. Translated by John Oman. London: Kegan Paul, Trench, Trübner. Translation of *Über die Religion: Reden an die Gebildeten unter ihren Verächtern*. 2nd ed. Berlin: Johann Friedrich Unger, 1806. Orig. ed., 1799.

Schlottmann, Konstantin. 1851. *Das Buch Hiob*. Berlin: Wiegandt und Grieben.

Schmid, Hans Heinrich. 1966. *Wesen und Geschichte der Weisheit: Eine Untersuchung zur altorientalischen und israelitischen Weisheitsliteratur*. Berlin: A. Töpelmann.

Schmid, Konrad. 2007. Innerbiblische Schriftdiskussion im Hiobbuch. Pages 241–61 in Krüger et al. 2007.

Schnurrer, Christian Friedrich. 1789. *Disputatio philologica ad Psalmum centesimum septimum*. Tübingen: Litteris Sigmundianis.

Scholnick, Sylvia Huberman. 1975. Lawsuit Drama in the Book of Job. Ph.D. diss., Brandeis.

Schultz, Hermann. 1869. *Alttestamentliche Theologie: Die Offenbarungsreligion auf ihrer vorchristlichen Entwickelungsstufe*. 2 vols. Frankfurt: Heyder & Zimmer.

Schultz, Richard L. 2014. Qoheleth and Isaiah in Dialogue. Pages 57–70 in Dell and Kynes 2014.

Schwáb, Zoltán S. 2013. *Toward an Interpretation of the Book of Proverbs: Selfishness and Secularity Reconsidered*. JTISup 7. Winona Lake, IN: Eisenbrauns.

Schwienhorst-Schönberger, Ludger. 1997a. Kohelet: Stand und Perspektiven der Forschung. Pages 5–38 in Schwienhorst-Schönberger 1997b.

Schwienhorst-Schönberger, Ludger, ed. 1997b. *Das Buch Kohelet: Studien zur Struktur, Geschichte, Rezeption und Theologie*. BZAW 254. Berlin: de Gruyter.

Schwienhorst-Schönberger, Ludger 2013. Alttestamentliche Weisheit im Diskurs. *ZAW* 125:118–42.

Scott, R. B. Y. 1960. Solomon and the Beginnings of Wisdom in Israel. Pages 262–79 in *Wisdom in Israel and in the Ancient Near East*. VTSup 3. Edited by M. Noth and D. Winton Thomas. Leiden: Brill.

Scott, R. B. Y. 1961. Priesthood, Prophecy, Wisdom, and the Knowledge of God. *JBL* 80:1–15.

Scott, R. B. Y. 1970. The Study of Wisdom Literature. *Int* 24:20–45.

Scott, R. B. Y. 1971. *The Way of Wisdom in the Old Testament*. New York: Macmillan.

Seitz, Christopher R. 2007. *Prophecy and Hermeneutics: Toward a New Introduction to the Prophets*. Grand Rapids: Baker Academic.

Sellin, Ernst, and Leonhard Rost. 1959. *Einleitung in das Alte Testament*. 9th ed. Heidelberg: Quelle & Meyer.

Seow, C. L. 1995. Qohelet's Autobiography. Pages 275–87 in *Fortunate the Eyes that See: Essays in Honor of David Noel Freedman in Celebration of His Seventieth Birthday*. Edited by Astrid B. Beck et al. Grand Rapids: Eerdmans.

Seow, C. L. 1997. *Ecclesiastes*. AB 18C. New York: Doubleday.

Seow, C. L. 2013. *Job 1–21: Interpretation and Commentary*. Illuminations. Grand Rapids: Eerdmans.

Seybold, Klaus. 1996. *Die Psalmen*. Tübingen: Mohr.

Sharp, Carolyn J. 2009. *Irony and Meaning in the Hebrew Bible*. Bloomington: Indiana University Press.

Sheehan, Jonathan. 2005. *The Enlightenment Bible: Translation, Scholarship, Culture*. Princeton: Princeton University Press.

Shelton, Pauline. 1999. Making a Drama out of a Crisis? A Consideration of the Book of Job as a Drama. *JSOT* 83:69–82.

Sheppard, Gerald T. 1980. *Wisdom as a Hermeneutical Construct: A Study in the Sapientializing of Old Testament Traditions*. BZAW 151. Berlin: de Gruyter.

Sheppard, Gerald T. 1983. Review of *Wisdom in the Old Testament Traditions*, by Donn F. Morgan. *JBL* 102:479–80.

Sheppard, Gerald T. 2000. Biblical Wisdom Literature and the End of the Modern Age. Pages 369–98 in *Congress Volume: Oslo 1998*. VTSup 80. Edited by André Lemaire and Magne Sæbø. Leiden: Brill.

Shields, Martin A. 2006. *The End of Wisdom: A Reappraisal of the Historical and Canonical Function of Ecclesiastes*. Winona Lake, IN: Eisenbrauns.

Shields, Martin A. 2013. Qohelet and Royal Autobiography. Pages 117–36 in Boda, Longman, and Rata 2013.

Shupak, Nili. 2015. The Contribution of Egyptian Wisdom to the Study of the Biblical Wisdom Literature. Pages 265–304 in Sneed 2015c.

Shveka, Avi, and Pierre Van Hecke. 2014. The Metaphor of Criminal Charge as a Paradigm for the Conflict between Job and His Friends. *ETL* 90:99–119.

Siegfried, C. 1898. *Prediger und Hoheslied*. HKAT II 3,2. Göttingen: Vandenhoeck & Ruprecht.

Sinding, Michael. 2002. After Definitions: Genre, Categories, and Cognitive Science. *Genre* 25:181–219.

Sinding, Michael. 2004. Beyond Essence (or, Getting over "There"): Cognitive and Dialectical Theories of Genre. *Semiotica* 149:377–95.

Sinding, Michael. 2005. Genera Mixta: Conceptual Blending and Mixed Genres in Ulysses. *NLH* 36:589–619.

Sinding, Michael. 2011. Framing Monsters: Multiple and Mixed Genres, Cognitive Category Theory, and Gravity's Rainbow. *Poetics Today* 31:465–505.

Sinding, Michael. 2012. Blending in a *baciyelmo*: *Don Quixote's* Genre Blending and the Invention of the Novel. Pages 147–71 in *Blending and the*

Study of Narrative: Approaches and Applications. Edited by Ralf Schneider and Marcus Hartner. Berlin: de Gruyter.

Sinding, Michael. 2014. Toward a Cognitive Sociology of Genres. Pages 39–58 in *Cognition, Literature, and History*. Edited by Mark J. Bruhn and Donald R. Wehrs. New York: Routledge.

Ska, Jean Louis. 2014. Abraham, maître de sagesse selon l'idéal des Proverbes. Pages 18–29 in *Wisdom for Life*. BZAW 445. Edited by Nuria Calduch-Benages. Berlin: de Gruyter.

Skehan, Patrick. 1967. Wisdom's House. *CBQ* 29:468–86.

Skehan, Patrick W., and Alexander A. Di Lella. 1987. *The Wisdom of Ben Sira*. AB 39. Garden City, NY: Doubleday.

Smalley, Beryl. 1986. *Medieval Exegesis of Wisdom Literature: Essays*. Atlanta: Scholars Press.

Smend, Rudolf. 1962. Universalismus und Partikularismus in der Alttestamentlichen Theologie des 19. Jahrhunderts. *EvT* 22:169–79.

Smend, Rudolf. 1995. The Interpretation of Wisdom in Nineteenth-Century Scholarship. Pages 257–68 in Day, Gordon, and Williamson 1995.

Smith, Yancy Warren. 2009. Hippolytus' Commentary on the Song of Songs in Social and Critical Context. Ph.D. diss., Brite Divinity School.

Sneed, Mark. 2002. (Dis)closure in Qohelet: Qohelet Deconstructed. *JSOT* 27:115–26.

Sneed, Mark. 2011. Is the "Wisdom Tradition" a Tradition? *CBQ* 73:50–71.

Sneed, Mark. 2012. *The Politics of Pessimism in Ecclesiastes: A Social-Science Perspective*. AIL 12. Atlanta: SBL.

Sneed, Mark. 2015a. "Grasping after the Wind": The Elusive Attempt to Define and Delimit Wisdom. Pages 39–67 in Sneed 2015c.

Sneed, Mark. 2015b. *The Social World of the Sages: An Introduction to Israelite and Jewish Wisdom Literature*. Minneapolis: Fortress.

Sneed, Mark, ed. 2015c. *Was There a Wisdom Tradition? New Prospects in Israelite Wisdom Studies*. AIL 23. Atlanta: SBL.

Snyder, John. 1991. *Prospects of Power: Tragedy, Satire, the Essay, and the Theory of Genre*. Lexington, KY: University Press of Kentucky.

Sommer, Benjamin D. 1998. *A Prophet Reads Scripture: Allusion in Isaiah 40–66*. Stanford, CA: Stanford University Press.

Sparks, Kenton L. 2005. *Ancient Texts for the Study of the Hebrew Bible: A Guide to the Background Literature*. Peabody, MA: Hendrickson.

Starowieyski, Marek. 1993. Le Livre de l'Ecclésiaste dans l'antiquité chrétienne. Pages 405–40 in *Gregory of Nyssa: Homilies on Ecclesiastes*. Edited by Stuart George Hall. Berlin: de Gruyter.

Steiert, Franz-Josef. 1990. *Die Weisheit Israels—ein Fremdkörper im Alten Testament? Eine Untersuchung zum Buch der Sprüche auf dem Hintergrund der ägyptischen Weisheitslehren*. Freiburger theologische Studien 143. Freiburg: Herder.

Steinberg, Julius. 2006. *Die Ketuvim: Ihr Aufbau und ihre Botschaft*. BBB 152. Hamburg: Philo.

Steiner, George. 1979. Tragedy: Remorse and Justice. *The Listener* 18:508–10.

Steinhoff, Anthony J. 2008. *The Gods of the City: Protestantism and Religious Culture in Strasbourg, 1870–1914*. Leiden: Brill.

Stewart, Anne W. 2016a. *Poetic Ethics in Proverbs: Wisdom Literature and the Shaping of the Moral Self*. Cambridge: Cambridge University Press.

Stewart, Anne W. 2016b. Wisdom's Imagination: Moral Reasoning and the Book of Proverbs. *JSOT* 40:351–72.

Stone, M. E. 1984. Apocalyptic Writings. Pages 383–441 in *Jewish Writings of the Second Temple Period*. Edited by M. E. Stone. Van Gorcum: Assen.

Stone, Timothy J. 2013. *The Compilational History of the Megilloth: Canon, Contoured Intertextuality and Meaning in the Writings*. FAT II 59. Tübingen: Mohr Siebeck.

Sturm, Richard E. 1989. Defining the Word "Apocalyptic": A Problem in Biblical Criticism. Pages 17–48 in *Apocalyptic and the New Testament*. JSNTSup. Edited by Joel Marcus and Marion L. Soards. Sheffield: Sheffield Academic.

Swales, John M. 1990. *Genre Analysis: English in Academic and Research Settings*. Cambridge: Cambridge University Press.

Sweeney, Marvin A., and Ehud Ben Zvi, eds. 2003. *The Changing Face of Form Criticism for the Twenty-First Century*. Grand Rapids: Eerdmans.

Swete, Henry Barclay. 1902. *An Introduction to the Old Testament in Greek*. Cambridge: Cambridge University Press.

Talmon, Shemaryahu. 1963. "Wisdom" in the Book of Esther. *VT* 13:419–55.

Tanzer, Sarah J. 2005. Response to George Nickelsburg, "Wisdom and Apocalypticism in Early Judaism". Pages 39–49 in *Conflicted Boundaries in Wisdom and Apocalypticism*. SBLSymS 35. Edited by B. G. Wright and L. Wills. Atlanta: SBL.

Tappenden, Frederick. 2010. Aural-Performance, Conceptual Blending, and Intertextuality: The (Non-)Use of Scripture in Luke 24:45–8. Pages 180–200 in *Biblical Interpretation in Early Christian Gospels Volume 3: The Gospel of Luke*. LNTS 376. Edited by Thomas R. Hatina. London: T&T Clark.

Tavares, Ricardo. 2007. *Eine königliche Weisheitslehre? Exegetische Analyse von Sprüche 28–29 und Vergleich mit den ägyptischen Lehren Merikaras und Amenemhats*. OBO 234. Fribourg: Academic Press.

Terrien, Samuel L. 1971. The Yahweh Speeches and Job's Responses. *RevExp* 58:497–509.

Terrien, Samuel L. 1978. *The Elusive Presence: Toward a New Biblical Theology*. Religious Perspectives 26. San Francisco: Harper & Row.

Ticciati, Susannah. 2005. *Job and the Disruption of Identity: Reading beyond Barth*. London: T&T Clark International.

Todorov, Tzvetan. 2000. The Origin of Genres. Pages 193–209 in Duff 2000b. Translation of "L'origine des genres" (1976). Pages 44–60 in *Les genres du discours*. Paris: Seuil, 1978.

Toombs, Lawrence E. 1955. O.T. Theology and the Wisdom Literature. *JBR* 23:193–6.

Toorn, Karel van der. 1991. The Ancient Near Eastern Literary Dialogue as a Vehicle of Critical Reflection. Pages 59–75 in *Dispute Poems and Dialogues in the Ancient and Mediaeval Near East: Forms and Types of Literary Debates in Semitic and Related Literatures*. Orientalia lovaniensia analecta 42. Edited by G. J. Reinink and H. L. J. Vanstiphout. Leuven: Department Oriëntalistiek.

Toorn, Karel van der. 2007a. *Scribal Culture and the Making of the Hebrew Bible*. Cambridge, MA: Harvard University Press.

Toorn, Karel van der. 2007b. Why Wisdom Became a Secret: On Wisdom as a Written Genre. Pages 21–9 in *Wisdom Literature in Mesopotamia and Israel*. Edited by Richard J. Clifford. Atlanta: SBL.

Tov, Emanuel. 2008. The Biblical Texts from the Judean Desert: An Overview and Analysis. Pages 128–54 in *Hebrew Bible, Greek Bible and Qumran: Collected Essays*. TSAJ 121. Edited by Emanuel Tov. Tübingen: Mohr Siebeck.

Treves, Marco. 1995. The Book of Job. *ZAW* 107:261–72.

Trigg, Joseph Wilson. 1998. *Origen*. London: Routledge.

Troxel, Ronald L., Kelvin G. Friebel, and Dennis R. Magary. 2005. *Seeking Out the Wisdom of the Ancients: Essays Offered to Honor Michael V. Fox on the Occasion of His Sixty-Fifth Birthday*. Winona Lake, IN: Eisenbrauns.

Tull Willey, Patricia. 1997. *Remember the Former Things: The Recollection of Previous Texts in Second Isaiah*. SBLDS 161. Atlanta: Scholars Press.

Tversky, Amos. 1977. Features of Similarity. *Psychological Review* 84:327–52.

Uehlinger, Christoph. 1997. Qohelet im Horizont mesopotamischer, levantinischer und ägyptischer Weisheitsliteratur der persischen und hellenistischen Zeit. Pages 155–235 in Schwienhorst-Schönberger 1997b.

Uehlinger, Christoph. 2007. Das Hiob-Buch im Kontext der altorientalischen Literatur- und Religionsgeschichte. Pages 97–163 in Krüger et al. 2007.

Umbreit, Friedrich. 1824. *Das Buch Hiob: Übersetzung und Auslegung*. Heidelberg: Mohr.

Umbreit, Friedrich. 1826. *Commentar über die Sprüche Salomo's*. Heidelberg: Mohr.

Van der Lugt, Pieter. 1995. *Rhetorical Criticism and the Poetry of the Book of Job*. OtSt 32. Leiden: Brill.

Van Leeuwen, Raymond C. 1990. The Sage in the Prophetic Literature. Pages 295–306 in Gammie and Perdue 1990.

Van Leeuwen, Raymond C. 1992. Wealth and Poverty: System and Contradiction in Proverbs. *HS* 33:25–36.

Van Leeuwen, Raymond C. 1993. Scribal Wisdom and Theodicy in the Book of the Twelve. Pages 31–49 in *In Search of Wisdom: Essays in Memory of*

John G. Gammie. Edited by Leo G. Perdue, Bernard Brandon Scott, and William Johnston Wiseman. Louisville: Westminster/John Knox.

Van Leeuwen, Raymond C. 1997. The Book of Proverbs: Introduction, Commentary, and Reflections. Pages 19–264 in *Introduction to Wisdom Literature, Proverbs, Ecclesiastes, Song of Songs, Book of Wisdom, Sirach*. NIB 5. Nashville: Abingdon.

Van Leeuwen, Raymond C. 2000. Building God's House: An Exploration in Wisdom. Pages 204–11 in *The Way of Wisdom*. Edited by J. I. Packer and Sven K. Soderlund. Grand Rapids: Zondervan.

Van Leeuwen, Raymond C. 2003. Form Criticism, Wisdom, and Psalms 111–112. Pages 65–84 in Sweeney and Ben Zvi 2003.

Van Leeuwen, Raymond C. 2010. Cosmos, Temple, House: Building and Wisdom in Ancient Mesopotamia and Israel. Pages 399–421 in *From the Foundations to the Crenellations: Essays on Temple Building in the Ancient Near East and Hebrew Bible*. AOAT 366. Edited by Mark J. Boda and Jamie Novotny. Münster: Ugarit-Verlag.

Van Seters, John. 2004. *The Pentateuch: A Social-Science Commentary*. London: T&T Clark International.

Vatke, Wilhelm. 1835. *Die biblische Theologie wissenschaftlich dargestellt*. Berlin: Bethge.

Vatke, Wilhelm. 1886. *Historisch-kritische Einleitung in das Alte Testament*. Bonn: Emil Strauss.

Vayntrub, Jacqueline. 2016. The Book of Proverbs and the Idea of Ancient Israelite Education. *ZAW* 128:96–114.

Vayntrub, Jacqueline. Forthcoming a. *Beyond Orality: Performance and the Composition of Biblical Poetry*. London: Routledge.

Vantrub, Jacqueline. Forthcoming b. Ecclesiastes and the Problem of Transmission. In *Biblical Literature in Writing and Scribalism: Authors, Audiences, and Texts in Social Perspective*. Edited by Mark Leuchter. New York: T&T Clark.

Veldhuis, Niek. 2003. Sumerian Literature. Pages 29–43 in *Cultural Repertoires: Structure, Function and Dynamics*. Edited by Gillis J. Dorleijn and Herman L. J. Vanstiphout. Leuven: Peeters.

Vinel, F. 1998. Le Texte Grec de l'*Ecclésiaste* et ses Caractéristiques: Une Relecture Critique de l'Histoire de la Royauté. Pages 283–302 in *Qohelet in the Context of Wisdom*. BETL 136. Edited by Anton Schoors. Leuven: Leuven University Press.

Volz, Paul. 1911. *Weisheit (Das Buch Hiob, Sprüche und Jesus Sirach, Prediger)*. Göttingen: Vandenhoeck & Ruprecht.

Waltke, Bruce K. 2004. *The Book of Proverbs*. 2 vols. NICOT. Grand Rapids: Eerdmans.

Wassell, Blake E., and Stephen R. Llewelyn. 2014. "Fishers of Humans," the Contemporary Theory of Metaphor, and Conceptual Blending Theory. *JBL* 133:627–46.

Watts, Duncan J. 2003. *Six Degrees: The Science of a Connected Age*. New York: Norton.

Watts, James W. 1999. *Reading Law: The Rhetorical Shaping of the Pentateuch*. Sheffield: Sheffield Academic.

Weeks, Stuart. 1994. *Early Israelite Wisdom*. Oxford Theological Monographs. Oxford: Oxford University Press.

Weeks, Stuart. 1999. Wisdom in the Old Testament. Pages 19–30 in *Where Shall Wisdom Be Found? Wisdom in the Bible, the Church and the Contemporary World*. Edited by Stephen C. Barton. Edinburgh: T&T Clark.

Weeks, Stuart. 2005. Wisdom Psalms. Pages 292–307 in *Temple and Worship in Biblical Israel*. Edited by John Day. London: T&T Clark International.

Weeks, Stuart. 2007. *Instruction and Imagery in Proverbs 1–9*. Oxford: Oxford University Press.

Weeks, Stuart. 2010a. *An Introduction to the Study of Wisdom Literature*. New York: T&T Clark.

Weeks, Stuart. 2010b. Predictive and Prophetic Literature: Can *Neferti* Help Us Read the Bible? Pages 25–46 in *Prophecy and Prophets in Ancient Israel: Proceedings of the Oxford Old Testament Seminar*. LHBOTS 531. Edited by John Day. New York: T&T Clark.

Weeks, Stuart. 2012. *Ecclesiastes and Scepticism*. LHBOTS 541. New York: T&T Clark International.

Weeks, Stuart. 2013. The Limits of Form Criticism in the Study of Literature, with Reflections on Psalm 34. Pages 15–24 in *Biblical Interpretation and Method*. Edited by Katharine J. Dell and Paul M. Joyce. Oxford: Oxford University Press.

Weeks, Stuart. 2014. The Inner-Textuality of Qoheleth's Monologue. Pages 142–53 in Dell and Kynes 2014.

Weeks, Stuart. 2015. Wisdom, Form and Genre. Pages 161–77 in Sneed 2015c.

Weeks, Stuart. 2016a. Is "Wisdom Literature" a Useful Category? Pages 3–23 in *Tracing Sapiential Traditions in Ancient Judaism*. JSJSup 174. Edited by Hindy Najman, Jean-Sébastien Rey, and Eibert J. C. Tigchelaar. Leiden: Brill.

Weeks, Stuart. 2016b. The Place and Limits of Wisdom Revisited. Pages 3–23 in *Perspectives on Israelite Wisdom: Proceedings of the Oxford Old Testament Seminar*. LHBOTS 618. Edited by John Jarick. London: Bloomsbury T&T Clark.

Weiner, Andrew D. 1991. Sidney / Spenser / Shakespeare: Influence / Intertextuality / Intention. Pages 245–70 in *Influence and Intertextuality in Literary History*. Edited by Jay Clayton and Eric Rothstein. Madison, WI: University of Wisconsin Press.

Weinfeld, Moshe. 1967. Deuteronomy: The Present State of Inquiry. *JBL* 86:249–62.

Weinfeld, Moshe. 1972. *Deuteronomy and the Deuteronomic School*. Oxford: Clarendon.

Weinfeld, Moshe. 1988. Job and Its Mesopotamian Parallels—A Typological Analysis. Pages 217–26 in *Text and Context: Old Testament and Semitic Studies for F. C. Fensham*. JSOTSup 48. Edited by W. Claasen. Sheffield: Sheffield Academic.

Wellmon, Chad. 2015. *Organizing Enlightenment: Information Overload and the Invention of the Modern Research University*. Baltimore: John Hopkins University Press.

Westcott, B. F. 1896. *A General Survey of the History of the Canon in the New Testament*. London: Macmillan.

Westermann, Claus. 1981. *The Structure of the Book of Job: A Form-Critical Analysis*. Translated by Charles A. Muenchow. Philadelphia: Fortress. Translation of *Der Aufbau des Buches Hiob*. Mohr: Tübingen, 1956.

Westermann, Claus. 1984. *Ausgewählte Psalmen*. Göttingen: Vandenhoeck & Ruprecht.

Westermann, Claus. 1995. *Roots of Wisdom: The Oldest Proverbs of Israel and Other Peoples*. Translated by J. Daryl Charles. Louisville: Westminster John Knox. Translation of *Wurzeln der Weisheit*. Göttingen: Vandenhoeck & Ruprecht, 1990.

Wette, W. M. L. de. 1807. Beytrag zur Charakteristik des Hebraismus. Pages 241–312 in vol. 3 of *Studien*. Edited by Carl Daub and Friedrich Creuzer. Heidelberg: Mohr & Zimmer.

Wette, W. M. L. de. 1830. *Lehrbuch der hebräisch-jüdischen Archäologie nebst einem Grundrisse der herbräische-jüdischen Geschichte*. 2nd ed. Leipzig: Vogel.

Wette, W. M. L. de. 1831. *Biblische Dogmatik: Alten und Neuen Testaments: oder kritische Darstellung der Religionslehre des Hebraismus, des Judenthums und Urchistenthums*. 3rd ed. Berlin: Reimer. Orig. ed., 1813.

Wette, W. M. L. de. 1869. *Lehrbuch der historisch-kritischen Einleitung in die kanonischen und apokryphischen Bücher des Alten Testamentes*. 8th ed. Edited by Eberhard Schrader. Berlin: G. Reimer. Orig. ed., 1817.

Whedbee, J. William. 1971. *Isaiah and Wisdom*. Nashville: Abingdon.

Whedbee, J. William. 1977. The Comedy of Job. *Semeia* 7:1–39.

Whybray, R. N. 1968. *The Succession Narrative: A Study of II Samuel 9–20; I Kings 1 and 2*. London: SCM.

Whybray, R. N. 1974. *The Intellectual Tradition in the Old Testament*. Berlin: de Gruyter.

Whybray, R. N. 1982a. Prophecy and Wisdom. Pages 181–199 in *Israel's Prophetic Heritage*. Edited by R. Coggins, A. Phillips, and Knibb M. Cambridge: Cambridge University Press.

Whybray, R. N. 1982b. Qoheleth, Preacher of Joy. *JSOT* 23:87–98.

Whybray, R. N. 1989. *Ecclesiastes*. NCBC. Grand Rapids: Eerdmans.

Whybray, R. N. 1995a. *The Book of Proverbs: A Survey of Modern Study*. Leiden: Brill.

Whybray, R. N. 1995b. The Wisdom Psalms. Pages 152–160 in Day, Gordon, and Williamson 1995.

Whybray, R. N. 1998a. *Job*. Readings: A New Biblical Commentary. Sheffield: Sheffield Academic.

Whybray, R. N. 1998b. Qoheleth as a Theologian. Pages 239–65 in *Qohelet in the Context of Wisdom*. BETL 136. Edited by Anton Schoors. Leuven: Leuven University Press.

Whybray, R. N. 2005. Slippery Words. IV. Wisdom. Pages 6–9 in *Wisdom: The Collected Articles of Norman Whybray*. Edited by Katharine J. Dell and Margaret Barker. Farnham, Hants: Ashgate.

Wilken, Robert Louis, ed. 1975. *Aspects of Wisdom in Judaism and Early Christianity*. Notre Dame, ID: University of Notre Dame Press.

Williams, Ronald J. 1981. The Sages of Ancient Egypt in the Light of Recent Scholarship. *JAOS* 101:1–19.

Williamson, H. G. M. 2007. Once upon a Time? Pages 517–528 in *Reflection and Refraction: Studies in Biblical Historiography in Honour of A. Graeme Auld*. VTSup 113. Edited by Robert Rezetko, Timothy H. Lim, and W. Brian Aucker. Leiden: Brill.

Williamson, Robert, Jr. 2010. Pesher: A Cognitive Model of the Genre. *DSD* 17:336–60.

Wilson, Gerald H. 1984. "The Words of the Wise": The Intent and Significance of Qohelet 12:9–14. *JBL* 103:175–92.

Wilson, Gerald H. 1992. The Shape of the Book of Psalms. *Int* 46:129–42.

Wilson, Leslie S. 2006. *The Book of Job: Judaism in the 2nd Century* BCE*: An Intertextual Reading*. Studies in Judaism. Lanham, MD: University Press of America.

Wilson, Robert P. 1999. Who was the Deutronomist? (Who Was Not the Deuteronomist?): Reflections on Pan-Deuternomism. Pages 67–82 in McKenzie and Schearing 1999.

Winkler, Mathias. 2017. *Das Salomonische des Sprichwörterbuchs: Intertextuelle Verbindungen zwischen 1 Kön 1–11 und dem Sprichwörterbuch*. HBS 87. Frieburg: Herder.

Winston, David. 1979. *The Wisdom of Solomon*. AB 43. Garden City, NY: Doubleday.

Witte, Markus. 2007. Die literarische Gattung des Buches Hiob: Robert Lowth und seine Erben. Pages 93–123 in *Sacred Conjectures: The Context and Legacy of Robert Lowth and Jean Astruc*. LHBOTS 457. Edited by John Jarick. London: T&T Clark.

Witte, Markus. 2012. "Weisheit" in der alttestamentlichen Wissenschaft: Ausgewählte literatur- und theologiegeschichtliche Fragestellungen und Entwicklungen. *TLZ* 137:1159–76.

Witte, Markus. 2013a. Does the Torah Keep Its Promise? Job's Critical Intertextual Dialogue with Deuteronomy. Pages 54–65 in Dell and Kynes 2013.

Witte, Markus. 2013b. Job in Conversation with the Torah. Pages 81–100 in Schipper and Teeter 2013.

Wolfers, David. 1995. *Deep Things out of Darkness: The Book of Job, Essays and a New Translation*. Kampen: Kok Pharos.

Wolff, Hans Walter. 1964. *Amos' Geistige Heimat*. WMANT 18. Neukirchen-Vluyn: Neukirchener.

Wolff, Hans Walter. 1973. *The Old Testament: A Guide to Its Writings*. Translated by Keith R. Crim. Philadelphia: Fortress. Translation of *Bibel—Das Alte Testament: Eine Einführung in seine Schriften und in die Methoden ihrer Erforschung*. Stuttgart: Kreuz, 1970.

Wright, Benjamin G. 2010. Joining the Club: A Suggestion about Genre in Early Jewish Texts. *DSD* 17:289–314.

Wright, Charles H. H. 1891. *Introduction to the Old Testament*. 2nd ed. London: Hodder and Stoughton. Orig. ed., 1890.

Wright, G. Ernest. 1952. *God Who Acts: Biblical Theology as Recital*. London: SCM.

Wright, G. H. Bateson. 1883. *The Book of Job*. London: Williams & Norgate.

Wright, J. Robert. 2005. Introduction to Proverbs, Ecclesiastes and Song of Solomon. Pages xvii–xxix in *Proverbs, Ecclesiastes and Song of Solomon*. ACCS 9. Edited by J. Robert Wright and Thomas C. Oden. Downers Grove, IL: InterVarsity.

Wurgaft, Benjamin Aldes. 2014. To the Planetarium—There Is Still Time! *History and Theory* 53:253–63.

Yoder, Christine. 2005. Forming "Fearers of Yahweh": Repetition and Contradiction as Pedagogy in Proverbs. Pages 167–83 in Troxel, Friebel, and Magary 2005.

Zabán, Bálint Károly. 2012. *The Pillar Function of the Speeches of Wisdom: Proverbs 1:20–33, 8:1–36, and 9:1–6 in the Structural Framework of Proverbs 1–9*. BZAW 429. Berlin: de Gruyter.

Zaharopoulos, Dimitri Z. 1989. *Theodore of Mopsuestia on the Bible: A Study of His Old Testament Exegesis*. New York: Paulist.

Zahn, Molly M. 2012. Genre and Rewritten Scripture: A Reassessment. *JBL* 131:271–88.

Zimmerli, Walther. 1962. *Das Buch des Predigers Salomo*. ATD 16.1. Göttingen: Vandenhoeck & Ruprecht.

Zimmerli, Walther. 1964. The Place and Limit of the Wisdom in the Framework of the Old Testament Theology. *SJT* 17:146–58. Translation of Ort und Grenze der Weisheit im Rahmen der alttestamentlichen Theologie. Pages 121–37 in *Les Sagesses du Proche-Orient Ancien. Colloque de Strasbourg, 17–19 mai 1962*. Edited by Centre d'Études Supérieures Spécialisé d'Histoire des Religions de Strasbourg. Paris: Presses Universitaires de France, 1963.

Zöckler, Otto. 1867. *Die Sprüche Salomonis*. Bielefeld: Velhagen und Klasing.

Zuckerman, Bruce. 1991. *Job the Silent: A Study in Historical Counterpoint*. Oxford: Oxford University Press.

Subject Index

Author Index

Ancient Sources Index

Printed and bound by CPI Group (UK) Ltd, Croydon, CR0 4YY